Taxation
and Latin
American
Integration

**Vito Tanzi, Alberto Barreix,
and Luiz Villela**

Editors

Inter-American Development Bank

**David Rockefeller Center for Latin American Studies
Harvard University**

© 2008 Inter-American Development Bank
1300 New York Avenue, N.W.
Washington, D.C. 20577

Co-published by David Rockefeller Center for Latin American Studies
Harvard University
1730 Cambridge Street
Cambridge, MA 02138

Produced by the IDB Office of External Relations

To order this book, contact:
IDB Bookstore
Tel: (202) 623-1753
Fax: (202) 623-1709
E-mail: idb-books@iadb.org
www.iadb.org/pub

The views and opinions expressed in this publication are those of the authors
and do not necessarily reflect the official position of the Inter-American
Development Bank.

**Cataloging-in-Publication data provided by the
Inter-American Development Bank
Felipe Herrera Library**

Taxation and Latin American integration / Vito Tanzi, Alberto Barreix, and
Luiz Villela, editors.

      p. cm.
      Includes bibliographical references.
      ISBN: 978-1-59782-058-5

1. Taxation—Latin America. 2. Latin America—Economic integration.
3. Free trade—Latin America. 4. Globalization—Latin America. I. Tanzi,
Vito. II. Barreix, Alberto. III. Villela, Luiz Arruda. IV. Inter-American Development Bank. V. David Rockefeller Center for Latin American Studies.

HJ2460.5 .T84 2007   LCCN: 2007940766

Cover Design: Ultradesigns.com

Contents

Foreword

When countries' economies were relatively closed, tax systems reflected purely and exclusively national characteristics. Policymakers worried about the capacity of their tax systems to generate needed revenue, about the ability of their tax administrations to administer the national taxes, and perhaps even about the equity and efficiency of their tax systems. They did not give much thought to the impact that their systems could have on other countries' economies or to the impact that foreign tax systems could have on their own economy. Globalization started changing that environment and, together with the movement toward economic integration for groups of countries, it highlighted the need to consider the ways in which uncoordinated tax systems can become major obstacles to an efficient allocation of resources in the open setting that accompanies economic integration.

Coordination of taxation among countries can also be important for countries to protect their tax base. Exchanging information, signing tax treaties, and agreeing not to engage in unfair practices to attract foreign direct investments (FDI) are more and more relevant as globalization advances. In addition, by agreeing to make certain characteristics of their tax systems similar, though not necessarily identical, groups of countries can together allocate resources more efficiently and become more attractive for FDI than the countries would be individually.

All of these issues indicate that the borderline between trade policy and tax policy is breaking down. Analytical work done to date has shown how uncoordinated tax systems have become a major obstacle to full integration in Europe, and how taxes interfere with the free and efficient allocation of labor, capital, and other resources among the European Union countries. The European experience also indicates that it is better to prepare the ground early than to wait until integration has advanced a great deal, when removing obstacles is more difficult. In Latin America, analysis on these subjects is lacking, perhaps because integration has been feeble.

In order to provide valuable insights to policymakers in Latin America, this book presents studies on different aspects of taxation as it relates to economic integration. The chapters were written by renowned experts in their respective fields, and the book was edited by Vito Tanzi, Alberto Barreix, and Luiz Villela.

Some of the important issues discussed are the need for tax reform in developing countries as a result of globalization, the degrees of tax harmonization in Latin America and the Caribbean, the importance of capital income tax coordination, tax incentives for FDI, and the portability of pension systems as economic integration proceeds. The book also addresses the fiscal impact of trade liberalization, issues and models of tax treaties and transfer pricing legislation, the conflicts between fiscal decentralization and economic integration, and the need for and the limits to exchange of tax information to curb unfair practices.

Santiago Levy
Vice President, Sectors and Knowledge
Inter-American Development Bank

Acknowledgments

This work is the result of a collective effort by various tax experts, but we are especially grateful for Peter Kalil's unwavering encouragement and to Antoni Estevadeordal, Vicente Fretes Cibils, and Mario Marcel Cullell, who enthusiastically supported us in the preparation of this book and provided the resources needed to undertake it. Additionally, we are grateful to Maricela Cruz, our office assistant, Patricia Abad, our diligent research assistant, and the resourceful aid of the IDB Library staff. Also, we would like to acknowledge the contributions of Julia Benseñor, responsible for translating two of the chapters into English, and Andrew Crawley, who diligently reviewed and prepared the manuscript for publication.

Vito Tanzi, Alberto Barreix, and Luiz Villela

1

Introduction

Vito Tanzi

This book aims to provide an introduction to issues that arise when a group of countries that had been wholly independent and economically autarchic embarks on a path that one day could lead to their full economic integration. The final destination may be unknown at the outset, but it is enough that policymakers in the different countries decide that more integration is a desirable good. They do not have to agree on how far they wish to go on this road. The final goal, of course, might be to establish a single economy that includes all the participating countries.

Different groups of countries or territories have moved toward economic, and even political, integration in the past. Some of these movements were determined by historical developments, as happened, for example, in Germany, Italy, the United States, and other places where separate regions, states, or colonies decided to form a political entity. Others took different paths.

In the past half-century, a movement toward economic integration has been most evident in Europe. In 1957, six European countries (Belgium, France, Germany, Italy, Luxembourg, and the Netherlands) signed the Treaty of Rome and thereby began a historic movement toward economic integration. Initially slow, the process accelerated, and the number of interested countries grew to the 27 that today compose the European Union (EU). The EU members adopted a common trade policy toward the rest of the world and began eliminating intra-European trade barriers, especially those affecting goods (many restrictions on services still persist). The member states also instituted policies that would create a common economic climate. The EU, as a single entity, now has the largest total income of any economic unit in the world. Furthermore, 12 EU countries have gone so far as to replace their national currencies with a common European currency, the euro.

The harmonization—or more often the coordination—of economic policies in the EU has been particularly significant in the area of public finances, especially taxation. Taxes can be major obstacles to economic exchanges among countries that trade with each other. Hence it is important for countries that become members of a commercial union to remove those aspects of taxation that create obstacles to cross-country (but inter-union) exchanges. Trade taxes must be the first to be eliminated, but other taxes can also be barriers to the development of a single market, and they merit attention. Europe has made significant progress in the area of indirect taxes, such as value-added taxes (VAT) and excises. Less progress has been made on the coordination of direct taxes, such as those on personal income and company profits, and much remains to be done in this area.

In the Americas, and especially in country groups in South and Central America, a movement toward further economic integration has begun. In Europe in the first half of the twentieth century, the integration process derived urgency and impetus from devastating wars between some countries. Those wars prompted a conviction among political figures that economic integration of European countries would remove the causes of conflict. As some put it, when goods cross borders freely, soldiers do not have to. In the Americas there is no such stimulus, and thus the integration movement may be slower. Nonetheless, Latin American and Caribbean countries may now be at a point similar to that at which the European countries found themselves half a century ago.

Some actions geared to economic integration have been or are being taken. Others are likely to follow. Those actions may one day become part of a process that could create a single economy including several Latin American and Caribbean countries, or even all the countries of the region. They are activities that have, and increasingly will have, significant implications for policies related to public finances and especially the countries' tax systems. To help make the process smoother and to foster a better understanding of the policy actions required, the Inter-American Development Bank (IDB) embarked on a project to produce several studies that could be collected in a book. The 12 studies included in this volume address various matters related to the impact of trade integration on taxes. Some of them were written by IDB staff and some by external specialists. Some deal directly with the countries of the region, while others tackle issues that are, or will become, germane to the region's integration process.

Chapter 2, by Luiz Villela, Jerónimo Roca, and Alberto Barreix, mainly examines the impact of trade liberalization on the tax revenue of Latin American and Caribbean countries. This is the issue that has attracted the most attention and made some policymakers in these countries reluctant to agree to greater economic opening for fear of losing income from taxes. The authors of this wide-ranging chapter discuss several matters related to the impact of globalization on tax systems and tax revenue, and they provide empirical estimates of that impact for particular countries. Some of the topics they introduce are examined in greater detail, or from different perspectives, in other chapters.

Villela, Roca, and Barreix provide a great deal of useful statistical information on the foreign trade taxes of the countries of the region and show that, in most countries, customs duties have been losing the importance they had as recently as two decades ago. Beginning in the 1980s, many Latin American countries saw the advantages of tariff reduction. They recognized that excessive protection of domestic activity can harm a country's economic efficiency, especially in an integrating world. The reduction in customs duties, however, led to a decline in foreign trade taxes. In most countries, the revenue losses were offset by other taxes, and especially by a more intensive use of VAT. Hence the removal or lowering of tariffs undoubtedly had a revenue effect, but many (though not all) countries were easily able to make up for this loss. The potential revenue losses attendant on the removal of tariffs, therefore, should not be viewed as a valid reason for failing to proceed with trade integration.

The chapter offers empirical estimates of the direct revenue losses arising from trade agreements that various regional groups have concluded with the United States. Those losses are larger for smaller countries and are particularly significant for Caribbean countries, which are substantially reliant on foreign trade taxes. In the Bahamas, the loss was estimated to be as high as 4.5 percent of gross domestic product (GDP).

Chapter 2 also discusses the impact of tariff reduction on the countries' fiscal sustainability and equity. It presents various tax options that countries can use to compensate for the revenue lost when they engage in trade liberalization. There are several alternatives, but VAT is inevitably the strongest or best candidate. Obviously, not all the options are equally easy to implement in every country, and thus different governments can be expected to make different choices.

Chapter 3, by Vito Tanzi, addresses some issues that are similar to those examined in Chapter 2. However, instead of centering on taxes and Latin America, Chapter 3 deals more broadly with the impact of trade liberalization on fiscal balances. It extends the discussion from a focus on taxes to one that takes account of both taxes and public spending. It also takes a more general equilibrium approach to the issue of trade liberalization, with a view to considering all of its important effects and to drawing conclusions about how they may affect the fiscal balance.

The chapter stresses that the decline in trade taxes during recent decades should not be attributed directly or solely to trade agreements, since the falling trend began in the 1950s and has affected all countries, irrespective of whether they were members of a customs union. The trend was identified in the "theory of tax structure change" developed by various writers in the 1950s and 1960s. The theory predicted that as countries developed, they would gradually eliminate foreign trade taxes because of the taxes' distorting effects on economic activities, and they would replace them with more modern and more neutral taxes.

Chapter 3 also argues that trade liberalization cannot fail to affect the spending side of the budget, since the government will inevitably feel pressure from those who lose the protection of high tariffs or quantitative restrictions. The chapter surveys several studies that have examined the effects of trade liberalization on tax revenue, and it concludes that the impact is not always a decline in income.

Chapter 4, by Fernando Velayos, Alberto Barreix, and Luiz Villela, opens with a brief review of the literature on tax harmonization and addresses the important questions of what harmonization means and what instruments are needed to achieve it. The authors point out that there are different definitions and degrees of harmonization. The situation is somewhat similar to that described in *Alice in Wonderland*, where words did not have a precise or objective meaning because their significance was decided by those using them. Obviously, this can make communication difficult. The authors of Chapter 4 point out that neither a dictionary nor descriptions by experts are particularly helpful. There are different degrees and definitions of harmonization, but there are also different instruments available to attain it—or more often to attain coordination, which is less demanding.

An important part of the chapter is the construction of a "tax harmonization (or integration) scale." The authors list several steps toward tax harmonization, reflecting descending levels of political commitment: (1) standardization, (2) compatibility, (3) coordination, (4) cooperation, and (5) convergence. After explaining these steps, Velayos, Barreix, and Villela attempt to apply them to four Latin American and Caribbean regional organizations in order to assess progress toward integration. The four organizations are the Andean Community (CAN), the Caribbean Community (CARICOM), the Southern Common Market (MERCOSUR), and the Central American Customs Union, which is now getting under way. The authors note that these customs unions have used different instruments to proceed toward integration and harmonization. Much remains to be done, but progress is being made.

Chapter 5, by Eduardo Wiesner, tackles a different kind of integration: tax coordination among different regions of the same country. This coordination takes place at the same time that national governments may be pursuing coordination at an international level. Tax competition can arise not only between countries but also within a country when different regions, with some power to tax, use the tax system to attract investment and economic activity. This problem of tax competition has attracted much attention in Brazil, the United States, and elsewhere.

Wiesner shows that the taxes controlled by regions have been rising as a share of the countries' gross national product (GNP). He sees this as a positive development because it brings spending decisions closer to citizens, who thus have greater oversight of what and whom to tax and how to use tax revenue. Wiesner accepts a thesis made popular by Dani Rodrik, which asserts that the increasing risks that are assumed to accompany globalization promote higher government spending. However, while more trade integration increases public spending, it may reduce tax revenue and thereby cause macroeconomic problems. Pointing out that public spending has risen more than taxes as a share of GDP in Latin America, Wiesner discusses the controversial issue of whether fiscal decentralization raises public spending and taxes as shares of output. Positions have diverged on this issue. James Buchanan, for example, has argued that fiscal decentralization reduces public spending, an outcome that Wiesner deems desirable. However, many other scholars argue the contrary—that decentralization increases public spending. Ad hoc evidence seems to support the latter position.

Chapter 6, by Reuven Avi-Yonah, deals broadly with globalization and tax competition and their implications for developing countries. The chapter accepts the view that tax competition forces countries to lower taxes on capital, because of the latter's mobility. Consequently, unless other income can be secured (by taxing labor, real estate, or consumption, for example), tax competition leads to a decline in public revenue. Thus governments are forced to cut public services. Avi-Yonah sees this as a significant problem because of governments' great need for tax revenue in both developed and developing countries. Tax havens are seen as contributing to this outcome.

Avi-Yonah mentions that tax incentives are often used by countries as a protective measure against tax competition. He suggests that it would be better if all developing countries were to abolish them. Bilateral tax treaties are not particularly helpful, and multilateral tax treaties would thus be needed. As yet, however, there are no such treaties. The author concludes that the key to finding a solution to the tax competition problem is to attack it on a broad multilateral basis. He believes that the Organisation for Economic Co-operation and Development (OECD) is the natural choice to lead such an effort, but the OECD represents a relatively small share (about 15 percent) of the world's countries. It is unlikely that the 85 percent of countries that are not represented, including large countries such as China, India, Brazil, and Indonesia, would agree to the OECD playing this role. The issue of an international institution that could deal globally with tax matters that damage other countries is addressed further in Chapter 13.

Chapter 7, by Richard Bird, deals with tax incentives for foreign investment in Latin America and the Caribbean and considers whether tax incentives need to be harmonized. The chapter opens with a description of how attitudes toward tax incentives have changed over the past half-century. Tax incentives were very popular in the 1950s and 1960s but are much less so today. Since the 1980s and the so-called supply-side revolution, and especially after the 1986 U.S. tax reform that promoted broad-based taxes, including, conceptually, flat-rate taxes, there seems to be less justification for tax incentives, because in order to be powerful, they would require high tax rates. The higher the rates, the greater the potential impact of incentives on resource allocation. In a world of low tax rates, tax incentives lose much of their force. Nonetheless, tax incentives survive in the real world, and countries still use them despite the negative attitude of tax experts.

Bird concedes that tax incentives can be useful in particular circumstances, especially in a world where capital movements have increased the importance of tax differences in determining the location of investments and of economic activities in general. But fundamental factors (stability and transparency of rules, good macroeconomic policy, proximity to markets, and so on) are still more important than tax incentives. The author believes that some of the importance of tax incentives stems from "signals" they send to foreign investors, indicating that the country welcomes investment. He also addresses the important question of whether tax competition is good or bad. In an examination of whether and how tax incentives could be coordinated regionally, he concludes that incentives should be few, simple, and transparent. Moreover, he recommends keeping good records of who gets the incentives and making those records public. Bird also suggests that estimates of the revenue losses arising from the granting of tax incentives should be made public, so that policymakers and citizens can assess not only the presumed benefits but also the costs of the incentives.

Chapter 8, by Peter Byrne, examines tax treaties in Latin American countries, a topic that has attracted relatively little attention from economists but much more from tax lawyers and accountants. Byrne refers to the negotiation of the U.S.-Mexico tax treaty, initiated in 1990, as "a watershed." Previously Mexico had been reluctant to conclude such agreements. This treaty, based on the OECD model, lessened Mexico's concern with tax revenue—always a major preoccupation for developing countries—and prompted greater Mexican attention to the impact of the treaty on foreign investment. Byrne assumes that developing countries have an acute need for foreign investment. In developing countries, policymakers' main argument against tax treaties has been that the agreements cause revenue losses because they tend to put the interests of foreign investors, who traditionally have been from developed countries, ahead of the interests of developing countries.

Byrne argues that it would be preferable to conclude a general tax treaty that is accepted by all countries, rather than take the "spaghetti bowl" approach of bilateral agreements. Some countries, such as Chile, Mexico, and Venezuela, have concluded many treaties, but other countries are still reluctant to negotiate them. Is it important to have tax treaties? Byrne's answer is a resounding yes. He offers several reasons, the main one being that income should be taxed only once, and treaties pursue that goal. Arguments can be made against treaties, however, and especially against bilateral accords: they are costly to negotiate, especially for small countries that lack specialists in these matters; larger countries are better prepared to secure advantageous terms; and developing countries may lose tax revenue when treaties prevent them from taxing foreign investors. Tax treaties are also important inasmuch as they require or guarantee the exchange of information between countries. This is an important issue discussed in a later chapter by Claudino Pita.

Chapter 9, by Amparo Mercader and Horacio Peña, discusses transfer pricing and Latin American integration. The chapter begins by pointing out that production chains have become progressively more globalized in recent decades, and thus there is greater need to appraise the value of inputs that are often imported from other countries or from branches and subsidiaries of multinational companies. When imported goods or services are product-specific, as they often are, there may not be competitive or arm's length prices that can be relied upon. This circumstance enables companies to engage in price manipulation and to shift profits to countries where they are taxed at a lower rate. Mercader and Peña point out that polls indicate that "transfer pricing, whether its justification, its evaluation, or settlement of disputes regarding it, is one of the most important issues on the agendas of many tax executives" (Chapter 9).

This was not always the case. In Latin America, the enactment of transfer pricing legislation is a recent development that began in Mexico in 1997. Many other countries of the region have taken the same path since then. Except for Brazil, all Latin American countries that have transfer pricing legislation adhere to the arm's length principle in setting values. Mercader and Peña mention other methods, but the arm's length principle is the most solid and popular. The chapter lists the types of transactions that are subject to transfer pricing and discusses the various methods that can be used to determine acceptable transfer prices. Companies sometimes reach pricing agreements with governments for particular periods in order to avoid conflict, but this practice risks transforming corporate income taxes into presumptive taxes.

The chapter briefly describes transfer pricing legislation in various Latin American countries. Given the lack of tax system harmonization and the growing globalization of production, this issue will certainly become more important as the Latin American economies integrate further.

Chapter 10, by Claudino Pita, deals with an issue that has been attracting ever more attention: the exchange of information between tax administrations. At least in theory, this could play an important and useful role in resolving tax problems created by globalization and tax competition. The exchange of information on the economic activities of individuals and enterprises could reduce tax evasion connected with these activities. It could also help level the international playing field, which is often uneven because different enterprises have different opportunities to evade taxes. Pita discusses the scope and forms of tax evasion and the distinctions between tax fraud, tax evasion, and tax avoidance. Legal systems may consider these differences important, but their effects on tax revenue and tax competition tend to be the same: governments obtain less revenue, and the taxpayers who engage in these activities, however defined, enjoy competitive advantages over competitors who do not.

Pita addresses the challenges that arise in particular from transfer prices, electronic commerce, and tax havens, and he provides a useful discussion of dumping and subsidies. He outlines the different means of exchanging information and examines the double taxation agreements or models provided by the OECD, the United Nations, and the Andean Pact. All these models make provisions for information exchange, but they all place limits on that exchange. The author finds that these models impose excessive constraints on efforts to fight tax evasion by exchanging information. Their main goal is to prevent double taxation, not to combat evasion. Hence he argues that specific agreements on information exchange are needed, in addition to double taxation treaties. Accords on the exchange of information would give more power to tax administrations and less to the lawyers who negotiate the double taxation treaties.

Such agreements already exist in the EU, among countries in northern Europe, and between the Council of Europe and the OECD. The problem is that some of these treaties are simply "executive agreements" that fall far short of making information exchange mandatory. Mandatory exchanges, of course, would pose significant legal and economic problems. Many countries' legal systems would make them impossible. And for reasons of competition, some countries might be reluctant to provide others with information on companies operating in their territory. In some cases, moreover, tax administrations might incur high costs in obtaining the information. It is generally costlier to provide information than to request it.

Chapter 11, by Francisco Delmas González, deals with economic integration and pensions. Generally, though not always, governments provide pensions to individuals working in their countries who have paid social security contributions for a required minimum number of years. Many important issues arise in connection with pensions and pension systems. These include the systems' sustainability in the face of demographic changes and increasing life expectancies, the adequacy of pension benefits, the proportion of the population covered by the systems, the tax treatment of contributions or benefits, and so on. This chapter addresses several of these issues.

Thus far in Europe there has been little coordination among the systems, which raises questions about whether a single market can be fully developed in these circumstances. European pension systems are mature, and it would be very complex to coordinate or standardize the regulations that control them. If it were possible to do so, workers would be able to move freely from country to country in the EU without losing benefits. Delmas González refers to the European Directive on the activities and supervision of occupational pension funds, which is a limited but important step forward toward an internal market for occupational pensions.

In Latin America, greater challenges are posed by the different development levels of pension systems among groups of countries. Pension systems are well developed in the MERCOSUR countries, but elsewhere they are much less so. Delmas González mentions MERCOSUR's founding treaty, which makes reference to "social justice," and to the Andean Community's Andean Social Security Instrument, which calls for protection of individuals covered by social security. This is an area that will require attention as the countries make further progress on integration.

Chapter 12, by Harry Huizinga, addresses capital income tax coordination in the EU and whether the European experience can be a blueprint for Latin America. The author provides detailed background on the gradual coordination of national tax policy in the EU. He reports on the slow progress achieved there and the reasons why, which essentially are the lack of consensus and the need for unanimity in decision making. Huizinga describes the increasingly important role of the European

Court of Justice in forcing changes to aspects of tax systems that are seen as obstacles to capital mobility among the European countries. He states that "the existence of multiple and separate capital income tax systems entails large efficiency costs" and points out that Latin America has no equivalent of the European Commission or the European Court of Justice to promote tax coordination. Hence coordination of capital income taxes will be more difficult unless other institutions or international trends provide impetus in that direction.

Huizinga indicates that there is still wide dispersion in tax rates in the EU, and taxes on capital incomes have not fallen in recent years. The evidence does not support the view that tax competition is lowering tax levels. Huizinga argues that this may be because foreigners own a large share of European capital assets, and thus European governments are not reluctant to impose high taxes on those assets. Additionally, low labor mobility makes it possible for European countries to maintain very high taxes on labor income. The result, of course, is lower employment and a high level of underground economic activities. The EU has tried to develop a code of conduct to protect tax bases from being raided by other countries, and it has issued a Savings Tax Directive that requires countries to provide information on interest paid to citizens of other member countries. Special provisions had to be made for Austria, Belgium, and Luxembourg to give them time to implement the agreement.

So far, efforts to introduce a common corporate income tax base for all the EU countries have failed. Such a tax base would enable the countries to use whatever rates they desire to tax corporate income, but it would dramatically reduce compliance costs for enterprises operating in more than one European country. There has also been some discussion of developing an EU model tax treaty, but to date the OECD model continues to guide negotiations on tax agreements. An important point to emerge from Huizinga's chapter is the significance of EU-wide institutions such as the European Commission, the European Court of Justice, and the European Parliament in pushing forward the process of tax coordination. Latin America, of course, lacks such institutions. For this reason, regional multilateral organizations, especially the IDB and the

Economic Commission for Latin America and the Caribbean (ECLAC), would have to play a role.

The final chapter in this volume, "Globalization, Tax Systems, and the Architecture of the Global Economic System" by Vito Tanzi, does not deal specifically with Latin America but with the impact of globalization, in all its aspects, on tax systems. Indirectly, the chapter concerns the economic roles of the state. It argues that various current developments—globalization, for example, and technological and policy changes—are likely to make it ever more difficult for governments to choose the tax structure they want and to collect the revenue they wish. Tanzi maintains that tax systems are now suffering from the existence of "fiscal termites." These, like real termites, may damage foundations—in this case the foundations of tax systems. It may take some time for these effects to become fully visible, but a lack of statistical evidence of these effects should not be interpreted as proof of their absence.

The chapter contends that the architecture of the global economic system lacks a basic element: an international organization responsible for overseeing national tax practices that harm other countries. Negative externalities arising from tax policy receive little attention, and no international institution keeps track of them. As tariffs and quantitative restrictions on trade are reduced, countries will likely rely more on instruments that they still control (indeed, this is already happening). Such instruments could be elements of the tax systems, and thus the negative externalities could become more powerful. An international organization that follows tax developments, identifies trends, calls attention to practices that might harm other countries, and provides a forum for senior national representatives to discuss tax reforms could be of global benefit.

The Fiscal Impact of Trade Liberalization

*Luiz Villela, Jerónimo Roca, and Alberto Barreix**

Introduction

The tax systems of Latin America and the Caribbean (LAC) were set up in the 1960s and 1970s, when most countries were applying import-substitution policies and barely beginning the processes of commercial and financial opening. Since economic conditions changed substantially in the 1990s, many of these systems do not efficiently promote trade and investment.

The prospects for a far-reaching, hemisphere-wide trade agreement that could permanently change economic structures in LAC are gloomy, given the stagnation of negotiations for the Free Trade Area of the Americas (FTAA). Most countries in the region are pursuing bilateral trade agreements, particularly with more developed economies, in order to expand their access to large external markets. Eventually this strategy will have to be accompanied by significant adjustments to most countries' tax structures, including both the tax system and its administration. In 2004, for example, about 46 percent of LAC's trade was with the United States.[1] The United States was also the leading source of foreign direct invest-

*The authors would like to thank Vito Tanzi and Fernando Velayos for comments and suggestions, and Patricia Abad for her assistance in compiling the tax data.

[1] According to estimates from the Inter-American Development Bank's trade databases for Latin American and Caribbean countries.

ment (FDI) in the region, accounting for 40 percent of total investment in 2005 (ECLAC, 2005a).

Tax Effects of Trade and Financial Liberalization

The intensification of trade and financial liberalization, and the subsequent deepening of economic integration processes, have significant implications for tax policy:

1. Providing impetus to sectors with comparative advantages, but also to those that are hard to tax.
2. Confining sectoral policies to tax incentives policies.
3. Posing difficulties in taxing financial capital, the most mobile production factor.
4. Heightening the importance of taxes on international activities.

Impetus to Sectors with Comparative Advantages, but Also to Those That Are Hard to Tax

In general, trade theory is very straightforward. It says, for example, that good and large-scale investment prompts growth, or that without growth, systematic indebtedness is not viable. The idea of comparative advantages in international trade, however, is subtle. In short, the theory holds that each country should export those goods that it can produce with a relatively greater cost advantage (or relatively lesser disadvantage), and import those goods in which it has a relatively lesser cost advantage (or relatively greater disadvantage). In other words, if two countries produce two goods and one country is more efficient in the production of both, the welfare of both countries will increase if each specializes in the production of the good at which it is relatively most efficient.

The emphasis on production in sectors with comparative advantages in LAC tends to lead to an increase in primary products (agricultural goods and nonrenewable natural resources) and a partial decline in the industrial sector (Barreix and Alvarez, 2001). Other trends, moreover, such as the outsourcing of services and the attendant proliferation of small businesses and microenterprises, give rise to a new distribution of value added among the three main economic sectors. Between 1980 and 2004, the share of manufacturing in LAC's gross domestic product (GDP) fell from 32 percent to 24 percent, and that of services increased from 54 percent to 66 percent—although the wholesale and retail trades declined from 17 percent to 13 percent (ECLAC, 2000b, 2005b). This has significant effects on tax policy and administration, since the majority group of taxpayers comprises those who are "hard to tax," especially farmers and urban microenterprises (Shome, 1999). It is likely that this circumstance might be partially offset by greater concentration of economic output, since in most countries of the region, less than 1 percent of taxpayers provide almost 75 percent of the tax take.

Confining Sectoral Policies to Tax Incentives Policies

Reduced and uniform customs tariffs have substantially lowered the effective protection of national production. This has triggered strong pressure for new incentives and fiscal benefits to protect sectors or regions, leading to significant tax waivers. Hence the proliferation in LAC of free zones, duty-free shops, and benefits for the tourist hotel industry, mining, and forestry. Nonetheless, most assessments of sectoral or regional policies based on tax incentives conclude that they have virtually no investment-promotion effect; they are simply conducive to tax evasion and, above all, avoidance, thereby damaging the economy as a whole. This has led to a "porous" income tax with fiscal loopholes through which taxable earnings leak. Hence income tax, especially on business, has high nominal rates (close to those of the developed countries), but real takings (effective tax rates) are very low, at about a third of the nominal value.

In small countries, moreover, it is harder for the tax administration to specialize because of problems of scale. This complicates the management of the exemptions, be they special import regimes (classification and origin problems) or sectoral and regional incentives. Thus it would be much more transparent to manage them with direct and temporary subsidies.

Finally, there is a tendency to engage in harmful tax practices. When tariff barriers are eliminated, it is no longer necessary to be installed in a market in order to supply it, and fiscal benefits become a means of retaining and attracting FDI. This is evidenced by the efforts of Brazilian states to induce automakers to set up local factories by offering fiscal incentives, a practice emulated by some provinces in Argentina.[2] Given the increase in tax expenditure, however (revenue lost because of the exemptions), the federal government is trying to amend the law so as to impose greater discipline on the states.

Difficulties in Taxing Financial Capital, the Most Mobile Production Factor

The liberalization of exchange controls and capital flows, in conjunction with the development of new financial instruments and communications technologies (which lowered marginal transaction costs), have given capital substantial relative mobility (Avi-Yonah, 2000). Between 1991 and 2000, gross capital flows between industrialized countries expanded by 300 percent, while the GDP of industrialized countries increased by 26 percent and international trade rose by 63 percent (Evans and Hnatkovska, 2005).

First, more sophisticated mechanisms for fiscal planning of the financial structure (such as replacing dividends with interest when the latter is untaxed), in tandem with new financial products (derivatives and similar instruments), enhance the prospect of arbitrage and heighten the tendency toward erosion of the income tax base.

Second, capital volatility and fiscal planning—using instruments such as "financial centers," offshore banking, hedge funds, and intercompany loans—have spurred competition between jurisdictions, which reduce the tax burden in order to retain and attract savings.

As a result, the liberalization of trade and capital flows has eroded the bases of taxes on external trade and nonwage income, which have been offset in Latin America by an increase in taxes on consumption and

---

[2] For the details of the "fiscal war" in Brazil, see Barreix and Villela (2003b).

wages.[3] These trends are similar to those in the member countries of the Organisation for Economic Co-operation and Development (OECD), and they have adverse effects on the equity of the tax systems.

The Heightened Importance of Taxes on International Transactions

The increase in transactions between affiliates in different countries has allowed intercompany prices to be set in a way that evades the tax authorities and the payment of tax.[4] According to the Economic Commission for Latin America and the Caribbean (ECLAC), the sale of transnational companies' affiliates increased in the 1990s at a much higher rate than global exports, and their production levels rose from 5 percent of GDP in 1982 to 10 percent in 2000 (ECLAC, 2000a). The stock of FDI, meanwhile, increased from 10.3 percent of GDP in 1990 to 36.7 percent of GDP in 2005, according to the United Nations Conference on Trade and Development (UNCTAD, 2006). Moreover, regional economic integration is creating a new kind of transnational: the "regional strategist," comprising regional companies or global companies with a regional strategy.[5] There are still no appropriate, region-wide regulatory frameworks in the tax field, either to benefit such firms (avoidance of

---

[3] According to Barreix and Alvarez (2001, *n* 1), between 1980 and 1997, for a representative set of Latin America countries, there was a 10 percent and a 4 percent decline, respectively, in the share of external trade taxes and income tax in the total collected. At the same time, consumption and payroll taxes increased by 11 percent and 5 percent, respectively.

[4] Highly skilled professionals supplying value in a knowledge-based economy are becoming more aware of the differential tax rates applied to their earnings and regard this as a significant factor in their decisions to emigrate.

[5] The great majority of multinationals (320 out of 380 for which data are available) gain, on average, 80 percent of all their sales in their home region of the triad (Japan, the European Union, and the United States/Canada). Only a handful of multinationals (nine) operate across all the regions of the triad. There are 25 biregional multinationals and another 11 geared toward a particular "host" country. Global markets are not becoming homogenized except in a few sectors, such as consumer electronics, for which a global strategy of economic integration is viable. In most other manufacturing fields, like the automobile industry, and in all services, regional strategies are required (Rugman, 2003).

double taxation, for example) or to control them so as to obviate their exploitation of trade facilities with a view to evading tax.

In addition to intercompany operations and new international financial instruments, significant progress in the area of information and communications technology is promoting international transactions in new and intangible goods and services, especially through the Internet, by means of e-commerce. Cross-border transactions have increased in volume and changed in nature.

Electronic commerce in intangible goods and services has a series of features that distinguish it radically from traditional operations: the division of activities in the international network increases the chances that producers will not be physically located; thus the principle of territoriality (which is fundamental to determining tax borders) becomes hazy, while the internationalization of transactions makes it hard to determine the tax base.[6] As a corollary, it becomes very difficult for tax policymakers and the tax administration to set and levy taxes on activities that originate outside their jurisdiction if the tax authorities in other countries do not cooperate (Byrne, 2001).

Tax policy and administration face a series of additional problems attendant on the internationalization of economies:

1. Assigning the tax base of multinational companies' income.
2. Tax on earnings and capital gains.
3. Information exchange.
4. Double taxation agreements.
5. Offshore centers and harmful incentive regimes.

Most LAC countries have not tackled these issues at the policy level, and, even worse, their tax administrations lack response capacity. In addition to the fall in the tax take, constraints on the control of these activities

---

[6] Credit card–branded products (special trademarks that are sold on credit card promotions) in Latin America hit a record sales volume of more than \$2.8 billion in 2005. This represents a growth rate of 42 percent over 2004.

confer a relative advantage on international companies receiving a high level of professional advice, since they can exploit the situation.

The Tax System under Pressure

In the final quarter of the twentieth century—as a result of structural adjustments triggered by the external debt crisis in developing countries, the abandonment of the state-led economic model, and the increase in trade and capital flows between countries—there was an unprecedented convergence of tax systems. In general, countries have adopted very similar systems. The six kinds of tax that have become the pillars of the export-promotion model applied in LAC since the 1970s are as follows: (1) value-added tax (VAT), which replaced myriad minor taxes on sales; (2) income tax on the earnings of both individuals and companies; (3) a small number of excise taxes exploiting the low price elasticity of some goods and services; (4) social security contributions (mainly calculated on the basis of nominal wages); (5) property tax, especially on real estate; and (6) tariffs, whose share of the total fell with greater unilateral trade opening and then again because of subregional integration.

Despite such similarities, the LAC countries adopted significantly different regulations (tax base, exemptions, rates, procedures, and so on), because there was no equivalent development in the consolidation of institutions that ensure a market economy, the depth of its markets, and the management capacity of the tax administrations. This has led to very different collection structures and levels of fiscal pressure.

In some countries of the region, moreover, the need to finance the permanent growth in public spending, coupled with exchange rate/financial crises, has demanded a substantial fiscal effort that in some cases might exceed taxpaying capacity. This excess burden has distorted the tax system as an instrument of the development strategy (trade openness with export-promotion) for which it was created. The "tax spiral" of continuous tax packages in response to the demands of growing public spending has

1. "Sullied" the tax systems. For example, some countries have fallen back on saturated tax bases like the payroll, levying inefficient

taxes such as those on bank debits and exports set by arbitrary rulings, and they have used sales taxes that have cumulative effects. This "tax activism" has given rise to technically poor taxes or increased the burden of distortionary taxes that undermine competitiveness.

2. Increased the system's unfairness. Because of limits on the extent to which the mobile factor (capital) can be taxed, and because of limited administrative capacity, the burden has fallen on consumption and wages. Excessive pressure on wages, through payroll or personal income taxes, undercuts the propensity to work (in the formal sector) and constrains national savings.

Recent Trends in Tariffs

Since the start of the 1980s, and especially since the Uruguay Round, unilateral trade liberalization has reduced average tariffs and their dispersion (standard deviation) in LAC, and tariff revenue has therefore declined (IDB, 2002). Further trade agreements in the Western Hemisphere and beyond should not lead to a significant loss of fiscal revenue (except in the Caribbean and some Central American countries) because levels of nominal protection are now very low. Table 2.1 shows the striking reduction in average nominal rates in LAC between 1985 and 2004.

Table 2.2 shows the clear trend towards the diminishing importance of import taxes throughout the world, and in Latin America in particular, in a context where the total tax burden has tended to increase slightly. It should be noted that despite the significant decline, tariff income is still more important in LAC than in developed countries, which use quota systems or nontariff barriers to protect crucial sectors.

A Comparison of Tax Structures and Trends

Table 2.3 offers a panoramic snapshot of taxation and of the total revenue of the nonfinancial public sector (NFPS) in LAC. Total average NFPS revenue (including social security contributions and revenue from

Table 2.1. Simple Average Tariff Rate and Its Deviation

Country	1985 average (%)	2000 Average (%)	2000 Standard deviation	2004 Average (%)	2004 Standard deviation
Argentina	28.0	13.3	6.7	10.7	7.5
Brazil	80.0	14.1	6.8	11.9	6.8
Chile	36.0	9.0	0.5	6.0	0.8
Colombia	83.0	11.6	6.3	11.9	7.2
Ecuador	50.0	11.3	6.4	11.3	6.4
El Salvador	53.2	7.3	8.6	7.5	8.9
Guatemala	50.0	7.1	8.0	6.0	6.7
Mexico	34.0	16.3	14.1	16.0	15.2
Nicaragua	54.0	4.2	5.8	5.5	6.9
Panama	41.3	9.2	10.1	8.6	10.6
Peru	64.0	13.5	3.7	10.4	5.2
Uruguay	32.0	12.5	6.8	11.4	6.5
Venezuela	30.0	12.0	6.0	12.0	6.1

Source: UNCTAD Trade Analysis and Information System.

Table 2.2. Import Duties in Selected Countries
(percentage of GDP)

Country	1985	1995	2000	2004
Latin America and the Caribbean				
Argentina	2.29	0.73	0.65	0.73
Bahamas	13.84	12.24	10.70	7.30
Bolivia	1.67	1.09	1.17	1.00
Brazil	0.62	0.80	0.77	0.50
Chile	3.06	2.07	1.29	0.60
Colombia	1.97	1.04	1.06	0.88
Costa Rica	4.38	3.06	1.03	1.14
Dominican Republic	3.69	5.87	3.89	4.79
Mexico	0.65	0.61	0.55	0.40
Nicaragua	2.56	5.25	1.38	0.96
Peru	3.26	1.75	1.47	1.20
Uruguay	2.78	0.98	0.83	1.30
Venezuela	3.86	1.50	1.21	0.99
Other countries				
Australia	1.36	0.75	0.68	0.69
Austria	0.48	0.01	0.00	0.00
Canada	0.89	0.37	0.25	0.23
France	0.01	0.00	0.00	0.02
Italy	0.01	0.00	0.00	0.00
Spain	1.29	0.00	0.00	0.01
Sweden	0.23	0.27	0.02	0.00
United States	0.30	0.27	0.21	0.20

Sources: IMF; ECLAC; various governments; OECD.

Table 2.3. Tax Structure, 2004

Group and country	GDP (PPP, US$ millions)[1]	Total NFPS revenue	Total tax revenue (excluding social security)	Tax burden (% of GDP)							Share of total tax revenue (%)				
				Social security	Direct taxes	Indirect taxes					Direct taxes	Indirect taxes			
						All	General goods and services	Excise	Import taxes			All	General goods and services	Excise	Import taxes
MERCOSUR	**2,078,734**	**34.5**	**27.6**	**6.2**	**8.5**	**19.2**	**8.2**	**1.8**	**0.6**	**30.8**	**69.2**	**29.7**	**6.9**	**2.4**
Argentina	510,266	28.7	24.3	3.0	9.5	14.9	6.9	2.1	0.7	38.9	61.1	28.5	8.7	3.0
Brazil[2]	1,507,106	36.8	29.2	7.4	8.3	20.9	8.7	1.7	0.5	28.5	71.5	29.8	5.9	1.8
Paraguay[3]	28,960	22.2	11.9	1.1	2.2	9.8	4.7	2.4	2.2	18.3	81.7	39.1	20.4	18.2
Uruguay	32,402	29.8	22.9	8.5	5.2	17.7	8.5	3.1	1.3	22.7	77.3	37.1	13.5	5.8
Chile[4]	175,323	36.3	17.3	1.4	4.2	13.2	8.4	1.7	0.6	24.0	76.0	48.4	10.1	3.3
Mexico[5]	**1,017,529**	**23.0**	**10.0**	**1.4**	**4.7**	**5.3**	**3.7**	**1.2**	**0.4**	**47.1**	**52.9**	**36.9**	**11.8**	**3.9**
Andean Community	**716,485**	**25.5**	**15.0**	**2.1**	**5.7**	**9.4**	**5.9**	**1.6**	**1.0**	**36.2**	**63.8**	**40.9**	**10.7**	**7.1**
Bolivia[6]	24,501	27.5	15.7	1.9	3.6	12.1	6.6	2.1	1.0	22.9	77.1	42.0	13.6	6.4
Colombia[7]	325,915	30.3	17.6	2.8	8.4	9.2	5.9	2.0	0.9	47.6	52.4	33.5	11.6	5.0
Ecuador[8]	51,681	26.7	15.9	3.3	2.9	12.9	6.2	0.9	1.6	18.4	81.6	39.3	5.6	9.8
Peru[9]	156,511	17.8	13.3	1.6	3.9	9.5	5.4	2.0	1.2	28.9	71.1	40.7	14.7	9.0
Venezuela[10]	157,877	22.6	11.1	0.6	3.1	8.0	6.4	0.7	1.0	27.9	72.1	57.0	6.2	8.9
Central America	**190,361**	**18.7**	**12.5**	**2.9**	**3.7**	**8.9**	**5.1**	**2.2**	**1.2**	**29.8**	**70.2**	**40.8**	**16.5**	**10.0**
Costa Rica[11]	40,325	22.8	13.9	6.2	4.0	9.9	5.5	3.2	1.1	28.5	71.5	40.0	23.1	8.2
El Salvador[12]	34,088	16.3	11.5	1.7	3.5	8.0	6.0	0.5	1.1	30.2	69.8	52.3	4.1	9.7
Guatemala[13]	53,027	11.0	10.6	0.2	2.7	7.9	4.8	1.1	1.1	25.5	74.5	45.3	10.4	10.4
Honduras[12,14]	20,273	28.7	17.2	1.1	4.6	12.6	6.2	5.0	1.4	26.5	73.5	36.0	29.2	8.2
Nicaragua[11,12]	19,538	22.3	15.7	3.5	4.4	11.3	6.4	3.9	1.0	28.2	71.8	40.7	24.9	6.1
Panama[12,15]	23,110	21.3	9.5	5.6	4.3	5.2	1.8	1.8	1.6	45.3	54.7	18.9	18.9	17.6
Caribbean[16]	**123,013**	**19.2**	**17.6**	**0.4**	**6.0**	**11.6**	**4.2**	**2.4**	**3.9**	**30.1**	**69.9**	**24.0**	**14.8**	**25.9**
Bahamas[13]	6,147	16.6	14.8	2.2	0.7	14.1	0.0	3.4	7.3	4.7	95.3	0.0	23.0	62.8

(continued on next page)

Table 2.3. Tax Structure, 2004 *(continued)*

Group and country	GDP (PPP, US$ millions)[1]	Total NFPS revenue	Total tax revenue (excluding social security)	Tax burden (% of GDP)						Share of total tax revenue (%)				
				Social security	Direct taxes	All	Indirect taxes			Direct taxes	Indirect taxes			
							General goods and services	Excise	Import taxes		All	General goods and services	Excise	Import taxes
Barbados[17]	4,288	32.7	30.9	2.3	13.4	17.5	9.4	4.2	3.1	43.2	56.8	30.5	13.6	10.0
Belize	2,093	22.5	20.4	2.3	5.3	15.2	5.7	0.5	3.6	25.7	74.3	27.7	2.3	17.4
Dominican Rep.[18]	65,315	16.4	15.3	0.0	3.4	11.9	3.9	2.9	4.8	22.1	77.9	25.7	19.2	31.3
Guyana[19]	3,278	28.8	28.7	4.0	14.1	14.7	10.6	0.4	2.3	49.0	51.0	37.0	1.4	8.0
Haiti[18]	14,333	8.9	8.9	0.0	1.9	7.0	2.6	0.8	2.5	21.3	78.7	29.2	9.4	28.1
Jamaica[20]	10,727	28.4	24.6	0.7	9.7	14.9	6.7	2.5	2.4	39.4	60.6	27.2	10.2	9.9
Suriname[13]	2,696	32.4	28.4	1.2	13.5	15.0	5.7	3.0	4.7	47.5	52.8	20.1	10.6	16.5
Trinidad and Tobago[17]	14,136	27.0	23.7	0.6	16.3	7.5	3.4	1.5	1.6	68.5	31.5	14.4	6.1	6.6
Latin America and the Caribbean	**4,301,445**	**29.2**	**20.0**	**4.1**	**6.7**	**13.3**	**6.5**	**1.7**	**0.7**	**35.2**	**64.8**	**34.4**	**9.5**	**4.6**

Sources: IMF, ECLAC, various governments, Inter-American Development Bank Department of Integration Consultancies.

[1] PPP = purchasing power parity.
[2] For taxes on goods and services, the ICMS (Impuesto a la Circulación de Mercancías y Servicios) was considered.
[3] Total revenue refers to the consolidated public sector revenues (IMF data). Total tax revenue refers to the central government.
[4] Total revenue includes copper. Total tax revenue excludes copper (data from IMF and Chile's Servicio de Impuestos Internos [SII]). Estimation of direct taxes is based on SII data including income, estate, inheritance, and gift taxes.
[5] Total revenue includes oil revenue in addition to other nontax and non-oil revenue (including public enterprises). Total tax revenue excludes public enterprises' oil revenue and includes excise taxes on oil.
[6] Total tax revenue excludes hydrocarbons.
[7] Total revenue refers to the combined public sector (IMF data). Total tax revenue includes taxes on oil.
[8] Total revenue includes oil. Total tax revenue excludes oil revenue.
[9] Total revenue refers to the nonfinancial public sector (IMF data). Total tax revenue refer to the central government.
[10] Total revenue refers to the central government, including oil. Total tax revenue refers to the non-oil central government.
[11] Total revenue refers to the combined public sector (IMF data).
[12] Total tax revenue refers to the central government.
[13] Total revenue and tax revenue refer to the central government (IMF data).
[14] Total revenue refers to the combined public sector and includes the nonfinancial public sector and the quasi-fiscal deficit of the central bank (IMF data).
[15] Total revenue refers to the nonfinancial public sector, excluding operations of the Panama Canal Authority.
[16] Weighted average for social security revenue in the Caribbean excludes Guyana.
[17] Data are for 2003. Total revenue and tax revenue refer to the central government.
[18] Total revenue and tax revenue refer to the central government.
[19] Data are for 2003. Total revenue and tax revenue refer to the central government. Taxes on goods and services include consumption taxes on both domestic and imported goods and services.
[20] GDP is for 2003. Other data are for the 2002/03 fiscal year. Total revenue and tax revenue refer to the central government.

the exploitation of natural resources) accounts for almost 30 percent of the region's GDP, while the average tax burden (without social security) reached about 20 percent in 2004.[7]

Table 2.3 reveals the significant differences between country groups. The Southern Common Market (MERCOSUR) has the highest averages (27.6 percent for the tax burden and 34.5 percent NFPS revenue), followed by the Caribbean (17.6 percent and 19.2 percent), the Andean Community (15.0 percent and 25.5 percent), and Central America (12.5 percent and 18.7 percent).

In LAC, indirect taxes account for 65 percent of the tax take. Consumption taxes, generally VAT, account for more than half of that share. Income from excise taxes is about 50 percent higher than that from taxes on imports. These proportions, however, vary substantially between the regions. The burden of general consumption taxes is much lower in the Caribbean, where it accounts for 25 percent of tax revenue; it runs to about 40 percent in the rest of Latin America.

As regards import taxes, the level of dependence is reasonably low for the LAC weighted average, standing at just 6 percent of tax revenues. Again, however, this varies substantially between the regions. In MERCOSUR, the average is 2 percent (high only in Paraguay, at 18 percent); in the Andean Community, it accounts for around 7 percent; in Central America, for 10 percent; and in the Caribbean, for 26 percent. The Bahamas is an extreme case (63 percent). In the Caribbean countries, in fact, import tax revenue is very close to revenue from general consumption tax. Finally, note that revenue from import taxes in Central America is about two-thirds of that from excise taxes, and only a quarter of that from VAT.

Remember that Table 2.3 is an overview of the tax structure in LAC for 2004. There are substantial differences among countries, and three important characteristics should be highlighted. First, as regards the

---

[7] GDP, measured in terms of purchasing power parity, was used to weight the individual tax burdens. It should be recalled that the difference between the tax burden and the total revenue of the NFPS is smaller in countries with mixed or privately run social security systems or where natural resources are not important or are exploited by the private sector.

different jurisdictions with the power to tax, unitary systems (which include only the central and municipal levels of government) should be distinguished from federal systems, which include a third level (state or provincial). LAC has four federal countries: Argentina, Brazil, Mexico, and Venezuela.[8] In the latter two, subnational state revenue is less than 5 percent of total tax income. In Argentina, by contrast, provincial tax revenue is equivalent to almost 4 percent of GDP and accounts for a sixth of total income. In Brazil, state taxes are equivalent to 11 percent of GDP and almost a third of tax revenue. Colombia is unusual in regard to decentralization. Although the country is a unitary republic, about 15 percent of tax is collected at the subnational level. While the provinces account for a growing share, they secure only a small part of tax revenue, with the bulk coming from municipalities.

A second characteristic is the importance of income from public enterprises, especially from nonrenewable natural resources, a circumstance that very much influences the total revenue of the NFPS. For Ecuador, Mexico, Trinidad and Tobago, and Venezuela, the income from oil and natural gas represents a substantial share of revenues. Similar is the income from copper in Chile, from hydroelectricity in Paraguay, from the Canal in Panama, and from state monopolies in Brazil, Costa Rica, and Uruguay.

Finally, note that contributions to social security are particularly significant in Uruguay, Brazil, and Argentina, accounting for 8.5 percent, 7.4 percent, and 3.0 percent of GDP, respectively. Costa Rica is similar: social security contributions account for 6.2 percent of GDP. It should be recalled, however, that in countries like Bolivia, Chile, El Salvador, and Mexico, social security is privately managed (with a minimal public contribution) on actuarial bases. Thus the contributions do not feature in the fiscal accounts. Circumstances are similar in Argentina, Colombia, Peru, and Uruguay, where a public system based on intergenerational solidarity is complemented by a privately run system based on individual accounts.[9]

---

[8] Peru has an incipient fiscal decentralization process.

[9] According to the International Association for Supervisory Organizations of Pension Funds (http://www.aiosfp.org/), in countries where all or part of social security

The Tariff Cost of Integration

Many economists accept the proposition, borne out by many successful experiences, that trade liberalization improves economic efficiency and fosters development. However, the fact that free trade can lead to a decline in public revenues is an issue that demands special attention. In countries with severe fiscal imbalances, a common circumstance in LAC, any loss of revenue requires careful assessment.

In addition to certain sectors' loss of protection, the countries must face a fiscal problem that arises when they decide to intensify their trade links with the rest of the world: the impact of the elimination of tariff barriers on public sector income. This is particularly important in developing countries with limited capacity to collect direct taxes, whose public finances therefore depend to a significant extent on revenue from taxes on external trade.

The Tax Effects of Trade Integration

The income effects of regional integration, and of trade liberalization more generally, can be uncertain (Tanzi, 1989), and in the final analysis the net outcome will depend on empirical assessment. The effects depend on initial conditions in each country and the kind of tariff reform it undertakes.[10] For the purposes of this analysis, changes in trade policy have five kinds of effects on tax earnings:

---

is in privately managed individual accounts, the amounts of funds managed in 2004 were as follows (as a percentage of GDP): Argentina, 12.0; Bolivia, 20.5; Chile, 59.1; Colombia, 10.3; Costa Rica, 2.7; Dominican Republic, 1.9; El Salvador, 13.7; Mexico, 5.8; Peru, 11.0; and Uruguay, 16.1. The average for these countries was 11.8 percent (*Boletín Estadístico AIOS* 12, December 2004). Private social security contributions for 2004 were as follows (as a percentage of GDP): Argentina, 0.74; Bolivia, 2.15; Chile, 3.43; Colombia, 1.10; Dominican Republic, 0.65; El Salvador, 1.48; Mexico, 1.22; Peru, 1.67; and Uruguay, 1.10. Countries such as Colombia and Brazil (not included) have contributions to pension funds managed by provinces or state-owned enterprises.

[10] For a traditional approach to estimating the impact of trade liberalization, see Ebrill, Stotsky, and Gropp (1999).

1. *Direct:* the loss of income associated with the reduction or elimination of nominal tariff rates on products subject to the trade
   agreement.
2. *Indirect:* the decline in revenue from other taxes based on cost, insurance, and freight (CIF), plus import tariff values (particularly
   VAT and excise taxes on consumption), associated with the fall in
   the tariff rate.
3. *Elasticity:* the net result of the probable increase in the volume of
   goods imported with lower or no tariffs, which are now cheaper,
   and the corresponding increase in internal taxes.[11]
4. *Substitution:* the decline in revenue attendant on trade diversion,
   since imports facing tariffs are displaced by purchases from the
   partners in the agreement (see Box 2.1).
5. *Induced:* the change in the collection of all taxes as a result of the
   new structure of production and consumption that springs from
   the new form of commercial insertion.

The first two effects, direct and indirect, are concomitant with the
process of tariff reduction. The other three effects arise with greater
or lesser intensity and at different stages after the reduction in tariff
rates.

The direct (tariff reduction) and substitution (trade diversion) effects entail a loss of revenue. The substitution effect is negative for the
public coffers because purchases from trade partners for which the tariff
has been lowered displace taxed imports from third countries.

The overall fiscal impact of the indirect effect and the elasticity effect will depend on the market structure. While the indirect effect of
tariff reduction diminishes the VAT base (and that of excise taxes, as
the case may be), the decline can be offset at later stages in the market-
ing process (depending on the good's demand elasticity), and there is

---

[11] Although the goods are not completely tariff-exempt, the price-effect reduction
leads to an increase in imported value and in the corresponding customs and internal
taxes. As with any other tax, moreover, tariff reduction also has an income effect: more
income is available because of the lower import cost.

Box 2.1. The Substitution Effect

Broadly speaking, it can be said that the reduction of tariffs on imports from a particular country (the result, for example, of a trade agreement) has two effects: trade creation and trade diversion.

Trade is created in the sense that, because of the tariff preference, goods of a lower relative cost from the trade partner with which an agreement is concluded displace goods of a higher relative cost produced within the country itself. Trade is diverted in the sense that goods of a higher relative cost from the trade partner with which an agreement is concluded displace goods of a lower relative cost from third countries that do not enjoy tariff preferences.

The impact of trade diversion on tax revenue is negative because purchases from trade partners for whom the tariff has been lowered displace taxed imports from third countries.

The scale of the diversion will depend on (1) the extent of the fall in relative prices prompted by the tariff reduction; and (2) the elasticity of substitution of the goods imported from partner countries, relative to the rest of the world.[a] The elasticity of substitution measures the relative reaction of the relationship between imports from two countries, A and B, in a context of percentage changes in the relative prices of the imports.

If M_A and M_B are the imports from A and B, respectively, and P_A and P_B are the prices of those imports, then the elasticity of substitution is

$$\varepsilon_S = \left[\Delta(M_A / M_B)/(M_A / M_B)\right]/\left[\Delta(P_A / P_B)/(P_A / P_B)\right]$$

The elasticity of substitution is an empirical matter, and thus quantification of the effect demands a more specific analysis of each market. As a general criterion, however, and given most countries' low share of extra-FTAA imports, it is not tendentious to aver that the revenue losses arising from this effect will be minor.

[a] The British economist John Hicks introduced the concept of elasticity of substitution in 1932 in order to measure the relative reaction of the capital-labor ratio in the context of percentage changes in the marginal rate of technical substitution of capital for labor.

even a chance that the tax take will rise. The fiscal result of the elasticity effect, as well as being dependent on demand (like the indirect effect), will also be influenced by the structure of the market for the product in question. If the importer has a monopsony, for example, he can appropriate much of the tariff reduction. Thus the final price falls little, other taxes will be marginally affected, and the benefit to the consumer is less.

The induced effect is macroeconomic and thus should be analyzed using general equilibrium models. Moreover, this effect is more uncertain because it affects production and consumption throughout the economy, as well as trade patterns, and hence the total of all the taxes levied.

Assessments of the fiscal impact of the final four effects require fieldwork: specific analyses of each market are needed to assess the indirect, elasticity, and substitution effects, and an examination of the whole economy is required to gauge the induced effect. This chapter therefore confines itself to estimating only the direct effect of tariff reduction, which is the most significant in the short term.

From the fiscal perspective, the challenges of trade liberalization and tariff reduction are (1) quantitative assessment of the measures' fiscal effects, and (2) deciding what to do about fiscal policy in general—that is, offsetting revenue losses with other taxes, cutting expenditure, or accepting a wider deficit.

Trade Liberalization or Marginal Tariff Reduction

From the perspective of fiscal effects, it is helpful to distinguish between two kinds of tariff adjustments that have been experienced and are being experienced in the region. They depend on the scale of the change in the trade openness of the country in question.

One case, trade liberalization, is that of a quite closed economy with a high level of tariff and nontariff protection, which decides to remove many of its trade barriers. This is a discrete substantive change, and thus estimates of elasticities using historical data are of little use in calculating income—because of, among other things, the significant change in the level and composition of imports. In this context, a simplistic calculation might be highly distorted because many tariff rates are redundant at the outset ("water" or redundant protection in the tariffs). The other case is the marginal reduction in rates or the conclusion of trade agreements with partners who are not important to the country's trade. In this case, the reduction effect is less through rate level or import coverage; its fiscal impact therefore tends to be negative and generally easier to estimate.

Chile reduced tariffs in the mid-1970s, as Table 2.4 shows, and there were practically no fiscal effects. Only when the rates were harmonized at about 15–20 percent (lowering nominal protection) did successive reductions begin to cause significant revenue losses.

Currently, and almost without exception, the LAC countries do not have tariff structures of such a scale that they could be classified as redundant protection. In general the economies are fairly open to foreign trade and feature very few nontariff barriers, and the tariffs have almost no "water."

In recent decades, almost the entire region has moved toward lower protection levels, reducing tariffs, lowering nontariff barriers, and eliminating "water" from the tariffs. This suggests that the fiscal effects of trade agreements will be a net loss in revenue. In most of the Caribbean countries, where some tariffs remain high, their main purpose is to generate revenue, not to protect domestic production.

Nonetheless, and as mentioned earlier with regard to the five tax effects, the impact is hard to estimate accurately because it will depend on different and complex economic reactions. While it is difficult to generalize, the demand for final consumer goods is more elastic than that for intermediate goods and raw materials. In developing countries, imports of finished goods are less important than raw materials and capital goods, but they habitually face higher tariffs. The elimination of such higher

Table 2.4. Chile: Tariff Rates and Taxes on External Trade

Year	Nominal tariff rate (%)[1]	Taxes on external trade	
		Percentage of imports	Percentage of GDP
1975	49	13.9	2.9
1980	10	7.5	1.4
1985	26	17.1	3.2
1990	15	9.0	2.2
1995	11	7.6	1.9
2000	9	5.5	1.4
2001	8	4.5	1.2
2004	6	2.3	0.6

Sources: Vial (2003); UNCTAD Trade Analysis and Information System, tariff rate 2004; government tax data.
[1] Note that nontariff barriers as well as tariffs were lowered.

tariffs on consumer goods can lead to significant revenue losses, but these can be partially offset by the increase in import volumes, which entails higher revenue from domestic taxes because of the high elasticity.

Tariff Exemptions and Tax Evasion

It should also be recalled that when the tariff structure changes, its design has a constraining determinant, as with any other tax: the capacity to administer it. This has been shown empirically in studies, such as that by Pritchett and Sethi (1994), which reveal the nonlinear link between legal tariffs and those actually levied. The argument is that the higher the tariff, the greater the incentive to seek an exemption. Thus income does not rise in line with tariff increases, just as reducing high tariffs does not lead to a proportional decline in income. When the tariff is high, moreover, there is an incentive to classify imported goods as lower-tariff or exempted products, or to engage in smuggling, which also entails a decline in internal taxes.

Estimate of the Direct Loss of Tariff Revenue Caused by Trade Agreements

In the last few years, mainly as a result of the stagnation of the FTAA negotiations, several LAC countries have negotiated or are considering negotiating bilateral or regional trade agreements, especially with the United States and the European Union (EU), but also between regional blocs. Table 2.5 presents an estimate of the loss of import tariff revenue for some LAC countries that have concluded trade agreements with the United States or are considering doing so. In the cases of the Central American Free Trade Agreement (CAFTA) signatories, along with Colombia and Peru, the estimates were based on the agreed concessions when fully implemented. In the cases of the Caribbean Community (CARICOM) countries, along with Panama and Uruguay, a zero tariff in transactions between the agreement's signatories was assumed, so as to discern the scale of the final impact of the tariff-reduction process.

Table 2.5. Projected Annual Loss of Import Tariff Revenue from Trade Agreement with the United States

Country	Import tariff revenue loss (% of GDP)[1]	Tax revenue (% of GDP)	Import tariff revenue loss/tax revenue (%)
CARICOM countries			
Bahamas	4.50	14.80	30.41
Guyana	1.30	28.74	4.52
Haiti	1.50	8.90	16.85
Suriname	1.70	28.40	5.99
Trinidad and Tobago	0.60	23.74	2.53
CAFTA countries[2]			
Costa Rica	0.62	13.88	4.44
El Salvador	0.52	11.50	4.56
Guatemala	0.65	10.60	6.09
Honduras	1.08	17.06	6.32
Nicaragua	0.47	15.70	2.98
Andean countries[3]			
Colombia	0.55	17.57	3.10
Peru	0.28	13.34	2.11
Others[4]			
Panama	0.70	8.77	7.95
Uruguay	0.09	22.90	0.39

Source: Authors' estimates based on IDB data.

[1] In all cases of tariff rate quotas, tariffs are levied beyond the quota, and thus only the amount over the restriction is subject to the tariff schedule of the trade promotion agreement. Because the quota for any given item is no more than 5 percent of total imports from the United States, and also because imports over the quota are usually taxed at higher rates than the average, we assumed no losses on these items.

[2] Calculations are based on a basket of goods from each country and 2003 imports. Import tariff revenues are calculated on the basis of nominal tariff rates that appear in each country's offer. This does not include any subjective benefits available.

[3] Calculations are based on 2004 imports.

[4] Calculations are based on 2005 imports.

The estimates for the CARICOM countries are the preliminary results of a study commissioned by the Inter-American Development Bank (IDB) as part of a technical cooperation project to assess the fiscal impact of trade liberalization in that region. The database was extracted from the actual import transactions conducted at each country's customs in 2004.

As regards the other countries, the estimates of revenue losses were based on tariff rates obtained from each country schedule and on import values taken from the database of the IDB's Institute for the Integration of Latin America and the Caribbean (INTAL). It should be noted that the imports and their corresponding tariffs were considered item by item—that is, at the highest level of disaggregation of the tariff nomenclature. Similarly, the tariff-reduction schedules negotiated by each CAFTA and Andean country were used.

The tariff revenue losses estimated in the table stem solely from the first, direct effect of eliminating tariffs that were previously positive, assuming that the level of imports before the elimination remains constant. Hence this is a static comparison.

The lost revenue is expressed as a percentage of each country's GDP and total tax revenue. To assess the scale of the loss, the table also shows the total tax burden relative to GDP. For the same percentage loss in tax income, the implications differ according to whether a country has a high or low level of taxation.

The CARICOM and CAFTA countries experience the most significant fall in tariff revenue. The decline in the two Andean countries is lower. Uruguay suffers only a negligible loss, especially when its total tax burden is taken into account.

The results are quite widely dispersed among the CARICOM countries. The revenue losses are significant in countries such as the Bahamas (30.4 percent of tax revenue), Haiti (16.9 percent), and Suriname (6.0 percent), and less so in Guyana (4.5 percent) and Trinidad and Tobago (2.5 percent). There is less dispersion in CAFTA countries, where the total loss of revenue at the end of the tariff-elimination schedule will be between 3 and 6 percent of total tax revenues; Honduras is the most affected and Nicaragua the least. Of the two Andean countries, Colombia should lose more since it is more dependent on trade with the United States than Peru. Panama, which also conducts a significant level of trade with the United States and has relatively high tariffs, would lose a significant amount of revenue (8 percent). Circumstances would be quite different in Uruguay, where a trade agreement with the United States would have almost no impact on revenues.

Tables 2.6 and 2.7 present estimates of the loss in import tariff revenues for the CAFTA countries and the two Andean countries during their negotiated tariff-reduction schedules, indicating the reasonable time frame they will have in order to make the necessary adjustments in their domestic tax policies to offset the lower import tax take.

For some CARICOM countries, Table 2.8 presents preliminary estimates of the total potential loss of tariff revenue and the type of adjustment in domestic taxes that could offset those losses.

Fiscal Challenges

Irrespective of the challenges posed by trade liberalization, treasuries in LAC may face difficulties in spite of the current tax buoyancy due to a very positive phase of the cycle (quite favorable terms of trade, sustained world economic growth [demand], relatively low interest rates, etc.). Hence integration adds to the demands made on the traditional

Table 2.6. CAFTA: Estimated Hypothetical Loss of Import Tariff Revenue from Trade Agreement with the United States[1]

	Loss at the end of each period (% of GDP)					
Country	1 year	5 years	10 years	15 years	20 years	Total loss
Costa Rica	0.31	0.43	0.56	0.59	0.61	0.62
El Salvador	0.18	0.29	0.42	0.43	0.43	0.52
Guatemala	0.27	0.37	0.53	0.53	0.53	0.65
Honduras	0.29	0.47	0.68	0.69	0.70	1.08
Nicaragua	0.21	0.31	0.38	0.39	0.39	0.47

Source: IDB data.
[1] Calculations are based on a basket of goods from each country and 2003 imports. Import tariff revenues are calculated on the basis of nominal tariff rates that appear in each country's offer. This does not include any subjective benefits available.

Table 2.7. Colombia and Peru: Estimated Hypothetical Loss of Import Tariff Revenue from Trade Agreement with the United States[1]

	Loss at the end of each period (% of GDP)					
Country	1 year	5 years	10 years	15 years	20 years	Total loss
Colombia	0.45	0.51	0.55	0.55	0.55	0.55
Peru	0.22	0.26	0.28	0.28	0.28	0.28

Source: IDB data.
[1] Calculations are based on 2004 imports.

Table 2.8. CARICOM: Estimated Loss of Import Tariff Revenue from Trade Agreement with the United States and the Policy Response Considered

Country	Annual loss (% of GDP)	Tax reform considered
Bahamas	4.5	Introduction of VAT at 13.4%
Guyana	1.3	Introduction of VAT at 14.4% and adjustment of excises
Haiti	1.5	Increase of VAT from 10.0%to 15.8%
Suriname	1.7	Introduction of VAT at 17.5% and adjustment of excises
Trinidad and Tobago	0.6	Increase of VAT from 15.0% to 18.9%

Source: IDB.

functions of fiscal policy, and especially tax policy. Tax policy should meet the sufficiency criteria to (1) finance traditional spending and investment, be they in social areas or infrastructure; (2) finance temporary spending, such as stabilization of the economic cycle or crises in the external sector; (3) finance contingencies, such as financial or exchange rate crises; and (4) tackle the fiscal impact of trade liberalization and integration. One function is permanent: replacing tariff revenue; the other is temporary: compensating "losers" among the sectors and regions that are currently protected. To address these challenges in the most effective way, the tax authorities could institute a new instrument: minimum coordination of national tax policy and administration by means of international cooperation.

Compensation for Losses and for the "Losers" in a Process of Greater Trade Opening

While trade opening yields significant economic benefits over the long term, the timing and scale of the impact on the existing productive structure could cause losses and transitional costs that endanger the political viability of the reforms. To ensure that they are implemented correctly, therefore, and to attenuate the social costs, there is a need for sectoral and regional support and restructuring programs based on objective economic criteria. These represent an additional cost for public finances. These compensations to reconvert the losers, and the facilitation of assistance and infrastructure to support the new opportunities conferred by expanded trade, usually have relevant fiscal impacts.

Finally, these temporary restructuring and assistance programs might be needed to guarantee that the transition to free trade is successful. Above all, they should be designed so that market forces steer the resources in the economy to activities that promote high growth and long-term job creation (Abed, 1998).

The Need for Minimum Coordination among the Members

The EU is an example of successful cooperation. It is the only integration process that has made some progress on fiscal coordination, mostly on indirect taxation. In meeting deep integration objectives, there are three basic lessons to be drawn from the EU experience of tax.

The first, in line with the principles of nondiscrimination between domestic production and imports, is to harmonize indirect taxes because they directly affect trade and to ensure transparency that reduces the discretionary power of national authorities, thereby strengthening investors' property rights. This requires the prior harmonization of tax bases and procedures, as well as the equalization of rates, which can vary within a certain range.

The second lesson is that the process of harmonizing direct taxes is more difficult than the process of harmonizing indirect taxes. However, while direct tax harmonization has been sluggish in the EU, it has yielded some important agreements, such as the common taxation of cross-border distribution of dividends between associated companies (the Parent-Subsidiary Directive) and the Savings Directive. The latter makes use of the institutional apparatus that encompasses

- The Council of the EU (member states' economy and finance ministers, known as the Ecofin, and a range of lower-level groups), which decides on tax policy proposals and works as a platform for tax policy coordination.

■ The European Commission, which facilitates the Council's difficult decision-making process by setting up technical discussion groups that pave the way for actual tax policy proposals. The Commission also carries out technical work in the field of tax cooperation (the Standing Committee on Administrative Cooperation, the Fiscalis program, and so forth) in order to fight tax evasion and ensure that the income from intra-EU operations is fairly divided.[12]

■ The European Court of Justice, which, more than settling disputes, rightfully applies the EU *acquis*—that is, the treaties, principles, and regulations.

The third lesson to be drawn from the EU's experience is that there is a need for a compensation system, which could cover sectors and regions in the various countries. There are two reasons for fiscal compensation. The first is to temporarily compensate the less developed regions that are affected by closer integration and trade liberalization. The second involves a system of fiscal transfers to compensate for asymmetries in the overall negotiations, such as excluded sectors or special treatment, as with the EU's common agricultural policy. Income from the common external tariff (CET) and a percentage of national VAT is used to finance these activities.[13]

The EU sought to create a common market after having made substantial progress in the area of macroeconomic coordination (which

---

[12] For more on this issue, see Barreix and Villela (2003a).

[13] Since the founding in 1951 of the European Coal and Steel Community, which set levies on coal and steel production, there have been common sources of financing. The same was true for the European Economic Community and then the EU. Initially, national contributions were set as a percentage of the member states' budget spending. In 1970 this system was replaced by another, whereby contributions came from levies on agriculture, taxes on sugar production, customs duties received at the Community's external borders, and 1 percent of the VAT base collected by each member. In 1985 the Community's budget needs gave rise to an increase in the VAT contribution from 1.0 percent to 1.4 percent. This led in 1988 to the creation of a complementary system based on the members' gross national product (GNP). After the VAT contribution fell back to 1 percent in 1999, the members agreed on the need for supplementary financing—confined to 1.27 percent of each country's GNP—in order to guarantee a balanced budget grounded in the GNP-based contribution. It is

gave rise to a single currency), as well as in areas such as regulation and social policies. It should also be acknowledged that in the field of external trade, the EU has protected strategic productive sectors, mostly primary products, by means of tariff quotas, production subsidies, and, in some cases, export subsidies.

In Latin America, with a few significant exceptions, there has been virtually no tax harmonization. Nonetheless, the Andean countries recently agreed to harmonize their VAT taxable base within 10 years (Arias et al., 2005).

Tariff Replacement Options

Once possible losses from fiscal income have been estimated, the authorities must decide on the direction of fiscal policy: to offset the revenue loss, reduce spending, or accept a deficit by increasing public indebtedness. The various options will differ for each country according to the amount of compensation needed, the characteristics of each economy, the current (and politically feasible) structure of internal taxes, and the capacity of the tax administration. The higher deficit alternative is increasingly unviable in LAC, where average indebtedness levels are already high. Cutting spending is feasible only in conjunction with a much greater effort to increase public sector productivity, given the immense social needs and the demand for better infrastructure. Offsetting the losses by raising other taxes demands a country-by-country analysis of the tax strategy to be pursued.

The following sections offer some general guidelines, with particular attention to those countries deemed to be the most fiscally vulnerable in their trade liberalization process. The first two sections concern immediate effects, and the next three assume a substantial medium-term effort. In principle, it seems reasonable that tariff replacement be based on a higher burden of indirect taxes (VAT and excise taxes), as discussed in the first two sections. For the fiscal sustainability and legitimacy of the integration process, however, it is important to have

---

important to note that the VAT contribution and the complementary GNP contribution finance more than 80 percent of EU expenditures.

an effective increase in direct tax revenue. Finally, the improved performance of income and real estate taxes over the medium and long term will improve the horizontal and vertical equity of the system (the chapter's last three sections).

The Semantic Correction: Tariffs Disguised as Excise Taxes

It is true that high customs tariffs were a feature of the import-substitution policy implemented by many countries, including the United States in the 1800s and LAC countries between the 1930s and the 1980s. The aim was to protect infant industries and allow them to consolidate before they faced international competition.

Some LAC countries never pursued that goal, especially small countries with limited capacity to develop competitive industries, and for whom tariffs were essentially a convenient and simple form of tax collection. The region's small and open economies, such as several in the Caribbean, still collect the greater share of internal taxes (like VAT and excise taxes) in customs during the import process. For many of these economies, therefore, customs remains the natural place to collect tax, and the tariff is the most convenient and most used device. If there is no need to protect a domestic productive sector, however, the term "tariff" is purely semantic. Much of the revenue collected as an import tariff could continue to be collected in the same customs as, for example, an excise tax. This is clearly the case for the small economies that do not produce fuels, vehicles, or cigarettes but do impose high taxes on imports of those goods. A simple change of nomenclature would allow the same amounts to continue to be collected in the same customs, but as excise taxes.

To a large extent, this is what happened in Cyprus during the many years it was preparing to accede to the EU. The country took the opportunity to embark on a wide-ranging tax reform, introduce VAT, and impose excise taxes on a range of products that previously bore high tariffs. Cyprus, a small island country and one heavily dependent on its trade with and tourism from Europe, serves as an example for the LAC economies (Jenkins and Kuo, 2002).

VAT: The Strongest Candidate

Most theoretical studies and practical experience concur that introducing or increasing VAT, either by raising the rate or expanding the base, may be the most efficient way of offsetting tariff revenue losses. Dixit (1985) established that the optimal way for a small and open economy to collect revenue and maximize its welfare is to reduce tariffs to zero and depend wholly on destination-based consumption taxes (taxing imports and exempting exports). In a more recent study, Keen and Ligthart (1999) advance an elegant theory on coordination between the reduction in tariffs and domestic tax reform. They show that in small "normal" economies, any tariff reduction that boosts productive efficiency, in conjunction with a reform of consumption tax that keeps consumer prices unchanged, will trigger an increase in both welfare and public income. These conclusions support strategies of upgrading (or introducing) VAT in combination with tariff reform. To a large extent this happened in Chile and Cyprus, with the former raising proportional rates and the latter introducing VAT as part of trade liberalization and economic integration.

Of the countries in Table 2.5 that appear most vulnerable to revenue losses stemming from trade liberalization agreements with the United States, three do not have VAT but partial forms of domestic consumption tax (the Bahamas, Suriname, and Guyana), and two have low VAT rates (Haiti and Panama). The introduction of VAT alone is not the solution for the first three countries, but it is hard to imagine some way of offsetting the estimated potential losses that does not include VAT as part of a reform package. Other measures to increase income from excise taxes and income tax will also be needed.

The CAFTA countries need to raise domestic tax revenue, and that should lead to a slight rise in the proportional rate of VAT and, mainly, an increase in its productivity. This is especially true for Costa Rica, Guatemala, and Nicaragua. Ecuador, with the same VAT rate as Guatemala (12 percent), has a productivity rate of 52 percent, well above Guatemala's 40 percent (see Table 2.9). To move forward, Guatemala should expand its VAT base and strengthen the tax administration.

Table 2.9. Tax Indicators, 2004

Country	GDP per capita (PPP, US$)	Total tax revenue (excluding social security) (% of GDP)	Direct taxes/ indirect taxes (%)	VAT revenue/total tax revenue (excluding social security) (%)	VAT rate (%)	VAT productivity[1] (%)	Income tax revenue/total tax revenue (excluding social security) (%)	Corporate income tax/total income tax[2] (%)	Business income tax rate (%)	Personal income tax rate (%)
MERCOSUR										
Argentina	13,302	24.3	45.1	28.5	21.0	33.0	21.6	70.3	35	9 to 35
Brazil[3]	8,194	29.2	39.2	29.8	21.8	39.9	25.1	62.8	34	15 to 27.5
Paraguay[4,5]	4,813	11.9	22.4	39.1	10.0	46.7	17.8	100.0	30/10	10.0
Uruguay[6]	9,445	22.9	29.4	37.1	21.5	39.5	20.5	53.2	30	—
Chile[7]	11,583	17.3	31.6	48.4	19.0	44.0	23.7	53.7	17	0 to 40
Mexico[8]	9,776	10.0	89.2	36.9	15.0	24.6	45.0	34.0	29	32.0
Andean Community										
Bolivia[9]	2,735	15.7	29.8	42.0	14.9	44.3	15.3	87.5	25	13
Colombia[10]	7,299	17.6	85.0	33.5	16.0	36.7	34.1	81.7	39	20 to 38.5
Ecuador[11]	4,050	15.9	22.5	39.3	12.0	51.9	18.3	—	25	5 to 25
Peru[4]	5,679	13.3	40.6	40.7	19.0	28.6	28.5	65.8	30	15 to 30
Venezuela[12]	6,042	11.1	38.7	57.0	16.0	39.7	19.7	90.9	15 to 34	6 to 34

(continued on next page)

Table 2.9. Tax Indicators, 2004 (continued)

Country	GDP per capita (PPP, US$)	Total tax revenue (excluding social security) (% of GDP)	Direct taxes/ indirect taxes (%)	VAT revenue/total tax revenue (excluding social security) (%)	VAT rate (%)	VAT productivity[1] (%)	Income tax revenue/total tax revenue (excluding social security) (%)	Corporate income tax/total income tax[2] (%)	Business income tax rate (%)	Personal income tax rate (%)
Central America										
Costa Rica	9,466	13.9	39.9	35.3	13.0	37.7	23.8	60.6	30	10 to 25
El Salvador[4]	5,085	11.5	43.2	52.3	13.0	46.3	29.3	50.4	25	10 to 30
Guatemala[4,13]	4,318	10.6	34.2	45.3	12.0	40.0	24.5	80.8	31	15 to 31
Honduras[4,14]	2,876	17.2	36.1	36.0	12.0	51.7	30.8	67.9	25	10 to 25
Nicaragua[4]	3,646	15.7	39.3	40.7	15.0	42.6	28.2	—	25	10 to 30
Panama[4]	7,340	9.5	82.7	18.9	5.0	36.0	37.9	30.6	30	4 to 30
Caribbean										
Bahamas[4,15]	20,200	14.8	5.0	0.0	—	—	—	—	—	—
Barbados[16]	15,720	30.9	76.2	30.5	15.0	62.9	37.2	39.1	36 (maximum)	40 (maximum)
Belize	7,405	20.4	34.6	27.7	13.0	43.5	24.6	1.4	25 (maximum)	25.0
Dominican Republic[4]	7,234	15.3	28.4	25.7	12.0	32.8	20.5	44.6	25	15 to 25
Guyana[17]	4,377	28.7	96.2	37.0	—	—	46.8	38.6	45 (maximum)	33.3 (maximum)
Haiti[4]	1,777	8.9	27.1	29.2	10.0	26.0	21.3	42.1	—	—
Jamaica[16]	4,163	24.6	65.1	27.2	16.5	40.6	39.4	19.6	33	25

(continued on next page)

Table 2.9. Tax Indicators, 2004 (continued)

Country	GDP per capita (PPP, US$)	Total tax revenue (excluding social security) (% of GDP)	Direct taxes/ indirect taxes (%)	VAT revenue/total tax revenue (excluding social security) (%)	VAT rate (%)	VAT produc- tivity[1] (%)	Income tax revenue/total tax revenue (excluding social security) (%)	Corporate income tax/total income tax[2] (%)	Business income tax rate (%)	Personal income tax rate (%)
Suriname[4,18]	6,552	28.4	90.0	20.1	—	—	45.1	57.8	—	—
Trinidad and Tobago[19]	11,835	23.7	201.3	16.8	15.0	26.7	68.0	69.3	30 (maximum)	25 to 30

Sources: Revenues: IMF; ECLAC, various governments, Inter-American Development Bank Department of Integration Consultancies. Rates: ECLAC—Instituto Latinoamericano y del Caribe de Planificación Económica y Social (ILPES); Deloitte; World Bank's *World Development Indicators*. GDP per capita: World Bank's *World Development Indicators*; UNESCO.

Note: — = Data not available.

[1] Productivity is the quotient between VAT revenue over GDP divided by the general rate of the tax.

[2] Total income tax is the sum of corporate income tax and personal income tax plus capital gains in some cases.

[3] The VAT rate is an average rate for the ICMS (Impuesto sobre la Circulación de Mercancías y Servicios), a state tax. For VAT revenue and calculations on productivity, ICMS revenues were considered. For the calculation of corporate income tax/total income tax, the numerator includes corporate income tax and Contribucion S. Lucro Liquido plus an estimate on withholding, which applies to both corporations and individuals. The business income tax rate includes rate of 25% plus 9% for social security.

[4] Tax revenues refer to the central government.

[5] There was no personal income tax in Paraguay until 2005.

[6] In Uruguay, there is no direct personal income tax (IRPF). There is a tax on personal revenues that taxes passive or active earnings (IRP) in addition to other taxes that apply to individuals and taxes such as those on commissions.

[7] Tax revenues exclude copper.

[8] Total tax revenue excludes public enterprises' oil revenues and includes excises on oil. The VAT rate does not include the rate in border zones of 10%. Corporate income tax includes estimated income tax revenue from withholdings, which applies to both corporations and individuals.

[9] Total tax revenue excludes hydrocarbons.

[10] Total tax revenue includes taxes on oil. Personal and business income tax rates include 35% plus an additional 10%.

[11] Total tax revenue excludes oil revenue.

[12] Tax revenues refer to the non-oil central government.

[13] Corporate income tax includes other income taxes charged on corporations carrying out trade or agricultural activities.

[14] In Honduras, the GDP is currently being revised upward. Corporate income tax includes some revenue from taxes on net assets, a temporary contribution for solidarity, and taxes on revalued assets.

[15] GDP per capita is for 2005 from World Bank (2006).

[16] GDP per capita is UNESCO data for 2003. Other data refer to the 2002/03 fiscal year. Tax revenues refer to the central government. Total income taxes include taxes on income and profits. Corporate income tax includes bauxite/aluminum taxes and taxes on other companies.

[17] Data including GDP per capita are for 2003. Tax revenues are for the central government. Taxes on goods and services include taxes on the consumption of both domestic and imported goods and services. Total income tax is for taxes on income, profits, and capital gains. Corporate income tax estimate includes other income taxes (turnover tax, withholding tax, capital gains tax, and tax on insurance premiums.

[18] GDP per capita is for 2003 from UNDP (2005) based on World Bank estimates.

[19] Data including GDP per capita are for 2003. Total tax revenues refer to the central government. VAT productivity calculations are based on 2004 data for VAT revenue and rate. Total income tax is for taxes on income, profits, and capital gains. Corporate income tax also includes unemployment levy and estimate of revenue from "other" taxes on income, profits, and capital gains.

Table 2.9 also shows that the VAT rate is very low in Panama. An increase in it will be necessary to offset, at least partially, the 8 percent tax revenue losses that could result from a trade agreement with the United States.

Honduras is a different matter. It introduced VAT at a rate of 12 percent, and the tax is very productive (52 percent). Assuming that GDP is not underestimated, the maneuvering room to raise VAT is clearly limited to no more than one or two percentage points. Even then, it will be difficult to secure approval. Revenue collection by means of excise taxes is already reasonable. Hence the way to cover the potential fiscal gap caused by CAFTA will be to increase direct tax (on income and property), which is still low, or to substantially improve its administration.

In Guatemala, the same VAT rate of 12 percent yields a lower percentage of income relative to GDP than in Honduras,[14] which suggests that measures to expand the tax base and strengthen the tax administration are needed. Direct tax is very low here too, and should be improved.

In the Andean countries, VAT performs very differently. Ecuador has the best VAT productivity, suggesting that in the event of a trade agreement with the United States, one possible option is a small rise in the VAT rate, despite past experiences suggesting that this will be politically difficult. It should be part of a package, so that the population is fully aware that there will be an attendant reduction in tariffs. Moreover, Ecuador should increase excise taxes, which now account for 6 percent of total tax revenue and 0.9 percent of GDP (Table 2.3). This is less than half the Andean Community average (not considering Venezuela).

Colombia and Peru, which have concluded their trade negotiations with the United States, should improve the productivity of their VAT. Peru has a rate of 19 percent and collects almost the same as Ecuador, whose rate is 12 percent. Colombia's position is worse: its tariff revenue losses will be higher than Peru's, its VAT productivity is low, and, unlike its Andean neighbors, it imposes various VAT rates, making its tax administration much more complex and inefficient.

---

[14] However, it is worth noting that recent estimates from the respective central banks suggest that Guatemalan GDP may be overestimated by about 12 percent, while that of Honduras may be underestimated by a quarter.

In Search of Lost Income

Economic integration can offer opportunities to the LAC economies, but it also poses a series of challenges. Countries' economic decision making is increasingly constrained by actions and developments beyond their borders, a fact that is as true for small countries as for large ones.

The only ways to tackle the problem of lost income are (1) an exchange of information among tax administrations, so as to obviate international evasion; (2) the proper treatment of transfer prices, in order to avert under- or overbilling; (3) bilateral agreements that facilitate the distribution of income received in two jurisdictions, thereby forestalling double taxation; and (4) as part of a trade agreement, a multilateral accord eliminating harmful tax practices (a "peace clause" like the EU's Code of Conduct on Business Taxation [Commission of the European Communities, 1997]).

It is important to stress that little progress has been made in recent years on the exchange of information among tax administrations, with a view to averting the possibility that a multinational taxpayer might exploit the asymmetry of information to evade tax. Clauses on information exchange are generally part of agreements to avoid double taxation, but such accords are uncommon in LAC and are always bilateral. It is time to conclude multilateral agreements on information exchange, especially when groups of countries are engaged in a process of economic integration to strengthen trade and investment.

It is no coincidence that during the North American Free Trade Agreement (NAFTA) negotiations, the U.S. and Mexican fiscal authorities concluded a taxation agreement in parallel to the trade talks. They realized that such an accord would be essential to support the growth in trade and (above all) investment between the two countries.[15]

---

[15] Additionally, effective collaboration between Mexican and U.S. taxing agencies (Servicio de Administración Tributaria, the Internal Revenue Service, and the U.S. Customs Service) has led to the significant and mutual professional development of their auditors.

Finally, it is worth noting that although income taxation is crucial for sufficiency and equity, it will not solve either of these problems. Vertical equity is far better achieved by poverty-targeted public expenditures, as discussed in many editions of ECLAC's *Social Panorama of Latin America*, especially the 2006 report, and in Villela, Roca, and Barreix (2006). On sufficiency grounds, corporate income taxes (CIT) usually account for about 3 percent of GDP around the world. Latin America is no exception: CIT revenues stand at between 2 and 3 percent of GDP in most countries. Personal income tax (PIT) is quite weak in the region, except for the English-speaking Caribbean countries. Although Latin America has relatively lower financial income per capita (and thus a narrower taxable base) than developed economies, collection seldom surpasses 2 percent of GDP. Mexico, for example, has a sophisticated income tax system including full integration between PIT and CIT, updated and active international taxation, and sophisticated capital income levy—but collection is still less than 5 percent of GDP, and the country has the least productive VAT in the region (0.25, with meager revenue of 3.8 percent of GDP in 2004).

Tax Expenditures and Foregoing Taxes for Incentives

The notion of tax expenditure was conceived in 1967 by Stanley Surrey (1973), then the Assistant Secretary for Tax Policy in the U.S. Treasury Department. Surrey stressed that deductions, exemptions, and other income tax benefits were not part of the tax structure. They were, in fact, government spending effected through the tax system rather than directly, through the budget. For this reason, he called them "tax expenditures."

This way of perceiving fiscal benefits—as comparable to budgetary spending but effected through the tax system—was novel. Analysis of tax expenditure rests on the premise that any form of tax has two components: (1) one that covers all the legal provisions that make up the tax regulations; and (2) the special provisions that represent a departure from those regulations.

The former are crucial to the definition of the tax itself: taxable base, passive subject, rate structure, payment conditions, jurisdiction, and ancillary taxpayer obligations required by the tax administration (controlling evasion). The special provisions are departures from the regulations thus defined, and are designed to meet the government's goals in areas other than tax. They offer fiscal benefits in the broad sense of the term—that is, they include tax incentives as well as benefits that are not incentives.

For a long time, but particularly in the last two decades, it has been standard practice in developing and developed countries to grant incentives in order to attract FDI. These incentives lower the tax burden on businesses so as to alter their behavior and induce them to invest in particular sectors or regions. Exceptions to the general tax system, they include reductions in the income tax rate, tax holidays, accelerated depreciation regimes, specific deductions of certain earnings in income tax liquidation, deductions for reinvestment, and lower social security contributions (Villela and Barreix, 2002).

The main advantage of the concept of tax expenditure over the traditional notion of fiscal incentive is that it introduces the idea that the reduction or selective elimination of taxes has a fiscal cost. Only rarely, however, is that cost gauged, and when it is, the estimates are rough.

Given the need to increase the level of public revenue to offset the possible loss of tariff income, one of the measures that must be adopted is a complete review of tax expenditures in current tax legislation. In other words, the special provisions that represent a departure from the tax regulations must be identified, and their fiscal cost must be measured. This exercise is known as a tax expenditure budget. It allows policymakers to set priorities and, by eliminating nonessential fiscal benefits, to foster a higher level of revenue and equity without necessarily creating new taxes or raising existing taxes. This policy is advisable for all LAC countries, especially when they are seeking new ways of offsetting the potential income losses attendant on trade liberalization.

Intergovernmental Fiscal Relations and Weak Property Tax

Most LAC countries will have to undertake fiscal adjustment in order to adapt to a globalized world and address the fiscal impact of trade liberalization. It is worth noting that the countries that suffer the greatest revenue losses due to tariff reduction—those in the Caribbean and Central America—tend to have strong tourism sectors. Although this sector is based on real estate development, property taxation collections are meager—usually less than 0.3 percent of GDP. Hence the adjustment will demand a change in their intergovernmental fiscal relations—that is, with their subnational jurisdictions. To a greater or lesser extent, irrespective of whether they have a federal structure, in almost every country the central government transfers resources to other levels of government, of which there might be two or three. In most cases these transfers are automatic; they are established by law, or even by the constitution.

This means that additional government efforts to raise revenue through domestic taxes, as a means of offsetting tariff losses, must be matched by further increases to meet the legal need to transfer resources to provinces, states, municipalities, districts, boroughs, and so on.

Since import tariffs seek to regulate external trade and/or protect national production, in many cases they are not listed among the revenues shared with subnational governments (Varsano, Ferreira, and Afonso, 2002). Thus when the loss of the import tariff is offset by domestic taxes, there might be substantially greater need for additional income from VAT, income tax, or selective consumption taxes.

Moreover, subnational taxation in many LAC countries is of very poor quality. Property tax is generally of little importance, and the municipalities use and abuse taxes on economic movement (sales), with cumulative effects of taxes over taxes. In many cases these taxes undermine the countries' competitiveness relative to their trade partners. The fiscal solution might therefore be complex, involving wide-ranging tax reform, an adjustment in the powers to tax, and changes to the systems for intergovernmental transfers or joint resource-sharing, on the grounds that the arrangements do not "fit."

Conclusions

Economic integration, like globalization and commercial and financial opening, creates opportunities for the more efficient transfer of goods, services, technology, and capital. It thereby fosters greater labor productivity, which is the prime source of long-term per capita income growth. At the same time, integration makes a country more dependent on its partners, and thus requires institutional development that promotes competitiveness. To adapt to this new form of international insertion, countries will have to change their tax policy and administration.

While taxes on external trade have fallen substantially in Latin America, those taxes are still a significant source of public revenue in countries whose public finances are in a critical state. Any tariff reduction in free trade agreements must therefore be assessed in detail, so as to measure its positive and negative effects in each case. Since income is lost permanently, countries will have to coordinate a set of measures that have a lasting fiscal impact and are consistent with long-term fiscal sustainability. This is possible only if there are significant groups in favor of greater trade liberalization, which regrettably is not the case in many countries.

In some cases the loss of tariff revenue is serious, but it is a problem that can be solved with a reasonable effort. It should therefore not pose a new obstacle to integration by adding an internal front (negotiation between each country's trade and treasury authorities) to international trade talks. Nonetheless, it is short-sighted to believe that a country might have to miss the integration boat, which is sailing toward greater economic development, because it is unable to meet the fiscal cost of the ticket. On the contrary, for fiscal policy, and for tax policy in particular, wide-ranging trade integration should be seen as a significant opportunity to rectify tax structures, systems, and administration. The old goals of efficiency and equity persist, but there is a new one: international cooperation, which is a key instrument to deal with the inevitable globalization that has already affected tax structures significantly.

With the gradual phasing out of tariffs as a significant source of revenues, taxation in LAC will be supported by three main pillars—VAT, income tax, and social security contributions—as well as two supports—excises and property tax. These would be complemented by levies on nonrenewable natural resources. Excises are limited when operating as user fees; such is the case of fuel taxes because of the competitiveness implications. The same is true when excises operate as an externality corrector; such is the case of taxes on alcoholic beverages and tobacco products, because of smuggling. Property tax, albeit underused in LAC, also has limited revenue potential. Social security contributions based on payroll affect competitiveness and employment. Moreover, there is a trend toward the use of individual accounts (actuarial method) and not the pay-as-you-go system, a circumstance that limits the tax potential of payroll taxes. Thus VAT and income tax will constitute the core of the region's tax systems. International competition and enhanced factor mobility will push these taxes toward a broad base and low rates.

To conclude, taxation is crucial to the functioning of a country at all levels of government. It generates transfers that finance essential public goods, while avoiding adverse effects on economic efficiency and at the same time improving income distribution to some extent. Apart from technical options, therefore, taxes are determined by political considerations of how to distribute an economy's income.[16] The fiscal cost of economic integration, however, includes the additional factor of international coordination, and thus poses a greater challenge. As an instrument to foster economic growth in a context of supranational institutions, international coordination should be grounded in professional and academic developments, but the main responsibility for its proper use falls squarely on political decision makers.

---

[16] There are two main approaches to the study of the political economy of taxation. One regards taxes as an imperfect exchange between citizens and their government aimed at securing financing for public goods and services. This approach emphasizes the collective mechanisms for pricing public goods and the methods and institutions governing income distribution and public spending. The other approach views taxation as the coercive appropriation of resources to finance unspecified government activities. This approach stresses minimizing the efficiency costs of a social planner's policy choices, which may include distributional considerations. See Winer and Hettich (2004).

References

Abed, G. T. 1998. "Trade Liberalization and Tax Reform in the Southern Mediterranean Region." IMF Working Paper 98/49. Washington, DC: International Monetary Fund.

Arias, L., A. Barreix, A. Valencia, and L. Villela. 2005. "The Harmonization of Indirect Taxes in the Andean Community." INTAL-ITD Occasional Paper SITI-07. Buenos Aires: Special Initiative on Trade and Integration, IDB-INTAL.

Avi-Yonah, R. 2000. "Globalization, Tax Competition, and the Fiscal Crisis of the Welfare State." *Harvard Law Review* 113(7):1573–1676.

Barreix, A., and D. Alvarez. 2001. "Cambios en el contexto internacional y sus efectos en la tributación en América Latina y el Caribe." Paper presented at the XIII Seminario Regional de Política Fiscal, Santiago, January 24–29.

Barreix, A., and L. Villela. 2003a. "Tax Policy Challenges Related to Regional Economic Integration." Paper presented at the 2nd Plenary Meeting of the Inter-Parliamentary Forum of the Americas, February 20–21. Available at www.dgroups.org/groups/fipa/public/docs/Working_document_1_Group_I_ENGLISH.pdf.

———. 2003b. *Tributación en el MERCOSUR: Evolución, comparación y posibilidades de coordinación.* Special Reports Series. Buenos Aires: IDB-INTAL.

Byrne, P. 2001. "U.S. Tax Rules for Latin America." Unpublished paper. Inter-American Development Bank, Washington, DC.

Commission of the European Communities. 1997. *Code of Conduct on Business Taxation and Fiscal State Aid.* Brussels: European Commission.

Dixit, A. 1985. "Tax Policy in Open Economies." In *Handbook of Public Economics*, ed. A. J. Auerbach and M. Feldstein. Amsterdam: North-Holland.

Ebrill, L., J. Stotsky, and R. Gropp. 1999. "Revenue Implications of Trade Liberalization." IMF Occasional Paper 180. Washington, DC: International Monetary Fund.

ECLAC (Economic Commission for Latin America and the Caribbean). 2000a. *Foreign Investment in Latin America and the Caribbean, 2000*. Santiago: ECLAC.

———. 2000b. *Statistical Yearbook for Latin America and the Caribbean*. Santiago: ECLAC.

———. 2005a. *Foreign Investment in Latin America and the Caribbean, 2005*. Santiago: ECLAC.

———. 2005b. *Statistical Yearbook for Latin America and the Caribbean*. Santiago: ECLAC.

Evans, M., and V. Hnatkovska. 2005. "International Capital Flows Returns and World Financial Integration." NBER Working Paper 11701. Cambridge, MA: National Bureau of Economic Research.

IDB (Inter-American Development Bank). 2002. *Beyond Borders: The New Regionalism in Latin America*. Economic and Social Progress in Latin America: 2002 Report. Washington, DC: Inter-American Development Bank.

Jenkins, G., and G. Kuo. 2002. "Tax Reform for Human Development in Central America: Belize Chapter." Unpublished report. Inter-American Development Bank, Washington, DC.

Keen, M., and J. Ligthart. 1999. "Coordinating Tariff Reduction and Domestic Tax Policy." IMF Working Paper 99/93. Washington, DC: International Monetary Fund.

Pritchett, L., and G. Sethi. 1994. "Tariff Rates, Tariff Revenue, and Tariff Reform: Some New Facts." *World Bank Economic Review* 8(1):1–16.

Rugman, A. 2003. "The Reality of Globalisation: The Rise of the Regional Multinational." Templeton Executive Briefing. Oxford: Templeton College, University of Oxford.

Shome, P. 1999. "Taxation in Latin America: Structural Trends and Impact of Administration." IMF Working Paper 19. Washington, DC: International Monetary Fund.

Surrey, S. 1973. *Pathways to Tax Reform*. Cambridge, MA: Harvard University Press.

Tanzi, V. 1989. "Impact of Macroeconomic Policies on the Level of Taxation and the Fiscal Balance in Developing Countries." IMF Staff Paper 36. Washington, DC: International Monetary Fund.

UNCTAD (United Nations Conference on Trade and Development). 2006. *World Investment Report 2006.* New York: United Nations.

UNDP (United Nations Development Programme). 2005. *Human Development Report 2005—International Cooperation at a Crossroads: Aid, Trade and Security in an Unequal World.* New York: UNDP.

Varsano, R., S. Ferreira, and J. R. Afonso. 2002. "Fiscal Competition: A Bird's Eye View." Paper presented at the International Conference on Federalism 2002, St. Gallen, Switzerland, August 22–24.

Vial, J. 2003. "Efectos fiscales de la política exterior." In *The Fiscal Impact of Economic Integration,* ed. A. Valencia, A. Barreix, and L. Villela. Lima: General Secretariat of the Andean Community, and Washington, DC: Inter-American Development Bank.

Villela, L., and A. Barreix. 2002. "Taxation and Investment Promotion." Background note for the World Bank's *Global Economic Prospects 2003.* Washington, DC: Inter-American Development Bank. Available at www.iadb.org/INT/Trade/1_english/2_WhatWeDo/1_PublicationsFrame.htm.

Villela, L., J. Roca, and A. Barreix. 2006. *Equidad fiscal en los países andinos.* Lima: General Secretariat of the Andean Community, and Washington, DC: Inter-American Development Bank.

Winer, S., and W. Hettich. 2004. "The Political Economy of Taxation: Positive and Normative Analysis When Collective Choice Matters." In *The Encyclopedia of Public Choice,* ed. C. Rowley and F. Schneider. Amsterdam: Kluwer Academic.

World Bank. 2006. *World Development Indicators.* Washington, DC: World Bank.

3

Trade Liberalization and Fiscal Balances: Exploring Obvious and Less Obvious Channels

Vito Tanzi

Introduction

Traditional societies used to rely significantly on foreign trade taxes. In the nineteenth century, for example, the United States secured more than half its total tax revenue from import duties. These taxes have lost their importance in developed countries, but they retain their importance in developing countries, and particularly so in some of them. But in recent decades these taxes, which had accounted for almost a third of developing countries' total revenue, began to be replaced by domestic taxes. Latin American countries had traditionally relied less than other developing countries on such taxes, but even in Latin America, foreign trade taxes have been reduced over the years. Nonetheless, they remain important in most Caribbean countries, where they still account for substantial proportions of GDP (see Table 3.1).

Regional integration programs now under way in various parts of the world have had, and probably will continue to have, some impact on these revenues. Hence policymakers in some countries have expressed concern that the impact could be significant and negative. In some cases, these concerns may mask policymakers' lack of enthusiasm for trade liberalization. For countries that do not start the liberalization process with healthy public accounts, significant revenue losses could aggravate macroeconomic difficulties. Hence policymakers have been less disposed to open up their countries' economies to foreign trade.

Table 3.1. Import/Export Taxes
(percentage of GDP)

Country	1990	1991	1992	1993	1994	1995	1996	1997	1998	1999	2000	2001	2002	2003	2004
MERCOSUR															
Argentina	1.4	0.8	0.9	1.1	1.1	0.7	0.9	1.0	1.0	0.8	0.7	0.6	2.0	3.0	3.1
Brazil	0.4	0.4	0.4	0.4	0.5	0.8	0.5	0.6	0.7	0.8	0.8	0.8	0.6	0.5	0.5
Paraguay	1.7	1.8	1.6	1.6	1.8	2.7	2.2	2.2	2.1	1.6	1.8	1.7	1.5	1.6	—
Uruguay	2.3	2.1	1.9	1.1	1.1	1.0	1.0	1.1	1.1	0.9	0.8	1.0	1.0	1.2	—
Chile	2.4	2.2	2.1	2.1	2.0	2.1	2.0	1.7	1.7	1.6	1.5	1.2	1.1	0.7	0.6
Mexico	0.9	1.1	1.2	1.0	0.9	0.6	0.6	0.6	0.6	0.6	0.6	0.5	—	—	—
Andean Community															
Bolivia	—	—	—	1.5	1.4	1.4	1.3	1.4	1.5	1.3	1.3	1.1	1.1	1.0	—
Colombia	0.3	0.3	0.5	0.8	1.1	1.0	0.9	1.1	1.2	1.0	1.0	1.2	1.1	1.0	0.9
Ecuador	2.2	1.8	1.5	1.4	1.6	1.5	1.2	1.8	2.6	1.9	1.4	1.7	0.7	1.5	1.6
Peru	1.8	1.0	1.0	1.2	1.4	1.5	1.5	1.6	1.7	1.6	1.6	1.4	1.2	1.2	1.2
Venezuela	1.3	1.9	2.0	1.8	1.6	1.5	1.4	1.6	1.5	1.3	1.2	1.2	1.0	0.7	1.1
Central America															
Costa Rica	—	—	3.8	3.6	3.3	3.8	2.2	1.8	1.6	1.0	0.9	1.0	—	—	—
El Salvador	1.7	1.9	1.7	1.6	1.8	2.1	1.6	1.3	1.2	1.2	1.1	1.1	—	—	—
Guatemala	1.5	1.4	2.1	1.8	1.6	1.9	1.5	1.4	1.4	1.3	1.2	1.2	1.2	1.2	1.1
Honduras	5.6	5.7	5.1	4.7	4.5	4.3	3.8	3.5	3.0	2.6	2.4	2.5	2.2	—	—
Nicaragua	—	—	4.0	4.0	4.2	4.8	4.7	5.5	6.7	2.2	2.1*	—	—	—	—
Panama	—	—	2.5	2.2	2.3	2.4	2.3	2.5	2.7	2.5	1.7	1.4	1.5	1.5	1.6*

(continued on next page)

Table 3.1. Import/Export Taxes (continued)
(percentage of GDP)

Country	1990	1991	1992	1993	1994	1995	1996	1997	1998	1999	2000	2001	2002	2003	2004
Caribbean															
Bahamas	—	9.5	10.1	10.1	9.5	11.2	10.8	11.1	10.7	11.0	11.4	10.6	9.4	9.0	9.3*
Barbados[1,2]	—	—	4.8	4.5	4.8	4.7	3.9	3.1	3.1	3.0	2.9	3.1	3.3	—	—
Belize[1,3]	13.4	12.8	12.0	11.6	11.6	11.4	6.7	7.2	7.0	6.5	6.9	7.8	8.7	—	—
Dominican Republic[4]	4.1	4.0	5.7	5.5	4.4	4.0	3.8	4.2	4.3	4.5	4.3	2.7	2.8	—	—
Guyana	—	4.2	4.5	5.7	4.6	4.7	4.7	4.1	4.1	3.8	2.7	3.2	—	—	—
Haiti	1.4	1.7	0.9	0.8	0.4	1.1	1.1	1.9	1.7	1.9	1.9	2.1	—	—	—
Jamaica[1]	—	—	5.6	7.1	6.5	8.0	6.7	6.8	7.4	7.9	7.4	7.0	6.7	7.2	—
Suriname[5]	—	—	—	—	—	—	—	—	7.9	8.6	8.3	10.1	8.7	9.5	—
Trinidad and Tobago	—	—	2.5	2.8	2.1	1.6	1.5	1.7	2.0	1.9	1.7	1.4	1.5*	—	—

Sources: Prepared by IDB/INT using data from IMF, ministries of finance, central banks, IDB studies, and national tax collecting agencies. OECD data were used for Mexico. ECLAC data were used for some Venezuela figures.

Note: — = Data not available. * = Projected. Most countries include all taxes on international trade.
[1] Fiscal year starts on April 1 of year listed and ends in March of the following year.
[2] Data include taxes on all international transactions, including import duties and stamp tax.
[3] Data include taxes on all international trade transactions.
[4] Data do not include foreign exchange commission.
[5] 1990 figure reflects 1982 amount because no earlier data were available. Data include all taxes on international trade except for sales tax on imports.

The links between trade liberalization and tax revenue constitute a matter of particular interest, one that has attracted increasing attention in recent years. Several studies have analyzed these links for individual countries and groups of countries. Their conclusions have not been unanimous, but most have agreed that trade liberalization can lead to revenue losses.

To set the stage for a proper discussion, it should be stressed at the outset that policymakers' main concern should not be the impact of trade liberalization on the revenue from foreign trade taxes, but on total taxes. To take the analysis to its logical conclusion, the concern should perhaps be even broader—namely, what happens to the public accounts, since trade liberalization could also affect public spending. Those who have examined the issue have generally ignored this latter effect.

If the reduction in trade taxes were marginal or if it could easily be offset by increases in domestic taxes, and if the impact on public spending were small, then the public finance effect of trade liberalization could be ignored. But if the fall in trade taxes were substantial, and if it were difficult for administrative, political, or technical reasons to offset the revenue loss with increases in domestic taxes, then the policymakers' concerns would be more legitimate. Those concerns would be even more justified if trade liberalization forced governments to increase their public spending, as argued by Rodrik (1998).

The impact of trade liberalization on the fiscal accounts is likely to reflect conditions and characteristics that vary by country. A general discussion, therefore, can be useful only in indicating the relevant questions that ought to be raised in an analysis of the relationship between trade liberalization and the fiscal accounts. It cannot indicate what would happen in a particular country. The relationship between trade liberalization and total tax revenue (or, even better, between liberalization and the fiscal accounts) is much more complex than some studies have suggested. The reasons for this complexity are as follows:

1. Trade liberalization may affect foreign trade taxes (revenue from import duties and export taxes) either positively or negatively; the impact is not necessarily negative.

2. Trade liberalization is likely to have a positive effect on the revenue from value-added tax (VAT), which is often substantially dependent on the value of imports in domestic currency, especially in developing countries. In many developing countries, more than 50 percent of VAT revenue comes from imports. There are several reasons why VAT revenue may increase when a country opens itself up to trade. Trade liberalization increases the *volume* of imports, and especially the value of consumption goods subject to VAT. It also increases the domestic value of imports because of the likely devaluation of the exchange rate that accompanies the lowering of trade restrictions. The presence of a VAT, therefore, is an important element in determining the impact of trade liberalization. The larger the VAT base and the higher its basic rate, the more trade liberalization will contribute to VAT revenue. A country without a VAT will not benefit from this effect. About half of developing countries have a VAT. Small island countries that lack a VAT are more likely to be affected negatively by trade liberalization. A counterpoint could be a situation in which the structure and volume of imports are little affected, while the VAT is imposed on the import values that reflect the import duties. In this case, the reduction in import duties may reduce the VAT base.

3. Trade liberalization will affect revenue from excise taxes on imported products for the same reasons as for the VAT. Again, there may be circumstances in which the excise taxes are imposed on an import base that includes the import duties.

4. Trade liberalization will affect other taxes, such as those on income, because of changing economic activities stimulated by the liberalization process itself. It might affect taxes on properties if the properties are closely linked to export activities, as may be the case with agricultural land used for export commodities. Once more, countries that do not have income taxes or property taxes will not experience this effect.

5. Finally, trade liberalization could also affect public spending, especially if it is introduced too quickly and if it leads to unem-

ployment and distress for sectors that manage to persuade the government to provide subsidies.

Some of these effects could be significant, and hence they ought to be taken into account in a comprehensive analysis of the tax (and public finance) impact of trade liberalization. The effects are likely to differ across categories of countries. They will depend on the country's size, its level of development, its administrative sophistication, the tax system already in place, the country's geographical position, and the government's role in the economy. Obviously, given these factors, the political process will determine the outcome (see IDB, 2004). For these reasons, studies that seek to draw conclusions by analyzing the average behavior of taxes for large groups of countries may be less illuminating than their authors believe.

The Theory of Tax Structure Change

Trade liberalization does not take place all at once. Rather, it proceeds in phases and can take a long time to be fully implemented. This raises the problem of separating its effects on tax revenue from those that would have occurred without specific trade liberalization agreements. Starting in the 1950s and continuing in the following two to three decades, several public finance economists interested in economic development paid a lot of attention to the way in which tax systems change over time. They focused on the *taxable* capacity of countries and the *composition of tax revenue*. How did tax burdens and their reliance on different tax categories change over time? The attention paid to tax burdens reflected the model of economic development then popular, largely inspired by the work of economists such as Roy Harrod and Evsey Domar. That model linked economic growth almost exclusively to the accumulation of capital: a country would grow if it invested more and accumulated more capital. Since it was believed that the private sector would not be able to contribute adequately to the accumulation of capital, the need for government intervention seemed clear.

Economists held that the public sector should (1) raise as much tax revenue as possible, (2) contain the growth of current public spending, and (3) invest the difference between ordinary public revenue (mostly taxes) and *current* expenditure. Increasing public sector saving would allow for the increase in capital accumulation. This capital accumulation would be associated with the building of physical infrastructure and with public enterprises. Tax incentives to the private sector could play some role in increasing private investment, but they would also reduce tax revenue and, therefore, investment by the public sector. Hence the increase in tax revenue was the real driving force.

Reflecting the preoccupation with the level of taxation, in the early 1960s, at the time of the Alliance for Progress—the U.S.-financed program within the Organization of American States (OAS) to promote growth in Latin America—the Inter-American Development Bank (IDB), the OAS, and the United Nations joined forces to promote tax reform in Latin America. They created the Joint Tax Program, active throughout the 1960s and early 1970s, which was jointly sponsored but run from within the OAS. By means of tax missions, various publications, and important conferences, the program played a significant role in encouraging countries in the Western Hemisphere to reform their tax systems, and especially to raise more public revenue.

This predated the period when trade liberalization became a desirable policy goal. When the Joint Tax Program was active, import substitution (pursued through high tariffs and quantitative restrictions on imports) was still a popular policy in Latin American and Caribbean countries. Even then, however, many economists were aware that trade taxes were less efficient and desirable than taxes on domestic activities. The reason was that in addition to raising revenues, import duties sometimes gave unwanted or excessive protection to domestic activities. Hence a country that needed more tax revenue, and that therefore increased its level of import duties, automatically and inevitably raised the level of protection provided to domestic activities, thereby increasing the distortion in resource allocation.

Economists thus began to advocate a shift away from foreign trade taxes toward domestic taxes, including income taxes, property taxes, excise taxes, and the newly discovered and recently introduced VAT. This means that before the trade liberalization movement gained momentum (a movement that would require the lowering of tariffs), several countries had already started reducing foreign trade taxes and, when necessary, replacing the lost revenue with revenue from *domestic* taxes. In this period, export taxes almost disappeared in Latin America, while import duties started to be lowered. This was seen as an inevitable historical development, one largely unconnected to trade liberalization. This development makes it difficult for econometric studies based on time series to separate the ongoing trend from the effects of trade liberalization. Such liberalization could be blamed for revenue losses that had little to do with it.

In the 1960s and 1970s, an extensive literature documented several trends. Time-series approaches that studied countries over long periods showed that foreign trade taxes became progressively less important as countries developed and those taxes were replaced by domestic taxes. Cross-sectional approaches dealing with groups of countries showed that, all other things being equal, higher-income countries tended to rely less than lower-income countries on foreign trade taxes. These studies also showed that smaller and potentially more open economies relied more on foreign trade taxes. Thus was born a "theory of tax structure change during economic development" (see Tanzi, 1973). This theory implicitly promoted the progressive replacement of foreign trade taxes with domestic taxes.

The theory of tax structure change recognized that as countries became more developed, they acquired greater freedom to choose a tax structure that better reflected their preferences. When countries are poor and relatively underdeveloped, and thus have unsophisticated tax administrations, they tend to rely on taxes that are easy to collect. Most tax experts agree that foreign trade taxes are among the easiest to collect, especially in a world where most output is associated with tangible commodities and not with services or intangible products—a change that has occurred in recent years. For this reason, traditional societies had little choice but to rely on foreign trade taxes.

As Richard Musgrave (1969) put it in a book written almost four decades ago, foreign trade provided a convenient "tax handle," especially for poor countries. The reason is that imports and exports, and especially traditional agricultural exports and imports of consumer goods, are channeled through a few strategic points (harbors, border passes, airports), a circumstance that makes it easy for governments to control physical movements and to collect revenue from the values of these flows. Obviously, to the extent that in the modern world many products are losing their physical characteristics, and services that are often intangible are slowly replacing tangible products in importance, the advantage of foreign trade as a convenient "tax handle" is slowly disappearing. This trend will continue in the future and will affect countries' capacity to collect high revenue from foreign trade flows.

Small island countries, for which trade flows are a large share of GDP because of their limited domestic productive capacity, have traditionally found it convenient to collect a large share of their tax revenue from imports. This explains their particular reluctance to see a decline in revenue from foreign trade taxes. Nonetheless, these countries could continue to focus their tax administration on border activities, but, within certain limits, they could change the character of their taxes from import duties to excises. As mentioned earlier, moreover, tangible products' share of consumption is falling, and the same must be true of their share of total imports. Progressively, trade flows are being dominated by services (financial, health-related, tourism, and so on), and thus a redirection of tax systems away from trade taxes may not have the same revenue consequences as in the past, even for small island countries.

It follows from the foregoing description that the need to reduce or remove trade taxes is not strictly a consequence of the movement toward trade liberalization. But, of course, in recent years that movement may have accelerated the trend, and in particular cases it may have given more urgency to the removal and replacement of trade taxes. Policymakers ought to welcome this stimulus to reform. They should use the opportunity to modernize their tax systems, a change that can only benefit their economies. They should promote such change regardless of trade agreements.

Obviously, not all countries will find it politically or administratively easy to replace trade taxes with other revenue. Tax reform is never easy, and in some ways it remains the most political of all economic reforms. Changes can be difficult to enact and time-consuming to implement because of the existing economic structure, the sophistication of the tax administration, and political obstacles, including the resistance to change that comes from vested interests. Indeed, some would argue that "old taxes are good taxes," because the structure of the economy and the economic operators have adjusted to them. As argued above, however, the structure of economies is now changing.

Trade Liberalization and Taxes: General Issues

Countries that are contemplating trade liberalization should address, systematically and in an informed way, the potential impact on tax revenue of the progressive elimination of trade restrictions, including import duties. By anticipating that impact and dealing with its fiscal consequences, they can avoid unpleasant surprises. Trade liberalization, by potentially changing the structure of the economy, will not just affect tax revenue and the tax structure but will also inevitably call into question the public sector's role in the economy and, consequently, the role of public spending. It is unlikely that a country would agree to open its economy to the rest of the world without simultaneously introducing other reforms.

Countries that have liberalized their trade significantly (Chile, for example) have also made many other important structural reforms. This is one of the reasons why it is difficult to predict the impact of trade liberalization on the fiscal accounts (that is, on both sides of the budget) and not just on tax revenue or, even more restrictively, on revenue from foreign trade taxes. The partial analysis generally followed in empirical studies is a useful first step, but it cannot capture all the effects (direct and indirect) that trade liberalization sets in motion.

Before addressing the fiscal impact of trade liberalization more directly, it might be helpful to discuss two related issues. These are the *pattern* and *degree* of trade liberalization. Both of these play a role in determining the fiscal consequences of opening the economy.

Let us first consider degree. No economy ever becomes totally open to foreign trade, in the sense that it has absolutely no barriers to imports and exports. Sometimes hidden barriers replace recognized ones. Thus opening is only a question of degree, and it may not be possible to put an objective value on how much a country has opened its economy, although it is generally easier to determine the sense of direction.

Moving from the degree to the pattern of opening, there is no rigid path toward trade liberalization. Different roads may lead to similar final outcomes. If trade liberalization is not a spontaneous initiative on the part of the country but results from agreements among groups of countries, the agreements are likely to determine the path to be followed. In the absence of such agreements, however, there is a normal, logical, or almost optimal sequence that could be followed. This sequence is described below, along with some speculation about its impact on revenue from foreign trade taxes. Of course, this is a partial analysis. It ignores the other structural reforms that are likely to accompany the process of economic opening, and it disregards the effect of the latter on non-trade taxes and on public spending.

The first logical step would be the removal of quantitative restrictions (QRs) on the importation of various products in many countries. These restrictions could be removed all at once or gradually. They could be replaced by tariffs with the same restrictive power on imports, or by lower tariffs. This "tariffication" of QRs can be expected to have a positive impact on tax revenue because it would replace a policy (QRs) that did not *directly* generate any revenue with one that does. Of course, the level of the duties imposed on the imports that are now allowed, together with the level of the imports, would determine the impact of the policy change on trade taxes. There will be other effects, however, that are often ignored but that should be recognized.

Part of the additional foreign trade taxes that the government receives, after the replacement of QRs with tariffs, will effectively be a transfer to the government from those who, behind the wall of the QRs, were producing goods similar to those kept out by the QRs or close substitutes. The lower the new tariffs imposed on those previously forbidden imports, the greater the impact on domestic producers. Some domestic enterprises may have to close or reduce their activity. Some employees who had earned their incomes from their work in these activities may find themselves unemployed. Consequently, the government might lose some tax revenue (taxes on income and sales taxes) that it had been receiving from these domestic activities.

Additionally, at least in the short run, the government may face pressures for additional spending from the owners and/or employees of these enterprises, who will demand compensation for the lost incomes. Hence the *net* revenue gain from this change may not be as large, or necessarily as positive, as assumed in studies that have looked at tariffication only from a partial equilibrium viewpoint. Obviously, it is impossible to generalize, because these effects will vary from country to country. They will depend on the speed of the liberalization process and on the government's responsiveness to the pressure for help from the losing enterprises and the displaced workers.

A second logical step would be a reduction in the *number* of customs duties (tariff rates), accompanied by a lowering in the level of those rates, especially the highest ones. The final outcome of this process, which normally takes several or many years to complete, may be the replacement of many rates by one or a few low rates, or even a zero rate. This has been the case in Chile and some other countries. Along the way, this process reduces or eliminates the gap between the initial highest rate (or rates) and the lowest rate.

If the initial highest rate (or rates) was very high, as was often the case in many Latin American countries, that rate probably (1) discouraged imports of the highly taxed products; (2) encouraged the smuggling of these products into the country; and (3) stimulated requests for exemptions, either for the products themselves or, more often, for the inputs needed by domestic producers to make import substitutes (see, for example, Pritchett and Sethi, 1994). The protection offered by the high import duties would have stimulated the domestic production of similar products, but this stimulation is unlikely to be equally important in all countries. It is much more important in large and more technically advanced countries, and much less important in smaller and less technically advanced countries. The latter countries are unlikely to experience this effect.

Reducing the high import duties significantly would (1) reduce the incentives for smugglers, thus curbing the inflow of smuggled goods on which customs duties are not paid; (2) reduce the domestic production (if any) of products that competed with the imported products; (3) diminish the pressure from some groups (diplomats and so on) for exemptions from the payment of the high duties; and (4) increase the importation of the commodities through official channels. Because of all these effects, and also because the exchange rate and the flow of imports and exports are likely to change, it would be difficult or even impossible to predict accurately the revenue impact of these changes, *even for import duties.*

The final step would probably be the unification of all or most of the rates around a single low rate. This last step is probably the most significant for revenue from trade taxes, and it is the one with the potential to result in significant revenue losses. As some writers have pointed out, however, the final impact on revenue from trade taxes will depend on the level of the final rate and the variance among the rates before they converged toward the final rate. If the initial rates had been so high as to discourage the importation of the relevant products, the reduction of the high rates could have a positive effect on revenue. But, of course, the lower the final rate, the greater the probable revenue loss.

Some studies have tried to estimate empirically the level of import duty at which a country begins to lose revenue from foreign trade taxes. Up to that level, the higher imports stimulated by the lower rates would compensate for the lower rates. For example, Ebrill, Stotsky, and Gropp (1999) have estimated that a country will begin to lose revenue when the *effective tariff rate* (that is, the average tariff as a percentage of imported goods) falls to about 20 percent. Other authors have set this level at about 40 percent (see Khattry and Rao, 2002). These estimates require some comments.

First, the estimates are quantitative averages for groups of countries, and hence they may have little relevance for specific countries or for other groups of countries. Second, the same effective tariff rate may be consistent with widely different dispersions of nominal rates. Thus, like most averages, they are useful only up to a given point. Third, as already pointed out, calculations related to revenue from foreign trade taxes ignore the impact of changes in trade flows on other taxes, especially VAT and excise taxes. Since not all countries have VAT, the impact of lowering customs duties is likely to vary by country and depend significantly on whether a VAT is in place and, if so, on its characteristics. Countries with a broad-based VAT and a high rate will benefit the most.

The degree of trade liberalization (how much has a country liberalized its trade?) is also hard to assess. There is no objective yardstick that measures how far a country has gone toward liberalizing its trade, since there is no objective measure of how restrictive a country's policies are. Some authors have attempted to devise measures (see, for example, Anderson and Neary, 1994, and IMF, 1998). The International Monetary Fund (IMF) developed a qualitative yardstick consisting of a 10-point scale. The accuracy of these measures, of course, depends on the knowledge and judgment of those who assign the values. It may be difficult to give a precise numerical value to a country's trade liberalization progress at a specific moment, but it is easier to determine the direction of the movement as long as the policy changes follow the optimal path described above. In general, a country would be assumed to be opening itself to the rest of the world if it increased its index of openness (described as the share of imports plus exports in GDP) and at the same time reduced the average import tariff.

Trade Liberalization and Taxes: Empirical Studies

Over the past two decades, since serious progress toward trade liberalization began, several studies have attempted to measure its impact on tax revenue. These studies' conclusions have not been uniform. In part, this is because the countries covered have varied from study to study. The focus of the studies has varied, too: some centered on the effect on *foreign trade taxes* and some on *total taxes*. In the latter case, of course, the analysis may attempt to measure the automatic (partial equilibrium) impact on other taxes, because trade liberalization will also affect domestic indirect taxes, as well as income and property taxes. Or the analysis may be unable to separate the automatic impact on non-trade taxes from the policy-induced impact. In other words, some countries' governments will take specific measures to neutralize the impact.

Another problem concerns timing. In some cases the response of other taxes may be immediate, while in others it may be delayed. This may affect the interpretation of the results. The present author, moreover, is unaware of any study that has also considered the impact of trade liberalization on public spending.

Early studies by Tanzi (1989) and Blejer and Cheasty (1990) found that no general conclusions could be drawn, and hence the impact of trade liberalization on tax revenue was basically an open and empirical question. Another early study by Greenway and Milner (1991) also concluded that a range of outcomes is possible. A later study by the IMF (1998) found an array of fiscal outcomes from trade liberalization. Some authors (Abed, 2000; Abed et al., 1998) stressed the need to link trade liberalization to the reform of domestic taxes. Others (Mitra, 1992; Datta-Mitra, 1997) stressed that more emphasis on revenue issues was needed when policies aimed at trade liberalization were initiated. On the other hand, some authors (see Rajaram, 1994) were satisfied with the attention paid to taxes.

More recent studies have reported some interesting results. A study on sub-Saharan Africa by Agbeyegbe, Stotsky, and WoldeMariam (2004: 25) has concluded that "there is a partial adjustment over time in tax revenue [for the loss in foreign trade taxes]." Furthermore, "the real exchange rate and inflation are both negative and significant factors, suggesting that real exchange rate appreciation and high inflation depress revenue, consistent with Tanzi's hypothesis (1989)" (p. 25). These authors conclude that "overall the results suggest that there is a strong persistence over time in total tax revenues and all components of revenue. Some evidence is found that trade liberalization has a positive effect on income tax revenue but otherwise is not strongly linked to total tax revenue or its components" (p. 25). Therefore, "trade liberalization, accompanied by appropriate supportive monetary policies, may preserve tax yield" (p. 27). A study by the IDB (2004) related to the U.S.–Central America Free Trade Agreement, concluded that "in most cases the fiscal revenue loss is small."

In a study dealing with regional trade integration in East Asia, Castro, Kraus, and de la Rocha (2004: 17) concluded that "the impact of forming a CU [customs union] on customs revenue is in general undetermined; it depends on a country's tariff levels prior to joining a CU, the CET [common external tariff], import demand elasticities, and export supply elasticities in the CU member states." Other studies for Central America (1991–2000) have shown that the increase in indirect taxes has more than compensated for the fall in trade taxes. In particular, the use of the VAT was important in offsetting the fall in import duties. The VAT, however, should be broad-based (see IMF, 1998). A study by Pelzman (2004) on Morocco and Jamaica also concluded that trade liberalization did not reduce tax revenue because the countries were able to raise other taxes, or "parafiscal revenue."

One extensive study, by Baunsgaard and Keen (2005), used panel data for 111 countries over a 25-year period. The authors concluded that countries (especially low-income countries) have been broadly unable to recover the revenue lost from trade taxes. They recover only about 30 cents for each dollar lost. This is an important study because it raises doubts as to whether poor countries in particular will be able to increase excise taxes and VAT. The authors' conclusion is that while high-income countries have been able to do this, poorer countries have not. The main reason is that the poorer countries have been less able to introduce VAT with the characteristics necessary to replace the lost revenue. Those characteristics are a broad base, minimal exceptions, and a reasonable threshold.

A study that covers 111 countries over a 25-year period is unlikely to be able to impart much information about the impact of a specific policy. The study is really not about trade liberalization but about what happens when, for a variety of reasons (such as inflation, overvaluation of the exchange rate, corruption, a decline in exports that reduces a country's capacity to import, and so on), a country's import duties fall relative to its GDP. If the decline is due to the kind of macroeconomic developments described by Tanzi (1989), then the results by Baunsgaard and Keen are not particularly informative about the impact of trade liberalization on tax revenue in normal times.

In addition to the various studies that have dealt with groups of countries, several have analyzed specific countries. Typical of such studies are those on Chile by Vial (2003), on Guatemala by Schenone and de la Torre (2005), and on Cyprus by Jenkins and Poufos (2002). Various general conclusions can be drawn from all of these studies, as outlined in the next section.

General Conclusions

The first conclusion is that it is difficult to generalize about the impact of trade liberalization on countries' tax revenue and fiscal accounts. All countries have different tax systems, different economic structures, different governments, and different macroeconomic conditions. For this reason, studies that draw conclusions from large groups of countries over long periods are not informative as to the impact of trade liberalization (a specific policy) on specific countries. These studies, sometimes unintentionally, tend to regard trade liberalization as responsible for conditions it may actually have little to do with, such as inflation, overvalued exchange rates, deteriorating tax administrations, falling commodity prices, and so on.

The second conclusion is that the nature of a country's existing tax system plays an important role in determining how total tax revenue responds over time to trade liberalization. If a country has only, or mostly, foreign trade taxes, and if it reduces trade restrictions by lowering both quantitative restrictions and import duties without doing anything else, at some point it will experience revenue losses, unless imports increase sufficiently to neutralize the impact of lower import duties. Earlier this chapter argued that to some extent, the transformation of quantitative restrictions into tariffs and the lowering of very high tariffs, up to a point, might even lead to higher revenue. For this to happen, however, imports must increase significantly, and customs duties must not fall below a certain level.

The third conclusion is that a country that embarks on the process of trade liberalization with a well-developed tax system—one that includes a VAT, excise taxes, and income taxes—is less likely than other countries to experience revenue losses, because the reduction of trade restrictions will lead to an increase in revenue from these other taxes. For this compensation to be significant, however, several conditions are necessary. First, the country should have broad-based taxes. This is particularly important for the VAT, which is very sensitive to import flows. A broad-based VAT that has few exemptions and relies mostly on one rate will prove a significant counterweight to the possible fall in trade taxes. Second, the trade liberalization process must not be so sudden as to have a negative impact on domestic activities (closing of enterprises, firing of workers), which in turn could lead to a decline in domestic taxes. Third, the government must not react to the reduction in trade restrictions by significantly increasing its spending (presumably to compensate the losers). This reaction is more likely if trade restrictions are removed in too short a period.

The fourth conclusion is that larger and more advanced countries will find it easier to cope with trade liberalization, since they will have greater freedom to choose their tax systems. Smaller and less sophisticated countries, which have relied significantly on import duties and have not felt the need to develop alternative taxes, will be more challenged. In these countries, the share of imports in GDP is typically very high. Imports have thus provided a useful "tax handle." The island countries of the Caribbean, for example, have come to depend largely on trade taxes. These countries may find it more difficult, but certainly not impossible, to introduce income taxes or even broad-based VAT. To some extent, however, they may transform the import duties into excise taxes. In theory, excise tax makes no distinction between domestically produced products and services and those that are imported. Thus, at least in a legal sense, this change is possible. Since many of the products used in these countries are imported, the countries' tax administrations would continue to collect the excise tax at the point of importation. For these countries, however, a question arises: What is the level of the import duties (which may have become excise taxes) at which tax revenue is maximized? Trade agreements cannot require these countries to impose "excise taxes" that are too low, because such agreements relate only to trade.

Finally, a few additional comments can be made about the impact of trade liberalization on public spending. Evidence indicates that unless countries reduce their trade restrictions because they are obliged to do so under terms-of-trade agreements (and not because their policymakers are convinced that opening the country to foreign competition can bring benefits), they will make other changes that will have implications for public spending. Some of these changes would probably increase the level of public spending, while others would reduce it. More specifically, public spending could rise for at least three reasons. First, as already indicated, when trade restrictions are removed, and especially when this is done in a short period, there will be negative effects on domestic enterprises that had operated behind the protection of the high tariffs. They and their workers will put pressure on the government for compensation. Second, an increase in trade flows and greater foreign competition will force the country to make some investments in infrastructure, both physical and institutional, in order to cope better with the new trade (see Tanzi, 2004). Ports may have to be built, roads widened, training and education improved, and so on. Hence the government may have to increase its spending. Finally, a country that has lived behind protective walls often has implicitly developed a primitive and inefficient "safety net," especially for urban workers. The opening of its borders may force it to replace regulations (minimum wages, wage controls, price controls, and so forth) with explicit public expenditures, which may spur higher public spending and higher taxes.

References

Abed, G. 2000. "Trade Liberalization and Tax Reform in the Southern Mediterranean Region." In *Trade Policy Development in the Middle East and North Africa*, ed. B. Hoekman and H. Kheir-el Din. Washington, DC: World Bank.

Abed, G., et al. 1998. "Fiscal Reforms in Low-Income Countries: Experiences under Fund Supported Programs." IMF Occasional Paper 160. Washington, DC: International Monetary Fund.

Agbeyegbe, T., J. Stotsky, and A. WoldeMariam. 2004. "Trade Liberalization, Exchange Rate Changes, and Tax Revenue in Sub-Saharan Africa." Working Paper 04/178. Washington, DC: International Monetary Fund.

Anderson, J. E., and J. P. Neary. 1994. "Measuring the Restrictiveness of Trade Policy." *World Bank Economic Review* 8(2):151–69.

Baunsgaard, T., and M. Keen. 2005. "Tax Revenue and (or?) Trade Liberalization." IMF Working Paper 05/112. Washington, DC: International Monetary Fund.

Blejer, M., and A. Cheasty. 1990. "Fiscal Implications of Trade Liberalization." In *Fiscal Policy in Open Developing Economies*, ed. Vito Tanzi. Washington, DC: International Monetary Fund.

Castro, L., C. Kraus, and M. de la Rocha. 2004. "Regional Trade Integration in East Africa: Trade and Revenue Impacts of the Planned East African Community Customs Union." Africa Region Working Paper 72. Washington, DC: World Bank.

Datta-Mitra, J. 1997. *Fiscal Management in Adjustment Lending.* Washington, DC: World Bank.

Ebrill, L., J. Stotsky, and R. Gropp. 1999. "Revenue Implications of Trade Liberalization." IMF Occasional Paper 180. Washington, DC: International Monetary Fund.

Greenway, D., and C. Milner. 1991. "Fiscal Dependence on Trade Taxes and Trade Policy Reform." *Journal of Development Studies* 27:95–132.

IDB (Inter-American Development Bank). 2004. "Integration and Trade in the Americas: Fiscal Impact of Trade Liberalization in the Americas." Periodic Note (January). Washington, DC: IDB.

IMF (International Monetary Fund). 1998. *Trade Liberalization in IMF-Supported Programs.* Washington, DC: IMF.

Jenkins, G. P., and G. Poufos. 2002. "Economic Integration and the Transformation of the Tax Mix." Unpublished. Inter-American Development Bank, Washington, DC.

Khattry, B., and M. Rao. 2002. "Fiscal Faux Pas? An Analysis of the Revenue Implications of Trade Liberalization." *World Development* 30(8):1431–44.

Mitra, P. 1992. "The Coordinated Reform of Tariffs and Indirect Taxes." *World Bank Research Observer* 7(2):195–219.

Musgrave, R. 1969. *Fiscal Systems.* New Haven, CT: Yale University Press.

Pelzman, J. 2004. "Trade Liberalization and Fiscal Reform: Evidence from Two Case Studies—Morocco and Jamaica—and a General Cross-Country Econometric Analysis." Unpublished study for the U.S. Agency for International Development. Available at http://www.fiscalreform.net/best_practices/pdfs/pelzman_final_10405.pdf.

Pritchett, L., and G. Sethi. 1994. "Tariff Rates, Tariff Revenues and Tariff Reform: Some New Facts." *World Bank Economic Review* 8(1):1–16.

Rajaram, A. 1994. "Tariff and Tax Reforms: Do World Bank Recommendations Integrate Revenue and Protection Objectives?" *Economic Studies Quarterly* 45(4):321–38.

Rodrik, D. 1998. "Why Do More Open Economies Have Bigger Governments?" *Journal of Political Economy* 106(5):997–1032.

Schenone, O., and C. de la Torre. 2005. "Guatemala: fortalecimiento de la estructura Tributaria." In *Recaudar para crecer: bases para la reforma tributaria en Centroamérica,* ed. M. Agosin, A. Barreix, and R. Machado. Washington, DC: Inter-American Development Bank.

Tanzi, V. 1973. "The Theory of Tax Structure Change during Economic Development: A Critical Survey." *Rivista di Diritto Finaniario e Scienza delle Finanze* 1:199.

———. 1989. "The Impact of Macroeconomic Policies on the Level of Taxation and the Fiscal Balance in Developing Countries." *IMF Staff Papers* 36(9):633–56.

————. 2004. "Globalization and the Need for Fiscal Reform in Developing Countries." *Journal of Policy Modeling* 26(4):525–42.

Vial, J. 2003. "Efectos fiscales de la política exterior." In *The Fiscal Impact of Economic Integration*, ed. A. Valencia, A. Barreix, and L. Villela. Lima: General Secretariat of the Andean Community, and Washington, DC: Inter-American Development Bank.

4

Regional Integration and Tax Harmonization: Issues and Recent Experiences

*Fernando Velayos, Alberto Barreix, and Luiz Villela**

Introduction

It is broadly acknowledged that a country's form of international insertion determines trade in goods and services, as well as investment flows. Hence it has a significant impact on a country's technological level and production structure, and it conditions its tax structure. Additionally, if, as Musgrave (1989: 208) holds, economic integration is "the process through which economic relations and interdependence among areas are broadened and deepened," it is evident that to attain integration, the barriers interfering with the process have to be removed. Since taxes may be barriers to the free movement of goods, services, or production factors, their adjustment to integration should be examined.

This chapter does not seek to review market integration theories or the effects of taxation on the market.[1] Rather, it takes the premise above as a given—that taxes may constitute a barrier—and it therefore analyzes and describes Latin American efforts to address the issue of fiscal barri-

---

* The authors are grateful to Vito Tanzi, José Manuel Calderón, Adolfo Martín Jiménez, and Jerónimo Roca for their useful comments. They also thank Patricia Abad and Maricela Cruz for assistance.

[1] For a summary of these issues and for relevant references, see Martín Jiménez (1999: 7–17).

ers. The formulas that have been suggested to remove fiscal barriers to integration are diverse, both in the degree of harmonization they have sought and attained and in the legal instruments used.

The next section of this chapter classifies different degrees of harmonization.[2] Its purpose is to build a conceptual framework that might allow for a more coherent presentation of harmonization experiences, particularly in Latin America. The chapter then reviews concrete harmonization experiences in the region, arranged in line with that classification. Next, in light of the Latin American experience, the chapter explores the interrelation among the different goals of integration, the levels of tax harmonization attained, and the legal instruments devised to reach such levels. Finally, we seek to draw some conclusions.

Toward a Scale of Harmonization

Reviewing the Literature

A brief review of the literature on tax harmonization reveals several interesting things. First, there is no consensus on the technical definition of tax harmonization.

■ To begin with, the dictionary is of little help, since the general dictionary definition does not address a technical issue such as this. It refers to "bringing into harmony [that is, "establishing a proper proportion and correspondence between some things and others"], or bringing into consonance two or more parts of a whole, two or more things that must concur to the same end." Etymologically, the word derives from *armos* in ancient Greek, which means "a fitting or joining." Perhaps the lesson to be learned from a linguistic analysis is that harmony, contrary to what some authors have held and in contrast to popular belief (Fairlamb, 2004), can-

---

[2] The term "harmonization" is difficult to define. This chapter pays some attention to the different conceptual approaches to the subject.

not be compared with uniformity. As in music, there are ways of combining and adjusting certain sounds with others so that the whole sounds pleasing.

■ Tax harmonization is not an explicit legal concept. In the European context, Article 94 of the Treaty of Amsterdam includes the term "harmonization," but the term is not defined there or in any other part of the treaty and is frequently used only in relation to indirect taxes. As to direct taxes, Article 95 refers only to "an approximation of laws," without expressly mentioning the word.[3]

■ The *IBFD International Tax Glossary* (Larking, 2005) defines tax harmonization as the elimination of differences or inconsistencies between the tax systems of different jurisdictions, or making such differences or inconsistencies compatible with each other. It should be noted that the second part of this definition is subsumed under the first, since the reconciliation of an inconsistency can mean nothing but that the inconsistency has already been removed.

■ Peggy Musgrave (1989: 14) defines tax harmonization as "the process of adjusting national fiscal systems to conform with a set of common economic aims."

■ The term has been used in varied ways. For instance, some authors associate the concept with the adoption of a common tax rate (see, for example, Krugman and Baldwin, 2002). Kopits (1992) adds slightly different shades of meaning when he refers to "con-

---

[3] Article 94 states: "The Council shall, acting unanimously on a proposal from the Commission and after consulting the European Parliament and the Economic and Social Committee, adopt provisions for the harmonisation of legislation concerning turnover taxes, excise duties and other forms of indirect taxation to the extent that such harmonisation is necessary to ensure the establishment and the functioning of the internal market." Article 95 states: "The Council shall ... adopt the measures for the approximation of the provisions laid down by law, regulation or administrative action in Member States which have as their object the establishment and functioning of the internal market. [This paragraph] shall not apply to fiscal provisions, to those relating to the free movement of persons nor to those relating to the rights and interests of employed persons." (The article numbers used here correspond to the 1997 consolidated version of the Treaty Establishing the European Community.)

certed" and "spontaneous" tax harmonization: the first being a convergence-oriented formal agreement (not necessarily meaning "equalization") and the second a convergence in response to competitive pressures.

In conclusion, the term "harmonization" has been defined in different ways, but the underlying notion is that different degrees of harmonization are possible, and these are related to the economic background—that is, the level of integration pursued. Tax harmonization, therefore, is instrumental to economic integration.

A second finding that emerges from a review of the literature is that the range of instruments (and hence the range of options) currently available to remove fiscal barriers to integration (that is, to accomplish tax harmonization) is wider.

- Pinder, reformulating an idea first advanced by Tinbergen, spoke in 1968 about "negative integration" (obligations not to do certain things, with a view to eliminating discrimination among economic actors) and "positive integration" (involving the design and application of common and coordinated policies). For a detailed analysis, see Martín Jiménez (1999).
- González Cano (1996) argues that there are two tax harmonization mechanisms: uniformity and compatibility. The second, in his opinion, is the one to be applied at the early stages of economic integration, when tax harmonization is also incipient. His position masks some confusion in the analysis of harmonization's aims and instruments: the fact that integration is at an incipient stage does not mean that the degree of tax harmonization, in terms of the obligations assumed or the sovereignty transferred by the state, should be equally weak or lacking in vigor. On the contrary, as argued below, the opposite is the case.
- Martín Jiménez (1999) analyzes the relationship between aims and instruments when he examines the role of "soft law" in the European Union's (EU's) scheme of tax harmonization instruments, but he does not do so in order to establish a classifica-

tion of tax harmonization or levels of action. Nor does he seek to analyze the relationship between phases of integration, degrees of harmonization, and the instruments most commonly used to attain each level.

■ Caamaño and Calderón (2002), like Martín Jiménez, note that developments in the international context, such as an aggressive environment, foster greater sophistication in the instruments available for bringing tax policies closer, thereby avoiding distortions.[4] Though Caamaño and Calderón provide interesting examples of what they call "tax coordination," they neither define the term nor establish its distinctive features relative to other mechanisms for approximating or harmonizing taxes (although this matter is not crucial for their analysis).

■ In contrast, James (2000) ventures a classification of degrees of harmonization ranging from "no harmonization" to complete "standardization." His analysis is based on the notion that the first step toward harmonization is to define a common set of taxes— that is, it is important to start by harmonizing the object of taxation. Absent such an endeavor, the only matter on which some action can be taken is the elimination or mitigation of double taxation (presumably as regards direct taxes, although the author does not explicitly say so).

James's analysis is interesting because he classifies tax harmonization in the form of a scale (that is, with various possible steps), thus overcoming the dual or quasi-dual concept that prevailed in earlier studies. But even though he briefly mentions the term "administrative cooperation," he does not examine the new phenomenon of nonformal harmonization (the broad-scope coordination sphere discussed by Caamaño and Calderón). Neither does he address the possible relationship between degrees of integration and the instruments available to policymakers to attain the

---

[4] These authors do seem to draw a distinction between planned harmonization and spontaneous approximation.

intended harmonization. His review of the degrees of harmonization merely describes the results obtained and fails to explain the methodology used (the guiding criterion seems to be the degree of standardization attained). In sum, his main concern is a different one: whether the coexistence of various types of taxes, such as local taxes and other harmonized taxes, is justified—in other words, whether there is a rational constraint to tax uniformity.

▪ Finally, Barreix and Villela (2003) explore the plausibility of adding a new feature—coordinability—to the classic four of a tax system (sufficiency, efficiency, simplicity, and equity). "Coordinability" can be defined as a tax jurisdiction's ability to coordinate with the jurisdictions of its main economic partners. Barreix and Villela develop the idea of more "coordinable" tax systems in the Southern Common Market (MERCOSUR) without extrapolating their conceptual framework beyond that network of countries. However, the idea implies the existence of a range of harmonization actions, from "uniformization" to "fiscal wars." The best alternative must be chosen from among this wide array of possibilities, keeping in mind the impact on the traditional features of a good tax system.

In sum, observers increasingly perceive a trend toward a far richer, more complex, and multifaceted spectrum of harmonization objectives or degrees, with their attendant instruments. All this tends to bring tax systems closer, perhaps imperfectly, and may lead to an "international tax system" (Caamaño and Calderón, 2002). But the tax-related literature has not yet clearly established a true scale of harmonization actions, with their corresponding regulatory instruments (in formal and nonformal law).

Moreover, although the economic evolution of the different degrees of integration has been well defined, particularly using the typology of Balassa (1961),[5] studies have not yet focused on whether there is any par-

---

[5] Balassa outlines the following degrees of integration. *Free trade area:* Countries undertake to eliminate tariffs and quantitative restrictions on traded goods, but maintain a separate external tariff. *Customs union:* A common external tariff is adopted. *Common*

allelism or inherent logical relationship between the levels of integration pursued, the degrees of tax harmonization required, and the regulatory instruments used. This chapter seeks not to establish a dogmatic classification but to help clarify the different degrees of harmonization and to apply them to the Latin American experience.

Building a Tax Harmonization Scale

The theoretical and practical background is sufficiently robust for an attempt to develop, on the basis of one criterion or more, a true scale (that is, a logical order) of the degree of tax harmonization. Later in this chapter, following the review of specific Latin American harmonization experiences, we examine whether harmonization aims and instruments may be correlated and, if so, what the rationale behind that correlation is.

The Scale

The first methodological matter to be considered in building the scale is the choice of the guiding criterion. There are several possible criteria: the status of the legal rule used, the political commitment assumed, the economic implications at stake, and so forth.

This chapter opts to classify harmonization actions according to the political commitment assumed. This is because certain actions (taking harmonization in its broadest sense) may involve the use of different legal instruments, or may not be reflected in any legal instrument, at least not in a single one that meets the classical criterion of the normative pyramid.[6]

---

market: The free movement of labor and capital is added to the free movement of goods and services. *Economic union*: In addition to the above features, national economic policies are coordinated to eliminate distortions caused by different policies. *Economic integration*: Monetary, fiscal, social, and counter-cyclical policies are unified.

[6] For an analysis of the soft law paradox, see Chapter 7 in Martín Jiménez (1999), which shows that it is hard to place modern harmonization instruments into a hierarchical order, particularly if a court (in the case analyzed by the author, the European Court of Justice), relying on the thesis contained therein, may inadvertently raise the status of any of the instruments.

Analyzing the potential economic importance of each harmonization action would require a methodology to measure its economic consequences, a task that might be not only extremely difficult but also highly variable, depending on the regional bloc in which harmonization is undertaken. It is not certain, for example, whether the establishment of a customs union may have a greater impact than the adoption of a harmonized value-added tax (VAT).

On the other hand, the political commitment criterion allows for a more consistent classification—a priori, the degree of political commitment behind each type of action is deemed universally comparable, although this may be a matter of opinion in some specific cases. The political commitment criterion also allows for the introduction of new regulatory instruments or new forms of coordination. And it permits a subsequent analysis of the harmonization "rationale"—that is, determining whether the means (measured at least by their "political cost") suit the purposes of integration. Thus, tax harmonization processes involve the following steps, arranged in descending order of political commitment:

Standardization. This consists of having the same tax or, as González Cano (1996: 26) puts it, "equalizing the tax burdens imposed on the same item, under equal circumstances." It is the highest degree of harmonization. An example is the adoption of a common external tariff (CET).

Compatibility. Quoting González Cano again (1996: 31), compatibility involves "adjusting the tax structure in order to … counteract or compensate for the distortionary effects caused by tax burden disparities upon the integration process." Although González Cano leaves it unstated, adjusting those elements in the tax structure does not mean that they should necessarily be identical. In fact, compatibility does not affect the tax rate or tax benefits, at least not to their full extent. The reason is that if this were the case, there would be almost no difference between this form of harmonization and the previous one, thus eliminating its distinctive features—that is, compatibility does not exhaust its capacity for harmonization, particularly with respect to an extremely sensitive element such as the tax rate, and it leaves more room for policymakers to make tax policy decisions.

In the classical, particularly European, literature, there is a tendency to confuse compatibility with harmonization in the strict sense of the word—that is, standardizing tax bases, connection points, and taxable items, but leaving some maneuvering room for tax rates, or even for exemptions. Compatibility, then, is somehow associated with more advanced integration objectives—that is, when internal tax distortions are detected.

But making tax regulations compatible may begin much earlier, with free trade areas. Mutual tariff benefits do not need to be granted uniformly (some countries can grant benefits on some products, while other countries do so for others), as long as all parties respect the "global reciprocity" principle in the concession of fiscal benefits and the gradual trend toward increasing the benefits granted.

Ideally, any compatibility scheme should involve an institutionalized follow-up mechanism to ensure its effective enforcement. Compatibility is more complex than equalization; since there are no strict definitions to determine what has and has not been made compatible, some state decisions comply with harmonization objectives but others do not. Therefore, it is highly advisable to establish a follow-up mechanism to keep track of what each country does in this respect, so as to ensure that the goal of harmonization is not adversely affected. An emblematic example of this kind of harmonization is the Sixth Directive of the EU on VAT harmonization.

Coordination. The concept of tax coordination is far from being accurately defined in the literature. For some authors, coordination appears to be any action transcending typical harmonization mechanisms, which might be confined to the two categories above. But this would bring the typology to an end when, in fact, the various tax-approximation methods tested so far allow harmonization to be broken down into more categories.

Perhaps the best way to define this "in-between" category (in the typology herein, it is the third of five) is as follows: coordination is everything that does not fit into any of the other four categories. Hence this chapter implicitly acknowledges, as do other authors, how difficult it is to define it accurately. As to the degree of the political commitment involved, it is a step forward relative to the two following categories, as can be easily inferred. There are various examples of coordination: codes of conduct are a case in point.

Cooperation. This is the provision of mutual assistance, either for reasons of reciprocity (for instance, one country supplies tax information in the expectation that it will receive information from its counterpart at some other time) or out of mutual interest (such as when double taxation is detected and two countries undertake to cooperate). A distinction can also be drawn between practical cooperation (as in the previous example) and theoretical cooperation (for example, providing assistance or sharing best practices in taxation). In any case, cooperation does not necessarily entail sharing a common tax policy (except for the fact that cooperation is a policy in itself). It might be argued that, since there is no sharing of policies, there is no approximation and no reason to include this mechanism in this category. A closer examination, however, reveals that existing bilateral and multilateral cooperation mechanisms, by creating more homogeneous tax administrations, are contributing to a more consistent application of tax systems, thus ensuring greater horizontal equity and leveling the playing field for economic actors. In addition, the creation of cooperation mechanisms makes countries aware of and willing to adopt the best solutions, in terms of both tax administration and policy. For instance, after relevant consultations, countries might adopt the same interpretation criteria in a complex case when laws are similar or there is a double taxation agreement.[7]

Convergence. Curiously enough, this end of the harmonization scale has not passed unnoticed by many of the authors mentioned (see Kopits,

---

[7] Caamaño and Calderón (2002) implicitly endorse this idea but classify these actions as coordination because in their view they derive from "backdoor rules"—pseudo-regulatory instruments devised by international organizations.

1992, and Caamaño and Calderón, 2002). Convergence is a spontaneous movement (sometimes inevitable, though unwanted) toward harmonization, as a result of globalization and competition. Convergence is classified as the lowest step on the scale because no particular harmonization action has been taken for reasons of political will.[8] Instead, the country simply cannot escape the trend, or it admits (probably unconsciously or against its own wishes) that this is the best approach to take. Hence, in spontaneous convergence, there is always an element of discomfort, or at least passivity.

The Harmonization Pyramid and Its Corollary, the "Coordinability" of the Tax System

On the basis of the harmonization actions described and classified in the pyramid (Figure 4.1), it may be inferred that coordinability with other jurisdictions is a desired feature of a modern tax system. "Coordinability" here means that the tax system is capable of including a significant number of harmonization actions—especially with its major trade and economic partners—without jeopardizing the other traditional properties of a tax system (sufficiency, efficiency, simplicity, and equity).

A globalized economy requires tax systems with a greater capacity to adapt to a changing and interconnected environment. Indeed, this is increasingly important as regional integration deepens and widens, creating larger economic and political blocs. In this context, tax harmonization should facilitate and support economic and trade liberalization.

However, legal, institutional, and cultural barriers adversely affect attitudes toward changing tax systems. Thinking turns rigid, and countries run the risk of lagging behind in the processes of modernization and integration. This chapter does not seek to analyze those obstacles, but the following examples should be noted:

---

[8] When there is political will, unilateral or not, it can always be seen to be based on the usually explicit conviction that adjusting to third parties is an appropriate way to respond to a concrete problem.

Figure 4.1 The Harmonization Pyramid

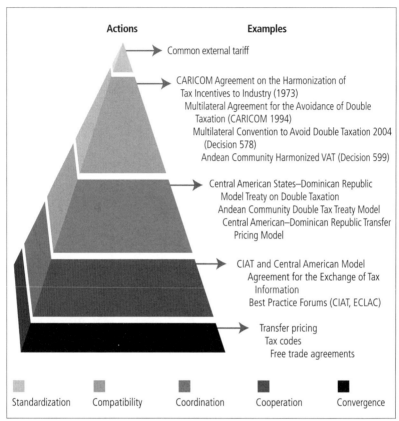

Note: CIAT = Inter-American Center of Tax Administration; ECLAC = Economic Commission for Latin America and the Caribbean.

- The state VAT in Brazil (the ICMS) not only harms the efficiency of Brazilian producers but also damages trade among MERCOSUR partners and constrains the prospects of completing a perfect customs union.
- Tax secrecy laws pose obstacles in Uruguay, and constitutional curbs in Guatemala (Article 4 of the constitution) limit the exchange of tax information. Although withholding tax is levied on passive income, there is only limited capacity to conclude double tax treaties and to tackle fraud in countries belonging to the same integration process. Similar issues arise in the tax and

bank secrecy regulations of certain EU countries (Austria, Belgium, and Luxembourg). This is hindering deeper integration in the area of savings taxation in the EU (2003/48/EC Directive of June 3, 2003, on the taxation of savings income in the form of interest—the Savings Directive—and its modification 2004/66/EC; see Martín Jiménez, 2006).

▪ A case of a "cultural" barrier is the level of excise taxes in the EU: while the northern European tradition penalizes alcoholic beverages with high tax rates, southern European countries resist this levy since it is inconsistent with their cultural patterns.

▪ The U.S. policy of rejecting the tax sparing clause for U.S. investors abroad gives rise to inflexibility in the negotiation of the country's tax treaties and clearly affects the coordinability of the U.S. tax system.[9]

Hence a new and desirable feature of a modern tax system, and one that is unavoidable if regional economic integration is to be deep, is its capacity to adapt to other tax jurisdictions (its economic partners)—in short, coordinability.

Latin American Experiences and the Tax Harmonization Scale

This section has a twofold purpose. First, it seeks to examine a number of experiences in order to show that Latin American economic history is also a history of tax harmonization. The interest in these experiences lies in noting and classifying them, although the latter endeavor may sometimes appear arbitrary. Hence, apart from more recent phenomena that may interest readers because of their novelty, this chapter offers brief accounts rather than thorough descriptions.

Second, this classification could be useful for examining, later in the chapter, the *ratio armonitatis* that might underlie integration—in other

---

[9] Neither in the U.S. Constitution nor in the tax code is there a provision that prohibits the acceptance of the tax sparing clause in a treaty. The Senate established this policy during the 1960s, and it has not been reviewed since.

words, for examining whether, in Latin America's turbulent integration movement, there is an intrinsic logic whereby identical or similar degrees of tax harmonization are attained when integration objectives are comparable.

Standardization

Common External Tariff and Customs Union

As mentioned earlier, a common external tariff is the paradigmatic example of tax law standardization. A customs union can be defined as "the merging of several customs territories into a single customs territory in order to consolidate the free movement of goods, regardless of their origin, provided the goods originating in third countries are cleared in any of the member states" (translated from SIECA, 2006: 9). Hence a customs union is an economic integration objective. The key element—though not the only one—in any true customs union is the adoption of a CET. This must be the same across the customs union's whole external border, because otherwise trade diversion and other perverse phenomena would occur.

There are four customs unions in Latin America, all of them of different scope: the Andean Community (CAN), the Caribbean Community (CARICOM), the Southern Common Market (MERCOSUR), and the Central American Customs Union (currently under way).

CAN. The CET applied by the CAN[10] is the result of a process involving three major milestones: Chapter VIII of the Andean subregional integration agreement (the Cartagena Agreement) of May 26, 1969; the establishment of a free trade area encompassing Bolivia, Colombia, Ecuador, and Venezuela, which came into effect in 1993 at the end of the process to eliminate trade barriers for goods; and the entry into force of a CET (through Decision 370) in 1995.

---

[10] Decision 370, like any other CAN decision, is binding on and directly applicable to all member states. Nonetheless, the CET is imperfect because of the exceptions and its different implementation in Bolivia and Ecuador.

CARICOM. The treaty establishing a CET took effect on the same date—August 1, 1973—as CARICOM's founding agreement, the Treaty of Chaguaramas. The latter was revised in 2001, and economic integration was strengthened by the inclusion of trade, tariff, and tax policy matters.[11]

MERCOSUR. Two major milestones can be highlighted: the Treaty of Asunción of March 26, 1991, and Decision 22/94 of the Common Market Council, which created the CET and regulated the exceptions to it.[12]

Central American Customs Union. This is under construction, but it has a founding text (adopted as an international treaty),[13] the economy ministries of the member countries of the Central American Economic Integration System (SIECA) have issued several important resolutions,[14] and technical teams are holding regular meetings. Nevertheless, the CET in the subregion has not been fully adopted: in July 2006, 6 percent of the items, mostly agricultural, had yet to be included (SIECA, 2006).

---

[11] As opposed to the CAN, the CARICOM, under its founding treaties (see revised Treaty of Chaguaramas, Articles 7 to 18, or the treaty establishing the CARICOM Court of Justice), has intergovernmental decision-making mechanisms; the member states thus retain a high degree of sovereignty. This does not prevent the establishment of a customs union and progress toward integration, but it does complicate the matter and slow down the process.

[12] The decisions adopted by the Common Market Council (as well as the resolutions adopted by the Common Market Group and the directives of the Trade Commission) are binding on the member countries but lack direct effects. Article 42 of the Ouro Prêto Protocol (December 17, 1994) states: "The decisions adopted by the Mercosur organs provided for in Article 2 of this Protocol shall be binding and, when necessary, must be transposed into the domestic legal systems in accordance with the procedures provided for in each country's legislation." In this respect, MERCOSUR can be said to be closer to the CARICOM than to the CAN. MERCOSUR's international legal nature has been described as a "special public international law system" (Rincón Eizaga, 2000) because some of its institutions include some elements of supranationality and rules that are binding on the member countries, although their effects are not directly enforceable (Sabsay, 1999).

[13] General Treaty on Central American Economic Integration, signed in 1960, and protocols thereof.

[14] For instance, the Central American Uniform Customs Code was approved as an international treaty. The text currently in force is dated May 2006.

For this analysis, it is worth noting that all these customs unions have used legal instruments to ensure the most uniform possible application of the CET and the other measures specified in the customs union regime. Although the degree of harmonization pursued has been the same, the instrument used has varied, depending largely on the degree of supranationality (how much sovereign authority has been ceded to common institutions). When supranationality is weak or still being introduced, as in Central America, the solution lies with intergovernmental approaches, wherein classical international agreements or treaties, duly ratified, impose commitments on the member states. When substantial authority has been ceded to relevant institutions,[15] they are responsible for completing the process.

Compatibility

As described earlier, the step below standardization is compatibility, which involves weaker political commitment (less cession of sovereignty). This degree of harmonization may be appropriate when a strong common discipline is required to avoid distortions, but when there is no need or desire to standardize every structural component of a tax. Examples in Latin America include the following.

Latin American Integration Association

In 1980 the Treaty of Montevideo established the Latin American Integration Association (LAIA)—a successor to the Latin American Free Trade Association (LAFTA), which was founded in 1960. Notwithstanding its name, LAIA is a typical free trade area, wherein countries grant regional trade preferences on a reciprocal basis (Article 5). The regional agreements resulting from the Treaty of Montevideo, particularly the agreement establishing the RTP, provide for a series of reciprocal tariff concessions that

---

[15] Without purporting to exhaust the subject, since it is beyond the scope of this chapter, it is worth noting that the only subregion currently seeking—at least on paper—a supranational structure is the Andean Community.

combine detail (an average 20 percent tariff reduction) with flexibility (national lists), and that may be categorized as "tariff compatibility."

CAN Decisions 40 and 578 (Multilateral Convention to
Avoid Double Taxation, 1970 and 2004)

In 1970 the Andean Community (Bolivia, Colombia, Ecuador, Peru, and, at that time, Chile but not Venezuela) adopted Decision 40, which already contained the key elements that were to be included in Decision 578. However, Decision 40 was never fully enforced, and it made no provision for correlative adjustments in the event of profits from transactions between related companies. It was therefore judged necessary to draft a new decision addressing this matter, together with other technical modifications, and to enforce a new regulation that would be beyond dispute. In 2004, Decision 578 was approved.

The features of Decision 578 are as follows:

I It is a multilateral agreement intended to avert double taxation.
I The tax is levied almost exclusively at source (except for goods transported by sea or air, or imported by diplomatic or consular employees).
I Although roughly modeled after the Organisation for Economic Co-operation and Development (OECD) and United Nations as regards income-related matters, the decision has certain peculiarities, such as the definition of key concepts that are subsequently used throughout the text: royalties, interest, capital gains, and others. Surprisingly, however, there is no definition of a resident or nonresident individual. There are also some peculiarities concerning the determination of connection points, especially as regards technical assistance services.[16] And none of its articles make

---

[16] Article 14 states: "Corporate income from services, technical services, technical assistance and consultancy services rendered. Income earned by businesses providing professional, technical, technical assistance and consultancy services shall only be taxable in the member country where the income from such services originates or is generated. Unless proof to the contrary is provided, the place where the income originates is presumed to be the place where the pertinent charge is made and recorded."

reference to the elimination of double taxation (a natural consequence of the fact that all the rights to tax are exclusive).

Several issues are pending:

- The decision does not automatically solve source disputes that arise when two countries believe that the income originated in their own territory. Suppose that a bank in country A has a branch in country B, and the branch is earning interest on a loan to a debtor who resides in country C. Under the decision, both B and C may argue that the income originated in their territory.
- There are no limits on the tax rates at source.
- The decision gives rise to tax planning, particularly among individuals whose direct taxes will become less progressive if a portion of their income (for example, their pension) originates in another member state.

In view of these considerations, the level of compatibility attained by the CAN in this matter may be deemed to be low, although not to the extent that these decisions could be said to fall in the domain of coordination rather than true compatibility. They belong to the sphere of compatibility because, even though rates are not harmonized, progress has been made with regard to pooling tax sovereignty, the technical definition of some concepts, and a shared vision of the need to eliminate double taxation.[17] In this respect, it could even be claimed that the Andean Community Court of Justice, since it has jurisdiction over this decision and all others, could act as the highest dispute settlement body.

---

[17] Decision 578, Article 6, concludes: "If a company operates in two or more member countries, each country may tax the income generated in its territory; for which purpose each country shall apply its own internal regulations to determine the tax base as if it were a distinct, independent and separate company, but shall avoid, however, generating double taxation under the provisions of this Decision." And Article 20 states: "The provisions of this Decision shall always be interpreted and applied bearing in mind that its fundamental purpose is to avoid the double taxation of the same income or equity at community level."

In short, the theoretical degree of integration resulting from this decision is significant. Moreover, according to data collected directly in Colombia and Peru,[18] this regulation is fully enforced at present in these two countries, regardless of the difficulties arising from the fact that this double taxation agreement scheme (with exclusive taxation at the source) has to coexist with other agreements, whereby the country of residence retains a great deal of sovereignty. Bolivia, Ecuador, and Peru have signed double taxation agreements of this sort, and Colombia is currently negotiating one. Hence, as far as harmonization is concerned, Decision 578 can be seen as an advance in the field of direct taxation in the CAN.

A different question is whether this decision meets (or would meet) a real need, given the prevailing level of integration, since it is curious that Andean integration, at least on paper, should make more progress in the field of direct taxation (Decision 40) than indirect taxation (the free trade area was not truly established until 1993, the CET entered into force in 1995, and actual VAT integration is more an endeavor than a reality). This circumstance may be explained by the fact that integration was—and to some extent remains—more formal than real, and it was easy to attain fiscal harmonization (compatibility) in those areas that had no practical implications. In fact, a review of the 1970s statistics shows that while there was little intra-subregional trade, there was even less intra-subregional direct investment, and thus Decision 40 was more of a virtual document than a legal text with actual effects. An analysis of the trade between the founding members of the European Economic Community—Germany, Belgium, France, Italy, Luxembourg, and the Netherlands—shows that intra-bloc trade accounted for 50 percent of total trade in the early 1970s. In contrast, trade among CAN member countries accounted for just 3 percent of the total in that period. At present it stands at about 15 percent, and intra-Andean investment is

---

[18] The Inter-American Development Bank is conducting a diagnostic survey of the international activities of tax administrations in some countries of the region, including Colombia and Peru (Project ATN/FG-9141-RS). The analysis has established that the tax administration and multinational companies are complying with this rule.

less than 1 percent of total foreign direct investment (FDI), revealing that there is no solid basis for trade integration. These considerations prompt a question to be discussed later in this chapter: what can be harmonized (in terms of political cost), and what must be harmonized (in terms of economic rationality)?

CARICOM Agreement on the Harmonization of Tax Incentives to Industry (1973)

This international treaty establishes a policy of tax incentives to industries. As regards its substance, the high level of detail is surprising. First, it covers many issues: time limits of all types; a classification of enterprises in terms of the "value they add" (which is also defined and measured) in order to be eligible for greater or lesser incentives; control and reporting obligations assumed on behalf of the CARICOM by the administrations responsible for the application of those incentives in each member state, and so forth.

Second, the agreement is striking because of the types of incentives it is designed to regulate or limit. As regards income tax, for instance, it specifies the general reduction that may be granted according to the type of activity—in particular, a table is provided for export activities—as well as minor matters (amortizations and tax incentives for dividends and interest). In addition, limitations for minor taxes, such as the tonnage tax, are specified.

As to the degree of harmonization, a legally binding text with such a high level of detail clearly fits within the category of compatibility. There is a real attempt to harmonize tax incentive policies, without regulating incentives completely or in minute detail, so countries still have significant maneuvering room.

Three other matters should be noted. First, this treaty imposes obligations on the member states under a typical CARICOM intergovernmental scheme.[19] As far as results are concerned, its high level of detail, coupled with the lack of penalties or legal consequences for noncompli-

---

[19] Article 17 states: "Member states shall be responsible for implementing this tax scheme through their own domestic legislation, in accordance with this agreement."

ance, led the countries whose tax incentive policies were different from this scheme to expend little effort on making the necessary adjustments. That, in turn, discouraged the other members who did strive for compliance. The result is that the text is ineffective today (Lecraw, 2003).

Finally, if the scheme may be deemed a failure, as it seems to have been, what failed: the objective or the instrument? Lecraw (2003: 34) suggests that both failed. On the one hand, the objective was overly ambitious, while the definition of a true investment policy for the region—and probably the actual economic integration of the Caribbean—was not framed within a consistent context. On the other hand, there were enormous practical problems in implementing the agreement because of the absence of coercive enforcement mechanisms. The biggest failure was the objective *as it related to* the instrument. CARICOM probably should not have embarked on such an ambitious policy[20] without the institutional instruments required to ensure the success—inherently difficult—of such an enormous undertaking at such an incipient stage of economic integration as that prevailing in 1973 in the Caribbean. Hence it was the rationale, the internal logic of integration, that actually failed.

CARICOM Multilateral Agreement for the Avoidance of Double Taxation and the Prevention of Tax Evasion and Fraud (1994)

This agreement draws on earlier CARICOM agreements adopted in 1973 and 1994. To a significant extent, however, this agreement resembles the CAN's Decision 578, adopted in 2004, which grew out of Decision 40 (1970). The CARICOM multilateral agreement has many features in common with Decisions 40 and 578 (taxation is exclusively at source, and technical assistance services are broadly defined and subject to taxation solely at source as well), but it has a distinctive feature of particular importance for the analysis here: it sets maximum withholding rates at the source for dividends, interest, royalties, and technical assistance

---

[20] If this agreement is akin to anything, it is the "Commission Notice on the Application of the State Aid Rules to Measures Relating to Direct Business Taxation," *OJEC* C. 384 of 10.12.1998, C 384/03.

services.[21] This is significant because it involves a higher degree of harmonization, and, as mentioned above, this is one of the main problems with the CAN's decisions.

Given the level of intra-subregional FDI in the Caribbean in 1973,[22] the question arises again as to whether this level of harmonization was a necessity in the context of Caribbean market integration. It may reasonably be asked whether "the cart was put before the horse."

The Andean Community Harmonized VAT

In 2004, after lengthy negotiations, the CAN approved Decisions 599 and 600, providing for the harmonization of VAT and excise taxes, respectively. The harmonization of indirect taxes is necessary to reinforce the CAN's customs union and minimize the asymmetries caused by competition under very dissimilar indirect tax regimes. The Andean VAT scheme may be summarized as follows:

1. The VAT is designed with the tax credit method, based on consumption, and the destination-country principle is applied at each production stage. This approach averts the cumulative effect, which is a normal feature of sales or income taxes that discriminate against specialized firms and favor vertically integrated ones.

2. A common list of exempted goods and services, especially sensitive services—such as education, health, and domestic transportation of passengers, except air transport—and financial intermediation services will be adopted in the long run. Exemptions or exclusions will be subject to domestic legislative decisions.

---

[21] See Articles 11–14 of the Agreement among the Governments of the Member States of the Caribbean Community for the Avoidance of Double Taxation and the Prevention of Fiscal Evasion with Respect to Taxes on Income, Profits or Gains, and Capital Gains and for the Encouragement of Regional Trade and Investment (1994).

[22] If intra-regional trade is considered the determinant of the level of FDI, the level of intra-community exports in the EU reached 70 percent of total exports in 1973 (when the EU had six members), while in CARICOM it is now slightly more than 26 percent—even though tourism services are much more significant than exports in the CARICOM countries.

3. Should there be multiple tax rates, they are to be reduced to no more than two—a general tax rate shall be equal to or lower than 19 percent, while the minimum preferential rate may not be lower than 30 percent of the general tax rate, in order to facilitate VAT administration. The limit imposed on the general tax rate derives from a political economy argument: if it were higher, pressure would follow as a result of differential rates and exceptions. Zero-rate VAT will be applied exclusively on exports of goods and services.

4. Specific regulations are adopted to protect taxpayers' rights, without limiting the tax administration's powers.

5. Coordination mechanisms for international transactions are implemented on the basis of the principle of nondiscrimination between domestic and foreign production.

The period within which member countries must comply with this regulation varies according to the measure in question, the maximum being 10 years. Member countries have undertaken to establish follow-up mechanisms to verify the progress made every two years.[23]

The VAT model adopted rests on three pillars. The first of these is the member countries' willingness to integrate, as reflected in the facilitation of intra-regional trade and the harmonization of the main tax at the base. The second is to bring the quality of the VAT (whose productivity is currently very low: see Table 4.1) up to the best international policy and management practices. This task will be undertaken with regional support. Finally, it has been observed that the general application of the VAT has very little impact from a distributional standpoint (Table 4.1).

The VAT has been designed in such a way as to favor neutrality and simplicity, tax rate competition, and preference for tax determined solely at the national level. First, priority was given to sectoral neutral-

---

[23] Decision 635 establishes 2008 as the date of entry into force, but it provides for an extension of that period, on request of a member country, for a maximum of three additional years.

Table 4.1. Tax Revenue Collection, Productivity, Progressivity, and Redistribution of the VAT in the Andean Countries, 2003

Indicator	Bolivia	Colombia	Ecuador	Peru	Venezuela
Tax revenue collection					
Total tax revenue (% of GDP)	13.7	14.3	12.0	12.9	8.7
VAT (% of tax revenue)	46.0	43.4	54.2	41.9	55.2
VAT productivity	42.4	38.9	54.6	29.7	30.0
([VAT revenue as % of GDP] /nominal rate)					
Progressivity					
Gini, income before VAT income	0.556	0.537	0.408	0.535	0.423
Quasi-Gini of VAT	0.547	0.469	0.445	0.358	0.473
Kakwani (regressive if < 0; progressive if > 0; neutral if = 0)	−0.009	−0.068	0.038	−0.177	0.050
Redistribution[1]					
Gini, income after VAT	0.557	0.541	0.406	0.547	0.427
Transfer from 50%⁻ to 50%⁺ (or from 50%⁺ to 50%⁻)	−0.05	−0.20	0.09	−0.60	−0.22
Losers (income decile)	2 and 3	1 to 6 and 9	9 and 10	1 to 8	10
VAT: Who Pays the Tax?[1]					
20%⁺ (richest)/40%⁻ (poorest)	8.9	4.0	3.7	2.3	6.2

Sources: Arias et al. (2005); Barreix, Roca, and Villela (2006).

[1] Data for Bolivia and Peru are for 2000.

ity and to a simplicity that should facilitate administration, establishing administrative mechanisms to combat tax evasion. Since almost all transactions are subject to taxation, tax control and audit activities are facilitated by keeping track of invoicing throughout the value-added chain. Table 4.1 illustrates the incidence of VAT relative to the total tax burden (the average for the region is about 50 percent) and its relatively low productivity in each country, notwithstanding the significant improvement in the quality of the region's tax administrations over the last decade.

Second, on average, tax in the subregion is slightly regressive on income but progressive on spending, in line with several studies in Latin America. Hence, if VAT revenue were collected mainly from higher-income sectors, its targeted use (through public spending) on behalf of the most vulnerable social sectors might make the VAT both progressive on income and an effective tool for well-targeted social spending. Studies on the Andean countries (Arias et al., 2005; Barreix, Roca, and Villela, 2006) show that the VAT paid by the wealthiest quintile is several times greater than the VAT paid by the two lowest-income quintiles, as Table 4.1 shows. This is because, in an open and competitive economy, the VAT has a greater impact on consumption.

Third, the member states retain enough fiscal autonomy to set the fiscal mix: setting their own rates for VAT collection purposes and establishing the level of public spending best suited for the country from the economic, social, and political perspectives.

Finally, the countries agreed that VAT would be defined at the national level and centrally administered.

Coordination

Attempts to identify coordination experiences are on slippery ground. As mentioned in the categorization of harmonization, "coordination" may only be defined in contrast to all the other established categories, whose boundaries are more clear-cut when placed in a hierarchy. Rather than developing a more accurate doctrinal definition of coordination, therefore, we offer an enumeration of all that has been deemed, reasonably, not to fit in the other four categories:

Central America–Dominican Republic Model
Double Taxation Agreement

This model agreement[24] was recently presented to the economy and finance ministers of Central America and the Dominican Republic. The document is not legally binding on the signatories, and the countries do not even expressly undertake to use it as a model in the event of negotiations. Still, it provides an interesting level of coordination on international tax policy for nonresidents, and even for the signatory countries, for the following reasons:

---

[24] The agreement includes Panama.

1. There is currently no double taxation agreement in force among the countries.[25] Hence it is illogical for them to depart from a text that they have previously discussed and analyzed and that they are comfortable with. In general, therefore, the text that they are submitting for negotiation with third countries will remain unchanged unless their domestic legislation requires otherwise or recommends that some adjustment be made (for instance, in the event that constitutional provisions on bank secrecy are approved).[26]

2. It is possible that some of these countries will engage in joint negotiations with third countries in the future. These third countries will have greater interest in negotiating with several small countries at the same time, while the latter gain negotiating capacity and bargaining leverage. The model thus becomes an element of cohesion, since no joint negotiation can be started if each co-negotiator departs substantially from the model.

3. The model contains interesting peculiarities that entail a departure from the UN and OECD models and that are attributable to these countries' characteristics (institutional weakness in tax administrations, revenue collection needs, a technological deficit, and so forth). From an economic viewpoint, therefore, it is sensible to keep this model as the pattern of taxation applicable to nonresidents.

In sum, this instrument has great potential and represents a major advance because (1) it indicates that the countries have decided to embark on a negotiating policy for double taxation agreements that will pose enormous challenges (negotiation, interpretation, effective application); (2) the countries have come to acknowledge the advantages of

---

[25] Partial agreements (on sea and air transport) are not included, nor is an old agreement between the Dominican Republic and Canada signed in 1976.

[26] One country in the group has even requested that an agreement that has already been signed—but has not yet entered into force—be renegotiated on the basis of this text.

working together, or at least the huge complications involved in undertaking this policy unilaterally; and (3) establishing technical teams to devise this instrument creates a sense of community that persists over the long term, thereby fostering a shared vision and enhanced coordination, particularly as regards three matters: tax policy for nonresidents[27] (Articles 6 to 21 of the model); the commitment (and to a large extent, the technical formulation) to avoid or correct international double taxation (Article 22); and mechanisms for cooperation between tax administrations (Articles 24 and 25).

To be clear, the tax regime for nonresidents earning income in these countries is not uniform in all of them. For example, the concept of permanent establishment is defined in the domestic legislation of some but not others, and there are different definitions of royalties, interest, and so on. Nonetheless, the way in which a double taxation agreement interacts with domestic legislation—solely as an instrument that delimits the substance of domestic law in specific cases, though preserving the application of that law in matters beyond the scope of the agreement (Vogel, 1997)—does not ensure that coordination will be complete. It is true, however, that countries have traditionally been prone to replicate the definitions used in double taxation conventions in their domestic laws in order to facilitate their application.

The Central America–Dominican Republic model agreement is inspired by the UN model. However, it provides for taxing at source "technical, legal, economic, financial, administrative or similar services, including consultancy services" on any occasion, irrespective of whether the services were rendered under permanent establishment.[28]

---

[27] Although the CAN's Decision 578 formally goes further than this model (since it is binding on and directly applicable to Andean countries), by providing for the source-country taxation of almost all income earned by nonresidents, it does not "harmonize" a common nonresident taxation policy. Additionally, it confirms the policies already being applied by each state in this respect. Moreover, and above all, Decision 578 has little real economic impact because the Andean countries themselves are far from being the leading investors in the subregion.

[28] If provisions are made for permanent establishment, they shall be deemed as such, without any further modification.

This, the most distinctive feature of the model, has a threefold rationale: (1) it preserves the taxation at source that the contracting parties
were unwilling to relinquish initially; (2) it simplifies nonresidents' operations, since they can be subject to resident withholdings and need
not be concerned about permanent establishment[29]—a hazy area that
causes legal uncertainty for those who approach it; and (3) it does not
involve, for tax administrations, any break from the management system used for nonresidents. Tax administrations are used to applying
a withholding tax to nonresidents, which enables them to retain this
general revenue collection system and make the appropriate refund in
the (rare) cases when the payment to the nonresident for the service
rendered cannot be taxed at the source under the double taxation
agreement. Tax administrations avoid having to discuss permanent
establishment in relation to the vast bulk of the services rendered by
nonresidents, thus maximizing the use of the few resources and minimizing litigation.[30]

The agreement has no peculiarity since all the signatories are countries with territorial income tax: all of them have retained the concept
of resident (domiciled or similar) and establish different forms of treatment for those who have resident status and those who do not. Addition-

---

[29] In this respect, some technical confusion is caused by the inclusion of an Article
5.3.b, equivalent to that in the UN model: "The furnishing of services, including consultancy services, by an enterprise through employees or other personnel engaged
by the enterprise for such purpose, but only if activities of that nature continue (for
the same or a connected project) within a contracting party for a period or periods
aggregating more than six months within any twelve-month period." This overlapping
may be solved by assuming that Article 5.3.b may be used by enterprises in order to
be taxed for their net income when they have a special interest therein, provided that
the minimum requirements for permanence and linkage to the territory established
in that provision are met.

[30] To conclude this issue, note that this proposal is not absolutely new in the region. As
early as 1970, Annex II of Decision 40 of the CAN introduced a model double taxation
agreement to be negotiated by CAN members with third countries. This provided for
the (unlimited) source-country taxation of technical assistance services. The CARI-
COM multilateral convention (see above) contains a similar provision to Decision 578,
although its actual impact is modest because of the low level of intra-subregional direct
investment in the Caribbean.

ally, a broad definition of certain connection points (especially service provision) and the incipient control of transfer prices may be causing international double taxation; hence it makes sense to include an article whereby the signatories pledge to eliminate it.

Unlike many other instruments analyzed here, this agreement is very recent. Thus it is difficult to appraise its scope and effectiveness. The Central American Free Trade Agreement (CAFTA) was the triggering factor, but it would be simplistic to think that this decision to coordinate taxes sprang from CAFTA alone; before and after CAFTA, progress was made on integration.[31] In fact, it is interesting to note how Central America's tax harmonization process has used an array of instruments, with different levels of sophistication, to keep moving forward at the pace that integration requires. The first stage of harmonization (customs union) is based on typical intergovernmental instruments,[32] and the most recent proposals, which can be said to fall under compatibility and/or coordination (the Central American VAT, tax codes, and the model double taxation agreement), propose more varied and sophisticated legal instruments.[33]

Central America–Dominican Republic Transfer Pricing Model[34]

The model was approved in the spring of 2007 by the authorities of Central America, the Dominican Republic, and Panama. It is a significant

---

[31] The website of the Secretariat for Central American Economic Integration (www. sieca.org.gt) gives an idea of integration activities undertaken before CAFTA. Since then, a notable effort is the treaty that the Central American countries are now negotiating with the EU, which resembles the Dominican Republic–CAFTA.

[32] Such instruments include the 1960 Central American General Economic Integration Agreement and various protocols—Protocols of Tegucigalpa (1991), Guatemala (1993), and so forth.

[33] As mentioned earlier, the model double taxation agreement, as its name indicates, is simply a guideline. By contrast the Central American VAT proposal (still under study) aims to be legally binding and recognizes the need for full enforcement. To that end, the authors of this interesting proposal are considering two instruments: to give the text the status of a Central American Code (which would apply directly to states and which the taxable subject could invoke), and to create a regional body responsible for its legal interpretation and dispute settlement (Thompson and Cornick, 2006).

[34] The model includes Panama.

step in the region's efforts to move toward a juridical tax framework that is more consistent with international standards and with an improvement in the countries' international insertion.

As with the model double taxation treaty, it is not legally binding on the signatories, and the countries involved do not assume a political commitment to ensure that their internal regulations comply with it. Nonetheless, it gives rise to an interesting degree of coordination on international tax policy, for the following reasons:

- The countries involved have reached agreement on certain bases for a common tax policy in the area of transfer prices, which were taken as a starting point in devising this model.
- The countries work jointly on tax administration with a view to creating or developing administrative structures that allow the regulations to be applied effectively. That joint endeavor in itself is a form of tax harmonization. In fact, the Inter-American Development Bank (IDB) is engaged in creating or strengthening tax administrations in Central America and the Dominican Republic in the field of international taxation.
- Much of the impetus for this undertaking originated in a regional working group, the Tax Policy Technical Group (TPTG). Now the countries can explore truly joint endeavors geared to widening the scope and cutting costs (such as the costs of acquiring highly specialized material and training staff).

The tax policy guidelines agreed upon by the TPTG, which are designed to prepare a model, can be summarized as follows:

1. *Overall objectives.* The TPTG's overall objectives are (1) developing general regulations consistent with international principles and standards; (2) granting equal importance to the goals of combating tax evasion/avoidance and eliminating double taxation; and (3) ensuring simplicity.
2. *The principle of free competition as an international standard.* As a subcomponent of tax policy, the TPTG supports the principle

of free competition and its qualifying factors through what is known as comparability analysis (characteristics of the goods and services, functional analysis, contractual clauses, economic circumstances, and commercial strategies).

3. *OECD guidelines.* The OECD guidelines are accepted as a technical reference for the proposal, although this is not explicitly stated for various reasons—one being that no country in the TPTG is an OECD member.

4. *Subjective, objective, and territorial scope of the future draft regulations.* The TPTG has agreed (1) to use well-developed criteria or a reasoning of linkages (related enterprises), including a completion regulation; (2) not to impose any restriction on the objective scope of the affected operations; and (3) to define the territorial scope of regulations covered by the model as encompassing all international operations and internal operations if they generate less tax or cause a tax deferral.

5. *Methods of appraising transfer prices.* The TPTG has agreed to establish a priority order of methods (following the international standard), but to mention that the objective method is the best.

6. *Safe harbor.* The TPTG has agreed to consider safe harbors for maquiladora activities and service companies. It has also agreed to limit the information requirements for small and medium-sized enterprises.

7. *Analysis of specific transactions.* The TPTG has agreed to regulate certain transactions in detail (intra-group services, cost-sharing agreements).

8. *Documentation.* The TPTG supports the inclusion of documentation requirements in the model, so that taxpayers have a means of demonstrating their compliance with the principle of free competition. The TPTG has accepted a "single model," since it prizes the economies of scale that such an approach offers. The idea is to impose documentation requirements that strike a balance between formal needs and the impossibility of effective control. In principle, everyone will be obliged to submit infor-

mation (in the form of tax returns). The documentation must be contemporaneous and must be available to the tax administration (although its submission is not automatic). The TPTG has agreed to leave some degree of flexibility in the time frame for submitting the information.

9. *Mutual agreement procedure and arbitration.* The member countries of the TPTG have approved a model double taxation agreement that includes these instruments. Hence they are deemed to be already available.

10. *Advance price agreements (APAs).* The TPTG has agreed to include and develop APAs in the model regulation.

Cooperation

Cooperation is the most cordial form of harmonization, since no policy rapprochement is involved. Sovereignty is respected, and cooperation happens only if there is a previously identified interest, be it reciprocal or mutual. The most typical example of this kind of harmonization is the exchange of information between tax administrations.

Information Exchange

The exchange of information in Latin America, including data on information exchange clauses and agreements currently in force, is discussed comprehensively by Claudino Pita in Chapter 10 of this book. Here we make a few general comments:

- Information exchange is a clear cooperation mechanism that has been used in the region, in different forms, for more than 30 years.[35]
- Recent years have seen the emergence of legal instruments that are more powerful as regards the type of information that can be requested and the purposes for which it can be used. They are

---

[35] Only the CAN's Decision 40 dates from 1970, but many double taxation agreements, especially those between Argentina and Brazil, also entered into force in the 1970s.

also more flexible in terms of the requirements for their approval and entry into force, since they are simple agreements between tax administrations and not classic international treaties.[36]

■ The actual number of information exchanges among countries in the region and with extra-regional countries is unknown. Nor is information available on the concrete outcomes of anti-fraud efforts as a direct result of such information exchange. Experts do not even know whether countries have undertaken any follow-up in this regard. Taxpayers' data, of course, must be protected with maximum confidentiality, but it would be helpful to have access to aggregate statistics that facilitate an assessment of the effectiveness and costs (and hence the efficiency) of such exchange.

■ In the absence of such data, and even though there may be an announcement effect that causes fraudulent conduct to be amended or moderated, fieldwork in the region's tax administrations and an IDB study on international tax administration in selected countries[37] reveal that this is only in its initial stage and must be strengthened.

Furthermore, in the exceptional cases where there is effective information exchange, it is usually asymmetrical—that is, the information goes to more developed tax administrations, which are usually in countries outside the region. Consequently, fraud and fraud networks are not discovered in domestic markets. An opportunity for harmonization and for closer subregional and regional economic integration is thus missed.

Best Practice Forums

Forums (institutionalized or otherwise) for sharing experiences and debating future strategies provide an interesting example of Latin American cooperation.

---

[36] The information exchange agreements between Argentina and Spain, Argentina and Peru, and Argentina and Brazil were drafted after the Inter-American Center of Tax Administrations model.

[37] Project ATN/FG-9141-RS.

Inter-American Center of Tax Administrations. The most renowned tax cooperation forum in the region is the Inter-American Center of Tax Administrations (CIAT).[38] There are other, equally prestigious forums, such as the Economic Commission for Latin America and the Caribbean (ECLAC), but their mission is broader (not only taxation) and their approaches are usually less operational, since they are devoted to studying the matter from a more doctrinal or academic perspective. CIAT's influence is enormous, to the extent that it has six European and two African countries among its members.[39]

Apart from the model for information exchange analyzed above, other examples of cooperation are the Model Tax Code (1997 and updated in 2006), work on tax and customs indicators (2002), the Audit Manual (2003), and the Model Code of Conduct (2005).

Some of these documents, mirroring the regulatory and institutional changes the region is undergoing, go beyond cooperation and approach coordination. CIAT is making a significant contribution to the standardization of the region's tax administrations. To some extent, this is a form of harmonization, since it ensures that similar efforts are made to combat tax fraud and evasion, thereby increasing horizontal equity.

This kind of cooperation, indirectly moving toward coordination by means of "backdoor rules," also includes the work undertaken for

---

[38] Founded in 1967 and headquartered in Panama, CIAT has 37 member states: 29 from the Americas, 6 from Europe, and 2 from Africa. Its mission is to encourage cooperation between tax and customs administrations of member states; to conduct research on tax systems, legislation, and administration; and to disseminate experiences through meetings, technical conferences, seminars, courses, and publications. It also provides technical assistance, organizes meetings, fosters the development of its member countries' administrations, and provides training to tax administration officials. Finally, it promotes and finances tax research studies, and issues a regular publication.

[39] There are other forums elsewhere with similar characteristics: the International Organization of Tax Administrations (IOTA), whose membership, despite the organization's international scope, is essentially European; the Centre de Rencontres et d'Etudes des Dirigeants des Administrations Fiscales (CREDAF), for French-speaking countries; and the Commonwealth Association for Tax Administrators (CATA), for British Commonwealth members. Probably none of them, however, has CIAT's significance, relevance, and influence.

decades by other international organizations to support the region in the fields of capacity building for tax administrations and technical assistance for tax reform processes.[40]

Convergence

Assuming that the definition of "convergence" provided earlier in this chapter is correct, a general review here prompts the conclusion that in Latin America, in this field, there is as much light as shadow. Sometimes there is an overall centripetal trend, suggesting that what is not done through conscious effort and explicit action is done simply because of the demands of circumstance. On other occasions, evidence points to a centrifugal force, one that tends toward "disintegration."

Transfer Pricing

Despite greater degrees of harmonization in some cases, such as the Central America–Dominican Republic transfer pricing model described above, this is probably one of the few fields in which there has been a trend—at least nominally—toward convergence. A review of what has happened in this area reveals a relatively uniform tendency toward the regulation of transfer pricing.[41] Except in Brazil[42] and the occasional means of calculating the market value of raw materials exports (Argentina's "sixth method"[43]), throughout the region the trend has been toward respect for the arm's length principle and, in general, for the principles set out in the OECD's transfer pricing guidelines.

---

[40] The Fiscal Affairs Department of the International Monetary Fund and the Inter-American Development Bank are the main actors in such activities in the region.

[41] See Chapter 9 in this book, which is devoted entirely to transfer prices.

[42] The Brazilian model (Law 9,430/96 and Regulatory Instruction 38/97) is based on the premise that transactions between related parties are invoiced at manipulated prices (higher or lower than the market price, depending on the specific case). Hence the model seeks to define objective transfer pricing criteria by establishing presumptive profit margins.

[43] Law 25784 introduces this pricing method for exports of raw materials (Chicago price).

As mentioned earlier, this convergence is more nominal than real and stems from the fact that legal texts, particularly in the absence of experience in the field, tend to look alike because of mimicry and prudence. But the extent of the respect for the arm's length principle will depend on the tax control policy applied to a multinational enterprise and its transactions. On the one hand, it is widely known that different tax administrations have different capacities; on the other hand, whenever a tax administration has concrete experience in the field (as those of Argentina, Brazil, and Mexico do), it is likely to depart from the OECD model and move toward a more protective and practicable formula for the tax base.

Free Trade Agreements

In the last 15 years, Latin America has pursued open regionalism through unilateral trade and financial liberalization, as well as economic integration, mainly at the subregional level. Hence a growing number of bilateral and multilateral free trade agreements have been signed or are being negotiated among Latin American countries or between countries in the region and third countries in North America, Europe, and Asia. These accords do not contain tax harmonization clauses, except for some very general concepts, and they have made little contribution to furthering harmonization.

For example, in the more than 15 years since it was signed, the Treaty of Asunción (creating MERCOSUR) has led only to agreements providing for nondiscrimination in trade in goods and services. Distortions persist in all the member countries, affecting competitiveness and the location of savings and investment (Barreix, Roca, and Villela, 2005).[44] Other agreements, such as the Dominican Republic–CAFTA, include a framework on indirect expropriation through taxes and introduce the concepts of investment, the obligation not to expropriate,

---

[44] The little progress made, such as the establishment of a procedure and of a general arbitration tribunal in Paraguay, has been geared to compliance with Article 7 of the Treaty of Asunción, which provides for equal tax treatment of goods and services traded between the member states (Barreix, Roca, and Villela, 2005).

and alternative dispute settlement mechanisms (Rodriguez, 2005). Despite this, in some cases, such as the North American Free Trade Agreement (NAFTA), the trade accord was negotiated in parallel to the double taxation agreement like in the case between the United States and Mexico. Note also that the Dominican Republic–CAFTA agreement is reviving positive integration in Central America by including the Dominican Republic and Panama.

In sum, except for the examples cited above, trade agreements have kept tax harmonization to a minimum, and the results have been in line with that circumstance.

Tax Codes

As pointed out earlier, tax administrations' structures and operations may follow either a path of coordination, especially in Central America, or a path of cooperation, based on the CIAT model and international organizations' studies. As regards taxpayers' rights and the authority vested in tax administrations to enable them to fulfill their tax collection and control tasks, these paths have led the administrations to adopt the best practices or highest standards known at the regional level. This is reflected in a widespread tax reform movement in the region and in current or imminent tax codes that are similar to each other or becoming so in many Latin American and Caribbean countries.[45]

Income Tax Model and Rates

In Latin America, a large number of income tax schemes (and rates) are applied to the three income tax components: personal, corporate, and international income. These schemes range from Mexico's Haig Simons income tax model (which includes worldwide income and features a so-

---

[45] Irrespective of the theoretical studies sponsored by the Organization of American States (excellent but outdated, since they were produced in 1967) and CIAT (1997, updated in 2006), the trend toward tax reform arguably started with successive amendments to the Dominican Republic tax code (2001, 2004, and 2005), was followed by the issuing of a new Bolivian tax code (August 2, 2003), and continues with a series of tax code reforms in the region. The reform of the tax codes of Haiti, Nicaragua, and Paraguay is currently under way, at various stages.

phisticated system for taxing capital gains adjusted for inflation and the full integration of personal and corporate incomes) to Paraguay's semi-flat income tax regime, which establishes a 10 percent personal income tax rate (equal to the general VAT rate) and a 20 percent corporate income tax rate, with ample margin for unlimited expense deductions (see Table 4.2).

International taxation is also diverse, though it is easier to group the different schemes used. The larger economies cover worldwide income, are subject to specific international legislation (such as that on transfer prices), and have bilateral agreements to avoid double taxation; the number of the latter depends on the country. Argentina, Brazil, Chile, Mexico, Peru, and Venezuela have such agreements. Smaller economies tend to tax income at source and use a dual-rate system to tax capital income. Since they use a final withholding tax system, usually they do not integrate corporate with personal income. In addition, they make use of few international tax laws and, with some

Table 4.2. Some Structural Elements of Income Tax in 10 Latin American Countries, December 2006

Country	Overall income	IIT & CIT integration	Capital gains	IIT rate (percent)	CIT rate (percent)	Interest rate on financial savings[1]
Argentina	Yes	No	No	9–35	35	No[2]
Brazil	Yes	No	25	15–27.5	34[3]	15
Chile	Yes	Yes	17 or 40[4]	0–40	17	4 or 35[5]
Colombia	Yes	No	Yes	20–38.5[6]	38.5[6]	No
Costa Rica	No	No	No	10–25	30	8
Honduras	Yes	No	10	10–25	25	10
Mexico	Yes	Yes	No	32	29	No
Paraguay	No	No	10	10	20	No
Peru	Yes	No	Yes[7]	15–30	30	No[2]
Uruguay	No	No	Yes	10–25	25	12

Note: IIT = individual income tax; CIT = corporate income tax.
[1] A percentage is indicated when it is a final withholding tax (dual income tax).
[2] The most common forms of savings income are exempted.
[3] Includes 25% plus 9% social security tax.
[4] 17% for corporations and 40% for individuals.
[5] 35% without tax treaty.
[6] Includes 35% plus additional 10% on the remaining income.
[7] Most capital gains are exempted.

exceptions, have signed very few tax agreements. This is true of the Central American countries, Panama, the Dominican Republic, Paraguay, and Uruguay.

Moreover, the reduction and standardization of tariffs attendant on "open regionalism" have significantly lowered the protection of domestic production. This has been accompanied by the governments' decision to progressively abandon sectoral and regional policies. In response, strong pressure has been exerted for the creation of new tax incentives and benefits aimed at protecting certain sectors or regions, which have resulted in significant tax concessions. This accounts for the proliferation of free trade zones and of fiscal benefits for the tourism, mining, and forestry industries in the region (Barreix, Roca, and Villela, 2005).

In the pre-2004 15-member EU there was also some diversity, but the differences were not so stark. The EU's institutional arrangements make a substantial difference, since the Union is equipped with instruments such as a supranational court (the European Court of Justice) and agreements such as the Code of Conduct for Business Taxation and the Taxation of Savings Income Directive. These have contributed to harmonization, particularly of the tax base.

With the accession of 10 new members, income tax diversity has widened in the EU. Some of the new members (Estonia, for instance) still have corporate income tax regimes that are heterodox in the European context. Worth mentioning, however, is that some of the EU's founding members are reacting to this by making the necessary adjustments to remain competitive in tax terms. For example, Germany has proposed lower corporate income tax rates, Spain has introduced a dual-rate system for income tax and a lowering of the corporate tax rate, and Sweden has reduced all direct taxes, among other tax-reduction and modification policies announced.

Another possible explanation for the growing income tax diversity is that income tax is more prone to harmonization in the face of intra-industry trade, as in the EU, where what really counts is specializing through economies of scale or agglomeration. In the EU, therefore, income tax has a greater impact on competitiveness than in Latin

America. In Latin American integration processes, the level of intra-bloc trade is relatively low, and most commerce is interindustry (Ricardian).[46] Europe's intra-bloc trade accounts for almost 70 percent of total trade, whereas in Latin America subregional trade is below 15 percent of the total.[47]

The Frustrated Harmonization of Taxes in MERCOSUR

At first glance, the tax systems of the MERCOSUR member countries (Argentina, Brazil, Paraguay, and Uruguay) appear to be very similar.[48] In all of them, general taxes on goods and services account for the major share of tax revenue, social security contributions account for a high proportion, and revenue from direct taxes is traditionally low (Barreix, Roca, and Villela, 2005) (Table 4.3). As Table 4.4 shows, however, the similarities are more apparent than real (Barreix and Villela, 2003).

Additionally, the MERCOSUR agreements provide for only a limited transfer of sovereignty. Given the absence of a joint trade policy and community institutions, the subregional group is simply an incomplete customs union. It features two different policies of international insertion: the "large country" policy adopted by Argentina and Brazil, and the "small country" policy adopted by Paraguay and Uruguay, which has significant fiscal implications.

Argentina and Brazil tax the worldwide income of their residents, both individuals and corporations. Their legislation does not provide for non–registered share corporations (only corporations with registered shares are allowed). In Brazil, capital (especially interest) gains are withheld at source. Tax and bank secrecy laws are less strict, enabling the two countries to sign double taxation and information exchange agreements (although in practice there is no effective automatic information

---

[46] In most Latin American integration processes, intra-bloc trade is encouraged by the diversion of trade resulting from tariff advantages granted to member countries.

[47] Exports from free zones are included for the Central American Common Market. Intra-NAFTA trade accounts for nearly 60 percent of total trade.

[48] Venezuela is currently in the process of becoming a full MERCOSUR member.

Table 4.3. MERCOSUR: 2003 Tax Burden, by Jurisdictional Classification, Disaggregated by Tax
(percentage of GDP)

Jurisdiction and tax	Argentina	Brazil	Paraguay	Uruguay
Central government	20.6	16.3	9.8	19.4
Taxes on goods and services	7.6	7.6	6.0	12.5
VAT or semi-VAT (Brazil)	5.3	4.8	4.2	9.3
Excise	2.2	2.5	1.8	2.5
Other	0.1	0.3	0.0	0.7
Income taxes	4.4	6.3	1.7	3.9
Individual	1.3	0.0	0.0	2.1
Corporate	2.6	0.0	1.7	1.8
Other	0.5	0.0	0.0	0.0
Property taxes	2.0	0.0	0.0	1.6
Other taxes	0.8	1.9	0.3	0.2
International trade taxes	3.0	0.5	1.8	1.2
Social security contributions	2.8	8.4	2.5	8.5
Subnational governments	3.8	10.5	0.2	3.2
Taxes on goods and services	2.4	8.1	—	0.3
Income taxes	0.0	0.0	—	0.0
Property taxes	1.0	1.2	—	2.4
Other taxes	0.4	1.2	—	0.5
Total	**24.4**	**35.2**	**12.5**	**31.1**

Sources: Authors' estimates based on data from Administración Federal de Ingresos Públicos (AFIP); Banco Nacional de Desenvolvimento Econômico e Social, Secretariat of Fiscal Affairs, and Receita Federal, Brazil; Finance Ministry and Central Bank of Paraguay, Paraguay; Dirección General Impositiva, Banco de Previsión Social, Central Bank, and Office of Planning and Budget, Uruguay; Ministry of Finance, AFIP and National Institute of Statistics, Argentina.
Note: — = Data not available.

exchange with any other jurisdiction). Additionally, these countries grant significant investment incentives, making use of the competitive advantage created by their large potential markets. This situation has triggered subnational competition, resulting in "tax wars" and causing tax-related expenses to rise, especially in Brazil. Incentives granted at the subnational level—with a strong indirect tax component—have offset the progressive abandonment of regional policies by the central governments of Argentina and Brazil.

Paraguay and, especially, Uruguay have pursued a "small country" strategy that consists of capturing foreign savings in the form of offshore bank deposits and related services, or asset management—through

Table 4.4. MERCOSUR Taxation: Main Asymmetries

Instruments	Point	Counterpoint
VAT and ICMS (Brazil's VAT)	VAT, national application, broad base, few tax rates, full credit leveraging: Argentina, Paraguay, and Uruguay.	ICMS (Brazilian VAT at state level) limited to goods and very few services, many different tax rates, limitations on the leveraging of certain credits originating from previous stages, complemented with PIS (1.65%) and COFINS (7.6%), which are federal-level, VAT-type levies.
Inefficient taxes as a result of cumulative effects	Uruguay and Paraguay do not have such taxes.	Brazil: PASEP (Civil Servants Saving Program), CPMF (tax levied on bank debits at 0.38%) and ISS (municipal tax on services). Argentina: Turnover Tax, represents more than 50% of the revenue income of provinces (2.2% of GDP) and Tax on Bank Debits and Credits (1.2%).
Excise taxes	Single-phase, applied to the producer or importer of the taxed goods: Argentina (internal taxes), Paraguay (excise taxes) and Uruguay (IMESI—specific internal tax). "Traditional" tax base: fuels, tobacco, alcoholic beverages, and motor vehicles (Argentina, Paraguay, and Uruguay).	Multiple-phase, noncumulative, VAT-type: Brazil (IPI—tax on industrialized products). In Brazil the IPI is not applied to fuels. Hence, in the ICMS, which levies fuels, high rates—more typical of excise taxes than a VAT—are applied.
Income tax	Brazil and Argentina tax individuals. Paraguay adopted a 10% flat income tax rate in 2005 and has a wide range of tax-deductible personal expenses.	Uruguay has applied a dual income tax as of July 2007.
	Brazil and Argentina apply the global income criterion, and dividends are not included in the income tax base to avoid double taxation.	Uruguay and Paraguay apply the "taxation at source country" criterion, taxing residents and nonresidents solely on their income from national sources.
Asset taxes	Brazil and Paraguay levy no such taxes.	Argentina and Uruguay apply overall taxes on the net worth or assets of individuals and companies. Argentina also levies taxes on assets abroad.

(continued on next page)

Table 4.4. MERCOSUR Taxation: Main Asymmetries *(continued)*

Instruments	Point	Counterpoint
Social security	Reforms and mixed systems in Argentina and Uruguay. Argentina: mixed system, with the possibility of opting for a public pension fund or a private pension fund. Uruguay: mixed system, with (1) a public pension fund that is mandatory for all pension fund participants, and (2) a private pension fund that is mandatory for pension fund participants whose income exceeds a given amount.	Public pension funds in Brazil and Paraguay.
Subnational transfers	Hardly significant in Uruguay and Paraguay (unitary states).	Highly significant in Argentina and Brazil. Argentina: State and municipal revenue collections account for 5% of GDP, and their revenue sharing accounts for 8% of GDP. Brazil: State and municipal revenue collections represent 11% of GDP, and 2% of GDP is transferred by the federal government.
Treaties	Argentina and Brazil have a bilateral treaty in place; in addition, they have more than 30 treaties signed with developed countries.	Uruguay and Paraguay do not have treaties with Latin American countries. They have information exchange agreements with very few developed countries.
Tax administrations	Argentina and Brazil: Customs and internal revenue administration are centralized in one single agency.	Uruguay and Paraguay: Customs and tax administrations are two separate entities.
Transfer prices	Paraguay has no legislation in this matter.	Argentina and Uruguay: Yes, adopting OECD guidelines, with some specific adjustments for Argentina, such as the procedure known as the "sixth method," applied to commodities. Brazil: Yes, according to (1) independent comparable prices, (2) resale price minus discounts and commissions, or (3) production cost plus margin.

non-registered share corporations having their assets abroad—protected by strong bank and tax secrecy laws. In Uruguay, since the financial liberalization of the 1970s and with the aim of making the country a financial leader in the region, the tax system was adjusted to follow the pace of offshore banking development and its related activities in free zones. In these special regimes, foreign savings or income earned abroad by residents is not subject to taxation, and tax secrecy is linked to bank secrecy, which can be lifted only by a court order. For this reason, it is highly complicated to exchange information with other jurisdictions.

Interrelation between the Objectives of Integration, Degrees of Tax Harmonization, and Legal Instruments

The best known scale of integration objectives is Balassa's (see note 5). The first part of this chapter proposed a harmonization scale and described the different degrees of harmonization. Here, a listing of all the legal instruments required to attain harmonization can be extracted from the different instruments mentioned earlier in the chapter: international treaties, decisions by bodies with supranational authority, codes of conduct (nonexistent in the region), models, theoretical and doctrinal studies, and so on.

Two questions arise. First, does a particular level of harmonization correspond to a particular stage of integration? Second, are the extant legal instruments associated with a specific degree of harmonization and with no other?

Pelkmans (1986: 324) answers the first question: "The first three stages of Balassa's model focus on the negative integration elements [basically, obligations not to do certain things, to avoid or eliminate discrimination], while the other two are associated with positive integration [that is, the design and implementation of common and coordinated policies]."

That assertion, however, should be nuanced by the following counterexample: the essential element of a customs union (one of the first phases of integration) is the CET, which is a clear example of a common policy or "positive integration."[49] In short, it is not always entirely clear that the initial integration stages require a lesser commitment to tax harmonization, at least if tariff policies are also expected to be harmonized.

Deepening the analysis in an effort to go beyond Pelkmans's theory, it can be said that the most refined stages of integration, where a more "positive integration" is required, are normally associated with more sophisticated degrees of harmonization. This is particularly true in the EU, but it has also been the case in various Latin American subregions. Some experiences of cooperation, coordination, and convergence have been described above.

This does not happen by chance: the highest level of economic integration entails two potentially antithetical consequences. On the one hand, market forces exert pressure for the progressive elimination of trade and investment barriers; as countries become more closely integrated, these barriers wane until they are no longer recognized. A good example might be the "second turn of the screw" that the EU has had to give to the directives on mergers and on the distribution of dividends between holding companies and their subsidiaries,[50] since the increasingly complex and diversified forms in which a company could own an interest in others no longer fit the rules established in the early 1990s. In short, from an economic viewpoint, there is a need to continue eliminating barriers to the creation of a true internal market in Europe.

On the other hand, the demand for greater tax harmonization entails political conditioning, since a high degree of tax policy autonomy is lost. This is why most countries retain veto powers in supranational organizations. To deal with this issue, harmonization has been pursued with subtle approaches (coordination or cooperation) or "involuntary" approaches (convergence).

---

[49] In addition, it should be kept in mind that the establishment of a free trade area (LAFTA-LAIA) involved fostering some compatibility among tariff policies.

[50] Council Directive 2003/123/EC of 22 December 2003 and Council Directive 2005/19/EC of 17 February 2005.

As for the second question (whether the legal instruments available are associated with specific degrees of harmonization and not others), the answer springs largely from the previous consideration. The availability of new instruments is essentially linked to the fact that there are new forms and degrees of harmonization. The subtler the latter, the more sophisticated the former (Martín Jiménez, 1999). It would not have been necessary to resort to such a creative imagination if it had not been concluded that traditional harmonization mechanisms were either obsolete or severely limited.

In other words, as integration approaches the sensitive matter of tax sovereignty—and even if this results from economic rapprochement—there is ever less prospect of settling the integration-sovereignty dispute in favor of integration, and more flexible legal or other instruments are needed to continue progress. It might be said that the centripetal forces of integration generate centrifugal tax policy solutions, in the sense that they avert the assault on the hard core of sovereignty.

These considerations merit particular attention in Latin America. The region has engaged in all kinds of experiments in integration, and the areas of integration are unclear. To some extent, therefore, and with the exception of Mexico's smooth inclusion in the North American integration process, all the other processes partially overlap each other, particularly at times when the CAN and MERCOSUR seem to be in (albeit intermittent) crisis.

Conclusions

This chapter began by distinguishing various levels of economic integration, degrees of tax harmonization, and legal or pseudo-legal instruments at the service of such harmonization. In particular, an effort has been made to classify harmonization experiences and arrange them into five large and predefined levels of harmonization consistent with the political commitment made by the countries—because the concept of harmonization herein goes beyond the classical dual scheme and is, rather, a complex and multifaceted arrangement.

In Latin America there are experiences of harmonization at all levels of the scale. Hence, although the economic integration of Latin

American markets is relatively modest even in the four integration areas (MERCOSUR, CARICOM, the Central American Common Market, and CAN), and tax harmonization is therefore also far from complete,[51] the trend toward more sophisticated forms and levels of harmonization is not exclusive to the EU or any other region. Thus it can be said that there is a kind of "harmonization inflation" in Latin America. The region has harmonized what it could (what did not involve true sacrifice or effort) rather than what it should, and certainly less than what it had promised.

Overall, integration processes in Latin America feature less intra-bloc trade than in the EU, along with more interindustry trade (Ricardian comparative advantage) than intra-industry trade (specialization by scale and agglomeration). Countries therefore tend to compete with each other to attract foreign investment rather than cooperate for mutual benefit.

Moreover, the region has relatively weak institutional arrangements. As the political scheme for cooperation among deeply rooted sovereign states becomes more sophisticated, there is an increase in the forms of harmonization and the instruments used to bring tax regulations into closer harmony with each other. The more refined and subtle the adjustment required, the more technically and politically complex is harmonization, not the reverse.

---

[51] Other chapters in this book focus on the causes of this anomaly, but here we can say the following about LAC's economic integration and its tax harmonization process:

- In its process, three problems exist: (1) indirect taxation has not been addressed as a priority—a huge dysfunction that is still not resolved; (2) the geopolitical delimitations of the integration areas are not definitively drawn; and (3) the U.S. strategy to sign bilateral agreements (in preparation for the Free Trade Area of the Americas) has introduced new distortions.
- Its mechanisms are plagued by generalized institutional weakness and the lack of a legal and institutional framework, which, even when there is political will, jeopardizes the result (Central America, for example).
- Its results are essentially erratic: insufficient VAT and excise taxes, and strange harmonization of direct taxes (for example, Decision 578 of the CAN triggered little harmonization that was conducive to effective integration and cross-investments). Convergence is a typical example of this situation.

Another noteworthy matter is that the conflict lies not in whether to harmonize or not, but in whether to standardize or retain sovereignty. This tension spurs a wide range of intermediate solutions, which foster harmonization but not standardization. Hence this chapter has defined the harmonization pyramid and its corollary, which prompts the proposal that a new and desirable feature of a tax system is its "coordinability" with other jurisdictions. Coordinability is a tax system's capacity to adapt to those of its main economic partners.

Finally, the lesson learned from Latin American experiences—which the harmonization pyramid sought to classify—is that it is difficult to determine whether integration or tax harmonization should go first. This is because there are cases in which tax harmonization efforts, though pioneering (such as Decision 40 of the CAN or CARICOM's tax incentive harmonization treaty), did not bring about closer integration; in other cases, Latin America still faces basic and unresolved problems of harmonization, such as the incomplete implementation of customs unions.

For all the above reasons, more effective harmonization outcomes will probably arise from focusing on less ambitious objectives and more limited instruments. One objective might be to protect tax revenue and avoid harmful incentive practices by enforcing codes of conduct. Another might be to foster cooperation among tax administrations (through efficient information exchange, for example) in order to control the rising number of transactions by multinational and regional companies. Such efforts might give a new impetus to harmonization for the region.

References

Arias, L., A. Barreix, A. Valencia, and L. Villela. 2005. "The Harmonization of Indirect Taxes in the Andean Community." INTAL-ITD Occasional Paper SITI-07. Buenos Aires: Institute for the Integration of Latin America and the Caribbean.

Balassa, B. 1961. "Towards a Theory of Economic Integration." *Kyklos* 14(1):1–17.

Barreix, A., J. Roca, and L. Villela. 2005. "Tributación en el MERCOSUR y la necesidad de coordinación." In *Tributación para la integración del MERCOSUR*, ed. V. Tanzi, A. Barreix, and L. Villela. Washington, DC: Inter-American Development Bank.

———. 2006. *Política fiscal y equidad en los países de la Comunidad Andina de Naciones.* Lima: General Secretariat of the Andean Community.

Barreix, A., and L. Villela. 2003. *Tributación en el MERCOSUR: Evolución, comparación y posibilidades de coordinación.* Buenos Aires: Institute for the Integration of Latin America and the Caribbean.

Caamaño, M. A., and J. M. Calderón. 2002. "Globalización económica y poder tributario: ¿Hacia un nuevo derecho tributario?" *Revista Española de Derecho Financiero y Tributario* 114:245–88.

Fairlamb, D. 2004. "Tax Harmony, EU Fracas." *Business Week*, May 31.

González Cano, J. 1996. *Armonización tributaria del Mercosur.* Buenos Aires: Instituto Universitario de Finanzas Públicas Argentinas.

James, S. 2000. "Can We Harmonise Our Views on European Tax Harmonisation?" *Bulletin for International Fiscal Documentation* 54(6):263–69.

Kopits, G. 1992. "Tax Harmonization in the European Community." IMF Occasional Paper 94. Washington, DC: International Monetary Fund.

Krugman, P., and R. E. Baldwin. 2002. "Agglomeration, Integration and Tax Harmonization." NBER Working Paper 9290. Cambridge, MA: National Bureau of Economic Research.

Larking, B., ed. 2005. *IBFD International Tax Glossary*, 5th ed. Amsterdam: International Bureau of Fiscal Documentation.

Lecraw, D. 2003. "Investment Incentives in CARICOM Member States: Improving Effectiveness and Harmonization." Unpublished draft. Inter-American Development Bank, Washington, DC.

Martín Jiménez, A. 1999. *Toward Corporate Tax Harmonization in the EU.* Boston: Kluwer.

———. 2006. "Loopholes in the EU Savings Directive." *Bulletin for International Taxation* 12:480–94.

Musgrave, P. 1989. "Fiscal Coordination and Competition in an International Setting." Unpublished draft. Department of Economics, University of California, Santa Cruz.

Pelkmans, J. 1986. *European Integration: Methods and Economic Analysis.* Harlow, U.K.: Pearson.

Rincón Eizaga, L. 2000. "La supranacionalidad en los esquemas de integracion. Especial referencia a la Comunidad Andina y MERCOSUR." Draft. Available at www.abogadoszulia.org.ve.

Rodriguez, A. 2005. "International Arbitration Claims against Domestic Tax Measures Deemed Expropriatory or Unfair and Inequitable." INTAL-ITD Occasional Paper SITI-11. Buenos Aires: Institute for the Integration of Latin America and the Caribbean.

Sabsay, D. 1999. "Integración y supranacionalidad sin considerar los desarrollos europeos recientes, bases constitucionales y límites. La experiencia del MERCOSUR." Paper presented at seminar, "Process of European and Global Constitutionalization," Berlin, May 15. Available at http://www.farn.org.ar/docs/a04/art4-1.html.

SIECA (Secretaría de Integración Económica Centroamericana). 2006. "Estado de situación de la integración económica centroamericana." Available at www.sieca.org.gt.

Thompson, E., and J. Cornick. 2006. Propuesta de IVA armonizado para Centroamérica. Unpublished draft. Inter-American Development Bank, Washington, DC.

Vogel, K. 1997. *On Double Taxation Conventions.* Boston: Kluwer.

5

Fiscal Decentralization and Regional Economic Integration in Latin America: Key Policy Linkages

Eduardo Wiesner

> *The ability of a country to take advantage of oppor-tunities offered by international economic integration depends on the quality of the state and the policies it follows.*
>
> —MARTIN WOLF, *Why Globalization Works*

First-Order Conceptual Linkages

A decentralization strategy within a given country is conceptually analogous to a process of economic integration within that country's spatial domestic territory. Similarly, a process of trade liberalization[1] or regional economic integration among a number of countries is akin to a deliberate process of decentralization involving several countries.[2] Both policy frameworks have the same underlying objective: to create

---

[1] The Inter-American Development Bank (1994: 179) observes that "a well designed decentralization strategy is akin to the opening or liberalization of the territorial do-mestic space to the market forces and to competition within the public sector."

[2] Wildasin (1995: 328) insightfully maintains that "although it is conventional to refer to national-level policies as 'centralized,' the country does not necessarily provide a natu-ral unit of analysis." For many purposes of public economics, such as the analysis of tax and transfer policies, the most economically appropriate unit of analysis is the area cov-ered by markets for the factors of production. The country is often not the natural unit

economic and welfare gains through the expansion of markets,[3] generate new information, enhance interjurisdictional competition,[4] and promote a better fit or convergence between supply and demand (Oates,
1999: 1121). The principles of openness[5] and subsidiarity[6] are common
threads in both policies.

Given these kindred conditions, it could be expected that both processes would complement each other as parts of a deliberately consistent
policy framework.[7] In general, however, this is not what seems to have
happened in Latin America (Wiesner, 2003a: 98). Judging by the results
so far, it is not easy to argue that the regional integration processes,[8] and
the decentralization drives in the 1980s and 1990s, were successful.

Global Framework and Objectives

What might explain these results? What flaws might each policy have
had? And what policy linkages to enhance complementarity might have

---

of analysis for trade and specialization issues. If factor markets become international
in scope (as seems increasingly to be the case), national governments are no longer
central governments in the relevant sense. On this topic see also Tanzi (1995).

[3] In the words of Winters, McCulloch, and McKay (2004: 108), "trade reform may be
one of the most cost effective anti-poverty policies available to governments. Certainly
the evidence suggests that, with care, trade liberalization can be an important component of a 'pro-poor' development strategy."

[4] Although interjurisdictional competition is usually examined within a country perspective (Fisher, 1991: 266), the essence of the argument is also largely valid when
several countries are competing for whatever activity or function they consider they
can perform more effectively.

[5] Throughout this chapter, "openness" refers to domestic decentralization and national
processes of economic integration, as well as analogous developments at the international level. After reviewing the complexities of defining and measuring openness, Berg
and Krueger (2003: 54) take "an eclectic approach to the measurement of openness."

[6] In Europe, proponents of fiscal decentralization refer to the "principle of subsidiarity." The precept is that public policy and its implementation should be assigned to the
lowest level of government with the capacity to achieve the objectives. This principle
has been formally adopted as part of the Maastricht Treaty. See Oates (1999: 1122).

[7] Since 1996, Ocampo (1996: 13) has warned that "each phase of economic integration
engenders demands for new policies and corresponding institutional innovations."

[8] For a review of the problems of the processes of regional integration, see IDB
(2002: 9).

been missed or underestimated? This chapter examines these questions and suggests policy recommendations geared to strengthening both processes individually and to enhancing their complementarity. The relevance of these questions is highlighted by the growing intensity of current trade negotiations between and among a number of Latin American countries and the United States. Globalization and its challenges provide the broad context (Stiglitz, 2002).[9] More specifically, this chapter will address the following questions:

1. Under which macroeconomic policy conditions were the decentralization and regional economic integration initiatives of the 1990s conducted?
2. What have been the recent fiscal decentralization developments in the region?
3. What policy principles should guide fiscal decentralization, on the one hand, and tax competition and regulation on the other?

The most important policy linkages run from macroeconomic policies to local fiscal decentralization frameworks and to "fiscal equivalences" at the country and international levels.[10]

The third set of questions refers to a situation in which, instead of different levels of government and little factor mobility across borders, there is a vertical structure corresponding to different countries and there is indeed factor mobility. Why should national policy principles be so different from international situations? Or, put another way, how much do conditions between countries under a regional integration process differ

---

[9] According to Aninat (2002: 6), "globalization holds the promise of enormous benefits for the peoples of the world. To make this promise a reality, however, we must find a way to carefully manage the process."

[10] Olson's classic concept of "fiscal equivalence" may help in framing the question of how to regulate tax competition under a regional economic integration process. Olson (1969: 483) posited that "there is a need for a separate government institution for every collective good with a unique boundary, so that there can be a match between those who receive the benefits of a collective good and those who pay for it. This match we define as 'fiscal equivalence.'"

Table 5.1. Public Sector Expenditures for Selected Latin American Countries
(percentage of GDP)

Country	1992	1995	2000
Argentina	18.9	20.0	22.0
Brazil	30.7	32.8	42.7
Colombia[1]	25.8	32.3	34.8
Costa Rica	21.9	24.0	32.5
Guatemala[2]	10.7	9.4	12.8
Mexico	25.4	22.9	22.9
Paraguay	16.3	18.3	31.8
Peru[2]	17.2	18.6	17.5
Uruguay	27.2	29.9	34.1

Source: Economic Commission for Latin America and the Caribbean (ECLAC).
Note: Calculated on the basis of figures in the national currency at current prices.
[1] Preliminary figures.
[2] Refers to the central government.

from taxation in a federal system? Wildasin (2004: 24) suggests that the "complementarity of factors of production such as labor and capital, and the impact of tax and expenditure policies on the supply of complementary factors, can mitigate or even reverse the predictions of the simplest models of tax competition."

What about tax competition between countries that differ in size? Should tax competition regulation be based on different policy principles? Kanbur and Keen (1993: 877) have examined these situations and have concluded that "the fully optimal response to freer cross-border trade may be to do nothing."

Latin America's Macroeconomic Context in the 1990s

The overarching macroeconomic characteristic of most Latin American countries during the 1990s was a soft budget constraint and substantial increases in public expenditures.[11] Table 5.1 shows that in Brazil, Colombia, Costa Rica, Paraguay, and Uruguay, public sector expenditures

---

[11] For a more detailed examination of Latin America's performance in the 1990s, see Fraga (2004).

grew very significantly. In Brazil they rose from 30.7 percent of gross domestic product (GDP) in 1992 to 42.7 percent in 2000. The increase in Colombia was also huge, from 25.8 percent to 34.8 percent. Mexico is a curious case, because public expenditures seem to have declined between 1992 and 2000. Peru remained stable. Guatemala's public expenditures grew from a low 10.7 percent to 12.8 percent.

Table 5.2. Latin America: Fiscal Deficits as a Percentage of GDP

Year	Deficit
1992	−1.4
1993	−1.7
1994	−2.0
1995	−1.6
1996	−1.6
1997	−1.3
1998	−2.2
1999	−2.9
2000	−2.7
2001	−3.3
2002	−3.1
2003	−2.7

Sources: For 1992, ECLAC (2001: Table A-7); for 1993 and 1994, ECLAC (2002: Table A-1); for 1995–2003, ECLAC (2004: Table A-25).

Although tax revenue also grew during the decade, it did not match the growth of expenditures. The result was the prevalence of fiscal imbalances in the region as a whole. Table 5.2 shows that in every year from 1992 to 2003, the region as a whole registered fiscal deficits as a percentage of GDP.

The key finding, in terms of its implications for decentralization and regional economic integration processes, is that there was no real macroeconomic budget constraint supporting these two developments. Given this overarching context, it should not be surprising that the results of decentralization and regional economic integration did not meet expectations.[12] After all, the "right" incentives can hardly emerge in an environment where there is no hard budget constraint. Fiscal deficits have been associated with a common-pool approach to fiscal deficits (Poterba and von Hagen, 1999: 3).[13] If economic and political actors can have ac-

---

[12] For a review of the problems of regional integration processes, see IDB (2002: 9). For a summary of the difficulties of decentralization drives in what he calls "first generation" policy frameworks, see Wiesner (2003b: 10).

[13] Jones, Sanguinetti, and Tommasi (1999: 148) have found that the common-property approach can explain Argentina's fiscal difficulties. In their view, "provincial governments tend to overexploit the common resource of national taxation."

cess to a common pool of unrestricted resources, why should they strive to do so through the more competitive incentive path?

Second-Generation Fiscal Developments

Given that decentralization assumes efficiency and welfare gains from the growing proximity of the supply of and demand for local public goods, the critical policy links to enhance those gains can be found in the fiscal and institutional governance structures connecting decentralized tax revenues and decentralized public expenditures. In principle, the larger the proportion of local public goods financed through local "own-taxes," the higher the efficiency gains obtained from such local public expenditure. This may explain why state and local taxes are relatively more important in many advanced countries than in developing countries.[14]

If fiscal links are the critical policy determinants of decentralization outcomes at the local level, decentralization can be defined and measured by the sustainable process through which the share of non-national tax revenue grows relative to both GDP and total tax revenue.[15] The critical policy instrument to induce effective decentralization consists of incentives that reward increased local tax authority and collection. This tax revenue criterion is preferable to a transfer-and-expenditure approach, because it induces stronger local institutional development, whereas transfers alone say little about the quality of expenditures or local preferences.[16] Transfers, however, can include transferring national

---

[14] Donahue (1997: 74) found that in the United States, "the sum of all federal spending other than defense, interest, and transfers dropped from 4.2 percent of GDP in 1980 to just 1.7 percent in 1996. Over the same period, state and local spending funded by state and local tax revenues has grown from 8.5 percent to 10.3 percent of GDP."

[15] On the importance of the unit of measurement of decentralization, see Ebel and Yilmaz (2002).

[16] Meloche, Vaillancourt, and Yilmaz (2004: 23) rightly point out that measuring subnational fiscal autonomy should be the key policy target. They state that "the degree of revenue autonomy of subnational governments does seem to be positively related to growth."

tax bases to local governments.[17] Ihori and Itaya (2004: 62) argue that in the case of Japan, these types of transfer have had a positive effect on fiscal discipline.

In certain countries—including Brazil, Chile, and, to some extent, Mexico and Colombia—a new approach to structuring and implementing decentralization policies seems to be evolving. This second-generation approach is characterized by (1) a tighter macroeconomic budget constraint, (2) a strong intergovernmental regulatory framework, (3) more intensive use of incentives at the sectoral level, and (4) a growing subnational GDP and total tax revenue share.

In Brazil, the 2000 Fiscal Responsibility Law provided a de facto, strong regulatory institutional framework for intergovernmental fiscal and financial relationships. In Chile, which followed a tight macroeconomic approach well before other countries adopted such a course, the emphasis is on using incentives at the regional and sectoral levels. In Mexico, a reform agenda is being developed that emphasizes greater subnational taxing autonomy and a rationalization of the transfer system, and it may also involve a new federal-state commission on fiscal federalism and a code of fiscal conduct (see Courchene and Díaz-Cayeros, 2000).

Although it would be premature to state that most other countries will follow a more market-based approach to decentralization, it is safe to say that countries like Argentina and Colombia are being forced to revise their existing decentralization frameworks. Such a policy change can stem from fiscal corrections or from a new perceived wisdom as to what does and does not work in decentralization.

National Fiscal Decentralization Experiences

Argentina

One of the chief explanations for Argentina's economic crisis in the late 1990s was excessive subnational spending and its adverse impact

---

[17] On the issue of mobile tax bases, see Janeba and Smart (2003: 276), which examines the conditions under which tax preferences are desirable or not.

Table 5.3. Argentina: Tax Shares by Level of Government

Level of government	As a percentage of GDP			As a percentage of total tax revenue		
	1995	2000	2002	1995	2000	2002
a. National	12.0	14.3	12.8	76.9	79.0	79.0
b. Subnational (provincial)	3.6	3.8	3.4	23.1	21.0	21.0
Total tax revenue (a + b)	15.6	18.1	16.2	100.0	100.0	100.0

Source: World Bank data, 2004.

on the national macroeconomic fiscal accounts. The country appears to exemplify the risks posed by a weak institutional regulatory framework governing the public finances of the public sector as a whole. In brief, it may be an example of a fragmented public sector.

Table 5.3 shows that between 1995 and 2000, the subnational (that is, the provincial) tax revenue grew slightly from 3.6 percent of GDP to 3.8 percent. But by 2002 it had fallen to 3.4 percent, below the level of 1995. As a percentage of the total tax revenue, subnational tax revenue fell from 23.1 percent to 21.0 percent between 1995 and 2000.

Given the depth of the Argentine crisis and the continuing process of adjustment, it is too early to comment on the outlook for "real" fiscal decentralization in the country. It will depend largely on what real incentives come to feature in Argentina's difficult public jurisdiction as a result of that process.

Brazil

Brazil has been governed as a centralist state throughout its history, dating back to 1808, when João VI, Regent of Portugal, arrived in Rio de Janeiro as head of the Braganza royal family. It is a major historical accomplishment that the country remained unified after Pedro I declared independence in 1822, considering the efforts that Portugal and England made to undermine its unity, as well as the number of regional insurrections and wars with other countries (Burns, 1970: 160). After all, Brazil is a vast country that easily could have spawned several republics, as did the neighboring Spanish Empire. However, Brazil has always been able to balance, and respond with collective wisdom to, the centrifugal and centripetal forces that have emerged from time to time. At the beginning of the twenty-first century, Brazil is deepening its federalization process and remains a solid and unified state.

Brazil is fast evolving into a truly federal state. Adequate use of macroeconomic incentives and fiscal incentives at the state and municipal levels has produced an effective decentralization process. Brazil provides a good illustration of precepts from neo-institutional economics—namely, that incentives can change economic and political behavior. It is at the municipal level that political and economic markets differ the least, and where incentives can be particularly effective in transforming fiscal and political behavior.

After a decade of macroeconomic and exchange rate volatility,[18] Brazil seems to have put stable fiscal rules in place after several attempts.[19] It has done so largely because of the approval in 2000 of the Fiscal Responsibility Law, which is a significant double achievement. First, in a technical and conceptual sense, it implies a broad recognition that without the "right" fiscal rules for the country as a whole, many other equity and economic policy objectives are compromised.[20] Second, the law implies there is a substantial political consensus on which to anchor technical and orthodox "positive" macroeconomic precepts. Paraphrasing Williamson (1996: 377), it could be said that a "credible commitment" has been reached at the political level.

As for the critical question of whether Brazil's recent decentralization process has occurred within a tight budget constraint, the answer is that from 1994 to 1998, budgeting at all levels of government could hardly be described as tight. According to the International Monetary

---

[18] GDP growth in Brazil fell from 3.3 percent in 1997 to about 0.2 percent in 1998. The consumer price index went from 15.8 percent in 1996 to 3.2 percent in 1998, and the overall fiscal balance was negative from 1996 to 2000, reaching –10 percent of GDP in 1999.

[19] The Real Plan of 1994 successfully tamed inflation and initially boosted the primary surplus. However, the fiscal stance deteriorated over 1995–98, and in early 1999 Brazil had to abandon the crawling-peg exchange regime in favor of a market exchange rate system.

[20] For a review of Fiscal Responsibility Laws in Latin America, see Webb (2004).

Fund (IMF), the nonfinancial expenditures of the central government increased by 2.8 percent of GDP during those years, and the sharp deterioration of the fiscal stance contributed to the abandonment of Brazil's crawling-peg rate regime in 1999.

From the mid-1990s onward, Brazil underwent a significant "tax correction" at all levels of government. Table 5.4 shows that from 1995 to 2003, the national and subnational tax shares grew as a percentage of GDP. Subnational tax revenue as a percentage of the total, however, declined in relative terms. But the municipal tax revenue kept constant as an important share of at least 4.5 percent of the total. This suggests that the country was able to maintain a "real" process of decentralization, even while the national tax share grew very significantly from 20.01 percent of GDP in 1995 to an estimated 24.63 percent in 2003.

The total tax share as a percentage of GDP grew enormously, from 24.62 percent in 1991 to 35.80 percent in 2003. This raises the question of the extent to which federalism may lead to high taxation levels. Keen and Kotsogiannis (2002: 369) consider that the answer depends on the relative strengths of vertical and horizontal tax externalities.[21]

Bolivia

In 1994 Bolivia embarked on an intensive decentralization initiative through its Popular Participation and National Dialogue laws. At the same time, it allocated resources from the Heavily Indebted Poor Countries (HIPC) initiative and other concessional sources to the subnational level of government.[22] The broad policy question is whether the basic

---

[21] Keen and Kotsogiannis (2002: 363) state that "since vertical and horizontal tax externalities are inherent in federal tax structures, recognizing and understanding the interaction between them is of considerable importance to the theory of fiscal federalism. They are likely to distort levels of taxation in opposite directions. Horizontal externalities tend to leave state taxes too low. Vertical externalities, in contrast, are likely to leave state taxes too high."

[22] In 1996 the World Bank and the IMF jointly adopted the HIPC initiative to reduce the debt burden of 41 eligible countries to sustainable levels, provided they adopted strong programs of macroeconomic adjustment and structural reform. In 1999 an enhanced HIPC initiative was launched to provide deeper and more rapid debt relief to

Table 5.4. Brazil: Tax Shares by Level of Government

Level of government[1]	As a percentage of GDP					As a percentage of total tax revenue				
	1991	1995	2000	2002	2003 estimate	1991	1995	2000	2002	2003 estimate
a. National	16.12	20.01	22.97	24.39	24.63	65.48	67.24	69.23	68.63	68.8
b. State	7.32	8.32	8.69	9.47	9.52	29.73	27.95	26.19	26.64	26.6
c. Municipal	1.18	1.43	1.52	1.68	1.65	4.79	4.81	4.59	4.73	4.6
d. Total subnational (b + c)	8.50	9.75	10.21	11.15	11.17	34.52	32.76	30.78	31.37	31.2
Total tax revenue (a + d)	24.62	29.76	33.18	35.54	35.80	100.00	100.00	100.00	100.00	100.00

Source: Afonso (2004).
[1] Includes the social security budget.

decentralization framework adopted can yield sustainable welfare gains for most of the population, particularly those living in the poorest jurisdictions. The short answer is that to a large extent, the decentralization process adopted was excessively oriented toward a straight parceling out of resources, grants, and subsidies. Insufficient priority was given to local fiscal performance and to the use of incentives to enhance the effectiveness of decentralized expenditure.

Bolivia's current institutional decentralization framework is the product of a major constitutional reform conducted in 1993, at the start of the Sánchez de Losada administration. In the following year, two key laws came into effect: the Popular Participation Law and the Decentralization Law. The former established that 20 percent of the national budget had to be distributed to the municipalities on the basis of their populations.

Bolivia's institutional decentralization context is a complex mix of rules and norms containing all sorts of intended and unintended incentives. The net picture is one of severe political economy restrictions

---

a larger group of countries. The enhanced HIPC initiative sought a tighter integration between debt relief and poverty reduction. See Andrews et al. (1999).

that limit the application of incentives or a market-like approach. The organizations that have emerged from this institutional set of rules have found incentives to become active in pursuing transfers, subsidies, and special regional projects. A "common pool" of resources, basically consisting of debt relief and other resource transfers, has been harvested by a varied mix of agents, rent seekers, and jurisdictions.

The 2001 National Dialogue Law offers worrisome examples of the "capture" of earmarked funds by public sector rent seekers. This law could create serious fiscal problems and high transaction costs in all management processes dealing with transfers, loans, poverty reduction, and decentralization.

If "real" decentralization is measured by the relative growth of subnational tax revenues as a percentage of GDP and of the total, Bolivia could, in principle, claim that it is moving in that direction. Table 5.5 shows that the subnational (which is really municipal) tax share of GDP rose from 0.7 percent to 1.1 percent between 1995 and 2000. Municipal tax revenue as a percentage of the total rose from 4.0 percent to 5.9 percent in the same period.

It is not clear, however, that this subnational tax development is truly the result of an additional real local tax effort. It may be just a statistical quirk, in the sense that the numbers simply reflect the effects of the 1994 Popular Participation Law, which decreed that 20 percent of national budget resources should be transferred to the municipalities.

Table 5.5. Bolivia: Tax Shares by Level of Government

	As a percentage of GDP		As a percentage of total tax revenue	
Level of government	1995	2000	1995	2000
a. National	16.8	17.4	96.0	94.1
b. Subnational (municipal)	0.7	1.1	4.0	5.9
Total tax revenue (a + b)	17.5	18.5	100.0	100.0

Source: Ministry of Finance, Fiscal Programming Unit.

Table 5.6. Colombia: Tax Shares by Level of Government

Level of government	As a percentage of GDP					As a percentage of total tax revenue				
	1990	1995	2000	2002	2003	1990	1995	2000	2002	2003
a. National	8.8	9.7	11.6	13.4	14.1	83.0	80.8	81.1	83.9	84.9
b. State	1.0	0.8	1.0	1.0	1.0	9.4	6.7	7.0	6.4	6.0
c. Municipal	0.8	1.5	1.7	1.5	1.5	7.5	12.5	11.9	9.6	9.0
d. Total subnational (b + c)	1.8	2.3	2.7	2.6	2.5	17.0	19.2	18.9	16.1	15.1
Total tax revenue (a + d)	10.6	12.0	14.3	16.0	16.6	100.0	100.0	100.0	100.0	100.0

Source: Ministry of Finance, Superior Council on Fiscal Policy, 2004.

Colombia

Recent developments in Colombia augur well for sustained corrections in its decentralization framework.[23] Municipal tax revenues have grown substantially, from 0.8 percent of GDP in 1990 to 1.5 percent in 2003 (see Table 5.6). As a percentage of the total, municipal revenue rose from 7.5 percent to 9.0 percent in the same period. Tax revenues at the state level have not shown the same vigor. This trend suggests that a critical component of real decentralization is taking place. The growth of tax revenue at the subnational level in the 1990s, however, was accompanied by large, unconditional transfers from the national level. All this led to unsustainable expenditures at the subnational level, generating fiscal deficits at this and the national levels. In the end, the national level had to bail out the subnational level (Echavarría, Rentería, and Steiner, 2002).

More recently, the authorities have been able to make important corrections through Law 549 of 1999, Law 617 of 2000, and Law 715 of 2001.[24] Through these new legal and constitutional rules, it is expected that subnational finances will be better managed. This has proven to be

---

[23] For the background to Colombia's decentralization framework, see Wiesner (1992, 1995).

[24] Law 715 followed from Constitutional Amendment No. 01 of 2001.

a tough challenge, however, given the difficulty of changing the structural components of the initial constitutional rules passed in 1991 (see Wiesner, 2004).

Chile

Chile has a long tradition of state centralism. Since its birth as a republic in the early nineteenth century, a strong presidential regime has been the norm. Over the past 20 years, however, there has been a significant process of political and fiscal decentralization. Decentralization began in earnest in 1976, when the country was divided into 13 regions, 52 provinces, and 325 *comunas*. In 1993 the Regional Government and Administration Law created the institutional entities of "regional government" and "regional council" as the two pillars of subnational government. Today, all municipalities have mayors and municipal councils elected by the local citizens.

In contrast with strategies that emphasize the role of growing and largely unconditional transfers, Chile gives priority to macroeconomic and fiscal restraint, as well as to the development of incentives for overall productive resource use. It also favors selective and sectoral decentralization more than wide-open devolution of resources and competencies. On the other hand, Chile's adherence to tight macroeconomic and fiscal constraint is akin to Brazil's recent fiscal correction and to its adoption of the Fiscal Responsibility Law in 2000. More specifically, Chile's approach to decentralization focuses on building institutions, developing processes, and nurturing the "right" incentives in the rules and norms that flow from such processes and institutions.[25]

At the municipal level, Chile has a unique system of intra-municipal transfers from fiscally strong *comunas* to fiscally weak and poor ones. Those transfers finance the Common Municipal Fund, which decentralizes resources and has a legal and institutional framework to ensure that

---

[25] It should be remembered that institutions "are" rules and that rules are, in fact, incentives. See Wiesner (2003b: 20).

transfers reach the neediest sectors of the population. A proportion of municipal own-tax revenues is exclusively earmarked for transfer from rich *comunas* to poorer ones.

Table 5.7 shows that the tax share of Chile's municipal level (there is no fiscally significant state or regional level) has been rising since 1990. As a percentage of GDP, this share increased from 1.09 percent in 1990 to 1.56 percent in 2002. As a percentage of total tax revenue, the municipal share rose from 7.23 percent to 8.58 percent in the same period. Total tax revenue increased from 15.05 percent of GDP to 18.17 percent. As a percentage of total tax revenue, the national share has declined from 92.77 percent to 91.42 percent, a clear sign of fiscal decentralization.

Chile, therefore, can be seen as an example of a country that is following a mutually reinforcing two-track approach to decentralization: first, one based on sectoral decentralization toward market-like conditions; and second, one based on local fiscal (municipal) development.

Ecuador

Ecuador's decentralization framework cannot be characterized as market-based or consistent with tight macroeconomic fiscal constraint. In the 1990s, and particularly in the second half of that decade, Ecuador had large fiscal deficits that reached 7.2 percent of GDP in 1999. The dollarization adopted in early 2000 did not resolve the underlying fiscal imbalances. It merely made it more difficult to use inflation or seignior-

Table 5.7. Chile: Tax Shares by Level of Government

Level of government	As a percentage of GDP				As a percentage of total tax revenue			
	1990	1995	2000	2002	1990	1995	2000	2002
a. National	13.96	15.54	16.31	16.61	92.77	92.64	91.42	91.42
b. Subnational (municipal)	1.09	1.23	1.53	1.56	7.23	7.36	8.58	8.58
Total tax revenue (a + b)	15.05	16.78	17.84	18.17	100.00	100.00	100.00	100.00

Source: Ministry of Finance, Directorate of the Budget, 2004.

age as a source of government revenue. But the structural fiscal problems largely persist, although they are currently masked by fast GDP growth and an oil-led investment boom.[26]

A Fiscal Responsibility Law (*Ley Orgánica de Responsabilidad, Estabilidad y Transparencia Fiscal*) was passed in 2002, though it is doubtful that this will balance revenues and expenditures. It may even open the door for new debt problems by allowing subnational jurisdictions to borrow if revenues fall short of expenditures (Frank, 2003: 409).

Ecuador's decentralization process has contributed to its fiscal problems, as transfers from the national government grew from 3.2 percent of GDP in 1996 to 6.6 percent in 2000. Most of these growing transfers were unconditional and were not accompanied by a corresponding transfer of responsibilities. The 15 percent Transfer Law of 1997 implied a corresponding increase in the fiscal deficit (Wiesner, 2000). An enormous share of government revenue is preassigned to specific sectors, institutions, and all sorts of rent seekers. The IMF (2000: 62) estimates that 64 percent of central government revenue was earmarked for specific purposes in 2000.

Compared to other countries in the region, Ecuador is highly centralized. In the 1990s, the national government accounted for more than 95 percent of all tax revenues (Table 5.8). However, the share of the subnational level has been growing as a percentage of GDP and of the total. The municipal level's share grew from 0.3 percent of GDP in 1990 to 0.58 percent in 2002. During the same period, this tax share as a percentage of the total rose from 3.5 percent to 4.47 percent. This is a significant development. After all, it took place in a period when the national share as a percentage of GDP grew substantially, from 8.3 percent in 1990 to 12.37 percent in 2002. Often, when the national tax share grows so robustly, it leaves little room for the subnational level.

---

[26] See Wiesner (2003b: 117) for a review of Ecuador's decentralization experience since the 1980s.

Table 5.8. Ecuador: Tax Shares by Level of Government

Level of government	As a percentage of GDP				As a percentage of total tax revenue			
	1990	1995	2000	2002	1990	1995	2000	2002
a. National	8.3	9.3	12.18	12.37	96.4	95.9	96.92	95.43
b. State	0.0	0.0	0.01	0.00	0.1	0.1	0.05	0.10
c. Municipal	0.3	0.4	0.38	0.58	3.5	4.0	3.03	4.47
d. Total subnational (b + c)	0.3	0.4	0.39	0.58	3.6	4.1	3.08	4.57
Total tax revenue (a + d)	8.6	9.7	12.57	12.95	100.00	100.00	100.00	100.00

Source: Central Bank, Ecuador.

Mexico

From an expenditure perspective, it has been argued (Courchene, Díaz-Cayeros, and Webb, 2000: 129) that Mexico is reaching decentralization levels comparable to those of Brazil and Argentina. But from a strictly local tax revenue perspective, whereby transfers or expenditures are not deemed as good a measurement of decentralization as subnational-owned tax collections, Mexico has a weak claim to being a federal country. The national level collected more than 97 percent of total tax revenue in 2000 (Table 5.9). The tax share collected at the subnational level declined from 0.43 percent of GDP in 1990 to 0.31 percent in 2000. And as a percentage of total tax revenue, the subnational share grew from 3.83 percent in 1990 to 5.51 percent in 1995, but fell to 2.84 percent in 2000.

Table 5.9. Mexico: Tax Shares by Level of Government

Level of government	As a percentage of GDP			As a percentage of total tax revenue		
	1990	1995	2000	1990	1995	2000
a. National	10.80	9.30	10.60	96.17	94.49	97.16
b. State	0.23	0.29	0.16	2.05	2.96	1.50
c. Municipal	0.20	0.25	0.15	1.78	2.55	1.34
d. Total subnational (b + c)	0.43	0.54	0.31	3.83	5.51	2.84
Total tax revenue (a + d)	11.22	9.79	10.90	100.00	100.00	100.00

Source: World Bank data, 2004.

Mexico, however, may well be moving toward decentralization in a crucial sense, which is that of responsibility and accountability. According to Webb (2001: 709), "since the mid 1990s, spending and borrowing decisions have been rapidly decentralized." But Webb also warns that "taxation is much more centralized than spending and probably more than is necessary for efficient administration."

Within this mixed picture, the global decentralization outlook is positive. Mexican policymakers know that they need to reform the basic structure of the tax and expenditure assignment problems. All this is a highly political process in a country currently undergoing even deeper political transformations. It will not be easy, but Mexico seems up to the task.[27]

The Overall Fiscal Decentralization Outlook

There is still ample room for policy corrections in the area of decentralization in Latin America. Still, the fact that subnational tax revenues seem to be growing relative to GDP and/or to total tax revenue is a positive sign that augurs well for decentralization in this region.

Table 5.10 shows that in the last 10 years, subnational revenues as a percentage of GDP have grown in Bolivia, Brazil, Chile, Colombia, and Ecuador. There has been a small decline in Argentina and a more pronounced fall in Mexico. As a percentage of the total, subnational tax revenues have grown in Argentina, Bolivia, Chile, and Ecuador. This share has fallen in Brazil, Colombia, and Mexico.

This global picture suggests some resilience on the part of local tax collection. Normally, it is less difficult for the national level of government to raise its tax intake, since it has stronger fiscal instruments. If the local tax share is able to hold its ground, that speaks well of the fiscal decentralization framework.

---

[27] See Webb and Gonzalez (2004) for recent developments in the process of balancing subnational tax assignments with earmarked transfers.

Table 5.10. Subnational Tax Revenue Shares of Selected Latin American Countries

Country	As a percentage of GDP			As a percentage of total tax revenue		
	1990	1995	2002	1990	1995	2002
Argentina	3.70[1]	3.60	3.40	17.19[1]	23.10	21.00
Brazil	8.50[2]	9.75	11.15	34.52	32.76	31.37
Bolivia	—	0.70	1.10[3]	—	4.00	5.90[3]
Colombia	1.80	2.30	2.60	17.00	19.20	16.10
Chile	1.09	1.23	1.56	7.23	7.36	8.58
Ecuador	0.30	0.40	0.60	3.60	4.10	4.50
Mexico	0.43	0.54	0.31[3]	3.83	5.51	2.84[3]

Sources: Tables 5.3–5.9.
Note: — = Data not available.
[1] 1993 data.
[2] 1991 data.
[3] 2000 data.

Critical Policy Linkages

In descending order, there are roughly three critical policy linkages that need to be monitored closely in order to ensure their consistency and timely adjustment as needed:

1. The links between autonomous macroeconomic policy objectives[28] and openness-related developments.
2. The links between fiscal decentralization objectives and the enabling institutional and regulatory framework for such a process.
3. The ways that national and subnational tax structures will affect, and be affected by, trade liberalization and regional economic integration. The key question is how to ensure policy consistency in this two-way incentive interaction.

---

[28] According to Linn and Wetzel (1990: 26), "in discussing trade and public finance policies, the many intricate relations between the two policy areas need to be explicitly considered. Failure to do so will likely lead to inconsistent and unsustainable policies, thus hindering a country's trade and development prospects."

Openness, Government Expenditures, and Macroeconomic Objectives

Greater openness to international trade can affect government expenditures—and hence macroeconomic policy objectives—through two interdependent routes.[29] The first is what Rodrik (1998: 997) calls "social insurance against external risk." He argues that the "relationship between 'openness' and government size is strongest when the terms of trade risk is highest." The second route is through a negative fiscal or tax revenue impact. In the first case, the "additional" expenditures could come from interventions to "protect" some private or public markets, or from "complementary" domestic agendas involving subsidies, as well as institutional and infrastructure enhancements. In the second case, if tax revenues fall as a result of trade liberalization and if public expenditures cannot adjust accordingly, the net effect will be higher expenditures than would otherwise be the case, along with fiscal imbalances and macroeconomic instability.

Independently of the robustness of Rodrik's correlation between openness and larger governments, in both cases the short-term pressures will be either to maintain a given fiscal stance or to "tolerate" a larger fiscal imbalance. These possible developments have broader and important policy implications: first, for the relationships between governments and markets, and second, through the effects of larger fiscal deficits on the relative exchange rate for tradable goods. This happened in Colombia during the 1990s, when transfers to the subnational level grew very substantially. Central government expenditures alone rose from 13 percent of GDP in 1990 to 19 percent in 1998. One result was an appreciation of the exchange rate and large increases in imports. Echeverry (2002: 53) has pointed out that the exchange rate appreciation was tantamount to an increase in salaries in terms of imported goods and services.

---

[29] Macroeconomic policy in general can be affected by trade liberalization in several unexpected ways. Faini (2004: 19) observes that it could reduce foreign direct investment, since firms no longer need investment to circumvent trade restrictions.

Generally speaking, openness should engender a greater role for markets, not for governments. Enhanced competitiveness should originate "mainly through increased efficiency in the allocation of resources" and not from unsustainable changes in the exchange rate (Blejer and Cheasty, 1990: 67). Whenever the exchange rate becomes misaligned, fiscal policy should be the first approach for correction (Calvo and Reinhart, 1999: 15).

There is little point in attempting to conclude whether the fiscal impact of trade liberalization is negative, neutral, or positive. This is an empirical question that has to be examined relative to each country's initial conditions. Much will depend on how open or not a given economy was, on its internal tax structure, and on import and export elasticities.[30] It should also be kept in mind that other, nonfiscal consequences of trade agreements have very important implications for the economy as a whole.[31] A study by the General Secretariat of the Andean Community on the experiences of Bolivia, Colombia, Ecuador, Peru, and Venezuela concluded that the trade liberalization processes of the 1980s did not reduce tax revenues (Valencia, Barreix, and Villela, 2003: 40).

Vial (2003: 12) suggests that trade policy has three types of fiscal effects: (1) direct effects related to lower custom duties; (2) indirect effects from other tax sources; and (3) indirect effects—arising from more macroeconomic responses—on income, imports, and exports. In Chile, policymakers decided to offset the loss of tax revenue from lower tariffs by other tax increases. In Colombia, which is now negotiating a free trade agreement with the United States, a study by the National Planning Department concluded that over the medium and long term, such an agreement would be beneficial to growth and employment (Departamento Nacional de Planeación, 2004).

Whatever the answer or forecast may be regarding the fiscal impact, there are two "higher-order" considerations: the need to maintain mac-

---

[30] For an estimation of the trade elasticities between Colombia, Venezuela, and the United States, see Rocha, Perilla-Jiménez, and López Soler (2004: 25).

[31] For a review of those effects in the case of Colombia, see Departamento Nacional de Planeación (2004).

roeconomic stability[32] and send the right signals to the markets; and the long-term objective of enhanced national competitiveness. These are overriding strategic policies, and they should prevail over other considerations.

Fiscal Decentralization and the Right Incentive Structure

Greater decentralization can affect (increase) government expenditures and macroeconomic stability in two related ways: first, by providing automatic and largely unconditional transfers, and failing to adhere to the principle of fiscal neutrality; and second, by not providing the right incentives to reward greater tax effort at the subnational levels. A combination of these characteristics will tend to increase total government expenditures over and above what would happen under another policy.

Generally speaking and in principle, all decentralization schemes should be fiscally neutral in their micro-institutional arrangements and financial implications. That is, they should not change the steadiness of fiscal balance. After all, the aim is to identify and exploit potential efficiency and welfare gains by applying the subsidiarity principle to any market that can function better at the closest intersection between supply and demand. As Bird and Vaillancourt (1998: 37) have aptly put it, "money should follow functions, not precede them."

As mentioned earlier, in the 1980s and part of the 1990s the decentralization frameworks adopted in several Latin American countries adversely affected most countries' macroeconomic balances. This was not only because constitutional rules introduced the "wrong" incentives and mandated unconditioned transfers to the subnational levels,[33] but also because of surreptitious transfers and bailouts in such cases as Argentina, Bolivia, Brazil, and Colombia (Echavarría, Rentería, and Steiner, 2002).

---

[32] On how the macroeconomic framework can contribute to exchange rate stability, and how the exchange rate regime may improve macroeconomic performance, see Calvo and Mishkin (2003: 99).

[33] Persson and Tabellini (2004: 42) have concluded that "rules and forms of government shape fiscal policy."

The large discretionary transfers and bailouts were, in effect, incentives for local governments to export taxes, to overspend, and to neglect the development of their own fiscal bases. This led to what was known in Colombia as "fiscal lethargy" (Wiesner, 1992: 25).

Just as trade liberalization raises questions about its fiscal impact, so decentralization raises the question of whether it leads to higher expenditures and taxation. At the theoretical level, Keen and Kotsogiannis (2002: 369) suggest that it all depends on the "vertical and horizontal tax externalities" of the federation in question, and on how each level of government manages the mobile tax bases. The degree to which this is still an open question is reflected in the authors' heuristic conclusion that the "tax interactions in federations are more complex than has often been supposed." In the particular case of Latin America, federalism and decentralization led to higher expenditures[34] rather than to than higher taxes. The net effect, as mentioned above, was larger fiscal deficits.

In the end, what matters for policymakers is not to lose track of the long-term objectives of greater national decentralization and international openness. Policymakers will not help their countries if they conclude that these goals justify higher spending, especially unsustainable public expenditures. It may not be a coincidence that Chile seems to have made the most progress in both of these areas.[35] Chile has also pursued a prudent fiscal policy for about 20 years.[36] The overarching priority should be the preservation of macroeconomic stability as the enabling environment for successful trade and decentralization openness.

In brief, sound national macroeconomic fiscal policies are indispensable to the success of trade liberalization (Krueger, 1978) and domestic fiscal and political decentralization. Without a tight budget constraint,

---

[34] Stein (1998: 17) makes the insightful observation that "the larger the degree of vertical imbalances, the larger the potential for a commons problem, since a large vertical imbalance increases the incongruence between those who benefit and those who pay for government programs."

[35] See Corbo (1990: 144) for an analysis of the role of public finance and trade in the adjustment experience of Chile in the 1980s.

[36] See Marcel (1999) for an analysis of the effectiveness of Chile's public sector.

which limits access to public resources, it is very difficult for the right incentives to support trade liberalization, regional economic integration, and decentralization processes in general.

Subnational Tax Coordination under National and Regional Openness

The search for the key policy linkages between subnational tax coordination and a process of regional economic integration should begin by addressing some important questions. Would a nation-state perspective and an open international framework differ greatly? Would the basic policy principles guiding each framework—and their interaction—be so distinct? What policy approach can be taken to deal consistently with the two processes?

It will be appreciated that the basic policy principles underlying both perspectives are not substantially different, and Latin American policymakers should give a higher priority to the complementarities between the processes than to their apparent differences.

The Tax Assignment Labyrinth in a Nation-State

The "tax assignment problem" in a process of fiscal decentralization or regional economic integration refers to the determination of the vertical structure of taxes that are best suited for the different levels of government (McLure, 1983; Oates, 1999: 1125). A full description of tax assignment involves not only addressing the matter of who should tax what, but also how. More specifically, it should aim at "providing answers to the following questions: (i) which level chooses the taxes a given level imposes; (ii) which defines the tax bases; (iii) which sets tax rates; and (iv) which administers the various taxes" (McLure, 2001: 341). According to McLure, "where subnational governments lack control over all these decisions—but especially control over tax rates— there will be vertical fiscal imbalance, even if subnational revenues are adequate to meet expenditure needs. Tax assignment is not so much about the overall adequacy of revenue as about *control over marginal sources of revenue.*"

These are the classic questions for a nation-state, but what about the situation under openness? Tanzi (2001: 34) answers by saying that "under globalization tax administrators and policymakers will face challenges that will change the ways in which taxes have been levied and collected." The complexities of the tax assignment problem become evident in the following considerations by three distinguished scholars.

1. "Tax assignments depend on history and are moving targets under evolving institutional arrangements and political contexts" (McLure, 2001: 339).
2. "The assignment of taxes may be understood only in the context of a system as a whole" (Bird and Vaillancourt, 1998: 35).
3. "The stability of a system of federalism governance is, in fact, a delicate balancing act" (Oates, 2004: 35).

With regard to (3), Oates (2004: 36) argues that "a stable and enduring federal structure must have, on the one hand, a central government that is sufficiently strong to rein in regional and local governments so that the system is not undercut by aggressive jurisdictional 'beggar-they-neighbor' policies, and, on the other hand, adequate constraints to keep the central government within its sphere."

Tax Competition and Regulation under Openness

Subnational tax coordination within a nation-state, as well as under greater international openness, quickly evolves into the regulation of tax competition under both degrees of openness. In other words, tax coordination is tantamount to the regulation of tax competition. The question that arises, as indicated above, is whether the key policy principles supporting the design of a regulatory framework for tax competition would be substantially different in a nation-state and in an open, international process.

Table 5.11 summarizes the main factors involved in regulating tax competition in a single country and in a regional economic integration process: for example, the factors that frame the tax assignment problem in Brazil (the state of São Paulo relative to Fortaleza) and those that

Table 5.11. Subnational Tax Coordination under Closed and Open Frameworks

Factors	Tax base within a nation-state		Tax base under a process of openenss	
	National	Subnational	National[1]	Subnational
Mobile factors				
Capital	Income tax	Share in VAT	Income tax	Share in VAT
Labor	Customs	User fees, transfers	VAT transfers	User fees
Immobile factors				
Real estate	Land taxes	Real estate tax	Land taxes	Share in VAT
Public services	Tariffs	User fees	Tariffs	User fees

[1] Refers to the governance structure regulating an economic integration process.

affect the tax assignment between Brazil and, say, Argentina or Bolivia. As a general rule, "the best candidates for assignment to the subnational level are taxes characterized by relatively low mobility, a fairly even distribution of the base over the national territory, and relative stability over the cycle" (Ter-Minassian, 1997: 22).

Is the taxonomy in Table 5.11 really firm? Can it really be argued that the left side mandates substantially different policy postures than the right side? Would the nation-state tax assignment problem really differ that much from the one that emerges in a process of external openness? Are they not both under an equivalent fiscal process of dynamic change?[37]

If these two policy maps[38] have fiscal equivalence (using the terminology of Olson, 1969) and are not so different, then the regulation of both should be based on similar principles and equivalent policy linkages, namely:

---

[37] Wildasin (personal communication, October 6, 2004) underscores the dynamic nature of the interactions between competitive tax structures.

[38] According to Oates (2004: 5), when governments at different levels provide "efficient levels of outputs of public goods for those goods whose spatial patterns of benefits are encompassed by the geographical scope of their jurisdictions," a "perfect mapping" is the outcome.

1. Make sure the right macroconstitutional framework is in place.
2. Make sure that the right incentives are offered at the national, sectoral, and subnational levels.[39]
3. Let the principle of benefit taxation guide fiscal policies at "decentralized" (national and international) levels of government.[40]

The key policy linkages go from institutions to the specific decentralization and openness frameworks. As Rodrik (2003: 10) has put it, "the quality of institutions is the key. Trade, or more specifically government policy toward trade, does not play nearly as important a role as the institutional setting."

In brief, get the institutional framework right and then let all jurisdictions compete. The private market (from trade and regional economic integration) and the public goods market will interact, inform each other, and deliver reasonable outcomes—most probably more efficient outcomes than those resulting from direct discretionary interventions. Tax competition and investment competition will not necessarily drive down tax rates or tax revenues.

A tentative "zero-sum tax competition theorem" could be articulated as follows: from a "closed" spatial tax potential base for either a nation-state or multiple countries, tax competition will not tend to reduce subnational tax rates or tax revenues as a whole. It will merely redistribute tax revenues according to how the private and local public

---

[39] For the subnational level, Bird (1999: 35) recommends three principles: "(1) more attention should be paid to matching expenditure and revenue needs; (2) more effort should be made to ensure that all governments bear significant responsibility at the margin for financing the expenditures for which they are politically responsible; and (3) subnational taxes should not unduly distort the allocation of resources."

[40] According to Oates (1999: 1125), "decentralized levels of government should avoid the taxation of highly mobile economic units (be they households, capital, or final goods). But this in itself is not correct. The real implication is that decentralized levels of government should avoid *nonbenefit* taxes on mobile units. Or, more accurately, the analysis shows that on efficiency grounds decentralized governments *should* tax mobile economic units with benefit levies (Oates and Schwab, 1991; Oates, 1996). Such economic units, in short, should pay for the benefits that they receive from the public services that local governments provide to them."

markets negotiate a "Coasean bargain" for the supply and demand of local public goods and services in exchange for user fees and investment.

The specifics of the trade liberalization and regional economic integration processes will determine which jurisdictions will be adversely or positively affected by the redistribution process. The "losers" and "winners" will result from the underlying market forces of long-term structural change as well as from how each jurisdiction is able to adjust to that process and to influence it.[41]

This may sound like a normative platitude with little operational value, which might be partially true. The challenge, therefore, is to ascertain whether the broad macroeconomic and micro-institutional contexts are positive and propitious environments for nurturing the specific sectoral goals pursued.

The Parallel Agenda

The concepts of openness and globalization should not be perceived as referring exclusively to the international arena. The relevance of these concepts begins first at home, within the national spatial and policy framework, and then abroad, in the larger international markets. Fiscal decentralization and decentralization in general, as well as regional economic integration at the national level, are the first building blocks of the preparation for trade liberalization and openness generally. Most Latin American countries need to do a lot more "homework" to gain access to the potential offered by globalization and international openness. In other words, external openness has some requirements.

---

[41] This theorem posits that tax competition does not necessarily lead to changes in the level of revenues in the aggregate; it only redistributes revenues. Oates and Schwab (1991) maintain that tax competition leads to Pareto-efficient outcomes if certain conditions are satisfied, most notably if all jurisdictions employ benefit taxes.

The Requirements of Openness

It has been argued that "the absence of adequate prior institutional reforms may limit the gains from openness" (Berg and Krueger, 2003: 74). Rodrik (2001) has gone so far as to suggest that the efforts made to implement trade reform would be better directed at institutional reform. This may be going too far. After all, the positive spillovers from openness to other reforms could jump-start the reform process. In any case, Berg and Krueger (2003: 74) argue that waiting for institutional reform "is not a good idea."

The chicken-and-egg causality discussion cannot go far without specifying what sort of institutional reform is being considered. Some reforms may be implemented as part of the trade reform package, but others may have to be established as preconditions—such as a stable and well-anchored macroeconomic environment.[42] This is a key message of this chapter, especially for Latin American countries.[43]

One precondition that is always difficult to implement is the need to educate the general public about the potential gains from openness. In many countries the average citizen has a hard time understanding why high tariffs and import quotas lower the average standard of living. According to Poole (2004: 3), two principles explain the gap between economists' views and the public's view of trade: the simultaneity principle and the political-favors principle. The first refers to the comparative static equilibrium analysis, wherein one position is preferred to another without reference to the process by which adjustment between equilibrium is achieved. Economists can see the transmission process, but to others this process is a kind of black box.

---

[42] Papageorgiou, Michaely, and Choksi (1991) argue that trade liberalization in the presence of chaotic macroeconomic environments and overvalued exchange rates is likely to be reversed.

[43] Clavijo (2004: 12), referring to Colombia, thinks that the fundamental institutional reforms in areas such as property rights, labor markets, and public purchases may be even more important than strictly trade issues.

The second principle simply recognizes that trade restrictions are inherently political. They stem largely from a political and legislative process, not from an anonymous market process. Governments tend to be expected to "protect" their citizens, particularly if their actions will directly affect the individual welfare, a firm, an industry, or an employee. Actors will then legitimately use all political means to protect their perceived interests.

The Right Sequence for Institution Building

Few debates are more intense than the one about the direction of causality between institutions and development, and even geography and history. For Acemoglu (2003: 27), "the two main candidates to explain the fundamental causes of differences in prosperity between countries are geography and institutions." Saffran (2003: 221) observes that "just as psychologists have their nature-nurture debate, development economists have their institutions-geography debate." And finally history, as North and Weingast (1989) have argued, is the ultimate explanation for differences in long-term economic performance.

With regard to the specific role of regional economic integration, Rodrik and Subramanian (2003: 32) argue that "once institutions are controlled for, integration has no direct effect on incomes, while geography has at best weak direct effects. These results are very robust."

Although the thrust of these arguments is clear (that institutions matter far more than other factors), the question remains as to how specifically to go about building institutions and where to begin. This chapter suggests that the right sequence is to start by ensuring macroeconomic stability through a tight fiscal budget constraint. Thereafter, other institutions and reforms may develop, but macroeconomic stability is important for nurturing the other "right" institutions.

That said, it should be admitted that this proposition assumes the existence of the most elusive of factors—namely, political demand[44] for

---

[44] To Hoff and Stiglitz (2004: 753), the explanation for the weak rule of law in post-communist countries was the feeble demand for the institutions that would protect public or even private property.

the public good that the "right" institutions are supposed to provide: in this case, low inflation, exchange rate stability, and a future that can be discounted in its different risks and present values.[45] Understanding what ultimately determines the emergence of the demand for the "right" institutions is a daunting challenge and remains a work in progress.[46]

Main Findings and Conclusions

During the last 10 to 15 years, several Latin American countries have undergone a rapid process of change on two policy fronts: first, fiscal decentralization, and second, trade liberalization and regional economic integration. These two processes imply a favorable policy disposition toward greater openness at the domestic, nation-state level, as well as at the international level.[47] The policy linkages between these two processes have not yet become a major policy issue, but as both of them proceed, the need for greater policy coordination will become evident—particularly in the areas of tax competition and tax regulation.

The outlook for such enhanced policy surveillance and design is framed by two positive developments and by a third that poses a significant challenge:

1. At the domestic level, the growth of subnational tax revenues bodes well for fiscal decentralization and closer economic integration. Although there is ample room for improvement, the current trend in several countries augurs well for their decentralization strategies.

---

[45] Wiesner (2004: 38) observes that in the case of Colombia there is no real political demand for macroeconomic stability.

[46] See Mistri (2003) for an application of procedural rationality as a possible source for the demand of institutions and for cooperative collective games.

[47] According to Ocampo (2004: 72), from 1990 to 2000, Latin American countries "became more integrated into the world economy."

2. In a region where centralization[48] and protectionism have deep historical roots, the incipient inclination toward some degree of openness is a positive development. It reveals awareness that most Latin American countries are too small to grow fast enough to provide adequate welfare standards to their increasing populations. Faster and more sustainable growth has to be sought in the export markets.

3. There are relentless political pressures to increase public expenditures beyond sustainable levels in the region. Important segments of the population still equate higher public spending with gains in equity and poverty reduction. Explaining the effects of fiscal deficits and macroeconomic instability on the poor and disadvantaged is a major and unresolved challenge.[49] Reforms are not easy in this political economy context (see Rajan, 2004).

These findings refer to an immensely varied regional and policy context. Although several Latin American countries have had some common historical antecedents and share a continental geography, their initial conditions were not similar and they have followed different historical paths. In the areas of decentralization and federalism, the different policy choices they made one or two centuries ago explain their diverse current circumstances. Brazil is very different from Mexico, and Costa Rica is very different from Bolivia. How they and other countries will manage their openness will largely depend on the characteristics of their institutions and their particular histories.[50]

---

[48] Veliz (1980: 16) suggests that such centralism may predate Columbus's arrival in the West Indies.

[49] Winters, McCulloch, and McKay (2004: 106) state that "theory provides a strong presumption that trade liberalization will be poverty-alleviating in the long run and on average. The empirical evidence broadly supports this view, and, in particular, lends no support to the position that trade liberalization generally has an adverse impact."

[50] According to McLure (2001: 357), "choices of tax assignment depend crucially on history and both reflect and determine the degree of sovereignty allowed (or enjoyed by) second-tier governments."

Policy Implications

The policy implications of the ongoing and growing process of domestic and international openness are the following:

1. The macroeconomic institutional framework and its attendant real incentives are the key determinants of specific policy outcomes in the interdependent areas of fiscal decentralization and regional economic integration.
2. Tax coordination should not be seen as an invitation for direct and discretionary interventions, but rather as a response to the need to regulate tax competition and as a challenge to design the right regulatory framework for tax competition.
3. Tax and investment competition will not necessarily drive down tax rates or tax revenues. The principle of benefit taxation implies that the suppliers and buyers of local public goods, in a context of adequate institutional and incentives strategies, will tend to negotiate "satisficing"[51] outcomes and are more likely to come to agree on "cooperative games."

Recommendations

Given these policy implications, the emerging recommendations are:

1. National policymakers in each country should focus on developing the right institutional frameworks and incentives to prompt public and private markets to seek efficient and sustainable outcomes. All of this begins by having a tight macroeconomic fiscal constraint.[52] While this is not enough to assure successful decen-

---

[51] Simon (1982) avers that in economics, optimal conceptual and operational solutions are seldom possible or necessary, and that progress is achieved gradually by marginal "satisficing" improvements.

[52] A leading Latin American policymaker, Arminio Fraga (2004: 105), considers that Latin America's "best course is to persevere with a sound agenda of reforms and to

tralization and economic integration, it is a necessary condition. Without it, not much is possible as a long-term development strategy.

2. On the whole, countries should stay the current course of strengthening their subnational tax bases and local fiscal institutions. This is a first-order priority as a prerequisite for successful interjurisdictional tax and expenditure competition in a regional economic integration process.

3. The key recommendation is that policymakers should adhere closely to basic economic and tax principles and priorities when nurturing the "right" complementarities between domestic and international openness.[53] Efforts to micromanage the process will expose it to opportunism and to the inclusion of the "wrong" incentives.

Concluding Remarks

This chapter has examined the fiscal relationships between decentralization and economic integration processes in Latin America. These two processes imply a broader policy framework of openness. Within this wider context, the unit of analysis is no longer the nation-state but the area covered by the factors of production. The overall policy framework to deal with openness in general should be anchored to a tight macroeconomic budget constraint and the right institutions to enforce it. Once this requirement is in place, national and subnational tax coordination should largely be left to evolve into the regulation of tax competition among all "local" jurisdictions.

---

avoid the temptation of looking for shortcuts in the past. The path forward must surely include a sound macroeconomic framework, a focus on education and health, on microeconomic efficiency and flexibility, on building institutions, on creating a culture of trust and respect for the rule of law."

[53] On the importance of relying on basic tax principles, see Tanzi (2004).

References

Works Cited

Acemoglu, Daron. 2003. "Root Causes: A Historical Approach to Assessing the Role of Institutions in Economic Development." *Finance and Development* 40(2):26–31.

Afonso, José Roberto. 2004. "Brasil: un caso aparte." Paper presented at ECLAC's Seventeenth Regional Seminar on Fiscal Policy, Santiago, January 24–27.

Andrews, David, Anthony R. Boote, Syed S. Rizavi, and Sukhwinder Singh. 1999. *Debt Relief for Low-Income Countries: The Enhanced HIPC Initiative.* Washington, DC: International Monetary Fund.

Aninat, Eduardo. 2002. "Surmounting the Challenges of Globalization." *Finance and Development* 39(1):4–7.

Berg, Andrew, and Anne Krueger. 2003. "Trade, Growth, and Poverty—A Selective Survey." In *Annual World Bank Conference on Development Economics: The New Reform Agenda*, ed. Boris Pleskovic and Nicholas Stern. Washington, DC: World Bank and Oxford University Press.

Bird, Richard, and François Vaillancourt. 1998. "Fiscal Decentralization in Developing Countries: An Overview." In *Fiscal Decentralization in Developing Countries*, ed. Richard Bird and François Vaillancourt. Cambridge: Cambridge University Press.

———. 1999. "Rethinking Subnational Taxes: A New Look at Tax Assignment." IMF Working Paper 99/165. Washington, DC: International Monetary Fund.

Blejer, Mario I., and Adrienne Cheasty. 1990. "Fiscal Implications of Trade Liberalization." In *Fiscal Policy in Open Developing Economies*, ed. Vito Tanzi. Washington, DC: International Monetary Fund.

Burns, Bradford. 1970. *A History of Brazil.* New York: Columbia University Press.

Calvo, Guillermo A., and Frederic S. Mishkin. 2003. "The Mirage of Exchange Rate Regimes for Emerging Market Countries." *Journal of Economic Perspectives* 17(4):99–118.

Calvo, Guillermo A., and Carmen M. Reinhart. 1999. "Capital Flow Reversals, the Exchange Rate Debate, and Dollarization." *Finance and Development* 36(3):13–15.

Clavijo, Sergio. 2004. "Crecimiento, comercio internacional e instituciones: reflexiones a raíz de las negociaciones TLC-ALCA." Carta Financiera 128. Bogotá: Bogotá Asociación Nacional de Instituciones Financieras.

Corbo, Vittorio. 1990. "Public Finance, Trade, and Development: The Chilean Experience." In *Fiscal Policy in Open Developing Economies*, ed. Vito Tanzi. Washington, DC: International Monetary Fund.

Courchene, Thomas, and Alberto Díaz-Cayeros. 2000. "Transfers and the Nature of the Mexican Federation." In *Achievements and Challenges of Fiscal Decentralization: Lessons from Mexico*, ed. Marcelo M. Giugale and Steven B. Webb. Washington, DC: World Bank.

Courchene, Thomas, Alberto Díaz-Cayeros, and Steven B. Webb. 2000. "Historical Forces: Geographical and Political." In *Achievements and Challenges of Fiscal Decentralization: Lessons from Mexico*, ed. Marcelo M. Giugale and Steven B. Webb. Washington, DC: World Bank.

Departamento Nacional de Planeación. 2004. "Efectos del tratado de libre comercio con Estados Unidos." Bogotá: Dirección de Estudios Económicos, Departamento Nacional de Planeación.

Donahue, John D. 1997. "Tiebout? Or Not Tiebout? The Market Metaphor and America's Devolution Debate." *Journal of Economic Perspectives* 2(4):73–81.

Ebel, Robert, and Serdar Yilmaz. 2002. "On the Measurement and Impact of Fiscal Decentralization." Policy Research Working Paper 2809. Washington, DC: World Bank.

Echavarría, Juan José, Carolina Rentería, and Roberto Steiner. 2002. "Decentralization and Bailouts in Colombia." Research Network Working Paper R-442. Washington, DC: Inter-American Development Bank.

Echeverry, Juan Carlos. 2002. *Las claves del futuro: economía y conflicto en Colombia*. Bogotá: Editorial Oveja Negra.

ECLAC (Economic Commission for Latin America and the Caribbean). 2001. *Balance preliminar de las economías de América Latina y el Caribe.* Santiago: ECLAC.

———. 2002. *Situación y perspectivas: estudio económico de América Latina y el Caribe 2001–02.* Santiago: ECLAC.

———. 2004. *Anexo estadístico del estudio económico.* Santiago: ECLAC.

Faini, Riccardo. 2004. "Trade Liberalization in a Globalizing World." CEPR Discussion Paper 4665. London: Centre for Economic Policy Research.

Fisher, Ronald. 1991. "Interjurisdictional Competition: A Summary Perspective and Agenda for Research." In *Competition among States and Local Governments,* ed. Daphne A. Kenyon and John Kincaid. Washington, DC: Urban Institute Press.

Fraga, Arminio. 2004. "Latin America since the 1990s: Rising from the Sickbed?" *Journal of Economic Perspectives* 18(2):89–106.

Frank, Jonás. 2003. "Decentralization." In *Ecuador: una agenda económica y social del nuevo milenio,* ed. Vicente Fretes Cibils, Marcelo M. Giugale, and José R. López-Cálix. Bogotá: World Bank and Alfaomega.

Hoff, Karla, and Joseph E. Stiglitz. 2004. "After the Big Bang? Obstacles to the Emergence of the Rule of Law in Post-Communist Societies." *American Economic Review* 94(3):753–63.

IDB (Inter-American Development Bank). 1994. "Fiscal Decentralization: The Search for Equity and Efficiency." In *Special Report: Fiscal Decentralization.* Economic and Social Progress in Latin America: 1994 Report. Washington, DC: IDB.

———. 2002. *Beyond Borders: The New Regionalism in Latin America.* Economic and Social Progress in Latin America: 2002 Report. Washington, DC: IDB.

Ihori, Toshihiro, and Jun-Ichi Itaya. 2004. "Fiscal Reconstruction and Local Government Financing." *International Tax and Public Finance* 11(1):55–67.

IMF (International Monetary Fund). 2000. "Ecuador: Selected Issues and Statistical Annex." Country Report 00/125. Washington, DC: IMF.

Janeba, Eckhard, and Michael Smart. 2003. "Is Targeted Tax Competition Less Harmful Than Its Remedies?" *International Tax and Public Finance* 10(3):259–80.

Jones, Mark P., Pablo Sanguinetti, and Mariano Tommasi. 1999. "Politics, Institutions, and Public-Sector Spending in the Argentine Provinces." In *Fiscal Institutions and Fiscal Performance*, ed. James M. Poterba and Jürgen von Hagen. Chicago: University of Chicago Press.

Kanbur, Ravi, and Michael Keen. 1993. "Jeux sans frontières: Tax Competition and Tax Coordination When Countries Differ in Size." *American Economic Review* 83(4):877–92.

Keen, Michael J., and Christos Kotsogiannis. 2002. "Does Federalism Lead to Excessively High Taxes?" *American Economic Review* 92(1):363–70.

Krueger, Anne O. 1978. *Liberalization Attempts and Consequences.* Cambridge, MA: Ballinger.

Linn, Johannes F., and Deborah Wetzel. 1990. "Public Finance, Trade and Development: What Have We Learned?" In *Fiscal Policy in Open Developing Economies*, ed. Vito Tanzi. Washington, DC: International Monetary Fund.

Marcel, Mario. 1999. "Effectiveness of the State and Development: Lessons from the Chilean Experience." In *Chile: Recent Policy Lessons and Emerging Challenges*, ed. Guillermo Perry and Danny M. Leipziger. Washington, DC: World Bank.

McLure, Charles, Jr. 1983. *Tax Assignment in Federal Countries.* Canberra: Australian National University.

———. 2001. "The Tax Assignment Problem: Ruminations on How Theory and Practice Depend on History." *National Tax Journal* 54(3):339–63.

Meloche, Jean-Philippe, François Vaillancourt, and Serdar Yilmaz. 2004. "Decentralization or Fiscal Autonomy? What Does Really Matter?" Policy Research Working Paper 3254. Washington, DC: World Bank.

Mistri, Maurizio. 2003. "Procedural Rationality and Institutions: The Production of Norms by Means of Norms." *Constitutional Political Economy* 14(4):301–17.

North, Douglass, and Barry W. Weingast. 1989. "The Evolution of Institutions Governing Public Choice in 17th Century England." *Journal of Economic History* 49(4):803–32.

Oates, Wallace E. 1996. "Taxation in a Federal System: The Tax-Assignment Problem." *Public Economics Review* 1(1):35–60.

———. 1999. "An Essay on Fiscal Federalism." *Journal of Economic Literature* 37(3):1120–49.

———. 2004. "Toward a Second-Generation Theory of Fiscal Federalism." Paper presented at "Fiscal and Regulatory Competition," 60th Congress of the International Institute of Public Finance, Università Bocconi, Milan, August 23–26.

Oates, Wallace E., and Robert M. Schwab. 1991. "The Allocative and Distributive Implications of Local Fiscal Competition." In *Competition among States and Local Governments*, ed. Daphne A. Kenyon and John Kincaid. Washington, DC: Urban Institute Press.

Ocampo, José Antonio. 1996. "Prologue." In *Las Américas: integración económica en perspectiva*. Bogotá: Departamento Nacional de Planeación.

———. 2004. "Latin America's Growth and Equity Frustrations during Structural Reform." *Journal of Economic Perspectives* 18(2):67–88.

Olson, Mancur. 1969. "The Principle of Fiscal Equivalence: The Division of Responsibilities among Different Levels of Government." *American Economic Review* 59(2):479–87.

Papageorgiou, Demetrious, Michael Michaely, and Armane Choksi. 1991. *Liberalizing Foreign Trade*. Vol. 7, *Lessons of Experience in the Developing World*. Cambridge, MA: Blackwell.

Persson, Torsten, and Guido Tabellini. 2004. "Constitutional Rules and Fiscal Policy Outcomes." *American Economic Review* 94(1):25–45.

Poole, William. 2004. "Free Trade: Why Are Economists and Noneconomists So Far Apart?" *Federal Reserve Bank of St. Louis Review* 86(5):1–6.

Poterba, James M., and Jürgen von Hagen. 1999. "Introduction." In *Fiscal Institutions and Fiscal Performance*, ed. James M. Poterba and Jürgen von Hagen. Chicago and London: University of Chicago Press.

Rajan, Raghuram. 2004. "Why Are Structural Reforms So Difficult?" *Finance and Development* 41(2):56–57.

Rocha, Ricardo, Juan Ricardo Perilla-Jiménez, and Ramiro López Soler. 2004. *Una aproximación a los efectos del ALCA sobre las importaciones de Colombia.* Documento CEDE No. 25. Bogotá: Centro de Estudios sobre Desarrollo Económico.

Rodrik, Dani. 1998. "Why Do More Open Economies Have Bigger Governments?" *Journal of Political Economy* 106(5):997–1032.

———. 2001. "The Developing Countries' Hazardous Obsession with Global Integration." Harvard University, Kennedy School of Government, Cambridge, MA. Available at http://ksghome. harvard.edu/~drodrik/obsession.pdf.

———. 2003. "What Do We Learn from Country Narratives?" In *In Search of Prosperity: Analytic Narratives on Economic Growth*, ed. Dani Rodrik. Princeton: Princeton University Press.

Rodrik, Dani, and Arvind Subramanian. 2003. "The Primacy of Institutions (and What This Does and Does Not Mean)." *Finance and Development* 40(2):31–34.

Saffran, Bernard. 2003. "Institutions and Development." *Journal of Economic Perspectives* 17(4):221–22.

Simon, Herbert A. 1982. *Models of Bounded Rationality.* Cambridge, MA: MIT Press.

Stein, Ernesto. 1998. "Fiscal Decentralization and Government Size in Latin America." Working Paper 368. Washington, DC: Office of the Chief Economist, Inter-American Development Bank.

Stiglitz, Joseph E. 2002. *Globalization and Its Discontents.* New York: Norton.

Tanzi, Vito. 1995. *Taxation in an Integrating World.* Washington, DC: Brookings Institution.

———. 2001. "Globalization and the Work of Fiscal Termites." *Finance and Development* 38(1):34–37.

———. 2004. "Globalization and the Need for Fiscal Reform in Developing Countries." *Journal of Policy Modeling* 26(4):525–42.

Ter-Minassian, Teresa. 1997. "Intergovernmental Fiscal Relations in a Macroeconomic Perspective: An Overview." In *Fiscal Federalism in Theory and Practice*, ed. Teresa Ter-Minassian. Washington, DC: International Monetary Fund.

Valencia, Alexis, Alberto Barreix, and Luis Villela, eds. 2003. *Impacto fiscal en la integración económica.* Lima: General Secretariat of the Andean Community and Inter-American Development Bank.

Veliz, Claudio. 1980. *The Centralist Tradition in Latin America.* Princeton: Princeton University Press.

Vial, Joaquín. 2003. "Efectos fiscales de la política de comercio fiscal." In *Impacto fiscal en la integración económica*, ed. Alexis Valencia, Alberto Barreix, and Luiz Villela. Lima: General Secretariat of the Andean Community and Inter-American Development Bank.

Webb, Steven B. 2001. "Decentralization." In *Mexico: A Comprehensive Development Agenda for the New Era*, ed. Marcelo M. Giugale, Oliver Lafourcade, and Vinh H. Nguyen. Washington, DC: World Bank.

———. 2004. "Fiscal Responsibility Laws for Subnational Discipline: The Latin American Experience." Policy Research Working Paper 3309. Washington, DC: World Bank.

Webb, Steven B., and Christian Y. Gonzalez. 2004. "Bargaining for a New Fiscal Pact in Mexico." Policy Research Working Paper 3284. Washington, DC: World Bank.

Wiesner, Eduardo. 1992. *Colombia: descentralización y federalismo fiscal; informe final de la Misión para la Descentralización.* Bogotá: Presidencia de la República and Departamento Nacional de Planeación.

———. 1995. *La descentralización, el gasto social y la gobernabilidad en Colombia.* Bogotá: Asociación Nacional de Instituciones Financieras, Departamento Nacional de Planeación.

———. 2000. "La descentralización, el ajuste fiscal y el desarrollo municipal en el Ecuador." Serie de Estudios Económicos y Sectoriales RE3-00-002. Washington, DC: Inter-American Development Bank.

———. 2003a. "La descentralización, la estabilidad macroeconómica y la integración económica regional: enlaces de política y mecanismos de transmisión." In *Impacto fiscal en la integración económica*, ed. Alexis Valencia, Alberto Barreix, and Luiz Villela. Lima: General

Secretariat of the Andean Community and Inter-American Development Bank.

———. 2003b. *Fiscal Federalism in Latin America: From Entitlements to Markets.* Washington, DC: Inter-American Development Bank.

———. 2004. "El origen político del déficit fiscal en Colombia: el contexto institucional 20 años después." Documentos CEDE 2135. Bogotá: Centro de Estudios sobre Desarrollo Económico, Facultad de Economía, Universidad de los Andes.

Wildasin, David. 1995. "Comments on 'Fiscal Federalism and Decentralization: A Review of Some Efficiency and Macroeconomic Aspects' by Vito Tanzi." In *Annual World Bank Conference on Development Economics,* ed. Michael Bruno and Boris Pleskovic. Washington, DC: World Bank.

———. 2004. "Competitive Fiscal Structures." Paper presented at "Fiscal and Regulatory Competition," 60th Congress of the International Institute of Public Finance, Università Bocconi, Milan, August 23–26.

Williamson, Oliver. 1996. *The Mechanisms of Governance.* New York: Oxford University Press.

Winters, L. Alan, Neil McCulloch, and Andrew McKay. 2004. "Trade Liberalization and Poverty: The Evidence So Far." *Journal of Economic Literature* 42(1):72–115.

Additional Reading

Caballero, Ricardo. 2001. *Macroeconomic Volatility in Reformed Latin America.* Washington, DC: Inter-American Development Bank.

Krugman, Paul. 1991. *Geography and Trade.* Cambridge, MA: MIT Press.

Tiebout, Charles. 1956. "A Pure Theory of Local Expenditures." *Journal of Political Economy* 64(5):416–24.

Weingast, Barry W. 1995. "The Economic Role of Political Institutions: Market Preserving Federalism and Economic Growth." *Journal of Law, Economics and Organization* 11(1):1–31.

Wiesner, Eduardo. 1997. "La economía neoinstitucional, la descentralización y la gobernabilidad local." In *Descentralización fiscal en*

América Latina: nuevos desafíos y agenda de trabajo, ed. Gabriel Aghón and Herbert Edling. Santiago: Economic Commission on Latin America and the Caribbean (ECLAC)/Gesellschaft für Technische Zusammenarbeit (GTZ).

6

Globalization and Tax Competition: Implications for Developing Countries

Reuven S. Avi-Yonah

The current age of globalization can be distinguished from the previous one (between 1870 and 1914) by the much higher mobility of capital than labor. In the previous age, before immigration restrictions, labor was at least as mobile as capital. This increased mobility has been the result of technological changes—the ability to move funds electronically—and the relaxation of exchange controls. The mobility of capital has led to tax competition, whereby sovereign countries lower their tax rates on income earned by foreigners within their borders, so as to attract both portfolio and direct investment. Tax competition, in turn, threatens to undermine the individual and corporate income taxes that remain major sources of revenue (in terms of the percentage of total revenue collected) for all modern states.

The response of both developed and developing countries to these developments has been, first, to shift the tax burden from (mobile) capital to (less mobile) labor, and second, when further taxation of labor becomes politically and economically difficult, to cut government services. Hence globalization and tax competition lead to a fiscal crisis for countries that wish to continue to provide those services to their citizens, at the same time that demographic factors and the increased income inequality, job insecurity, and income volatility attendant on globalization make such services more necessary.

This chapter argues that if government service programs are to be maintained in the face of globalization, it is necessary to cut the intermediate link by limiting tax competition. From both practical and normative perspectives, however, any limits on tax competition should be congruent with maintaining the ability of democratic states to determine the desirable size of their governments.

International Tax Competition and the Taxation of Capital

From its beginnings in the late nineteenth century, the modern state has been financed mainly by progressive income taxation. The income tax differs from other forms of tax (such as consumption or social security taxes) in that it theoretically includes income from capital in the tax base, even if it is saved and not consumed. Because the rich save more than the poor, a tax that includes income from capital in its base is more progressive (taxes the rich more heavily) than a tax that excludes income from capital, such as a consumption tax or a payroll tax. However, the ability to tax saved income from capital (that is, income not vulnerable to consumption taxes) is impaired if the capital can be shifted overseas to jurisdictions where it escapes taxation.

Two recent developments have dramatically heightened the ability of individuals and corporations to earn income overseas free of income tax: the effective elimination of withholding tax by developed countries, and the rise of production tax havens in developing countries (Avi-Yonah, 2000). Since the United States abolished its withholding tax on interest paid to foreigners in 1984, no major capital-importing country has been able to impose such a tax for fear of driving mobile capital elsewhere or increasing the cost of capital for domestic borrowers, including the government itself (Tanzi, 1995; Gardner, 1992). The result is that individuals can generally earn investment income free of host-country tax in any of the world's major economies (Avi-Yonah and Swartz, 1997; Cohen, 1998; May, 1996). Moreover, even developed countries find it exceedingly difficult to effectively collect the tax on the foreign income of their individual residents in the absence of withholding taxes imposed by host countries, because the investments can be made through tax havens with strong bank secrecy laws (Tanzi, 1995). Developing countries, with much weaker tax administrations, find this task almost impossible. Hence cross-border investment income can be earned largely free of either host- or home-country taxation (Kant, 1996; McLure, 1989).

Consider, for example, a wealthy Mexican who wishes to earn tax-free interest income from investing in the bonds of an American corporation. All he needs to do is set up, for a nominal fee, a Cayman Islands corporation to hold the bonds. The interest payments are then made to the Caymans corporation without any U.S. tax withheld, under the "portfolio interest exemption" provided by Internal Revenue Code section 871(h). The individual does not report the income to the Mexican tax authorities, and they have no way of knowing that the Caymans corporation is effectively an "incorporated pocketbook" of the Mexican resident. Nor are the exchange-of-information provisions of the U.S.-Mexico tax treaty of any help, because the Internal Revenue Service has no way of knowing that the recipient of the interest payments is controlled by a Mexican resident, and therefore cannot report this to the Mexican authorities. As a result, the income is earned completely free of tax (the Cayman Islands, of course, imposes no income taxes of its own).

Shifting attention from passive to productive investment, a similar threat to the taxing capacity of both home and host jurisdictions becomes evident. In the last decade, competition for inbound investment has led an increasing number of countries (103, as of 1998) to offer tax holidays specifically geared to foreign corporate investors (Vernon, 1998; UNCTAD, 1996). Given the relative ease with which an integrated multinational can shift production facilities in response to tax rates, such production tax havens enable multinationals to derive most of their income abroad free of host-country tax (Hines and Rice, 1994; Altshuler and Newlon, 1993). Moreover, most developed countries, including the United States, do not dare impose current tax (or sometimes any tax) on the foreign-source business income of their resident multinationals, for fear of reducing the multinationals' competitiveness relative to the multinationals of other countries (Peroni, 1997). If they did, new multinationals could be set up as residents of jurisdictions that do not tax such foreign-source income (Hines, 1991). Thus business income can also be earned abroad largely free of either host- or home-country taxation.

Intel Corporation, for example, one of the 10 leading multinationals, has operations in more than 30 countries. On its website in 1999, the company stated that "an Intel chip developed at a design center in Oregon might be manufactured at a wafer fabrication facility in Ireland, packaged and tested in Malaysia, and then sold to a customer in Australia. Another chip might be designed in Japan, fabricated in Israel, packaged and tested in Arizona, and sold in China." Intel has major manufacturing facilities in China, Ireland, Israel, Malaysia, the Philippines, and Puerto Rico. Outside the United States, therefore, all of Intel's manufacturing facilities are located in countries granting tax holidays. Furthermore, Intel does not pay current U.S. tax on its income from those foreign operations because, under U.S. law, active income earned by foreign subsidiaries of U.S. multinationals is not taxed until it is repatriated in the form of dividends, which Intel can delay for many years (Avi-Yonah, 1997). Hence the effective tax rate on Intel's foreign source income is far below the nominal U.S. corporate rate of 35 percent.

If income from capital can escape the income tax net, the tax becomes, in effect, a tax on labor. Several empirical studies have suggested that in some developed jurisdictions, the effective tax rate on income from capital approaches zero, and tax rates on capital have tended to fall sharply since the early 1980s, when exchange controls were relaxed (Owens and Sasseville, 1997; Rodrik, 1997). As a result, countries that used to rely on income tax revenue are forced to increase relatively regressive taxes.

In recent years, the two fastest-growing taxes in member countries of the Organisation for Economic Co-operation and Development (OECD) have been consumption taxes (rising from 12 percent of total revenues in 1965 to 18 percent in 1995) and payroll taxes (rising from 19 percent to 27 percent over the same period). Both of these are more regressive than the income tax (Owens and Sasseville, 1997). Meanwhile, personal and corporate income taxes have not grown as a percentage of total revenues: the personal income tax accounted for 26 percent of total revenue in 1965 and 27 percent in 1995, while the figures for the corporate income tax are 9 percent and 8 percent, respectively (Owens and Sasseville, 1997). Total tax revenue as a percentage of GDP in developed countries rose sharply during the same period, from an average of 28 percent in 1965 to almost 40 percent in 1994, an increase that is largely accounted for by the rise of consumption and payroll taxes (World Bank, 1994). Moreover, there is evidence among OECD member countries that as the degree of openness of an economy increases, taxes on capital tend to fall while taxes on labor rise. The income tax is imposed on both capital and labor, so its stability may mask this trend (Mendoza, Razin, and Tesar, 1994; Mendoza, Milesi-Ferretti, and Asea, 1996).

The same trends can also be observed in developing countries. In non-OECD member countries (outside the Middle East), total government revenue as a share of GDP rose from an average of 18.8 percent in 1975–80 to 20.1 percent in 1986–92 (World Bank, 1994). This growth was financed mainly by the contemporaneous growth of revenue from the value-added tax (VAT), which rose from 25.5 percent to 31.8 percent of total revenue). At the same time, revenues from both the individual and the corporate income tax were flat or declined (World Bank, 1994).

A recent study by Keen and Simone (2004) illustrates both the extent of this problem and its impact on developing countries. The authors show that from 1990 to 2001, corporate tax rates declined in both developed and developing countries. In developed countries, however, the fall in the rates was matched by a broadening of the tax base, and thus no decline in revenue can be observed (Griffith and Klemm, 2004). In developing countries, by contrast, during the same period, corporate tax revenue fell about 20 percent on average.

This decline is particularly important in light of the larger share of tax revenue produced by the corporate tax in developing countries—an average of 17 percent, as opposed to 7 percent for developed countries. Keen and Simone (2004) attribute most of this decline to the spread of targeted tax incentives for multinational enterprises (MNEs). Between 1990 and 2001, the percentage of developing countries granting tax holidays to MNEs grew from 45 percent to 58 percent. Similar trends are evident for tax breaks for exporters (granted by 32 percent of countries in 1990 and 45 percent in 2001), reduced corporate rates for MNEs (granted by 40 percent of countries in 1990 and 60 percent in 2001), and free trade zones (in place in 17.5 percent of countries in 1990 and

45 percent in 2001). These figures are particularly important because a companion paper by Altshuler and Grubert (2004) shows that tax competition seems to have driven the evolution of countries' effective tax rates in the period 1992–98, and U.S. manufacturers are increasingly determining where to invest based on tax considerations.

Tax Competition and the Developing Countries

The drawbacks of tax competition for developed countries are relatively clear, because such countries have an elaborate social insurance safety net that requires a high level of government expenditure and is threatened by tax competition (Roseveare et al., 1996). But how does tax competition affect developing countries?

First, note that developing countries need tax revenues at least as much as developed countries do, if not more. A common misperception is that only OECD member countries are confronted by a fiscal crisis as a result of the increasing numbers of elderly people in the population. In fact, dependency ratios (the ratio of the elderly to the working population) are expected to increase in other geographic areas as well, as fertility rates decline and health care improves (World Bank, 1994). Outside the OECD and the transition economies, the dependency ratio starts in the single digits in the 1990s, but rises to just below 30 percent by 2100 (McLure, 1997). Moreover, while direct spending on social insurance is much lower outside the OECD and the transition economies, other forms of government spending (such as government employment) effectively fulfill a social insurance role. In Latin America, for example, direct government spending on social insurance is much lower than indirect spending through government employment and procurement programs (Subbarao et al., 1997).

Furthermore, it seems strange to argue that developing countries need tax revenues less than developed countries because they have less developed social insurance programs. If the normative case for social insurance is accepted, it applies to developing countries with even greater force because the presence of widespread poverty means that losing a job can have much direr consequences (UNDP, 1997). But the need for revenues in developing countries goes far beyond social insurance. In some developing countries, revenues are needed to ensure the very survival of organized government, as the Russian experience demonstrates (*The Economist*, 1998). In other, more stable developing countries, revenues are needed mainly to provide for adequate education (investment in human capital), which many regard as the key to promoting development (Sen, 1997). For example, the United Nations has estimated that for only $30–40 billion, all people in the world can obtain basic social services such as elementary education (UNDP, 1997). Given current trends in foreign aid, most of these funds have to come from developing-country governments (UN General Assembly, 2001).

Second, economists' standard advice to small and open economies is that they should refrain from taxing foreign investors because such investors cannot be made to bear the burden of any tax imposed by the capital-importing country (Razin and Sadka, 1991). Hence the tax will necessarily be shifted to less mobile factors in the host country, such as labor and/or land, and it is more efficient to tax those factors directly. This argument seems quite valid as applied to portfolio investment, but less so with regard to foreign direct investment (FDI), for two reasons. First, the standard advice does not apply if a foreign tax credit is available in the investor's home country, which frequently would be the case for FDI (Viherkentta, 1991). Second, the standard advice assumes that the host country is small. An extensive literature on multinationals, however, suggests that typically they exist in order to earn economic rents (Hennart, 1991). In that case, the host country is no longer small in the economic sense. That is, there is a reason for the investor to be there and not elsewhere. Thus any tax imposed on such rents (as long as it is below 100 percent) will not necessarily cause the investor to leave, even if it is unable to shift the burden of the tax to labor or landowners.

This argument clearly holds in the case of rents that are linked to a specific location, such as natural resources or a large market. But what if the rent can be earned in a large number of potential locations (Dunning, 1988)? In this case, the host country will not be able to tax the rent if the multinational can credibly threaten to go elsewhere, although once the investment has been made, the rent can be taxed. This situation, which is probably the most common (Hennart, 1991), would require coordinated action to enable all host countries to tax the rent earned within their borders. Some possibilities for such action are described below.

This matter is related to the final argument, which is that host countries need to offer tax incentives to be competitive. An extensive literature has demonstrated that taxes play a crucial role in determining investment location decisions (Bond, 1981; Boskin and Gale, 1987; Hines, 1999). All of these studies, however, emphasize that the tax incentives are crucial *given the availability of such incentives elsewhere* (Guisinger et al., 1985). Hence it can be argued that, given the need for tax revenues, developing countries would generally prefer to refrain from granting tax incentives, if only they could be assured that no other developing country would be able to grant such incentives (Avi-Yonah, 2000).

Restricting developing countries' ability to compete in granting tax incentives, therefore, does not truly restrict their autonomy or run counter to their interests. That is the case whenever they grant the incentive solely because they fear competition from other developing countries, and would not have granted it but for such fear. Whenever competition from other countries drives the tax incentive, eliminating the competition does not hurt the developing country and may aid its revenue-raising efforts (assuming it can attract investment on other grounds, which is typically the case). Moreover, under the proposals described below, developing countries remain free to lower their tax rates generally, as opposed to granting specific tax relief aimed at foreign investors.

Two additional points should be made from a developing-country perspective. The first concerns the question of tax incidence. Since the tax competition that is most relevant to developing countries concerns the corporate income tax, it is important to attempt to assess the incidence of that tax in evaluating how its collection affects the welfare of the developing country. Unfortunately, after decades of analysis, there is no consensus on the incidence of the corporate tax. Older studies have tended to conclude that the tax is borne by shareholders or by all capital providers, but more recent studies have suggested that the tax is borne to a significant extent by consumers or labor (Fanning, 1967; U.S. Treasury, 1992). Another possibility is that the tax on established corporations was borne by those who were shareholders at the time the tax was imposed or increased, because thereafter it is capitalized into the price of the shares (Fanning, 1967).

This debate is unlikely to be decided soon. In fact, the incidence may be shifting over time, especially as globalization may enable corporations to shift more of the tax burden to labor. But from the perspective of a developing country that is deciding whether to collect taxes from a multinational, three of the four possible alternatives for incidence (current shareholders or capital providers, old shareholders, and consumers) are largely the residents of other jurisdictions, and thus from a national welfare perspective, the developing country gains by collecting the tax. Even if some of the tax is shifted to labor in the developing country, it can be argued that as a matter of tax administration, it is more efficient (as well as more politically acceptable) to collect the tax from the multinational than to attempt to collect it from the workers.

The second point to note is that a developing country may want to collect taxes from multinationals even if in general it believes that the private sector is more efficient than the public sector in using the resources. That is because in the case of a foreign multinational, the taxes that the developing country fails to collect may indeed be used by the private sector, but in another jurisdiction, and therefore they will not benefit the developing country. A possible solution, and one used by developing countries, is to refrain from taxing multinationals while they reinvest domestically, but to tax them upon remittance of the profits abroad. Such taxation of dividends and other forms of remittance, however, is subject to the same tax competition problem discussed above. Thus it seems that in most cases, it is in developing countries' interest to overcome the tax competition problem. The question remains as to how to do so in the face of the collective action problem described above.

Tax Competition and Tax Treaties: The Tax Sparing Problem

Bilateral tax treaties usually have little impact on tax competition, which is a quintessentially multilateral phenomenon. This has led several commentators to advocate for a multilateral tax treaty (e.g., Slemrod and

Avi-Yonah, 2002). The issue of the appropriate forum to address tax competition will be addressed below.

One aspect of tax treaties, however, is relevant to the tax competition issue and has been particularly important in Latin America—namely, tax sparing. Tax sparing refers to an agreement by a residence country, one that normally taxes its residents on a worldwide basis with a foreign tax credit, to grant such credits to taxes that would have been collected by a residence country but for a tax holiday or similar targeted measure.

Tax sparing is quite prevalent in treaties signed by European countries and Japan, although the OECD has questioned its usefulness (OECD, 1994). Moreover, Hines (1997) has shown that tax sparing is quite effective in promoting FDI. However, since 1959, when U.S. Treasury official Stanley Surrey persuaded the U.S. Senate to reject a proposed treaty with Pakistan that included a tax sparing provision, the United States has steadfastly refused to grant tax sparing in any of its treaties. As a result, the United States has far fewer treaties with developing countries than other developed countries do. In particular, in Latin America, the United States currently has treaties only with Mexico and Venezuela; it has terminated treaties with Honduras and Nicaragua and has negotiated but never ratified treaties with Argentina and Brazil.

The tax sparing issue has stymied efforts to negotiate treaties between the United States and the larger Latin American countries, even though such treaties would be beneficial to both sides and despite Latin American countries' increasing reluctance to rely on tax incentives. Fundamentally, the Latin American countries insist on their rights to adopt preferential measures to attract investments. They argue that in the absence of tax sparing, treaties would mean a transfer of revenue from their treasuries to the U.S. Treasury, which they regard as an unacceptable result.

But is this argument correct? Two aspects of U.S. domestic tax law indicate that a U.S. multinational enterprise (MNE) would normally benefit from a tax holiday granted in a Latin American country, even in the absence of tax sparing. The first is deferral. Under U.S. tax law, foreign subsidiaries of U.S. MNEs (so-called controlled foreign corporations, or CFCs) do not normally pay U.S. tax on their foreign-source income. Instead, U.S. tax on the income is deferred until the CFC remits it to its

U.S. parent. While the United States has several regimes that limit the scope of deferral, none of them apply to active business income earned from manufacturing operations, which is the typical form of income that benefits from tax holidays in developing countries. Given this situation, it is unsurprising that U.S. MNEs typically reinvest most of their foreign-source income and do not repatriate it. When this happens, the tax holiday is fully effective.

The second relevant aspect of U.S. domestic tax law is cross-crediting. By law, a U.S. MNE may claim a foreign tax credit for foreign income taxes imposed on its foreign-source income, but only up to a limit: no foreign tax can be credited if it exceeds the U.S. tax rate that would be imposed on the foreign-source income. Thus the key planning issue for U.S. MNEs is to ensure that the overall effective foreign tax rate on their foreign-source income does not exceed 35 percent (the current U.S. rate). Moreover, while taxes on different forms of income may not be averaged with each other, taxes on the same type of income from different countries may be averaged. Hence, if a U.S. MNE has (for example) $100 of active income from Japan taxed at 42 percent, it will not be able to credit more than 35 percent of the Japanese tax. If, however, it can also earn another $20 of active income from Brazil, which does not tax it because of a tax holiday, the foreign tax credit limit would rise from 35 percent to 42 percent (35 percent x 120) and the full Japanese tax will be creditable. The Brazilian tax holiday will therefore benefit the U.S. MNE despite the absence of tax sparing.

In general, for these two reasons, U.S. MNEs can benefit from tax holidays granted by Latin American countries. Thus Latin American countries would be ill-advised to insist on tax sparing as a condition for negotiating tax treaties with the United States. Given the evidence that tax treaties increase FDI to developing countries (Bloningen and Davies, 2004), they should negotiate such treaties without tax sparing.

What Can Be Done about Tax Competition?

The tax competition problem, therefore, is essentially a problem of coordination and trust. Each jurisdiction would prefer to tax investors from abroad to gain the revenue, but it fears that doing so would drive the investors to other jurisdictions that do not tax them. If there were a way to coordinate actions among the relevant jurisdictions, they all could gain added revenues without running the risk of losing the investment.

A good illustration of how this dynamic works is the history of German taxation of interest income. In 1988, Germany introduced a 10 percent withholding tax on the interest paid to bank depositors, but it had to abolish the tax within a few months because of the magnitude of capital flight to Luxembourg. In 1991, the German Federal Constitutional Court held that withholding taxes on wages but not on interest violated the constitutional right to equality. The government thereupon reintroduced the withholding tax on interest but made it inapplicable to nonresidents (Mutén, 1994). Nonresidents, however, may be Germans investing through Luxembourg bank accounts. To cope with this problem, the Germans have led a European Union (EU) effort to introduce either exchange of information or a withholding tax on all interest payments to EU residents (Council of the European Union, 1998). This proposal was adopted as a directive after a prolonged political fight, but it is still conditioned on the cooperation of Switzerland and the actual implementation of withholding taxes by Austria, Belgium, and Luxembourg (Cnossen, 2004).

Thus, the key to finding a solution to the tax competition problem is to attack it on a broad multilateral basis through an organization such as the OECD. Under current conditions, the OECD is the natural choice for leading such coordinated actions against tax competition, for three reasons. First, for individual investors to earn decent returns on their capital without incurring excessive risks, they need to invest in an OECD member country. Tax havens do not offer adequate investment opportunities, and developing countries are generally considered too risky for portfolio investment (other than through mutual funds, which do not offer tax avoidance opportunities). If all OECD members enforced taxation of portfolio investment, therefore, it could be subject to tax without requiring cooperation from the tax havens.

Second, about 85 percent of the world's multinationals are headquartered in OECD member countries. This is likely to remain the case for a while, because OECD members offer investors stable corporate and securities law protection that is lacking in other countries. Hence, if all OECD members agreed on a coordinated basis to tax their multinationals currently on their income from abroad, most of the problem of tax competition from direct investment could be solved.

Third, the OECD has the required expertise (its model tax treaty is the global standard), and it has already started on the path of limiting tax competition. In 1998 it adopted a report entitled *Harmful Tax Competition: An Emerging Global Issue* (OECD, 1998). The report is somewhat limited, because it addresses tax competition for financial activities and services only—ignoring, for example, Intel's manufacturing plants. Moreover, it does not address the taxation of investment income. But it represents an extremely useful first step and proves that a consensus can be reached on tax competition: Switzerland and Luxembourg abstained, but did not dare veto the adoption of the report by the other 27 OECD members.

The OECD makes a useful distinction between (1) tax competition in the form of generally applicable lower tax rates, and (2) tax regimes designed to attract foreign investors. This distinction is both normatively and pragmatically sound: restricting tax competition should not and cannot mean that voters in democratic countries lose their right to determine the size of the public sector through general tax increases or reductions. But it does mean that countries should not provide windfalls for foreign investors if that impedes welfare states from providing the public services their residents desire. Such limitations are particularly appropriate because those foreign investors themselves often reside in countries providing a high level of services, yet refuse to pay the tax price that the provision of such services entails.

Relying on the OECD to restrict tax competition, however, has three significant drawbacks. First, the OECD has only 30 members, and it is not clear that it can effectively impose its antitax competition rules on nonmember countries. Solutions that rely on where the parents of MNEs are located, for example, assume that no significant growth in MNEs will take place outside the OECD, and solutions that rely on the OECD as the market assume no significant markets outside the OECD. Either assumption may become wrong. When that is the case, solutions that rely on OECD enforcement will lose their effectiveness unless those emerging markets join the OECD. Several developing countries have joined the OECD recently, including South Korea and Mexico, but it is hard to imagine China or India doing so in the near future.

Second, relying on the OECD to implement solutions to the tax competition problem, even if those solutions are tailored to benefiting developing countries, may not be acceptable to those countries. The OECD has made a huge effort to include nonmembers in the tax competition project, but it is still identified as the rich countries' club. Thus developing countries may not be able to shed their suspicions that the OECD will not act in their interests, even if it can actually be made to do so. In fact, the OECD's efforts to develop a multilateral agreement on investments (MAI) foundered precisely because developing countries and left-leaning nongovernmental organizations coordinated a campaign against it, perceiving it to represent the interests of the rich countries and "their" MNEs.

Third, the OECD effort is limited at present to geographically mobile financial services and excludes real investments, although these constitute a significant part of the problem. In addition, even for the areas it does cover, the OECD has the power only to persuade, not to adjudicate.

From these perspectives, the World Trade Organization (WTO) is a more attractive candidate for "world tax organization." It has a much broader membership than the OECD, and developing countries are much better represented within it. They also have real clout, as shown by the recent struggle over the selection of the WTO's director general.

Moreover, WTO rules already cover and prohibit the form of tax competition that is most prevalent in developing countries—namely, granting targeted tax incentives to MNEs engaged in the manufacture of goods. As long as the goods are mainly intended for export, as would typically be the case for small developed countries, these targeted incentives arguably constitute a prohibited export subsidy (Slemrod and Avi-Yonah, 2002). Moreover, if the goods are mainly intended for the local market, there is much less pressure on the developing countries to grant tax incentives (which Argentina, Brazil, and China, for example, are now phasing out).

Nonetheless, there are several serious objections to including tax matters in the jurisdiction of the WTO. First, it has been argued that the WTO lacks sufficient tax expertise. That problem, however, can be remedied by hiring a sufficient number of tax experts to sit on the WTO's panels. In fact, as the WTO has expanded its jurisdiction to nontariff matters, its staff already includes tax experts who also understand trade issues.

Green (1998) has advanced a more serious objection, arguing that the costs of imposing the WTO's legalistic dispute resolution mechanism outweigh any benefits. Green argues that the need for the WTO to resolve trade disputes legalistically is based on two features that are typically lacking in the tax context: retaliation and lack of transparency. Retaliation is a feature of repeated prisoners' dilemma–type games and ensures that players have an incentive to cooperate. In an assurance (stag hunt) game, both players cooperate if they can be assured of the other player's cooperation. With retaliation, an organizational setting is needed to manage retaliatory strategies, while with assurance, it is needed to provide the information required for the assurance to exist.

In the context of tax competition, however, it seems that both retaliation and lack of information are serious problems. In the case of portfolio investment, for example, the United States began a race to the bottom by abolishing its withholding tax, and other countries responded (that is, retaliated) by abolishing their own taxes. Currently, no country dares reimpose its tax without adequate assurance that other countries will follow suit. Similarly, for direct investment, countries have adopted tax incentives or deferral and exemption rules for their resident MNEs in response to the actions of other countries, and they fear changing such policies without assurance that others will do the same. Thus, whether these developments are characterized as prisoners' dilemma or assurance games, they seem to present precisely the kind of problem that only a multilateral organization with rule-making power can effectively resolve.

Green, however, raises another objection to giving the WTO authority over taxes, one that in practice is likely to be far more potent: the problem of sovereignty. Countries are wary of relinquishing their sovereignty over tax matters, which lies at the heart of their ability to exercise national power. This concern is particularly acute in the United States and almost led to the failure of the entire Uruguay Round, as the United States insisted at the last minute on excluding direct taxes from the purview of the General Agreement on Trade in Services. Green argues that if the WTO dispute resolution mechanism is given authority over tax issues, this might lead to widespread noncompliance, particularly given the perception that the WTO is not transparent and lacks democratic legitimacy.

Green may be wrong about this matter, especially since the analysis above has shown that the WTO already has jurisdiction over most forms of harmful tax competition, and thus no further extension of its powers is necessary. But even if Green is right and sovereignty poses a real problem, there may be a solution to this as well. Under the General Agreement on Tariffs and Trade (GATT), all decisions had to be reached by consensus—that is, with the agreement of the party whose regime is at stake. Under WTO rules, on the other hand, all dispute settlement rulings are binding unless there is a consensus not to implement them—that is, when even the complaining party agrees to refrain from action. Perhaps the former rule is more appropriate for tax matters than the latter, because it gives the loser a veto if it feels that its sovereignty is truly at stake. Similar rules exist for tax matters in both the EU and the OECD. But, as shown by the Domestic International Sales Corporation case in the GATT and by the OECD's adoption of the tax competition report, a country will typically use its veto power sparingly—only when it perceives that an adverse result will severely constrain its sovereignty. In other cases, the stigma of disapproval is sufficient to ensure cooperation.

In the final analysis, therefore, it may be necessary to set up a multilateral organization with rules different from those of the WTO, but with a similarly broad membership. The United Nations is the obvious venue for such an organization, building on the important work of the League of Nations Fiscal Committee. The Current Ad Hoc Group of Experts on International Cooperation in Tax Matters should be upgraded to provide the basis for such an organization.

To sum up, as a result of globalization and tax competition, tax rules can no longer be set by countries acting unilaterally or by bilateral tax treaties. In a world where capital can move freely across national borders and multinationals are free to choose among many investment locations, the ability of any one country (or any two countries in cooperation) to tax or otherwise regulate such capital is severely limited. Any such unilateral move will be undercut by other countries, or not even attempted in the name of preserving national competitiveness. A multilateral solution is therefore essential if the fundamental goals of taxation or other regulation are to be preserved. Private market activities that span the globe can be regulated or taxed only by organizations with a similar global reach.

This chapter has tried to outline some of the ways in which global governance can be achieved in capital income taxation. Meeting this goal will not be easy, given the expected resistance of (1) private actors eager to preserve their freedom from taxation, and (2) governments protecting their sovereign ability to set their own tax rules. But limiting tax competition is not impossible. Moreover, because preserving the ability of developing nations to tax income from capital is essential to the achievement of important policy goals, it must be tried.

References

Altshuler, Rosanne, and Harry Grubert. 2004. "Taxpayer Responses to Competitive Tax Policies and Tax Policy Responses to Competitive Taxpayers: Recent Evidence." *Tax Notes International* 34(13):1349–62.

Altshuler, Rosanne, and T. Scott Newlon. 1993. "The Effects of U.S. Tax Policy on the Income Repatriation Patterns of US Multinational Corporations." In *Studies in International Taxation*, ed. Alberto Giovannini, R. Glenn Hubbard, and Joel Slemrod. Chicago: University of Chicago Press.

Avi-Yonah, Reuven S. 1997. "International Taxation of Electronic Commerce." *Tax Law Review* 52(3):507–55.

———. 2000. "Globalization, Tax Competition and the Fiscal Crisis of the Welfare State." *Harvard Law Review* 113(7):1573–1676.

Avi-Yonah, Reuven S., and Linda Z. Swartz. 1997. "Virtual Taxation: Source Based Taxation in the Age of Derivatives." *Derivatives* 2:247.

Bloningen, Bruce A., and Ronald B. Davies. 2004. "Do Bilateral Tax Treaties Promote Foreign Direct Investment?" In *Handbook of International Trade: Economic and Legal Analysis of Laws and Institutions*, ed. J. Hartigan. Oxford: Blackwell.

Bond, Eric. 1981. "Tax Holidays and Industry Behavior." *Review of Economics and Statistics* 63(1):88–95.

Boskin, Michael J., and William G. Gale. 1987. "New Results on the Effects of Tax Policy on the International Location of Investment." In *The Effects of Taxation on Capital Accumulation*, ed. Martin Feldstein. Chicago: University of Chicago Press.

Cnossen, Sibren. 2004. "Reform and Coordination of Corporation Taxes in the European Union: An Alternative Agenda." *Tax Notes International* 34(13):1327–47.

Cohen, Edmund S. 1998. "Individual International Tax Planning Employing Equity Derivatives." *Derivatives* 4:52.

Council of the European Union. 1998. "Conclusions of the ECOFIN Council Meeting on 1 December 1997 Concerning Taxation Policy." *Official Journal* (C 2): 1–6.

Dunning, John H. 1988. "Explaining International Production." *Journal of International Economics* 28(3–4):393–95.

The Economist. 1998. "Meltdown in Russia." August 29.

Fanning, James E. 1967. "Review of *Federal Tax Policy* by Joseph A. Pechman." *Journal of Finance* 22(1):135–36.

Gardner, Edward H. 1992. "Taxes on Capital Income: A Survey." In *Tax Harmonization in the European Community*, ed. George Kopits. Washington, DC: International Monetary Fund.

Green, Robert A. 1998. "Antilegalistic Approaches to Resolving Disputes between Governments: A Comparison of the International Tax and Trade Regimes." *Yale Journal of International Law* 23(1):79–94.

Griffith, Rachel, and Alexander Klemm. 2004. "What Has Been the Tax Competition Experience of the Last 20 Years?" *Tax Notes International* 34(13):1299–1315.

Guisinger, Stephen E., and associates. 1985. *Investment Incentives and Performance Requirements.* New York: Praeger.

Hennart, Jean-François. 1991. "The Transaction Cost Theory of the Multinational Enterprise." In *The Nature of the Transnational Firm*, ed. Christos N. Pitelis and Roger Sugden. London: Routledge.

Hines, James R. 1991. "The Flight Paths of Migratory Corporations." *Journal of Accounting, Auditing and Finance* 6(4):447–79.

———. 1997. "Tax Sparing and Direct Investment in Developing Countries." NBER Working Paper 6728. Cambridge, MA: National Bureau of Economic Research.

———. 1999. "Lessons from Behavioral Responses to International Taxation." *National Tax Journal* 52(2):305–22.

Hines, James R., and Eric M. Rice. 1994. "Fiscal Paradise: Foreign Tax Havens and American Business." *Quarterly Journal of Economics* 109(1):149–82.

Kant, Chander. 1996. *Foreign Direct Investment and Capital Flight.* Princeton Studies in International Finance, No. 80. Princeton, NJ: Princeton University, Department of Economics.

Keen, Michael, and Alejandro Simone. 2004. "Is Tax Competition Harming Developing Countries More Than Developed?" *Tax Notes International* 34(13):1317–25.

May, Gregory. 1996. "Flying on Instruments: Synthetic Investments and Withholding Tax Avoidance." *Tax Notes* 73(10):1225–34.

McLure, Charles E., Jr. 1989. "U.S. Tax Laws and Capital Flight from Latin America." *University of Miami Inter-American Law Review* 20(2):321–57.

———. 1997. "Tax Policies for the 21st Century (Keynote Paper)." In *Visions of the Tax Systems of the XXIst Century: Proceedings of a Symposium Held in Geneva in 1996 during the 50th Congress of the International Fiscal Association.* IFA Congress Seminar Series, vol. 21d. The Hague: Kluwer Law International.

Mendoza, Enrique G., Gian Maria Milesi-Ferretti, and Patrick Asea. 1996. "On the Ineffectiveness of Tax Policy in Altering Long-Run Growth." CEPR Discussion Paper 1378. London: Centre for Economic Policy Research.

Mendoza, Enrique G., Assaf Razin, and Linda L. Tesar. 1994. "Effective Tax Rates in Macroeconomics: Estimates of Tax Rates on Factor Income and Consumption." *Journal of Monetary Economics* 34(3):297–323.

Mutén, Leif. 1994. "International Experience of How Taxes Influence the Movement of Private Capital." *Tax Notes International* 8(11):743–50.

OECD (Organisation for Economic Co-operation and Development). 1994. *Tax Sparing: A Reconsideration.* Paris: OECD.

———. 1998. *Harmful Tax Competition: An Emerging Global Issue.* Paris: OECD.

Owens, Jeffrey, and Jacques Sasseville. 1997. *Emerging Issues in Tax Reform.* Paris: Organisation for Economic Co-operation and Development.

Peroni, Robert J. 1997. "Back to the Future: A Path to Progressive Reform of U.S. International Income Tax Rules." *University of Miami Law Review* 51(4):975–1011.

Razin, Assaf, and Efraim Sadka. 1991. "International Tax Competition and Gains from Tax Harmonization." *Economics Letters* 37(1):69–76.

Rodrik, Dani. 1997. *Has Globalization Gone Too Far?* Washington, DC: Institute for International Economics.

Roseveare, Deborah, Willi Leibfritz, Douglas Fore, and Eckhard Wurzel. 1996. "Ageing Populations, Pension Systems and Government Budgets: Simulations for 20 OECD Countries." OECD Economics Department Working Paper 168. Paris: Organisation for Economic Co-operation and Development.

Sen, Amartya. 1997. "Development Thinking at the Beginning of the XXI Century." In *Economic and Social Development in the XXIst Century,* ed. Luis Emmerij. Washington, DC: Inter-American Development Bank.

Slemrod, Joel, and Reuven Avi-Yonah. 2002. "(How) Should Trade Agreements Deal with Income Tax Issues?" *Tax Law Review* 55(4):533–54.

Subbarao, Kalanidhi, Kene Ezemenari, Aniruddha Bonnerjee, Soniya Carvalho, Jeanine D. Braithwaite, Alan Thompson, and Carol Graham. 1997. *Safety Net Programs and Poverty Reduction: Lessons from Cross-Country Experience.* Washington, DC: World Bank.

Tanzi, Vito. 1995. *Taxation in an Integrating World.* Washington, DC: Brookings Institution.

UNCTAD (United Nations Conference on Trade and Development). 1996. *World Investment Report.* Geneva: UNCTAD.

UNDP (United Nations Development Programme). 1997. *Human Development Report 1997.* New York: UNDP.

UN General Assembly. 2001. *Report of the Secretary-General to the Preparatory Committee for the High-Level International Intergovernmental Event on Financing for Development.* UN Doc. A/AC.257/12 (Dec. 18, 2000). New York: United Nations.

U.S. Treasury. 1992. *Integration of the Individual and Corporate Tax Systems: Taxing Business Income Once.* Washington, DC: U.S. Treasury.

Vernon, Raymond. 1998. *In the Hurricane's Eye.* Cambridge, MA: Harvard University Press.

Viherkentta, Timo. 1991. *Tax Incentives in Developing Countries and International Taxation.* Deventer, Netherlands: Kluwer Law and Taxation.

World Bank. 1994. *Tax Policy Handbook.* Washington, DC: World Bank.

7

Tax Incentives for Foreign Investment in Latin America and the Caribbean: Do They Need to Be Harmonized?

*Richard M. Bird**

> *The statesman, who should attempt to direct private people in what manner they ought to employ their capitals, would not only load himself with a most unnecessary attention, but assume an authority which could safely be trusted, not only to no single person, but to no council or senate whatever, and which would nowhere be so dangerous as in the hands of a man who had folly and presumption enough to fancy himself fit to exercise it.*
>
> —ADAM SMITH, *An Inquiry into the Nature and Causes of the Wealth of Nations*

N ot much has changed since Adam Smith wrote this in the eighteenth century. The case for letting capital markets do their job without interventions from governments remains as strong as the case for free trade. In the real world, however, protectionist policies and investment subsidies abound. The Latin America and Caribbean (LAC) region is no exception. For example, in 2004 Argentina established new tax incentives for investments in new capital assets used in industrial activities, as well as

*The author is grateful to Alberto Barreix and Duanjie Chen for helpful comments on an earlier draft of this chapter.

for investments in infrastructure projects (Messineo, 2005). Similarly, at the end of 2005 Ecuador was considering a new set of fiscal incentives for investments in various industrial activities (Deloitte, 2005).

Economists may be skeptical about the virtues of incentives for foreign investment, but they continue to exist in many LAC countries. An obvious question, therefore, is whether the region as a whole would be better off if such incentives were "harmonized." This question is not new. The context within which the issue of harmonizing incentives arises may have changed, but it is not clear that the appropriate answers have changed much. There remain considerable theoretical and empirical uncertainties about most of the key factors in the debate: whether and under what conditions tax incentives may succeed in attracting foreign investment; whether, if they do succeed in doing so, the benefits reaped are worth the costs incurred; whether interjurisdictional tax competition for such investment is beneficial or harmful; whether and how such competition should or can be effectively restrained; and, if so, how this might best be done.[1]

Given the continuing high degree of uncertainty about such key issues, a good working rule for policy economists would seem to be "first, do no harm." Prudence, not ideology or faith, should guide those devising fiscal incentive policies. As Messere (1999: 342) puts it, "tax policy is about trade-offs, not truths." The aim of this chapter is to sketch a framework within which countries can think about how such questions may be approached in a way that may both reduce the harm wrought by poor design and foster more judicious and reasoned consideration of the inevitable trade-offs facing tax policy designers.

The Rise and Fall and Rise of Tax Incentives

The history of investment incentives over the last 50 years may be viewed from two quite different perspectives.[2] From one standpoint, there has

---

[1] Blonigen (2005) provides a useful recent review of the empirical literature. For a comprehensive recent review of these questions in a regional developing-country context, see Bolnick (2004).

[2] Portions of this section are based on Bird and Chen (2000).

been a more or less steady trend away from the extensive reliance on incentives that characterized the initial development efforts in many countries in the 1950s and early 1960s (not least in Latin America). Instead, international experts now commonly recommend the nirvana of "incentive-free" tax systems, which a few countries, notably Indonesia, have actually put in place (see Gillis, 1985).[3] Similar, if less drastic, moves away from fiscal incentives were apparent in a number of Latin American countries in the 1970s and 1980s (Bird, 1992). Attitudes toward tax incentives by the end of the last century were markedly different than they had been in the early postwar period, when expert reports frequently favored tax incentives to channel investment in one desired direction or another (Goode, 1993). As skepticism grew with respect to both the efficacy of incentives and the wisdom of interventionist policies in general, attitudes changed and tax incentives fell into disfavor.

The palpable failure of central planning in Eastern Europe and elsewhere, the accumulated empirical evidence of the relative inefficiency and ineffectiveness of incentives, and the growth of economic knowledge all seemed to point in the same direction. The interventionist policy represented by incentives was replaced by the ideal of a uniform "level playing field" in which market forces rather than government officials made investment decisions.

Ideas about the role and efficacy of tax incentives thus changed markedly in the fourth quarter of the last century. The extent to which ideas influence policy, however, depends as much on chance and circumstance as on their inherent merit. The failed Soviet central planning dream was soon replaced in the minds of some by the "Asian miracle" dream of sensible, government-led interventionist policy. Although the Asian currency crisis at the end of the century dimmed the appeal of this model somewhat, new examples like the "Celtic tiger" (Ireland) continue to loom like mirages on the horizon, ever beckoning to those thirsting for

---

[3] For example, although the World Bank (1991) reluctantly recognized that tax concessions would continue to exist, its preference was clearly for a low-rate, broad-based system, with any incentives being limited in duration and distributed evenly across sectors and assets in order to avoid distorting investment decisions.

reasons to introduce fiscal incentives. Keen and Simone (2004) report not only that the variety of tax incentives currently found in developing countries is greater than that found in developed countries, but also that such incentives are more common in developing countries now than they were a decade ago.

The apparently sharp disparity between expert opinion and policy practice prompts several questions:

▪ First, are countries simply mistaken in thinking that tax incentives (and other policies fostering investment) have much to do with their growth success?

▪ Second, which tax policy works best to promote growth? Does the Hong Kong model of low and uniform taxes offer a surer path to success than the JKS (Japan-Korea-Singapore) model of fiscal (and other) interventionism? Some Asian analysts (such as Choi, 1997) have condemned the tax incentive approach and urged the adoption of a more neutral system. However, with the exception of Hong Kong, almost all the high-growth Asian countries have made extensive and prolonged use of specific tax (and other) incentives and continue to do so to some extent.[4] Of course, many other factors—such as macroeconomic stability, high and growing investment in human capital, and the market-driven (export) nature of growth—help explain the Asian success stories. Nonetheless, high investment levels clearly played a critical part (Young, 1993), and tax incentives appear to have played some role in achieving these levels.

▪ Third, why did incentives apparently fail in many Latin American countries although similar to the incentives employed in Asia? Were differences in political or social culture the reason?[5]

---

[4] For a recent study of Taiwan, for instance, see Jenkins, Kuo, and Sun (2003).

[5] Ishi (1993: 156), for example, suggests that sociocultural factors seem more likely than tax incentives to explain high savings rates in Japan. On the importance of institutions in determining tax levels and structures, see Bird, Martinez-Vazquez, and Torgler (2005).

Or differences in the institutional and macroeconomic context?[6] Or simply differences in the design and implementation of the incentives? For an example of the last point, consider a study of tax incentives in Belize a few years ago, which concluded that there were two major problems with the incentive package then in place:

> First, it is not and cannot be administered well for three re-lated reasons: (i) it is far too complex; (ii) it is completely non-transparent and non-standardized; and (iii) it is, in the end, completely discretionary. Second, and perhaps more easily remediable, it is replete with statutory loopholes that make it both a revenue "sink"—into which revenues flow but nothing necessarily comes out—and a potential revenue "bomb"—with the potential of devastating the normal rev-enue system in the long run. (Bird and Chen, 1997: 7)

Despite such strictures, not only does recent empirical work suggest that incentives in the right conditions may indeed increase investment flows (Zee, Stotsky, and Ley, 2002), but recent theoretical developments also cast a slightly more favorable light on incentives. The new emphasis in trade theory on imperfect markets and external economies, for exam-ple, reopens the case for selective government intervention in trade and factor markets. The real-world relevance of these ideas remains doubt-ful, however, because of the unclear importance in practice of external economies and the concern that governments may not be capable of implementing even beneficial interventions without opening the doors

---

[6] See, for example, Thirsk (1991) on the importance of sound exchange rate policy in determining the effectiveness of incentives. More broadly, as Bolnick (2004: 7–8) says, the countries usually cited as having relatively successful tax incentive policies "used tax incentives in conjunction with stable economic and political conditions, a well educated labor force, good infrastructure, open trade for exporters, dependable rule of law, and effective investment promotion systems." He concludes that "when these conditions are lacking, tax incentives are generally not sufficient to attract major flows of investment."

to dubious special interests and excessive rent seeking.[7] Such considerations are likely to be downplayed by special interest groups that stand to
gain from tax favors, but the exacting practical demands of implementing strategic trade theory make it an uncertain basis on which to advance
an argument for incentives.

Much the same may be said of the new literature on endogenous
growth. Incentives favoring research and development or machinery and
investment may, in certain circumstances, accelerate growth (Barro and
Sala-i-Martin, 1992). Moreover, there is some empirical support for this
proposition (Shah, 1995). Although increased growth may not always result in increased welfare, policymakers seeking a rationale for doing something they want to do have seldom worried about such refinements.

By the end of the century, therefore, incentives were again the flavor
of the month for some. The World Bank (1991) reflected the then-pre-
vailing conventional wisdom on tax incentives: they erode the tax base,
reduce investment efficiency (because they respond largely to pressure
from special interests), are ineffective and often inequitable, and facilitate rent seeking activities and tax evasion. Only a few years later, however, Shah (1995: 30) summarized an impressive set of empirical studies of
tax incentives carried out under World Bank auspices by noting, among
other things, that when it comes to foreign direct investment (FDI),
"once business confidence is restored and the credibility of the regime
is no longer in question, consideration can be given to well-targeted tax
policy interventions."

As the twenty-first century dawned, the incentive worm seemed to
have turned, at least to some extent. Tax experts still favored low-rate,
broad-based (LRBB) approaches to tax system design in general, but
tax incentives had again become relatively intellectually respectable. The

---

[7] As Krugman (1993: 364) puts it, echoing the passage from Smith quoted at the beginning of this chapter: "Free trade is a pretty good if not perfect policy, while an effort
to deviate from it in a sophisticated way will probably end up doing more harm than
good." See also Levy (1993) on the many political and organizational constraints that
make it unlikely that interventionist policies can be implemented effectively in most
developing countries.

new message was certainly heard by policymakers keen to attract more FDI. Tax holidays and other incentives remain an important feature of tax policy in many countries.

Why so many governments opt for incentives in the absence of any solid evidence that they produce economically meaningful results remains a puzzle to many economists. But perhaps it is not so puzzling. Policymakers are human. They are more influenced by concrete stories than by abstract and intuitively hard-to-follow facts.[8] One plausible story of a factory or head office "lost" to a rival, allegedly as a result of a better fiscal incentive package, often carries more weight than 15 refined analytical studies demonstrating that the net social effects of "winning" the investment in question are likely to be negligible or even negative. In the course of the last two centuries, economists have not managed to persuade most policymakers that unilateral free trade policy trumps protectionist interventionism. They should not be surprised at the continued strength of such arguments with respect to attracting foreign investment.

Policymakers in democracies are always driven to do something rather than nothing. A good way to appear to be doing something about providing jobs and encouraging growth is to offer incentives for such good things. In the 1960s, when Latin America was the major developing region in the foreign investment game, many LAC countries were ambivalent about foreign capital. Promised fiscal benefits were frequently accompanied by regulatory controls (such as on capital export) in order to make them more politically palatable. Now, however, when virtually every country in the world is in active competition for scarce FDI, incentive policies to encourage more FDI are more politically attractive—although, led by Venezuela's new oil-boosted self-confidence, this tide may again be turning in some LAC countries.

Moreover, a given incentive for FDI may actually be more effective now than in the past. With freer international trade regimes and freer

---

[8] The following summary of the political economy of incentives draws in part on Easson (2001) and Wells and Allen (2001).

international financial markets, fiscal differences now matter more. As Thirsk (1991) has noted, investment incentives are more likely to be effective in countries with lower variability in inflation, exchange rates, and growth rates. These conditions are now more prevalent in LAC than in the previous heyday of incentives in the 1960s. Tax incentives remain only one of many factors determining the magnitude of FDI in any country. Political stability, a favorable legal framework (trade policy, labor policy, and so on), and attractive economic conditions (including natural resources, infrastructure, domestic market, and the cost and quality of labor) are all probably more important. Nonetheless, when the nontax environment for investment is favorable, tax incentives undoubtedly add to a country's attractiveness. Although even the most generous incentives are unlikely to overcome a fundamentally unattractive environment, fiscal advantage clearly counts in attracting FDI in a competitive world.

In addition, in a noisy world, loud fiscal signals may be critical in attracting attention. In the European Union, for example, Ireland's tax policies sounded a very loud signal. They were clearly a factor in attracting investment and launching the country's impressive recent growth record (Haughton, 2002). In particular, the signaling effect of tax holidays in attracting investment has long been discussed in the theoretical literature (Bond and Samuelson, 1986), although most analysts (McLure, 1999) remain persuaded that any virtues that holidays may possess in this respect are outweighed by their myriad defects.

Finally, when bureaucratic and political interests coincide, policy is likely to move in the indicated direction. In a number of countries (Jamaica, for example), special agencies and bureaus have been established to foster and encourage foreign investment. Such agencies are judged by how successful they are in achieving their objectives. Understandably, they are eager to publicize the benefits resulting from their successes, and they have no incentive to mention any associated costs. As a rule, this behavior is made easy by the fact that no one monitors what actually happens. Politicians cheerfully report success in "creating" new jobs and opportunities, and officials readily take credit for doing so too. Unfortunately, it is in no one's interest to publicize, or even calculate, the costs of such "successes." This matter is discussed further in the section "Regional Economic Integration and Tax Incentives."

Taxes and Tax Incentives in Latin America and the Caribbean

Geographic location affects tax levels. Countries may follow their neighbors because they learn what possibilities exist in terms of services, or because tax levels in other countries provide political cover for tax rate increases. For example, taxes in Europe, which average nearly one-fourth of gross domestic product (GDP) (24.0 percent)—or a third of GDP (33.5 percent) if social insurance payments are included—are much higher than in other continents. In contrast, taxes in North America—an area Fox and Gurley (2005) define to include the Caribbean—average only 17.5 percent of GDP, and taxes in Latin America are even lower (averaging 16.3 percent), although not as low as taxes in Asia (14.7 percent).[9]

Over time, tax levels have crept up around the world. Tanzi (1987) reported that taxes were 17.8 percent of GDP for the 86 countries in his sample, which covered mainly developing countries in the early 1980s. For the 75 of his countries where overlapping data are available for the mid-1990s, the comparable percentage was 18.6 percent. Changes in tax burdens differ both by region of the world and by income level. While tax burdens have fallen in Asia, for example, the most pronounced increases have been in the Americas (both North and South), and Europe has also experienced a slight increase.

Taxes in general may have crept up a little in many Latin American countries over time, but in world terms, the region as a whole has relatively low corporate tax rates (Bird and Chen, 2000). On the other hand, it is not uncommon in Latin America to impose non-profit-related taxes on business (such as turnover tax and gross or net assets-based taxes). Except when such taxes are imposed as a minimum tax (as in Argentina,

---

[9] The figures reported here were calculated for 167 countries from IMF, World Bank, and OECD sources, and are simple averages for (generally) a six-year period in the mid-1990s.

Mexico, and Peru), usually they significantly increase the effective tax burden on capital investment. Similarly, some countries in the region (for example, Brazil, Chile, Mexico, and Peru) have mandatory employee profit sharing. Such plans are usually nondeductible for income tax purposes, and hence may significantly reduce net-of-tax profit and potentially discourage FDI. Both non-profit-based taxes and mandatory profit sharing are relatively uncommon in other regions. Moreover, property taxes, although not high in most LAC countries, are nonetheless higher than in most developing countries, and as a rule they fall particularly heavily on business property (Bird and Slack, 2004). Taxes on transfers of property are also relatively substantial in some countries of the region. Finally, payroll taxes (including social security contributions payable by the employer) are rather high in LAC compared with most developing countries. Particularly when imposed on total payroll without a ceiling, such taxes may be perceived as an obstacle to hiring more highly skilled workers, and hence may discourage potential foreign investment.

Despite these fiscal deterrents to FDI, Latin American countries on the whole appear to make less use of tax incentives than most developing countries. Most tax incentives in LAC focus on sectoral development (mining, agriculture) or on specific objectives such as exporting, tourism, or financial investments. That is, they appear to be instruments of what might be called industrial policy rather than growth-oriented development policy. The main tax incentives that encourage export and that are attractive to foreign investors are exemptions for transaction taxes levied on export-related inputs. Such incentives are generally applicable to free zones and assembly operations. A recent count, for example, found 29 countries in LAC with small free zones (less than 1,000 hectares), one country (Brazil) with a larger zone (encompassing some resident population), one (Mexico) with "performance-specific" zones (maquiladora) that may in principle be located anywhere, and four with "industry-specific" zones (mainly banking in some Caribbean countries).[10]

---

[10] This information is from the World Economic Processing Zones Association (www. wepza.org) as of January 19, 2006. See also Byrne (2003) for a description of tax incentives in the Southern Common Market (MERCOSUR).

Table 7.1. Effective Tax Rate on Direct Foreign Investment, 2000
(percent)

Case	Argentina	Brazil	Chile	Mexico	Peru
Manufacturing					
Regular taxable case	31.3	35.5	22.3/26.9	28.2	24.1
Impact of corporate income tax only	20.8	19.1	4.0/10.6	19.3	11.5
Effect of non-profit-based taxes	10.5	16.4	18.3/16.3	8.9	12.6
Tax relief from import duties	—	29.3	15.1/20.4	21.8	16.7
Free zones	—	22.3	12.0/17.0	21.8	0.9
Services					
Regular taxable case	38.8	39.1	28.0/31.8	29.2	24.5/29.2
Impact of corporate income tax only	22.7	17.1	2.6/9.4	17.6	6.9/13.7
Effect of non-profit-based taxes	16.1	22.0	15.4/22.4	11.6	17.6/15.5
Tax relief from import duties	—	—	—	—	—
Free zones	—	—	—	—	—

Source: Bird and Chen (2000).
Note: — = Data not available. When different rates apply to particular industries (such as tourism in Peru), two rates are shown in the relevant cells. See Bird and Chen (2000) for a full discussion of the meaning and limitations of the marginal effective tax rates reported in this table, which are calculated by aggregating all taxes (but not the mandatory profit-sharing plans) directly affecting the rate of return on capital earned by a typical investment project, and taking that figure as a proportion of the gross-of-tax rate of return on capital.

Table 7.1 reports some results from an illustrative study of the marginal effective tax rates (METRs) for five selected LAC countries. The basic case (row 1) shows that at the end of the century, Chile was the lowest-taxing country from a foreign investor's perspective when profits are not distributed, owing to the combination of its low statutory corporate income tax rate (15 percent) and a generous tax depreciation allowance for buildings. Chile's tax advantage deteriorates, however, when taxes on profit distribution are taken into account. In this case, Peru provided the most favorable tax system to foreign investors, particularly in tourism, since it had the second lowest statutory corporate income tax rate and the most generous tax depreciation allowance for machinery and equipment.[11]

Table 7.1 further shows that taxes other than the corporate income tax may also impinge strongly on investment. Taxes on asset values

---

[11] Favoritism to the tourism sector, of course, is by no means confined to Peru. It is especially important in a number of Caribbean countries (such as Jamaica).

(property taxes or gross receipts taxes) may constitute major charges on potential profits. Since value-added taxes on inputs are supposed to be refunded—though this mechanism does not always work as it should (Harrison and Krelove, 2005)—the main transaction taxes affecting effective tax rates are import duties levied on capital (and raw materials). Relief from such input taxes (especially import taxes) is almost a sine qua non for most foreign investors. As Table 7.1 (row 4) shows, except for Argentina, where no such incentives existed at the time of the study, the effective tax rate for the manufacturing industry in all countries was 5–6 percentage points lower as a result of exemptions of input taxes for exporting firms.

Row 5 in Table 7.1 goes further and simulates the METR imposed on FDI located in the free zones that flourish in much of the region. Such zones cover a range of possibilities, from bonded manufacturing warehouses to offshore financial centers and export-processing zones. In some countries (such as Honduras), these zones account for almost all FDI. Nontax incentives such as one-stop shopping, easier regulatory procedures, and subsidized infrastructure may also be important, but as a general rule, the distinguishing feature of such zones is their exemption not only from transaction taxes but also from various direct taxes through devices such as tax holidays and reduced tax rates. At the time of the study reported in Table 7.1, the additional tax incentives included a 40 percent income tax reduction in Brazil, a full income tax exemption in Chile, and a complete tax exemption for 15 years in Peru. As the table shows, the result was that the effective tax rate in free zones fell by between 3 and 16 percentage points compared to the general tax incentives for export promotion.

The main form of FDI initially attracted to free zones has generally been labor-intensive manufacturing—for example, textiles, garments, toys, and sporting goods. Subsequently, more consumer durable investment (appliances, automobile parts) may be attracted and, in the best of cases, as in some Asian countries, even the lower range of high-tech investment sectors such as electronics and precision engineering. A critical factor in such development, however, appears to be the availability of high levels of local skills as, for example, in Ireland, South Korea, and

Taiwan—all countries that have long invested heavily in educating their populations in the skills and knowledge needed to compete successfully in the modern world.

In the absence of such investment in human capital, even if the initial impact of FDI tends to raise employment and real wages, the inherently footloose assembly and low-tech industries attracted to these favored zones are likely to move on if an even lower-wage tax haven looms somewhere on the horizon. Mexico, for example, appears to have gained some industry for this reason, as countries like South Korea and Taiwan began to be priced out of the low-wage market. Countries using this approach to attracting FDI should pay much attention to forging links between zone activities and the development of their economies, and especially the knowledge and skills of their populations.[12] To develop a sustainable economic base over time, countries relying on tax-free zones to attract FDI need to spend more fiscal revenue on developing people and infrastructure. Unless the increased economic activity attracted by tax incentives results in increased fiscal revenue that is then directed to such growth-inducing activities, any initial favorable effect is unlikely to be large or sustained for long, as the most noted case in the region, Puerto Rico, suggests (Baumol and Wolff, 1996).

A few years ago, another study compared fiscal incentives in the mainly island countries of the Caribbean Community (CARICOM). Since all the countries included in the comparison are relatively small and all made extensive use of targeted tax incentives, this study complements the large-country (and relatively non–incentive intensive) analysis reported in Table 7.1.

---

[12] Mutti (2003) argues that the free-zone approach may be a useful way in which countries that cannot create a stable, rule-based tax system with a low marginal effective tax rate for all investment may at least be able to do so for some, by providing such conditions for a few lucky foreign investors. While perhaps superficially plausible, this argument is by no means persuasive, because reducing distortions for the few may not result in a net welfare gain for the many. Moreover, it is never a good idea to insulate from the ill effects of a bad system those who might carry considerable weight in changing it.

As an example, Table 7.2 shows that Belize (which is classified as a less developed country, or LDC, in CARICOM) has a somewhat more generous and less transparent version of the basic CARICOM LDC incentive package. For example, the main criteria for tax holidays under the general CARICOM harmonization scheme are export potential and local value added. Field observation in Belize suggested that much more emphasis was put on job creation and the total value of the investment, and, importantly, that the whole process was highly discretionary (Bird and Chen, 1997). Questions may be raised about criteria such as local value added, but they are surely both more relevant and easier to monitor than a criterion such as job creation in relation to capital

Table 7.2. Incentives in Central American and Caribbean Countries, 1995

Country	Corporate income tax rate (percent)[1]	Capital cost allowance[2]	Other incentives[3]	Years that loss carry-forward is permitted	Withholding tax rate (percent)[4]
Antigua	40.0	Yes	International base company	6	—
Barbados	40.0	Yes	Export	9	0–15
Belize	35.0	No	Yes	Indefinite	0
Costa Rica	30.0	No	Reinvest[5]	3–5	—
Dominican Republic	26.0	No	No	3	18
El Salvador	25.0	No	Export	0	—
Guatemala	34.0	No	Export	4	—
Guyana	35.0	Yes	Export	Indefinite	—
Honduras	35.0	No	Export	3	—
Jamaica	33.3	Yes	No	Indefinite	15.0–22.5
Panama	34.0	No	Export	3	5–15
St. Lucia	33.3	Yes	—	6	—
Trinidad and Tobago	45.0	Yes	—	Indefinite	15–20

Source: Boadway and Shah (1995).
Note: — = Data not available.
[1] Refers to the standard statutory corporate income tax rate in 1995.
[2] Indicates some form of accelerated depreciation, initial allowance, or investment allowance. Antigua has a 2 percent initial allowance on buildings; Barbados has a 4 percent initial allowance on industrial buildings; St. Lucia has a 20 percent initial allowance on industrial buildings and machinery; Guyana has a 70 percent investment allowance on equipment; and Jamaica has a 120 percent write-off of "market equipment cost" over time.
[3] Includes various special incentives for export industries. Some minor incentives for specific industries and locations are not indicated.
[4] Refers to the withholding tax rate on dividends paid to a treaty country. Rates often differ for royalties and interest, and rates are generally higher for all forms of payment to nonresidents in non-treaty countries.
[5] For Costa Rica, 50 percent of reinvested profits are deductible from income.

investment, for which there can be no standard across industries and regions.[13]

In other respects, too, the incentives in Belize departed from the general CARICOM package. For instance, the maximum duration of a tax holiday in other CARICOM countries is 15 years. In Belize, however, it was found that the period was as long as 25 years in law, and sometimes even longer in practice. More importantly, the duration of import-duty exemption in the CARICOM scheme is the same as that of the tax holiday. In Belize, however, these two incentives could be applied separately, which obviously complicates the application and approval process and increases administration and compliance costs. Another difference observed was that although the duration for carrying forward tax losses after the tax holiday in other CARICOM countries is limited to five years, it could be indefinite in Belize.[14] Finally, in contrast to the explicit provision on depreciation allowances in the CARICOM package, there were no specific investment-related incentives in Belize.[15] All in all, the existing system of incentives in Belize not only is on the generous side but suggests that the CARICOM incentive package has not provided a very firm guiding hand to local policymakers.

Of course, generous fiscal incentives have often been used elsewhere in the region. In Guatemala, for example, until recently, a wide and varied set of tax incentives was available for many investors, including investment allowances (deduction of more than 100 percent of cost of assets), 8- to 10-year tax holidays for up to 90 percent of profits, duty

---

[13] Local value added can be easily defined and measured as ex-factory sales minus the purchase of factor services from nonresident sources.

[14] In Belize, losses may be carried forward "as long as the trade, business, profession or vocation is carried on by the person who incurred the loss" (Laws of Belize, Chapter 46, Income Tax, Part I, Art.15). In contrast, the shorter carry-forward period normally more prevalent in countries that generally have shorter holiday periods is presumably intended simply to provide for hardship cases in which it may take a year or two of full operation before potentially taxable profits are realized. (Some other CARICOM countries also permit indefinite loss carry-forward.)

[15] An indefinite loss carry-forward provision will eventually allow the full write-off of all capital costs incurred during the holiday period, but this is not the same as an incentive geared specifically to capital outlays such as an initial or investment allowance.

exemptions, special exemptions for free trade zones, and a range of benefits for exporting firms. Although a 1993 tax reform eliminated most of these incentives—except those for exports—it left in force benefits already granted and introduced a new deduction for reinvested profits of up to 25 percent of taxable income (Bahl, Martinez-Vazquez, and Wallace, 1996).

Similarly, Jamaica has had a regime of tax holidays and other incentives since at least 1944, although its current system (set out in Table 7.2) largely reflects that permitted by the CARICOM agreement of 1974. Apart from a proliferation of minor incentives, the most important subsequent change occurred in 1981, when, under the auspices of the Jamaica National Investment Promotion agency, a more transparent and objective system was adopted for determining eligibility and the duration and amount of any benefits granted. Thirsk (1991: 722) concluded that although the incentives may not have been very effective in generating significant new investment per dollar of revenue forgone in the past, on the whole "Jamaica seems to have struck a reasonable balance between rules and discretion in its incentive program." However, a more recent study (Rider, 2004) is considerably less sanguine, noting among other things the extent to which various concessions appeared to be granted on a discretionary basis and the significant revenue loss apparently attributable to Jamaica's tax incentive schemes.

Tax Competition: Is It Good or Bad?

As global corporate tax rates decline, the debate on fiscal competition for foreign capital has heated up both in the theoretical literature and in practice. This debate raises several questions. Does tax competition help countries attract FDI? Is tax competition harmful to the regional or global economy? What would an efficient and competitive tax structure look like? And, finally, as discussed in the next section, how should this issue be handled in the context of regional economic integration?

A survey of interstate tax competition in the United States found that taxes have a small but statistically significant effect on interregional location behavior (Wasylenko, 1997). The effect of taxes depends not only on the tax elasticity of capital allocation but also on the extent to which one jurisdiction's overall tax levels are significantly different from the average of the jurisdictions it competes against. A large deviation from the average tax level, multiplied by the tax elasticity, will yield a large location, employment, or investment effect. Several studies have found similar results in the international sphere, with capital tending increasingly to flow to tax-favored areas.[16] This finding seems relevant in Latin America, given the variation in effective tax rates discussed earlier. Indeed, Mutti (2003) suggests that the more marked decline in both the level and the dispersion of effective tax rates in LAC compared to other regions suggests that tax competition may be particularly intense in the region. Tax factors may definitely affect a country's attractiveness to foreign investment, and hence in all likelihood its growth rate.

In 1998 the OECD published an attack on what it called "harmful tax competition" (OECD, 1998). This initial report was not well received by the OECD's Business and Industry Advisory Committee (BIAC). The latter argued that international tax competition is generally a healthy phenomenon from the viewpoints of both government and business (BIAC, 1999). These conflicting views illustrate the very different ways in which the issue of tax competition, whether within or between states, may be viewed.[17]

Often, tax competition has been attacked as wasteful and distorting, leading to such presumably undesirable outcomes as "tax jungles" that impose high compliance costs on society and spur "races to the bottom," as competing jurisdictions continually lower tax rates in an effort to retain their tax base. Less frequently, fiscal competition between jurisdictions has been said to provide both a useful check on the propensity of governments to expand and a stimulus to more efficient use of scarce fiscal resources. Despite the fervor with which proponents of both "harmful" and "beneficial" intergovernmental competition often state their positions, in reality—and as underlined in a magisterial recent review by Wilson and

---

[16] For a recent example, see Benassy-Quere, Fontagne, and Lahreche-Revil (2003).

[17] For a classic example of these two views, see the debate in Buchanan and Musgrave (1999).

Wildasin (2004)—neither the theoretical nor the empirical literature on this issue is conducive to such certainty.[18] Neither extreme position—that all intergovernmental competition is bad or that all intergovernmental competition is good—dominates. Assessing the argument depends on a variety of factors that need to be specified carefully with respect to each setting in which the question is considered.

Whatever philosophers may argue, some degree of fiscal competition seems an inevitable fact of life. The question, then, is whether there is a tax structure that can improve a country's competitiveness in a manner consistent with nonpredatory behavior. As noted earlier, there are broadly two fiscal approaches to attracting FDI. One is to apply standardized tax provisions to all investors, combined with low tax rates—the LRBB approach. The other is to tax various investment activities differently so as to achieve targeted goals such as sectoral development or export promotion. Although the second approach may attract foreign investment in the short run, particularly at an early stage of opening up an economy to the world, on the whole it seems likely that the first approach is more conducive to sustainable FDI inflow in the long term and hence may be more suitable for the relatively more developed economies of Latin America. Nonetheless, since neither the region as a whole nor any one country stands alone in the world, tax competition would still remain a matter of concern even if there were no such competition within the region.

Empirical studies at the subnational level in the United States provide conflicting evidence on the extent to which differential state-local tax regimes affect competitive behavior, as well as on the effectiveness of specific subnational tax incentives. A balanced survey of this literature plausibly concludes that "studies exist to buttress almost any case about tax incentives" (Wasylenko, 1996). Much the same can be said in the international sphere. This confusing literature suggests few firm conclusions. One conclusion that emerges fairly clearly, however, is that fiscal competitiveness is more likely to affect location choices within smaller areas than within larger areas. CARICOM thus seems correct in placing the need for a

---

[18] See also the recent discussion by Afonso, Ferreira, and Varsano (2003).

clearer "regional" policy on tax incentives near the top of its "To Do" list (Caribbean Community Secretariat, 2004). But it is far from clear that an even more detailed "regulatory" approach will be any better than the earlier attempts discussed previously in "Taxes and Tax Incentives in Latin America and the Caribbean." The next section suggests a quite different approach to "harmonizing" regional tax incentives.

Regional Economic Integration and Tax Incentives

Tax incentives for FDI have a long history in LAC. Many countries in the region have adopted a variety of fiscal incentives to encourage foreign investment. An important concern in most of the earlier attempts at regional economic integration—not just CARICOM but also the Central American Common Market (CACM), the Latin American Free Trade Association (LAFTA), the Andean Community, and MERCOSUR—was to institute some way of coping with what was perceived to be the wasteful fiscal competition for foreign investment by countries in the different groupings.[19] None of these attempts was particularly successful, however, and toward the end of the last century, some countries unilaterally replaced many incentives with a combination of lower-rate (and often broader-based) taxes and the removal of some of the nontax barriers to foreign investors that had continued to exist throughout the tax incentive era.

Nonetheless, tax incentives remain problematic in the region for a number of reasons, good and bad, and a new literature on what to do and how to do it is beginning to emerge (see, for example, Byrne, 2003; Caribbean Community Secretariat, 2004; IDB, 2004; Peters, 2002; Pita, 2003; Villela and Barreix, 2002; and Villela, Barreix, and Taccone, 2003). Taxes and tax incentives, of course, are only one factor affecting FDI inflows. A country that scores high enough in terms of nontax factors may attract foreign investors even though it has higher taxes and fewer tax incentives than most of its competitors. Most LAC countries, however, are not so fortunately situated, and thus are likely to continue to resort

---

[19] For an early study along these lines, see Watkin (1967).

to favorable tax treatment for potential investors. How can regional economic integration deal with such pressures?

Three main questions are often raised in this respect. Is regional coordination of incentives an essential part of leveling the playing field? If so, how can such coordination be effectively achieved? What are the minimal rules of the game for a workable economic union? This approach to the issue essentially assumes that the way forward is first to set out what should be done and then to consider how it can be done. Arguments along these lines often proceed by looking around the world for an example where the procedures deemed most desirable may be found and suggesting that the region should emulate that model—for example, by copying some of the procedures and institutions of the EU.

A quite different approach to the question of harmonizing regional tax incentives for FDI also deserves consideration. In this approach, the core issue relates to the extent to which countries can both adopt the fiscal systems they think best for their purposes and at the same time foster rather than fragment regional economic cooperation. In other words, in the terms used in the EU, "subsidiarity" (avoiding unnecessary intrusions on national sovereignty) rather than "uniformity" (which is how harmonization is often understood in these debates) should be the first concern. Approaching the issue in this way seems especially appropriate in a region like LAC, where thus far it has proven very difficult to build regional economic groupings that are both significant and sustainable.

Viewed from this perspective, the order of the three questions listed above is wrong. Both the sad history of attempts to establish effective regional agreements on incentives and the lack of any credible enforcement mechanism suggest that the key principle to keep in mind is the one implicit in the last question: what are the *minimal* rules of the game for a viable economic union (of whatever depth or degree desired)? Such minimal rules would seem to have two components. First, they would interfere as little as possible with national fiscal sovereignty. Second, in achieving this aim, transparency should substitute for overarching regional institutions whenever possible.

To illustrate, a common external tariff may or may not be an essential element of a regional union. There are also many nontariff ways in which countries may impose barriers to trade. Does this mean that all such barriers should be listed and all member countries prescriptively barred from using them? Must the equivalent of a unionwide regulatory authority be set up to police compliance with these rules? Must countries that are found to be in breach of the rules be brought to some union court so that proper punishment can be imposed? Some would answer yes to all these questions, as the EU has done to a considerable extent. Alternatively, however, it is possible to rely not on the creation of sufficiently formidable community institutions with the force of law behind them, but rather on the force of public opinion informed by transparent, comparable, and credible information. This alternative approach to dealing with incentive issues may seem to be both incredibly naïve in conception and probably ineffective in practice. The argument here, however, is that not only is it more sophisticated in conception than the usual command-and-control approach, but it may perhaps prove to be more effective in practice in the circumstances that seem to prevail in much of LAC.

The underlying idea is simply that the key to productive governmental competition, whether within or between countries, is to make the relevant decision makers as fully and publicly accountable for their decisions as possible. In turn, the key to effective accountability is to set out the rules clearly and to make relevant comparative information publicly available. The ultimate mechanism driving "good" intergovernmental competition is citizens' ability to do two things: (1) compare governments in terms of the services they provide and the tax prices they charge and (2) affect and alter government decisions (Breton, 1996).

Democracy without good information, of course, is not enough to ensure that intergovernmental competition will be beneficial rather than harmful, nor is information without democracy sufficient for success. Much of the recent decentralization in Latin America, for example, has been closely associated with the revival of democratic institutions throughout most of the region (IDB, 1997). But too little attention has so far been paid to the need for good information systems in order to ensure that this democracy is exercised in a responsive and responsible way (Bird, 1999). Transparency is critical in ensuring that the ultimate outcome of any fiscal incentives is socially beneficial.

The idea, therefore, is simply to establish some simple, clear, and transparent rules of the incentive game. The most important rule would ban secret deals between governments and also between governments and investors. The basic enforcement mechanism would be through public accountability of the sort outlined above. To illustrate, an important way to understand the OECD's recent initiative on harmful competition is precisely along these lines.[20] The usual command-and-control approach to incentive harmonization essentially assumes that since experts can draw the "correct" line, what needs to be done is to embody such expert opinion in union law and establish a credible enforcement mechanism. In reality, however, it is hard a priori and from outside to say what is "harmful," or how much harm a particular action might cause and to whom. Moreover, if countries choose to harm themselves by adopting bad policies, then that is their right. Finally, the credibility of regional enforcement in any LAC grouping seems unlikely to be great. In these circumstances, it is critical to ensure that any harm a country's policies may do to others is made as clear as possible.

Instead of attempting to define in advance the nature of the regional problems that may arise from tax incentives, a better approach might be simply to secure agreement that every country will lay out clearly what it is doing in terms of FDI incentives, so that all other interested parties (the member governments and their publics) can appraise, criticize, and react as they see fit. Of course, if all member states agree in advance that some particular practices (tax holidays, for example) are always and everywhere to be prohibited, so be it. Such cases, however, are likely to be the exception, and a long list of prescriptive rules should not be the norm. If the members of a regional union have so little trust in their fellow members and their own people that tackling problems through public disclosure and reasoned discussion seems ridiculously naïve, then the future of the union and the democratic status of its member states are probably precarious in any case.

---

[20] Daly (1999) offers a similar interpretation of the WTO's concern with certain aspects of members' tax policy in connection with the WTO's Trade Policy Review Mechanism.

An important first step toward making tax incentives transparent is to keep them simple. Complex provisions that seek to fine-tune incentives in order to achieve detailed policy goals are likely to be costly to administer and unlikely to produce the desired results at a reasonable cost. Moreover, few countries have sufficient information to design narrowly focused incentives well. Even fewer are capable of implementing them. If there are to be any tax incentives, it is in a country's own interest that they be few in number and as simple as possible in structure. Tax holidays, for example, give rise to serious tax compliance problems, since they create what are in effect onshore tax havens (McLure, 1999). Nonetheless, in principle—if almost never in practice—in some respects, tax holidays may be easier to monitor than more sensible investment incentives, and thus may be more transparent. Whether this argument is accepted or not, there seems no reason to bar (or prescribe) any particular form of incentives in a regional union. What *is* essential, however, is that the fiscal benefits bestowed (the "subsidy-equivalent") and the estimated associated costs of all specific FDI incentives granted by any member should be as fully, accurately, and publicly reported as possible.

To ensure transparency and accountability, good records are needed. Who gets what incentives? For how long? At what estimated cost in revenue forgone?[21] Problems will inevitably arise in gathering and interpreting such information. In its absence, however, fiscal incentives are likely to be, at best, a costly means of advertising for investment, and, at worst, a way of rewarding those considered politically worthy of receiving such favors. Of course, such considerations are really the concern mainly of the country in question. From a regional perspective, the problem is not to stop countries from hurting themselves but to prevent them from hurting each other. A regional union, therefore, should specify precisely what information is to be obtained, when, in what form, and to whom

---

[21] Presumably, the citizens of the country in question would also want some information on the benefits (jobs, investment) as well as the cost of incentives. Since it is only the costs that are relevant in the union context, however, the appropriate model is tax expenditure analysis, not cost-benefit analysis.

that information is to be provided. Equally importantly, it should also provide for regular publication of credible, comparative information on who has given what concessions to whom, for how much, for how long, and under what conditions. If a prospective member state of a union is unwilling to meet this minimal transparency criterion, either it should not join or a meaningful union is unlikely to emerge.

Successful compliance with these apparently simple rules is not easy. Most incentives in most jurisdictions are marked by complex legislation, poor implementation, and complete lack of accountability. This reflects political and institutional factors that are unlikely to be changed easily or soon in many countries. In the absence of transparent and objective rules, however, discretionary and opaque systems of fiscal incentives are unlikely to be optimal from any point of view. Since it is not in the direct interest of either politicians or officials involved in investment promotion to provide such information, they will not easily agree to comply with any regional transparency agreement. But in the absence of such an agreement, bad incentives will continue to be put in place in response to the cost-benefit calculus of local politicians. If any brave new note of self-restraint in granting incentives is sounded during the euphoric phase of creating a new regional grouping, it will soon be muted.

Even if fiscal incentives are well designed and well administered, experience suggests that they are seldom effective and often surprisingly costly in terms of undermining the creation and operation of an effective, modern business tax system. In principle, more or less the same degree of stimulus to investment (whether foreign or domestic) may be attained through simpler measures that focus on strengthening, simplifying, and stabilizing the basic tax system.[22] Countries within a regional union may thus reasonably choose to follow alternative incentive strategies.

---

[22] Blomstrom and Kokko (2003) suggest that it is not sensible to limit investment subsidies to FDI, because if externalities warrant such subsidies, then limiting them in this way simply limits the welfare gain. Perhaps more importantly, even leaving aside WTO and other possible legal constraints, it makes little sense in any case to distinguish between foreign and other investment, in part because of the practical impossibility of determining which investors are really "foreign."

They may, for example, follow the model of Hong Kong and Ireland by cutting the corporate tax rate. While obviously simple, and likely to be seen as a strong sign that a country is "open for business," such a policy may be costly in revenue terms and provide a weaker stimulus to investment than other alternatives. But that is the country's problem. There seems to be no reason for regional economic unions to attempt to dictate country tax rates. The global market has pushed capital tax rates down already and is likely to continue to do so. Countries that want to tax capital more than the regional norm can certainly do so if they are willing to bear whatever consequences ensue.

Similarly, if a country chooses not to tax capital or to tax it very lightly—to become, in effect, a regional tax haven—it is not clear why, if, or how it should be prohibited from doing so. The EU has not managed to agree on a uniform corporate tax rate after 40 years, and it is not obvious that it will or should do so, despite the continuing push from countries with relatively high taxes on capital (Eggert and Genser, forthcoming). Indeed, as Desai, Foley, and Hines (2004) have recently argued, regions as a whole may actually gain from permitting such havens, which, the authors demonstrate, seem to attract some net economic gains to non-haven countries in the region. Although this result may not withstand further analysis, it is perhaps intuitively plausible as long as there are some non-haven countries outside the region.

Alternatively, or as a complementary policy, from the perspective of any single country, import duties and other forms of indirect taxes that raise capital costs should be reduced or eliminated. The introduction of the value-added tax (VAT), of course, has already moved most Latin American countries well along this path, as has the generalized reduction of import tariffs. Nonetheless, confining the elimination of all input import taxes to firms operating in free zones, as is currently the rule in some countries, is neither a wise nor a necessary policy. Some such countries may jeopardize significant revenue if they follow the economically sensible path. The *regional* question, however, is simply whether countries in a regional economic union should be required to adopt similar policies in this and other indirect tax matters. Again, the answer appears to be no.

The EU mandated a uniform VAT structure for two reasons: first, to prevent countries from providing hidden subsidies to exports by over-re-funding input taxes; and second, to serve as a basis for financing community functions. Although the first of these arguments may be somewhat relevant in some LAC contexts (in MERCOSUR, for example), it is based on the mercantilist perspective that it is somehow bad for a country if its trading partners choose to provide it with subsidized goods. Making such bad economics mandatory does not seem a good idea. The second argument also seems unlikely to carry much weight, since it is presumably inconceivable that any realistic union in LAC would want to set up anything like the EU's expensive bureaucracy and agricultural policy. More recently, the EU has attempted to impose a range of acceptable VAT rates in order to discourage tax-based, cross-border shopping and thus protect the revenues of some relatively high-tax member states. Again, the relevance of such concerns in LAC seems remote.

Finally, should countries that choose to retain or establish direct tax incentives, even bad ones, be prevented from doing so? From the view-point of effectiveness, in principle fiscal incentives for investment should take some form such as full or partial expensing of new capital invest-ment (that is, an initial write-off of 100 percent or some smaller fraction of the cost of depreciable capital). The rationale for this approach is well established in the literature (McLure, 1999). Such a system would (1) be relatively easy to administer, (2) remove all (or much) of the tax deterrent to such investment, and (3) provide more stimulus to invest-ment per dollar of revenue forgone than either tax holidays or general reductions of corporate tax rates.

Nonetheless, this approach, too, may prompt questions, because of its relative favoritism to capital-intensive investment and the greater burden it imposes on the administration of the corporate income tax. Moreover, such an incentive may not benefit new firms that often incur operating losses and hence cannot use such tax allowances in their early years. Countries that want to entice new firms to bring in capital-inten-sive business may therefore find a reasonable investment tax credit to be a better choice. And of course some countries may find the superficial simplicity and signaling value of the traditional tax holiday approach attractive. Does any of this matter for the effective functioning of a union? Basically, as long as whatever is done is done sufficiently transparently and openly, it probably does not.

As mentioned earlier, the underlying argument for relying on transparency to solve any problems that may arise from the competitive use of tax incentives in regional economic unions may be simple, but it is not naïve. It has three components. First, it assumes that countries entering an economic union must trust each other to some extent. If they do not, then presumably they should not unite. Countries cannot sit at the negotiating table if they are unprepared to extend even minimal trust to their partners.

Second, even minimal trust, especially among neighbors, must be earned by performance and reciprocated if it is to endure. It is therefore critical to set up the rules of the game in a union, not so much to achieve the famed level playing field (something that the disparities inherent in the real world suggest will never exist in any significant sense, in the absence of a substantial and improbable regional equalization system), but rather to ensure that every country knows that it is obliged to comply with the rules when it uses tax incentives that may affect the interests of other members.[23] Achieving this aim requires meaningful transparency, which in turn requires regular, current, public, and standardized reporting. If countries do not comply with this requirement or are caught cheating, presumably they have breached trust and should be expelled. If the other members are unwilling to expel them, the union may continue to exist, but it will have little real substance.

Third, apart from this (forced) "exit" option—and of course the many opportunities for "voice" afforded by regular meetings and the work of whatever secretariat is established—there seems to be no need either for a formal, regional approval process for fiscal incentives or for detailed regional rules on precisely what is permitted. Some regional groupings may choose, as CARICOM did, to establish a uniform pat-

---

[23] All members, of course, as seems depressingly common in such matters, may agree to conceive and implement policies in ways that make little economic sense, but that, like everything else, is their choice.

tern of accepted incentives—although it is not obvious why any such future regional body would prove much more effective than CARICOM at monitoring, let alone enforcing, compliance. Other unions may, like the EU, choose to go further and establish both regulatory policies over subsidies and substantial compliance and enforcement policies to back them up. Neither of these approaches, however, seems logically necessary. Moreover, both seem likely to provoke so much prior discussion and so many negotiating games as to delay rather than foster effective moves toward regional integration in LAC.

Conclusion

Countries that want to prosper in today's world may have to do many things differently than they did in the past. One such thing may be to enter more seriously into regional economic unions of various sorts. Another may be to take more seriously the international aspects of taxation and tax incentives. In any case, many countries would be well advised to do the latter in their own interests. But if the prospect of entering an economic union spurs them to concentrate collectively and individually in this respect, that would be a beneficial outcome of the integration movement. The final outcome, however, is unlikely to be full harmonization (in the sense of uniformity) of incentives, nor should it be.

The key to successful regional integration is not to eliminate national borders, and with them fiscal sovereignty and the right of countries to do foolish things. Rather, it is to open borders to the free flow of (among other things) information on what exactly each country is doing that may affect the perceived interests of others, and to provide as objective and factual a basis as possible for rational discussion within the union on what countries can and cannot do while still remaining members. The critical task facing the policy designer is not to prescribe from the outset precisely what people or countries should do, but rather to establish *processes* that will facilitate and encourage reasoned and informed discussion through which those involved can decide their own fate.

What does this approach suggest a country should do when it faces, as it will, some high-profile firm "shopping" for fiscal benefits as it decides where to locate its regional base? The answer is simply that it should do whatever it wants to do—*provided that* it is ready to display to its own people and its neighbors the full nature of any deal it reaches, assessed in accordance with a regionally agreed-upon methodology. If a country is unwilling to do this, it should not make the deal. And if a company is unwilling to accept these terms, is the deal really likely to be worthwhile?

The best way to attract FDI, as has always been the case, is (1) to provide a favorable nontax environment; (2) to establish a solid LRBB tax system that provides stability to investors and a fair share to nationals; (3) to lower and simplify the hoops through which prospective foreign investors are expected to jump; and (4) only then, and only when there is a demonstrable (and demonstrated) net national payoff and no breach of regional norms, to provide such additional tax incentives to investors as the government thinks desirable. Incentives will be most effective only when the first three conditions are met. Unfortunately, it is precisely countries in which these conditions are not met that are most likely to resort to incentives. Most tax incentives thus make little sense.[24] But what matters from a regional perspective is less the details of what is done than the way in which it is done. If the right procedures are instituted, then whatever is done will be about as "right" as it can be. Prescribe in detail the optimal incentive regime, and in the absence of the right procedures, the prescription is meaningless.

Those concerned with furthering regional integration in LAC are right to be concerned about fiscal incentives. But the focus of this concern should not be to prescribe what particular forms of incentives are right or acceptable. Instead, the key point is to accomplish two tasks. The first is technical: to establish a sensible, practical, and accepted methodology for assessing the extent of the investment subsidy extended through incentives. The second and more important task is institutional:

---

[24] In a recent study of tax incentives in a regional context, Bolnick (2004: xiv) suggests that "since most tax incentive programs, worldwide, have not been very successful, it is very likely that cooperation to mitigate harmful tax competition can benefit SADC [Southern African Development Community] states." Education is to be supported, and no doubt discussing these issues in a regional forum may educate some, but regional integration is not about stopping countries from harming themselves.

to establish the national and regional institutional structures needed to carry out such multilaterally determined, rule-based assessments in a prompt, timely, and reliable fashion, and to ensure that all members of the union are fully informed about what all other members are doing. If prospective member states do not trust each other to operate in such an open and transparent way, then doubts arise as to whether a union will long flourish, regardless of how detailed and prescriptive its initial charter may be with respect to fiscal incentives.

References

Afonso, Jose Roberto, Sergio Guimaraes Ferreira, and Ricardo Varsano. 2003. "Fiscal Competition." In *Federalism in a Changing World*, ed. Raoul Blindenbacher and Arnold Koller. Montreal: McGill–Queen's University Press.

Bahl, Roy, Jorge Martinez-Vazquez, and Sally Wallace. 1996. *The Guatemalan Tax Reform*. Boulder, CO: Westview Press.

Barro, Robert J., and Xavier Sala-i-Martin. 1992. "Public Finance in Models of Economic Growth." *Review of Economic Studies* 59(4):645–61.

Baumol, William J., and Edward N. Wolff. 1996. "Catching Up in the Postwar Period: Puerto Rico as the Fifth 'Tiger.'" *World Development* 24(5):869–85.

Benassy-Quere, Agnes, Lionel Fontagne, and Amina Lahreche-Revil. 2003. "Tax Competition and Foreign Direct Investment." Working Paper 2003-17. Paris: Centre d'Études Prospectives et d'Informations Internationales.

BIAC (Business and Industry Advisory Committee to the OECD). 1999. "A Business View on Tax Competition." *Tax Notes International* 19(June):281–87. Also available at http://www.biac.org/statements/tax/htc.pdf.

Bird, Richard M. 1992. "Tax Reform in Latin America: A Review of Some Recent Experiences." *Latin American Research Review* 27(1):7–34.

———. 1999. "Fiscal Decentralization and Governmental Competition." In *Competition and Structure: Essays in Honor of Albert Breton*, ed. Gianluigi Galeotti, Pierre Salmon, and Ronald Wintrobe. Cambridge: Cambridge University Press.

Bird, Richard M., and Duanjie Chen. 1997. "Fiscal Incentives in Belize: An Evaluation." Unpublished report. World Bank, Latin America and Caribbean Region, Washington, DC.

———. 2000. "Tax Incentives for Foreign Investment in Latin America." In *XII Seminario de Política Fiscal, Compendio de Documentos 2000*. Santiago: Economic Commission for Latin America and the Caribbean.

Bird, Richard M., Jorge Martinez-Vazquez, and Benno Torgler. 2005. "Tax Performance in Developing Countries: The Role of Demand Factors." In *Proceedings of the 97th Annual Conference on Taxation*, ed. Laura Kalambokidis. Washington, DC: National Tax Association.

Bird, Richard M., and Enid Slack. 2004. *International Handbook of Land and Property Taxation*. Cheltenham, U.K., and Northampton, MA: Elgar.

Blomstrom, Magnus, and Ari Kokko. 2003. "The Economics of Foreign Direct Investment Incentives." Working Paper 168. Stockholm: European Institute of Japanese Studies.

Blonigen, Bruce A. 2005. "A Review of the Empirical Literature on FDI Determinants." NBER Working Paper 11299. Cambridge, MA: National Bureau of Economic Research.

Boadway, Robin W., and Anwar Shah. 1995. "Perspectives on the Role of Investment Incentives in Developing Countries." In *Fiscal Incentives for Investment in Developing Countries*, ed. Anwar Shah. New York: Oxford University Press.

Bolnick, Bruce. 2004. *Effectiveness and Economic Impact of Tax Incentives in the SADC Region*. Technical Report submitted by Nathan-MSI Group to USAID/RCSA SADC Tax Subcommittee, SADC Trade, Industry, Finance and Investment Directorate. Washington, DC: U.S. Agency for International Development.

Bond, Eric W., and Larry Samuelson. 1986. "Tax Holidays as Signals." *American Economic Review* 76(4):820–26.

Breton, Albert. 1996. *Competitive Governments*. Cambridge: Cambridge University Press.

Buchanan, James M., and Richard A. Musgrave. 1999. *Public Finance and Public Choice*. Cambridge, MA: MIT Press.

Byrne, Peter D. 2003. "Regímenes tributarias especiales en la región MERCOSUR: Implicancias de políticas tributarias y de comercio para la integración regional." Paper prepared for the Inter-American Development Bank, Integration and Regional Programs Department, Washington, DC. Available at http://www.iadb.org/INT/Trade/1_english/2_WhatWeDo/Documents/

d_TaxDocs/2002-2003/y_Regimenes%20Tributarios%20Espec
iales%20Mercosur.pdf.

Caribbean Community Secretariat, Economic Intelligence and Policy
Unit. 2004. "Proposals on Investment Policy Harmonisation
and Coordination in the Caribbean Community." Unpublished
paper submitted to Ninth Meeting of the Council for Finance
and Planning, Basseterre, St. Kitts and Nevis, March 24.

Choi, Kwang. 1997. "Tax Policy and Tax Reforms in Korea." In *Tax Reform
in Developing Countries*, ed. Wayne Thirsk. Washington, DC: World
Bank.

Daly, Michael. 1999. "Some Taxing Issues for the World Trade Organization: From the Standpoint of the Trade Policy Review
Mechanism." Paper presented at Conference on the Future
of Tax Reform, Adam Smith Institute, London, December
8–10.

Deloitte. 2005. *Latin America Tax Forum 2005*. Available at http://www.deloitte.
com/dtt/cda/doc/content/la_tax_taxforum_Fall05_171005.pdf .

Desai, Mihir A., C. Fritz Foley, and James R. Hines, Jr. 2004. "Economic
Effects of Regional Tax Havens." NBER Working Paper 10806.
Cambridge, MA: National Bureau of Economic Research.

Easson, Alex. 2001. "Tax Incentives for Foreign Direct Investment."
Bulletin for International Fiscal Documentation 55(7):266–74 and
55(8):365–75.

Eggert, Wolfgang, and Bernd Genser. Forthcoming. "Corporate Tax
Harmonization in the EU: Status and Perspectives." In *Essays in
Honor of Theodore Georgakopoulos.*

Fox, William, and Tami Gurley. 2005. "An Exploration of Tax Patterns
around the World." *Tax Notes International* 37(9):793–808.

Gillis, Malcolm. 1985. "Microeconomics and Macroeconomics of Tax Reform:
Indonesia." *Journal of Development Economics* 19(3):221–54.

Goode, Richard. 1993. "Tax Advice to Developing Countries: An Historical
Survey." *World Development* 21(1):37–53.

Harrison, Graham, and Russell Krelove. 2005. "VAT Refunds: A Review
of Country Experience." Working Paper 05/218. Washington,
DC: International Monetary Fund.

Haughton, Jonathan. 2002. "Trade Agreements and Tax Incentives: The Irish Experience." ITD-INTAL Tax and Integration Series. Washington, DC: Inter-American Development Bank.

IDB (Inter-American Development Bank). 1997. *Fiscal Decentralization in Latin America*. Washington, DC: IDB.

———. 2004. "Integration and Trade in the Americas: Fiscal Impact of Trade Liberalization in the Americas." Periodic Note, Integration and Regional Programs Department, January. Washington, DC: IDB.

Ishi, Hiromitsu. 1993. *The Japanese Tax System*. London: Oxford University Press.

Jenkins, Glenn, Chun-Yu Kuo, and Keh-Nan Sun. 2003. *Taxation and Economic Development in Taiwan*. Cambridge, MA: Kennedy School of Government of Harvard University and Chung-Hua Institution for Economic Research.

Keen, Michael, and Alejandro Simone. 2004. "Is Tax Competition Harming Developing Countries More Than Developed?" *Tax Notes International* [Special Supplement] 34(13):1317–26.

Krugman, Paul. 1993. "The Narrow and Broad Arguments for Free Trade." *American Economic Review, Papers and Proceedings* 83(2):362–66.

Levy, Brian. 1993. "An Institutional Analysis of the Design and Sequence of Trade and Investment Policy Reform." *World Bank Economic Review* 7(2):247–62.

McLure, Charles E., Jr. 1999. "Tax Holidays and Investment Incentives: A Comparative Analysis." *Bulletin for International Fiscal Documentation* 53(8):326–39.

Messere, Ken. 1999. "Half a Century of Changes in Taxation." *Bulletin for International Fiscal Documentation* 53(8):340–65.

Messineo, Alejandro E. 2005. "Taxation of Foreign Direct Investment in Argentina." *Bulletin for International Fiscal Documentation* 59(8):394–98.

Mutti, John H. 2003. *Foreign Direct Investment and Tax Competition*. Washington, DC: Institute for International Economics.

OECD (Organisation for Economic Co-operation and Development). 1998. *Curbing Harmful Tax Competition: Recommendation by the Committee on Fiscal Affairs*. Paris: OECD.

Peters, Amos C. 2002. "Exploring Caribbean Tax Structure and Harmonization Strategies." *Bulletin for International Fiscal Documentation* 56(5):178–93.

Pita, Claudino. 2003. "Harmonization and Tax Systems in the Americas." Paper presented at 2nd Plenary Meeting, Inter-Parliamentary Forum of the Americas, Panama City, February 20–21.

Rider, Mark. 2004. "Corporate Income Tax and Tax Incentives." Working Paper 04–28. Atlanta: International Studies Program, Andrew Young School of Public Policy, Georgia State University.

Shah, Anwar, ed. 1995. *Fiscal Incentives for Investment in Developing Countries.* New York: Oxford University Press.

Tanzi, Vito. 1987. "Quantitative Characteristics of the Tax Systems of Developing Countries." In *The Theory of Taxation for Developing Countries,* ed. David Newbery and Nicholas Stern. New York: Oxford University Press.

Thirsk, Wayne R. 1991. "Jamaican Tax Incentives." In *The Jamaican Tax Reform,* ed. Roy Bahl. Cambridge, MA: Lincoln Institute of Land Policy.

Villela, Luiz, and Alberto Barreix. 2002. "Taxation and Investment Promotion." Background note prepared for the World Bank's Global Economic Prospects 2003. Inter-American Development Bank, Integration and Regional Programs Department, Washington, DC. Available at http://www.iadb.org/INT/Trade/1_english/2_WhatWeDo/Documents/d_TaxDocs/2002-2003/j_Taxation%20and%20Investment%20Promotion.pdf.

Villela, Luiz, Alberto Barreix, and Juan José Taccone, eds. 2003. "Tributación en el MERCOSUR: evolución, comparación y posibilidades de coordinación." ITD-INTAL Special Reports Series. Washington, DC: Inter-American Development Bank.

Wasylenko, Michael. 1996. "The Role of Fiscal Incentives in Economic Development: How Ohio Stands Relative to Its Competitor States." In *Taxation and Economic Development: A Blueprint for Tax Reform in Ohio,* ed. Roy Bahl. Columbus, OH: Batelle.

———. 1997. "Taxation and Economic Development: The State of the Economic Literature." *New England Economic Review* (March/April):37–52.

Watkin, Virginia C. 1967. *Taxes and Tax Harmonization in Central America.* Cambridge, MA: Harvard Law School International Tax Program.

Wells, Louis T., Jr., and Nancy J. Allen. 2001. "Tax Holidays to Attract Foreign Investment: Lessons from Two Experiments." In *Using Tax Incentives to Compete for Foreign Investment: Are They Worth the Costs?* [FIAS Occasional Paper 15], ed. Louis T. Wells, Nancy J. Allen, Jacques Morisset, and Neda Pirnia. Washington, DC: International Finance Corporation and World Bank.

Wilson, John Douglas, and David Wildasin. 2004. "Capital Tax Competition: Bane or Boon?" *Journal of Public Economics* 88(6):1065–91.

World Bank. 1991. *Lessons of Tax Reform.* Washington, DC: World Bank.

Young, Alwyn. 1993. "Lessons from the East Asian NICs: A Contrarian View." NBER Working Paper 4482. Cambridge, MA: National Bureau of Economic Research.

Zee, Howell, Janet Stotsky, and Eduardo Ley. 2002. "Tax Incentives for Business Investment: A Primer for Policy Makers in Developing Countries." *World Development* 30(9):1497–1516.

8

Tax Treaties in Latin America: Issues and Models

Peter D. Byrne

The countries of Latin America are at a new crossroads in the area of treaties for the avoidance of double taxation and the prevention of fiscal evasion (referred to throughout this chapter as "tax treaties"). Before 1990, tax treaties were a rarity in Latin America. Brazil and Argentina had limited treaty programs, and the few other treaties throughout the region were not of great commercial importance. The negotiation of the U.S.-Mexico tax treaty, initiated in 1990, was a watershed. This first modern tax treaty between the United States and a Latin American country was made possible because Mexico agreed to negotiate on the basis of the Organisation for Economic Co-operation and Development (OECD) Model Treaty. Argentina and Brazil had accepted only treaties that were generally more favorable to the source country from a revenue viewpoint. Mexico's relatively close adherence to the OECD model represented a departure: Mexico had decided to analyze tax treaties not so much in terms of revenue, but rather as (1) a tool to attract investment, and (2) a strategy to become more integrated into the global tax community. Revenue concerns remained a priority, but they were not the only priority.[1]

---

[1] The willingness to forego some revenue in order to pursue a greater economic good also characterizes trade agreements. Indeed, trade agreements involve greater revenue sacrifices, but the economic impact of trade agreements is easier to measure.

Mexico's treaty negotiations with the United States were followed by many more, and Mexico now has a very active tax treaty program. The country tends to be the tax policy trendsetter in Latin America, and its initiative inspired several other countries to take a fresh look at tax treaties. The result was a new wave of activity in this field, centered on Venezuela, Chile, and, more recently, Peru. Argentina and Brazil have continued slowly to expand their treaty networks. As these countries continue to evaluate their tax treaty programs, the remaining Latin American countries are considering the issue, in some cases for the first time. The movement toward free trade has added urgency to the debate.

This chapter reviews the current situation and focuses on issues related to tax treaties for Latin American countries. To place the issue in its proper context, an overview of Latin American tax systems, and especially their treatment of international investment activity, is warranted.

Taxation in Latin America

General Overview

A general overview of the business income tax in the Latin American countries gives the impression that the countries of the region have tax systems that are conceptually similar to one another, are generally consistent with international norms, and offer relatively low tax rates. But this is only part of the picture. Closer observation reveals significant differences, and it is apparent that the common trends are progressing at very different speeds.

The business income tax in Latin America is a tax on *business* income, not *corporate* income: the choice of entity affects neither the calculation nor the rate of tax. The income tax calculation is consistent with international norms. Gross income is reduced by expenses, which include the standard items such as interest expense. Other standard features include depreciation, amortization, loss carry-forwards, and so forth. Low tax rates on business income (in the 25–30 percent range) are among the important common features. When combined with no or low withholding on dividends (0–5 percent), the total tax burden is competitive.

With few exceptions, Latin American countries do not allow consolidated filing for related companies. In the area of corporate reorganizations, there is a trend toward allowing deferral of gain, though several countries continue to treat reorganization-related transfers as taxable. Taxation of such transfers reflects the historical emphasis on the form of a transaction and the principle of "legal certainty" (*seguridad jurídica*), whereas the trend toward deferral reflects a different and broader move toward recognizing substance over form in legislation and, more critically, in enforcement.

Most Latin American countries impose significant taxes on businesses only at the national level. A few of them, notably Argentina and Brazil, levy substantial taxes at the state or local level. These taxes are not on net income, but they can affect a business's total tax burden considerably.

From a procedural viewpoint, Latin American tax systems generally have a tax *code* that is separate from the income tax *law*. The code covers procedural issues, and the law covers substantive tax rules. It is also common to include tax principles in other substantive areas of law. The mining code, for example, might contain mining-related tax rules, or the investment promotion law might contain tax incentives.

It is important to note an array of taxes that are not precisely on net income but still affect the net income of businesses and are sometimes part of the business income tax. Perhaps the most venerable is the Mexican assets tax, which operates as a minimum income tax: it is paid only when the assets tax calculation exceeds the income tax calculation, in which case the difference is paid. Assets taxes of this sort have appeared and disappeared in Latin America at a disconcerting rate over the last 15 years (Byrne, 1997). A tax on business assets to support the business income tax is not as common as 5 or 10 years ago, but is still used by Argentina, Peru, and other countries. Other noteworthy taxes include those on gross receipts (used in Brazil and elsewhere) and a tax on gross exports (only in Argentina). Taxes on financial transactions have spread to many countries in the region, notwithstanding their arbitrary nature.

The competence of the tax administrations in Latin America varies considerably. All of them lack the level of discretion found in most developed countries. For example, they have almost no discretion to waive interest or penalties, which tend to be extremely high. Nearly always, the relationship between the administration and taxpayers is highly adversarial. The quality of dispute resolution varies according to the quality of the judiciary, but specialized tax courts have a good track record in several countries. Administrations and courts alike are hampered by tax legislation that is vague, inconsistent, and constantly changing.

The Latin American countries share the heritage of the "territorial" tax system, which features exclusive taxation of income at source. Over the last 30 years, however, several countries have embraced the worldwide system, taxing their residents on their worldwide income. At the same time, they have held onto territorial principles and attitudes, using aggressive source rules and continuing to tax all income arising within their borders.[2] Furthermore, this trend in favor of the worldwide system is far from complete: though all of the larger economies in the region have adopted the worldwide system, nearly a third of the countries still have the territorial system.

Although less significant than the shift away from the territorial system, other important trends should be noted. In view of their relevance to the subject matter of this chapter, the most important trends related to international investment are discussed below.

International Issues

Transfer Pricing

Latin America ignored the whole subject of transfer pricing until 10 years ago. It was considered too esoteric for countries struggling to administer their basic income tax laws. But rising investment and government officials' greater familiarity with international tax principles and tax planning convinced those officials to address this difficult issue. In an age when 75 percent of international sales are between related entities, transfer pricing rules could no longer be delayed.

---

[2] It is fair to note that the United States and other developed countries also tax virtually all domestic source income in the absence of a tax treaty.

The larger Latin American economies have adopted transfer pricing rules in a relatively orderly fashion. Transfer pricing is viewed as a strictly technical field in which the interests of developing and developed countries, and capital-importing and -exporting countries, are not at odds. This view facilitated adoption of the OECD model transfer pricing rules, which most countries followed closely.[3]

Tax Haven Legislation

One of the most surprising developments of the last decade has been the emergence of anti–tax haven legislation in Latin America. For many years, tax havens have been an annoyance for capital-exporting countries, which have made unilateral and multilateral efforts to prevent their residents from using tax havens to hide income earned overseas. Little attention was paid to improper use of tax havens to reduce source-country taxation, especially in Latin America, where the territorial mentality tended to ignore extraterritorial tax issues.

Nearly half of the countries in the region now have some sort of tax haven legislation. Payments to tax havens are subject to penalties that include high rates of withholding and denial of deductions. Perhaps most innovative is the way in which some countries treat sales. Any sale to or from a tax haven is assumed—usually without the possibility of rebuttal—to be with a related party and therefore subject to the transfer pricing rules. This policy reflects the fact that it is extremely difficult to verify that a tax haven resident is unrelated. Developed countries have relied on severe penalties to prevent dishonesty, but Latin American countries apparently do not believe penalties to be a sufficient disincentive. Multinational companies that operate through tax havens with no illicit tax-reduction intent complain that these rules complicate their operations in the region. Such investors find it especially irritating to be denied a chance to demonstrate that a tax haven-based seller or purchaser is unrelated.

---

[3] Brazil initially introduced several significant departures from the OECD rules. It has retreated from some of them but its rules still have many features that are not in harmony with international norms.

Limits on Deduction of Interest/High Withholding

Debt has always been a useful strategy to reduce source-country taxation. As a deductible expense, interest reduces the business income tax burden, and the savings can be even greater in cases where the withholding rate on dividends is higher than that on interest (rare in Latin America, but not in other parts of the world). Of course, the tax reduction is of no benefit to the investor if the interest payments are to an unrelated party. After all, the interest is a true income-reducing expense. But the savings can be substantial if the parent company lends to its subsidiary. Many countries respond to this issue by imposing a high withholding rate on related-party loans.

Several countries in Latin America have dramatically reduced withholding on interest rates, for a simple reason: ordinarily, loans from banks are not profitable if there is a withholding rate higher than 5 percent.[4] Because banks can be a source of scarce investment capital, some countries want to ensure that the withholding rate on interest is not an obstacle to such loans.[5]

In view of the foregoing, many countries attempt to impose low withholding on loans from financial institutions and high withholding on related-party loans. It is not easy to resolve this issue because of "back-to-back" loans, a mechanism through which an investor channels what is essentially a related-party loan through a financial institution in order to obtain the preferential withholding rate.

Until recently, there was little control of back-to-back loans in Latin America. Several of the larger economies, however, have enacted legislation in an effort to control this practice. The controls vary, but the problem has been recognized and the effort to limit abuses qualifies as a trend.

---

[4] Because of the cost of funding a loan, the gross interest received (on which withholding is imposed) is far greater than the net profit on the loan. A withholding rate of 5 percent may be equal to a 50 percent tax on net income.

[5] Having the borrower assume the withholding tax is not a viable solution. It drives up the cost of funds and effectively imposes a tax on the borrower, not the lender. The tax is supposed to be on income, not on an expense.

Tax-Free Zones

Several Latin American countries, especially in Central America, have determined that attracting investment is a far higher priority than deriving tax revenue from investors. To this end, such countries have instituted "tax-free" zones.[6] By eliminating all taxes on qualifying investments for a period of 10–15 years or more, these countries hope to attract investment that would have gone elsewhere in the absence of the tax-free zone incentive. The reward is employment, tax revenue generated by taxes on employees, and the general increase in economic activity.

Many tax policy experts frown upon tax-free zones, but the combination of investment policy and political interests has often prevailed. It is probable that the number of tax-free zones will continue to decline over the next few years. The overwhelming experience with such zones as a tool for regional development has been that they are extremely costly to national treasuries and have attracted little investment. For this reason, Brazil and Argentina are phasing out these zones, and eventually the Andean countries will have to do the same.

Export-oriented tax-free zones have been particularly resilient in Central America. They are viewed as successful investment incentives. The World Trade Organization (WTO), however, is pressuring countries with such zones to curtail them, and no doubt they will be a problem in regional or bilateral free trade negotiations.

The struggle over tax-free zones is likely to continue for years. Such zones complicate the negotiation of tax treaties, as explained below.

Bank Secrecy/Bearer Shares

An unfortunate number of Latin American countries allow bearer shares and continue to protect bank information absolutely. Such institutions promote tax evasion. While bank secrecy regimes are supported by legitimate concerns, there are even stronger arguments for allowing limited

---

[6] Such zones exist in many other Latin American countries. The Central American countries are noteworthy because they offer great flexibility. Tax-free zones are available in Colombia, Peru, and Venezuela, for example, but in geographically unattractive areas.

access to bank information. In addition to tax concerns, absolute secrecy facilitates money laundering, drug trafficking, and even terrorism.

OECD pressure on tax havens to accept minimum standards have not been completely successful, but it is probable that the pressure will continue. Free trade agreements may require minimum standards of transparency, but there is no doubt that tax treaties will require access to bank information.

In the model treaties described below, and in the vast majority of tax treaties in force, information exchange is a critical component. International operations provide enhanced opportunities for tax evasion and tax avoidance, and information exchange is considered essential to control this important group of taxpayers. Interaction with other tax administrations also strengthens enforcement know-how. There is already information exchange in Latin America—not only through tax treaties, but also through a network of tax information exchange agreements that the United States has concluded with several countries in the region.

Latin American countries generally hope information exchange will help them detect tax evasion by identifying assets, such as bank accounts, that their residents may have in the United States. While information exchange has been successful in some cases (notably Mexico), most countries consider information exchange to be of limited use. The fewer treaties a country has, the less useful information exchange seems to be.

It should be noted that the information exchange provisions of tax treaties will require several Latin American countries to revise their bank secrecy legislation, and possibly other rules as well. These reforms are often sought by tax administrations for the purposes of domestic taxes. In summary, information exchange offers some limited benefits to tax administrations, and reforms related to information exchange may also be beneficial.

Andean Pact Tax Treaties

The Andean Pact Model Tax Treaty was formulated more than 30 years ago, when regional integration was in its infancy and the territorial system of taxation was still the norm in Latin America. The treaty follows the territorial principle (with the exception of transport), taxing all income exclusively at source. This model prevents double taxation by resolving potential source conflicts.[7] In the context of two countries with territorial systems of taxation, however, the model's overall impact on the substantive taxation of international investment is modest. Of course, this model allows information exchange that otherwise would not be possible.

The Andean Pact model came into effect for all cross-border investments from one Andean country to another with the adoption of Decision 40 of the Cartagena Accord. The model also served as the basis for two of Argentina's treaties in the 1970s, with Bolivia and Chile. After this flurry of activity, however, the model slipped into disuse: no new treaties have been based on the Andean Pact model for more than 25 years. Developed countries have shown no interest in a tax treaty based exclusively on source. More significantly, the territorial system that served as the foundation for this model has been in retreat for more than two decades.

Like the territorial tax system, the Andean Pact model looks increasingly like a historical relic, and it can reasonably be argued that the model is now little more than a distraction.[8] Even the Andean countries have adopted the worldwide tax system, making the UN or OECD models perfectly appropriate for treaties among the Andean countries. Notwithstanding this environment, the Andean Community recently launched a new model treaty, revised for the first time since the original model. The new version continues to follow the source principle.

---

[7] The most important source conflict relates to services. Some countries consider income to be domestic-source on the basis of where the services will be used; nearly all countries consider service income to arise in the country where such services are rendered. Hence there will be double taxation if services are rendered in one country for use in another. The Andean Pact treaty, like the OECD model, settles the issue in favor of the country where the services are physically rendered.

[8] This is not a criticism of the territorial system, but rather a statement of fact. Arguments in favor of the territorial system are overshadowed by the fact that the worldwide system is clearly the international norm and is likely to remain so for political, not tax policy, reasons.

The Andean Pact model must still be included as an important aspect of Latin American taxation, for the simple reason that it still applies in the Andean Community, and the Argentina-Bolivia and Argentina-Chile treaties remain in force.

OECD Model Tax Treaties

As noted at the outset, Mexico seized the initiative in 1990 and has maintained an active tax treaty program since then. Consistent with its membership in the OECD, Mexico has based its negotiations on the OECD Model Tax Treaty. In contrast to the Andean Pact model, that of the OECD seeks a rational division of tax revenue between the source country and the residence country. The Mexican tax administration's website currently lists over 40 treaties in various stages from "in negotiation" to "in force," with far more than half in force.[9] Hence Mexico alone now has approximately the same number of tax treaties in force that the entire Latin American region had in 1990.

Venezuela and Chile's treaty programs are almost as sweeping as Mexico's; each of them has dozens of treaties either in force or in negotiation.[10] Venezuela began its OECD-based negotiations shortly after Mexico, and Chile did so in the late 1990s. Venezuela's program has slowed recently, although negotiations continue with countries such as Cuba, Russia, and China (Venezuela has significant commercial links with China). Chile has marked out a negotiating strategy that places more emphasis on taxation at source, and negotiations with the United States have foundered as a

---

[9] See http://www.sat.gob.mx/nuevo.html; select "Indice temático," then "Convenios internacionales celebrados por México en materia fiscal." Mexico is part of a growing trend in which countries make their tax treaties publicly available on the Internet. Mexico even provides a comparative table.

[10] Venezuela has treaties with Barbados, Belgium, Canada, the Czech Republic, Denmark, France, Germany, Indonesia, Italy, Mexico, the Netherlands, Norway, Portugal, Spain, Sweden, Switzerland, Trinidad and Tobago, the United Kingdom, and the United States, and it is a signatory to the Andean Pact agreement. Chile has treaties in force with Argentina, Brazil, Canada, Denmark, Ecuador, Mexico, Peru, Poland, South Korea, Spain, and the United Kingdom. In addition, Chile has signed treaties with Croatia, France, Malaysia, New Zealand, Russia, and Sweden, and negotiations are in progress with another dozen countries.

result. Peru's treaty program is still in its infancy: three agreements are in force (other than the regional Andean Pact treaty), but many more are in negotiation. Brazil and Argentina have not significantly altered their treaty policies; they continue to negotiate at a deliberate pace.[11] Rounding out the region's seven largest economies, Colombia has been studying treaties sporadically for years, and has even taken the political decision to negotiate them, but it has never sustained such efforts. Colombia's first OECD Model Treaty (with Spain) was signed in 2005.[12]

The other countries of the region have varying levels of interest in tax treaties and relatively few agreements in force. Their smaller economies make it more difficult for them to capture the attention of potential treaty partners. To some extent, the territorial system has prevented progress. If the smaller economies persist, however, eventually they can establish treaty programs.

The question is whether tax treaties should be a priority for the countries of Latin America. The Mexican attitude has pushed the number of tax treaties in the region to more than 100, and dozens of others are being negotiated. Is the more aggressive approach of Mexico and Venezuela the proper model, or should countries follow the more cautious approach of Argentina and Brazil? Would this more cautious approach condemn the smaller economies to international tax isolation, and does this matter? As explained below, the answer to these questions depends on a combination of tax policy, investment policy, and, to a limited extent, trade policy. Since each country has different policies, the answer will vary from one country to another.

---

[11] Brazil is negotiating treaties with Argentina, Austria, Belgium, Canada, China, the Czech Republic, Denmark, Ecuador, Finland, France, Germany, Hungary, India, Italy, Japan, Luxembourg, Mexico, the Netherlands, Norway, the Philippines, Portugal, South Korea, Spain, and Sweden. As for Argentina, it has treaties in force with Australia, Austria, Belgium, Bolivia, Brazil, Canada, Chile, Denmark, Finland, France, Germany, Italy, the Netherlands, Norway, Spain, Sweden, Switzerland, and the United Kingdom. See http://www.deloitte.com/dtt/cda/doc/content/impuestos_en_argentina%281%29.pdf.

[12] See http://documentacion.meh.es/doc/C8/En%20Tramitacion/CDI%20Espa%C3%B1a%20y%20Colombia.pdf.

Perceived Advantages:
Investment Attraction and Information Exchange

Investors always consider taxation as a critical part of an investment decision, but it is only one of several considerations. Indeed, it is less important than several other factors, such the size of the internal market, infrastructure, and the labor pool. Taxation, however, is perhaps the most important factor that is fully within a government's control. The quality of infrastructure and the labor pool are necessarily the result of long-term policies, whereas a government can eliminate taxation for a particular investor in a matter of days if there is sufficient political will.

"Taxation," moreover, includes more than tax rates or even the tax burden. Other aspects include:

-   How the tax burden in a given country will affect the total tax burden worldwide.
-   Whether a country's tax system is stable or subject to constant reforms that will require attention and potentially increase the tax burden.
-   In the event of a dispute, whether a country's tax administration is competent, whether the courts are honest and efficient, and whether interest and penalties are reasonable.

As noted at the outset, the income tax rates in Latin America are generally competitive and do not impede investment. Tax treaties would do little to change this. Reductions in the interest and royalty withholding rates would lower the tax burden for these payments, and taxes would be eliminated for certain low-level activities—generally, services and sales activity where there is no permanent establishment. But most activities would not be affected.

There are cases where a low tax payment in the source country does not equal a lower tax payment on a worldwide basis. For example, a U.S. investor operating in a tax-free zone will usually have to pay tax on income the moment it distributes such income to the United States. In this case, the total forgiveness of tax may not save the investor any money on a worldwide basis.[13] Another example involves a noncreditable tax, such as a tax on assets or gross receipts. Since such taxes do not offset income tax in the investor's home country on a dollar-for-dollar basis, an investor might prefer to pay a higher income tax rather than a lower tax that is not creditable.

On the second point raised about taxation—stability—Latin America fares poorly. While this general statement is unfair to Chile and perhaps to a few other countries, most countries in the region are subject to constant "reforms" that often have no purpose other than to meet short-term revenue goals. "Extraordinary" or "temporary" taxes are common and cause instability by their very nature.[14]

The record is also mixed in the area of audit/dispute resolution. While tax administrations throughout the region have improved, there are many stories of poorly supported assessments and behavior that could be interpreted as intimidation. Intimidation can be a real factor in Latin America, where penalties for nonpayment are severe. Most foreign investors are assessed because the tax administration does not agree with the taxpayer's reasonable interpretation of a law. But most countries in the region impose the same harsh penalties whether the assessment arises from outright evasion or merely from a different reading of legislation. Once a penalty is imposed, there is normally no discretion to relieve it unless the taxpayer concedes the case.[15] The total liability, moreover, can multiply at a breathtaking rate, since interest on both the deficiency and the related penalties is typically imposed at a very high rate.[16]

---

[13] On the other hand, if the taxpayer has "excess" foreign tax credit (that is, the foreign tax paid is greater than the U.S. tax that would have been payable on its other foreign income), the tax savings from operating in the tax-free zone could be significant. There are numerous other situations where tax-free zones would permit significant tax savings.

[14] "Temporary" taxes also make long-term planning very difficult. Usually such taxes are initially set to last one or two years but are extended, prompting the quip that "there is nothing more permanent than a temporary tax in Latin America."

[15] Several recommendations for reforms could be offered, but they are outside the scope of this chapter.

[16] Paying the tax is not viewed as a sensible option to prevent interest from accumulating, because governments do not have a good track record for refunds, and paying the tax is often viewed as an admission of guilt. The logical compromise, making payment in escrow, is usually not an option.

In some of these areas, tax treaties can help to some degree. With regard to the tax burden, an important article (elimination of double taxation) operates to clarify or expand the foreign tax credit. Some countries (notably Canada) use this article to dispose of the foreign tax credit analysis and provide an exemption for certain types of income.[17] Treaty negotiations often reveal foreign tax credit problems that can be resolved unilaterally or in the treaty.

Tax treaties help provide stability by capping or exempting certain categories of income that otherwise might be taxed. For example, a country may not tax the sale of shares at the moment a foreign company makes an investment, but the country may subsequently amend its laws to include such sales proceeds as taxable income. A treaty would prevent this change from affecting the investor, at least under some circumstances. Similarly, a Latin American country might raise its withholding rate on dividends to 30 percent. Without a treaty capping the withholding at 5 percent or 15 percent, an investor is exposed.[18]

Perhaps most importantly, the mutual agreement procedure article of a tax treaty provides comfort to investors in the case of tax disputes that are treaty-related, by authorizing the intervention of the investor's own tax authority. For example, if the tax authority of a treaty partner taxes an investor where that investor believes there is no permanent establishment, or if the investor feels it is being taxed in a discriminatory manner, the investor's tax authority can become involved on behalf of the taxpayer. For investors concerned about the intimidation mentioned above, this intervention is critical. The associated enterprises article is extremely helpful in transfer pricing situations.

---

[17] In a high-rate country, this benefit is very important. If Canada's rate is 40 percent, for example, and the treaty partner's rate is 30 percent, the 10 percent difference accrues to the investor. At present, few developed countries offer such an attractive incentive in tax treaties. But where such an incentive is offered, countries often seize the opportunity. Canada has expanded its tax treaty network in Latin America dramatically, in large part because of this incentive.

[18] Again, the caps apply only to cross-border items; treaties never limit the business income tax, for example. Nor would punitive penalties or interest be affected unless imposed in a discriminatory manner.

It must be understood that communication between tax authorities regarding a particular taxpayer may be illegal or even criminal if there is no treaty.

For the foregoing reasons, multinational companies usually support tax treaties, especially with countries where they have significant investments. At the same time, it is important not to exaggerate the importance of treaties. Investors themselves cite several other factors as more important than tax treaties when they analyze investment location options. The only empirical study on the subject suggests that tax treaties may have a small, positive impact on investment (Bloningen and Davies, 2000).[19]

Tax treaties also help a country's tax administration operate more efficiently in a world where international activity plays an increasingly important role in each country's economy. There are two main areas where tax treaties help. The first is information exchange. A tax administration gains access to potentially useful information on the activities of its own residents in the other country, as well as information on foreign investors. Even if information is not exchanged regularly (which, unfortunately, is the norm), the psychological effect on potential tax evaders and overly aggressive tax planners can be significant.

Second, most international tax policymakers in Latin America agree that a tax treaty network facilitates tax administration by increasing know-how. Tax treaties address the taxation of most forms of international investment. It is through the treaty-negotiation process that Latin American tax officials learn the techniques used by international investors to reduce their tax burden in a completely legal manner. Perhaps the most important example of this is transfer pricing. It is not coincidental that transfer pricing legislation has developed in conjunction with tax treaty negotiations. In 1990, most Latin American countries were unaware that transfer pricing presented a problem.

---

[19] A critical assessment of the paper by Bloningen and Davies calls into question whether the impact of tax treaties on investment can ever be measured. After subsequent analysis, the authors have backed away from their conclusions.

Perceived Disadvantages:
Revenue Loss and Administrative Burdens

The most powerful argument against tax treaties has always been the supposed revenue cost. This problem arises because the investment flow tends to move from more developed to less developed countries.[20] Though tax treaties are reciprocal in application, this imbalance in investment flows leads to revenue consequences that are not reciprocal. The general approach of the OECD Model Treaty (and the UN model, though to a lesser extent) is to limit source-country taxation on certain types of activity.

If investment flows are generally reciprocal, as would be expected between two European countries or even between many Latin American countries, these limits on source taxation will not have a significant impact in either country: some of the tax savings in the source country will be collected by the residence country of the investor, and some of the savings will accrue to the investor. In all respects, the effect should be roughly reciprocal. But where the investment flow is nonreciprocal, the limitations on taxation at source fall disproportionately on the capital-importing country, and the revenue increase accrues disproportionately to the capital-exporting country. Accordingly, a static analysis of the revenue effect reveals negative revenue consequences for capital-seeking Latin American countries.

Three areas illustrate this effect. First, Latin American countries tend to impose high rates of withholding (most of them in the 25–30 percent range) on royalties paid to nonresidents. Developed countries usually insist on capping royalty withholding rates in the 10–15 percent range, or even lower if possible. Hence one-half of royalty withholding receipts may be sacrificed by entering into a tax treaty.

Second, cross-border services may also involve revenue sacrifice for developing countries. In the absence of a treaty, Latin American

---

[20] There are, however, exceptions to this rule. Venezuela has long been an important capital-exporting country, and Chile has recently become one.

countries impose withholding on services rendered by nonresidents at a rate of 20–30 percent, even on small amounts. Many countries impose withholding even where the service provider has not entered the country in which the services will be used. Ordinarily, a tax treaty will prohibit a country from taxing services rendered by residents of the treaty partner unless there is some minimum physical presence. Furthermore, a country may never tax services that are rendered by a person physically present in the other country, because tax treaties routinely deem the country in which such services are provided to be the source country. Needless to say, these limitations will cost Latin American countries revenue, though (unlike the area of royalties) there is a real possibility that some revenue loss will be offset by individuals from Latin American countries providing services in developed, treaty-partner countries.

Third, all Latin American countries aggressively tax any business activity carried out in their territory by nonresidents. The permanent establishment article of the OECD and UN models, by contrast, sets forth a range of activities that the "source" country cannot tax. Income from these activities can only be taxed in the country of residence if there is no "permanent establishment." If there is a permanent establishment, the business-profits article ensures that all reasonable deductions will be allowed.

It cannot reasonably be argued that these and other tax treaty provisions will not reduce tax collections in the absence of compensating factors. Such factors include tax revenue related to greater economic activity, and higher revenue from enhanced control of international operations. This type of dynamic analysis would be more useful than a static analysis to countries weighing a tax treaty program.[21] Because the impact of tax treaties on investment is uncertain, however, a dynamic analysis is necessarily speculative. On balance, it is sensible to accept that

---

[21] The futility of a static analysis can be demonstrated by a simple example: a static analysis of investment behavior and revenue in Central America would conclude that revenue would soar if tax-free zones were eliminated. Such an analysis does not account for the fact that investment behavior would change.

a tax treaty network will result in a net revenue loss for Latin American countries.[22]

A further consideration for some countries is the cost of negotiating treaties and then maintaining the treaty program. While the concerns of cash-strapped developing countries must not be underestimated, such costs should not be the decisive factor. The costs of negotiation can be reduced by careful planning and by resolving issues through correspondence. And the cost of training officials who will negotiate and manage the tax treaty program should not be an obstacle. This investment should be made even without a treaty program. When lost revenue is considered, the cost of not having at least one official skilled in international tax matters is certainly higher than the cost of having one.

One threat that cannot be ignored relates to the departure of skilled government personnel to the private sector after they have acquired the know-how that is so important to the government. This issue certainly is not limited to the international area, or even the tax area. Unless compensation that is competitive with the private sector is available, it may be necessary to oblige designated tax officials to remain in government service for a certain number of years in exchange for the training received.

Related Factors

While the unfortunate trade-off between investment attraction and revenue sacrifice has long been the essential question, an evolving economic environment constantly alters the equation. The continuing expansion of international trade and investment is the most important trend for the purposes of the tax treaty analysis.

Historically, the smaller Latin American countries have been unable to offer what most often drives investment location decisions: a significant

---

[22] It must be noted, though, that loss of revenue should not be a concern for the several countries that routinely offer tax holidays or tax-free zones to investors. As noted above, countries will probably be obliged to phase out such exemptions. Tax treaties may be a useful component of such countries' investment policies when these exemptions can no longer be offered.

domestic market. Small populations and low income levels combine to yield small internal markets in Central America and in countries such as Bolivia, Paraguay, and Uruguay. In the absence of a substantial domestic market, such countries often seek to attract export-oriented investments.

The free trade movement removes this serious obstacle to foreign investment. The internal market of Honduras, for example, will no longer be Honduras, but rather all countries where items produced in Honduras can be purchased without significant customs duties or other obstacles. Accordingly, free trade can make smaller Latin American countries more attractive as investment destinations.[23]

Tax policies related to foreign investment must be reviewed in light of this change of circumstances. On a very practical level, free trade agreements usually call for the elimination of tax-free zones. As noted above, the elimination of export-oriented tax-free zones is a priority for the WTO. In essence, smaller countries are being pressured to abandon their primary investment attraction mechanism at the same time as the door to significantly increased foreign investment is being opened.

Tax-free zones are doubtless a factor in the persistence of the territorial system in Latin America. Countries with the territorial system have largely forfeited their taxing jurisdiction outside their borders, which eliminates the need to coordinate with other tax systems. With the end of tax-free zones on the horizon, coordination with other countries' tax systems becomes an issue.

Tax treaties should be considered as part of a comprehensive package to facilitate the increased foreign investment that should accompany free trade. By their very design, tax treaties promote bilateral tax coordination. But other reforms are essential, and tax treaties can support those reforms.

Obvious reforms that should be undertaken by all countries that have not done so already are rules on transfer pricing and thin capitalization. How tax treaties can support these rules is explained below. Moving

---

[23] Ireland illustrates how a small country can prosper in a free trade environment. For an excellent summary of Ireland's experience, see Haughton (2002).

away from the territorial principle in favor of the worldwide system will be a more controversial reform. As noted, all the large Latin American countries have made this move already, which leaves the remaining territorial countries even more isolated. Whatever the merits of the territorial system, it is not sensible to be out of step with the rest of the world in a context of economic globalization. Moreover, the territorial system is a serious impediment to the negotiation of tax treaties.

A final important reform is related not to substance but rather to the process of harmonization. Efforts to harmonize taxation in Latin America have been limited. There has been some success at the regional bloc level to harmonize value-added tax (VAT) and customs issues, but income tax issues are addressed on a country-by-country basis. Similarities found in the region's income tax regimes arise from common legal traditions, informal exchanges, and tax policy advice received from influential institutions (the Inter-American Center for Tax Administrators, the International Monetary Fund, and the Inter-American Development Bank). Notwithstanding these factors supporting convergence, coordination is diminished by competition among neighboring countries. This is best exemplified by the competition for investment in Central America, where the "race to the bottom" has concluded and several countries have surrendered all taxing jurisdiction.

If an effort is made to adopt modern international tax norms, it would be advisable to act on a regional, uniform basis where possible. Mexico, or even the United States (with an economy 25 times larger than Mexico's), may be taken as a point of reference. Uniform rules across the federal states of both Mexico and the United States facilitate investment. Even commercial rules that are issued at the state level in the United States, rather than the national level, are largely uniform.[24]

Central America, with six Spanish-speaking countries whose combined populations and economies are significantly smaller than Mexico's, would be a logical place for harmonization to take place. To be competitive, Cen-

---

[24] The Internal Revenue Code, establishing federal taxes, applies to the entire United States. Each state of the United States generally follows the Uniform Commercial Code to ensure harmony in the area of commercial transactions.

tral American countries should consider ceding some of their sovereignty, just as the states of Mexico and the United States have done. Cooperation could solve the "race to the bottom" problem mentioned above.

It would be sensible to begin the process of harmonization with rules on international investment: transfer pricing rules, thin capitalization rules, and so on. From a technical viewpoint this should not be difficult, since the countries would be writing on a nearly blank slate. Addressing these issues as a group would allow resources to be pooled, thus reducing the cost and improving the quality of the final product. Once the precedent of harmonization is established, it may be possible to take further steps on other important issues, such as the territorial system and tax treaties. It should be noted that tax treaties, in turn, support harmonization. Tax treaties establish standardized rules for every important area of taxation related to cross-border economic activity.

Tax Treaty Issues

This section focuses on the most important parts of the OECD Model Tax Treaty. Latin American countries must understand the implications of these provisions in order to make an informed decision on tax treaties. Other model treaties (the UN and Andean Pact models) are not included in this discussion for a simple reason: Latin American countries cannot expect more than a few capital-exporting countries to negotiate a treaty based on the UN model (though most will consider specific items from the UN model). None will consider the Andean Pact model.

Before discussing the most important aspects of the OECD model, a few general items should be noted. The model reflects the fundamental concept that income derived by a resident of one country from activity in the other country should be taxed once. Both exemption and double taxation are to be avoided. Hence the treaty includes both legal and administrative solutions to potential double taxation, and information exchange to prevent double exemption. In addition to this fundamental goal, the treaty attempts to distribute tax paid on such income between the two countries in proportions that are fair to both the source country (for providing the economic environment that made the income possible) and the country of residence (as the origin of the capital that made the income possible). Priority is assigned to the source country: the residence country is obliged to offer a foreign tax credit for taxes paid in the source country.

The treaty, however, also places great emphasis on the promotion of cross-border economic activity. To achieve this goal, tax treaties exempt low levels of commercial activity and services from taxation in the source country. The main purpose of these provisions (the permanent establishment concept and the services articles) is not to reduce the taxpayer's tax burden, but rather to remove the compliance burdens that often impede limited cross-border activity.

Tax treaties never impose taxes, and they should not increase a taxpayer's liability. To ensure this, a taxpayer can usually choose to apply domestic rules rather than the treaty.

Permanent Establishment/Business Activity/ International Transportation Articles

Without a doubt, among the most important articles of the OECD model is Article 5, which establishes that a resident of one contracting state cannot be taxed in the other state unless it has a "permanent establishment." This article defines a permanent establishment as a fixed base where business activity is carried out. In negotiations, problems often arise when the parties begin to enumerate the specific activities that will or will not be considered permanent establishments. It is understood that the following constitute a permanent establishment: a branch, an office, a factory, a workshop, a store, a mine, and so on. A fixed base, however, will generally not constitute a permanent establishment if it engages in only one of the following activities: distribution, storage, showroom, purchasing, research, and so forth. There are also rules to ensure that tax cannot be avoided through the use of agents when the latter are not truly independent.

In some cases, the permanent establishment article does not change the definition of permanent establishment in a country's internal law. The importance of this article to Latin American countries relates to the *consequences* when the foreign business does not have a permanent establishment: under domestic law, this usually results in taxation of gross income. In the context of a treaty, the source country may not tax a foreign enterprise if it does not have a permanent establishment. The purpose of this article is to promote cross-border activity by eliminating the administrative burdens associated with the taxation of limited activity. There is value in the international standard established by a treaty: investors know the standard and are comfortable with it. In the absence of a treaty, by contrast, an enterprise must consult local specialists and then pay tax. Such burdens are often disproportionate to the income generated, and therefore may impede the activity.

Latin American countries fear that foreign investors will organize their activities in such a way as to avoid having a permanent establishment, and thereby not pay any tax in the source country. No doubt this will happen, but probably on a very limited basis for the following reasons: (1) the activities that do not constitute a permanent establishment are very limited; (2) most fixed-base activities that are not permanent establishments do not produce significant income; (3) in most cases, the foreign investor will have to pay tax in its country of residence, and thus not having a permanent establishment most often will not result in any tax savings; (4) tax rates in Latin American countries tend to be lower than those in developed countries, so again, having a permanent establishment will not increase overall tax liability; and (5) the lower tax rates in Latin America are a powerful incentive for a foreign investor to form a corporation in the country where it operates, because without a corporation, the investor will not receive the deferral benefit on the difference between the local rate and the tax rate in the residence country. Once there is a local corporation, the whole permanent establishment issue becomes moot.

When there is a permanent establishment, Article 7 ensures that the activity will be taxed on the same basis as similar local activities, and that all reasonable deductions will be allowed. Latin American countries often object to the obligation to allow deductions for expenses incurred in other countries. This concern is generally relieved when the officials understand exactly how this provision operates.

Article 8 addresses specific activities (air and sea transport, or containers) that are exceptions to the general rule stated above. Traditionally, such activities have been taxed only in the country of residence, and Latin American countries accept this treatment.

Services (Dependent and Independent)

Just as the permanent establishment concept seeks to facilitate limited levels of business activity by eliminating tax concerns, the set of tax treaty articles related to services, both dependent and independent, attempts to facilitate cross-border provision of services as long as the services are limited. A service provider will generally become subject to taxation in the source country if the provider has spent more than 183 days there in a one-year period. In the case of dependent services, there are rules for specific circumstances, such as whether the employer is a resident of the source country. In the case of independent services, the rule follows the permanent establishment concept of fixed base.[25] Having a fixed base leads to source-country taxation, but on a net basis. Other treaty articles address specific types of services, such as athletes and government services.

There is a stark contrast between these treaty rules and the territorial concept (even the Latin American countries that have moved to the worldwide system still tax services on a territorial basis). There is no minimum threshold of activity or presence required before Latin American countries will tax services: one day is sufficient. Furthermore, the aggressive source rules described above present numerous possibilities for double taxation. Clearly, tax issues of this sort will impede cross-border service activity. The possibility of double taxation will often lead to tax evasion.

The services articles are often a major reason why Latin American countries fail to pursue tax treaties. The revenue loss may be mitigated by increased tax collections from services provided by Latin Americans

---

[25] The OECD model has eliminated the independent services article, considering its substance to be covered by other articles, but the article is included in the great majority of treaties in force.

in developed, treaty-partner countries, but services provided by developed countries to developing countries are likely to remain more significant for years to come. To minimize revenue loss, Latin American countries strive to negotiate treaties that maintain as much taxation at source as possible. Special emphasis is placed on limiting situations wherein a source-country exemption is accompanied by a deduction for the related expense.

Dividends, Interest, and Royalties Articles

Historically, withholding rates on dividends, interest, and royalties have been among the most controversial topics in tax treaty negotiations between Latin America and the rest of the world. Thirty years ago, most Latin American countries had extremely high withholding rates on gross income, sometimes exceeding 40 or 50 percent. These levels reflected not only the higher rates on net business income that prevailed at the time, but also the territorial notion that the source country should have exclusive taxing jurisdiction, even with respect to nonresidents with passive investments. This situation has changed considerably. Most countries in the region unilaterally exempt dividend distributions, and some countries impose relatively low withholding rates on some categories of interest, in the 5–10 percent range. But withholding rates are still high on royalties and some categories of interest.

Latin American countries generally worry that lower rates will lead to tax planning to reduce source-country taxation. High withholding rates prevent such planning, because there is little difference between the value of the deduction received and the withholding tax paid. Developed countries have always insisted that the withholding rates on interest and royalties should be reduced in tax treaties, because high nominal rates on gross-income items such as interest and royalties convert into an unreasonably high tax on net income, and rate reductions therefore benefit investors. There is no doubt that both positions are valid: whether a reduced withholding rate facilitates improper planning or makes an unreasonably high rate more tolerable depends on the taxpayer. Proponents of tax treaties, however, point out that transfer pricing rules and information exchange reduce the risk of improper tax planning.

Tax treaties generally call for dividend withholding to be reduced to the 5–15 percent range. This involves little or no revenue sacrifice for Latin American countries. Interest withholding rates must be reduced to the 10–15 percent range, and the United States generally insists on a reduction to under 5 percent for bank loans. After studying the issue, Latin American negotiators generally accept that 10–15 percent is reasonable for most loans from unrelated parties. They recognize that a higher rate will be borne by the borrower and will impede the movement of capital. But related-party loans will always create the potential for tax planning. The revenue loss can be managed by debt-equity rules and information exchange, but some loss is inevitable.

Royalties pose the most difficult challenge in this area. Latin American countries generally impose withholding at a rate approximating the business income rate, reflecting the attitude that expenses associated with intangibles developed abroad should be deducted where they were incurred. Developed countries tend to have a different concept of royalties and intangibles, and in some cases, treaties between developed countries establish complete exemption from withholding. Developed countries, for example, believe that withholding on royalties impedes technology transfer. Some of these fundamental differences can be alleviated in negotiations through a better understanding of the other party's concerns. Nevertheless, successful negotiation of a treaty between a developed country and a Latin American country will involve compromises that may be painful. If a single rate of 10–15 percent is unacceptable, sometimes multiple rates (lower for cultural and technological royalties, and higher for popular films and music, for example) make an agreement possible.

Capital Gains

Tax treaties divide the right to tax the capital gains of nonresidents between the source country and the residence country of the person deriving the gain.[26] The source country always has the right to tax real estate gains, and many recent treaties allow the source country to tax major dispositions of stock, provided that the company whose shares are transferred is resident. But treaties call for most other capital gains to be taxed only in the residence of the seller. For countries with a territorial background, this principle is problematic, both as a matter of principle and as a matter of revenue (since such gains are realized by persons from developed countries).

Latin American countries do not favor the foregoing principle, but it should not be an insurmountable obstacle to a tax treaty. This is because of the capital formation and capital attraction policies that Latin American countries have pursued unilaterally. Most importantly, many countries now exempt gains arising from sales of shares, particularly transfers taking place on a stock exchange. An additional reason for exempting such transfers is that investors can escape the capital gains tax with relative ease by forming an intermediate company and transferring shares of the offshore entity.

General Principles: Articles on the Elimination of Double Taxation, on Nondiscrimination, and on Mutual Agreement Procedures

Three treaty articles—those that eliminate double taxation, prohibit discrimination, and provide for mutual agreement—do not necessarily alter any internal tax laws; rather, they offer guarantees that are not available in the absence of a treaty. These guarantees are especially important for companies investing in developing countries.

Elimination of double taxation can be important in identifying taxes that are problematic for the purposes of the foreign tax credit, either confirming the tax as creditable or explaining why it does not qualify. In Latin America, the assets tax is a perfect example. Some developed

---

[26] The source country is ordinarily determined by the location of the property sold. But some countries follow other rules, such as the residence of the seller, which leads to source conflicts and double taxation.

countries have included the assets tax in tax treaties with Latin American countries, confirming a foreign tax credit for their investors. The United States cannot accept this tax as creditable, but it has worked with countries to minimize the negative impact of the tax on U.S. investors.

The nondiscrimination article protects investors from discriminatory laws or practices. While laws discriminating against foreigners are not a serious threat at present, some foreign investors complain of discriminatory treatment by the tax administrations of Latin American countries. The nondiscrimination article, when combined with the mutual agreement procedure, provides investors with a great deal of comfort.

The mutual agreement article protects investors against unreasonable interpretations of treaty provisions. In the case of discriminatory treatment, for example, investors may enlist their own tax authorities as allies (if those authorities agree with the investors' position) in order to reach an understanding with the other tax administration. This provision makes it unlikely that investors will be subject to intimidation or other unfair treatment.

Taken as a group, these three articles alleviate the anxiety that some investors might have in a country that does not have a tax treaty with their country of residence. Hence investment may be facilitated even where taxes are not relieved.

Tax Administration

The main benefit of tax treaties for a country's tax administration is information exchange, which takes four general forms:

- *Automatic/routine exchange:* an ongoing exchange of computerized information (such as dividends paid to residents of the other country) that is collected by either country in the ordinary course of administration.
- *Specific request:* a request for information other than that provided under automatic exchange. The country receiving the request should use all of its powers to collect the information, as long as the request is reasonable.

- *Voluntary exchange:* one administration may offer unsolicited information to another if it believes the information may be of use.
- *Simultaneous audit:* two tax administrations may choose to audit the cross-border activities of a taxpayer on a joint basis. Such a procedure may be more efficient than separate audits, and it may help the taxpayer avoid double taxation resulting from inconsistent interpretations by the two administrations (on a transfer price, for example).

As noted earlier, Latin American countries generally have not found information exchange to be of much use. And, of course, information from another country is of little avail if the taxpayer involved has an exemption, or if a country has a territorial system. Information exchange, however, should become more useful as cross-border activity increases and Latin American countries continue to embrace international tax norms.

Synthesis

The fundamental question remains the same: does the potential increase in foreign investment associated with tax treaties justify the potential loss of revenue? On the basis of decades of experience, it is probably fair to say that neither investment nor revenue is dramatically affected. The extreme difficulty of measuring the impact of tax treaties on either foreign investment or tax collections makes a simple cost-benefit analysis impossible. The decision will always be somewhat subjective.

Nevertheless, the economic panorama in which the tax treaty decision is taken continues to change rapidly. Virtually all the changes strengthen the argument in favor of tax treaties. The changes include (1) increased competition for foreign investment; (2) greater opportunities to attract foreign investment arising from free trade zones; (3) the need for enhanced control of increased investment flows; (4) the need to replace traditional incentives such as tax-free zones with an attractive and modern tax regime; and (5) an understanding that tax rules inconsistent with international norms impede foreign investment.

All of these factors have played a role in the decision of countries such as Mexico, Chile, and Venezuela to pursue a tax treaty network, and they will continue to spur debate in the rest of Latin America. This does not mean that all Latin American countries should begin tax treaty negotiations. Nor should tax treaties be considered a "magic bullet" that will address all tax concerns presented by the new economic circumstances. On the contrary, tax treaties should be viewed as part of a package of reforms. Some of these reforms should be undertaken regardless of whether a tax treaty program is initiated, and others are prerequisites for a tax treaty network.

If a decision is made to move forward with tax treaties, many Latin American countries will confront several harsh realities. First, in most cases, there is no "foreign aid" element in tax treaty negotiations. In other words, the main aim of developed countries in the negotiations is to secure their own narrow interests—that is, their own fiscal interests and, to some extent, the interests of their resident investors who operate in the other country. By contrast, developing countries must protect their own fiscal interests and sacrifice revenue only where the tax reduction will benefit investors.

Second, in a negotiation between a Latin American country and a developed country, the developed country will usually have an experienced team of negotiators, whereas the Latin American country is likely to have a team that is still learning.[27] This imbalance is critical, given the conflicting interests mentioned above as well as a third fact: many developed countries attach little importance to tax treaty negotiations with smaller economies. The less economic activity between the two countries, the less pressure there is for a treaty, and the smaller the Latin American country, the less economic activity there is likely to be. Accordingly, the smaller countries in the region will have to undertake the necessary domestic reforms before moving forward, and choose their initial treaty partners carefully. Even so, they will have to be flexible in

---

[27] For this reason, it is wise to begin treaty negotiations with countries that are at a similar stage of development, or with countries that are not major investors, and later negotiate with countries like the United States and Spain.

negotiations. Even larger countries like Brazil and Argentina must be more flexible than in the past if they wish to expand their treaty networks. This flexibility will result in revenue loss if not offset by increased investment and enhanced enforcement (both of which are speculative, as noted earlier).

The more essential reforms include adoption of the worldwide system, transfer pricing rules, various anti-abuse rules, elimination of tax-free zones and other problematic tax incentives, and increased access to information. Tax treaties are an additional step that may be taken, a step that will support the other reforms and potentially attract foreign investment. To the extent possible, the foregoing reforms should be undertaken on a harmonized basis. Harmonized regimes will be attractive to investors, and a collective effort is likely to result in a superior set of rules. Tax treaties promote harmonization by establishing relatively uniform rules for the taxation of international activity.

References

Bloningen, B., and R. Davies. 2000. "The Effects of Bilateral Tax Treaties on U.S. FDI Activity." NBER Working Paper 7929. Cambridge, MA: National Bureau of Economic Research. Available at www.nber.org/papers/w7929.

Byrne, P. D. 1997. "The Business Assets Tax in Latin America—The End of the Beginning or the Beginning of the End?" *Tax Notes International* (September 22):941–48.

Haughton, J. 2002. "Trade Agreements and Tax Incentives: The Irish Experience." ITD-INTAL Tax and Integration Series. Washington, DC: Inter-American Development Bank.

9

Transfer Pricing and Latin American Integration

*Amparo Mercader and Horacio Peña**

Introduction

Since over 60 percent of the world's trade is carried out by multinational enterprises (MNEs),[1] it is no mystery that transfer pricing is the number one international tax issue.[2] There are several reasons for the increasing importance of transfer pricing.

First, with the liberalization and growth of international commerce, the sheer volume of intercompany trade among affiliates of MNEs has surged. In the last decade, more than ever MNEs have diversified their production chains across different countries and regions in an effort to enhance competitiveness. For instance, an MNE can produce goods in Brazil for resale in 15 different Latin American countries, sourcing raw materials from Argentina, using technology licensed from the United States, and be supported by a service center in Uruguay.

* The authors would like to thank Mariana Isturiz, as well as other members of the PricewaterhouseCoopers network, for their contributions: Juan Carlos Ferreiro and José María Segura (Argentina); Cassius Carvalho and Nélio Weiss (Brazil); Miguel Massone (Chile); Rafael Parra (Colombia); Fred Barrett, Mauricio Hurtado, and Claudia Margarita López (Mexico); Miguel Pua and Rudolf Roder (Peru); Jaime Esteves and Clara Dithmer (Portugal); Javier Gutiérrez Menduiña (Spain); and Juan Horowicz (Venezuela).

[1] By MNEs we refer to small to large multinational corporations that have at least one foreign affiliate.

[2] Ad Hoc Group of Experts on International Cooperation in Tax Matters, Transfer Pricing History, State of the Art, Perspectives Tenth Meeting, Geneva, 10–14 September 2001.

Political reasons have also played a role. Tax authorities in each of these countries want to make sure that they get a fair share of MNEs' income on which to levy their tax. Politicians from the United States and around the world have often alleged that foreign MNEs pay less tax than their local counterparts. Severe penalties and increasing audit risk in the United States have induced both U.S. and foreign MNEs to review their transfer pricing policies. In order to avoid losing more income than necessary to the United States, tax authorities around the world have responded with their own sets of rules and requirements.

What Is Transfer Pricing?

To put it simply, when cross-border transactions occur, each jurisdiction in which a product is bought or sold will receive a charge or remuneration. This is the transfer price. The transfer price will determine both direct and indirect taxes that should be paid by an MNE in each country. For this reason, there is a suspicion among governments that through aggressive transfer pricing planning, MNEs minimize taxes.

Evaluating transfer prices can be very simple or very complex depending on the nature and characteristics of the transaction. Unlike transactions among third parties there is not necessarily a price negotiation between subsidiaries of the same MNE. In some cases, a comparable product or benchmark is available in the competitive open market and that price can be used for intercompany transactions. However, if such a benchmark does not exist it may be difficult to determine an appropriate transfer price for an intercompany transaction. Consider a chip or production component that is only used in the production chain of a given MNE. A comparable price will not exist for such a product in the marketplace. However, that is just the starting level of complexity. An example of a more complex intercompany transaction is, for example, when one subsidiary of an MNE licenses to another the right to further develop an intangible property. Let's say that the affiliate licensing the technology was not able to profit from the idea, but that somehow the licensee is able to create a blockbuster product that has great commercial success. In this case, the royalty or payment to be made to the original owner of the intangible asset will be an interesting transfer pricing question.

MNEs are investing increasing resources in settling transfer pricing disputes. Surveys conducted by PricewaterhouseCoopers (PwC) show that transfer pricing, whether its justification, its evaluation, or settlement of disputes regarding it, is one of the most important issues on the agendas of many tax executives. In Latin America, PwC alone has about 250 specialists in the field of transfer pricing.

Regional Integration and Transfer Pricing

Transfer pricing is a direct result of global trade integration. Declines in external tariffs and the creation of regional trade blocs allow MNEs to exploit the comparative advantages of each jurisdiction in areas such as production, raw materials, and services.

MNEs do benefit from fiscal differences among countries. For instance, MNEs can generate higher income in countries where taxes are lower or in countries that offer specific benefits to lower their global tax burden, such as free trade zones. If there were no differences in tax rates across different jurisdictions, there would be less incentive for MNEs to use tax and transfer pricing to decrease their international tax burden. However, the vast majority of MNEs prefer to maintain a good relationship with the tax authorities in the countries where they operate.

The presence of harmonious taxing systems among jurisdictions of the same trade bloc is an incentive for MNEs to expand commerce. The risk of double taxation is lower across countries with similar fiscal systems and among those with tax treaties. Similarly, when transfer pricing requirements are similar among different jurisdictions, taxpayers face lower administrative burdens.

Finally, with increasing trade integration and the formation of regional trade blocs, governments are witnessing a reduction of tax revenue given the lower customs and duties. As a result, income tax has become more important for tax authorities around the world and transfer pricing is a fundamental tool in assessing whether MNEs pay appropriate income tax. Tax authorities in countries such as India are devoting increasing resources to monitoring transfer prices of MNEs to ensure their governments reap the benefits from foreign investment.

Basic Aspects of Transfer Pricing

One of the reasons transfer pricing has become such an important tool for tax authorities around the world is that not only does it govern the sale of tangible products but it also regulates all types of intercompany transactions that have an economic impact. Types of transactions include transfer or license of intangible assets and provision of services, as well as financing operations, to name just a few.

The Arm's Length Principle

The arm's length principle is the internationally accepted standard and most important concept in transfer pricing.[3] This principle establishes that transactions between related parties should be agreed upon at a price and under conditions similar to what would be agreed upon if they had been between independent, unrelated parties.[4] The provisions recognize that identical transactions between unrelated taxpayers are usually rare. It will be appropriate to consider comparable rather than identical transactions.

The arm's length principle was included in treaties concluded by France, the United Kingdom, and the United States as early as the 1920s. In a multilateral context it was formulated for the first time by the League of Nations in 1936.[5]

---

[3] The arm's length principle is the internationally accepted principle for evaluating the consistency of the transfer prices agreed upon in intercompany transactions. The most frequent international reference to the arm's length principle and its application is in the OECD Guidelines.

[4] See the OECD Model Tax Convention on Income and Capital, Article 9.

[5] See Ad Hoc Group of Experts on International Cooperation in Tax Matters, Transfer Pricing History, State of the Art, Perspectives Tenth Meeting, Geneva, 10–14 September 2001. (The paper was prepared by the United Nations Secretariat.)

However, prior to 1968 when the United States issued detailed regulations on the application of the arm's length principle, very little administrative guidance was available. The regulations issued by the United States impacted the Organisation for Economic Co-operation and Development (OECD)[6] discussion on transfer pricing. The OECD Guidelines on transfer pricing were published in 1995 and updated in 1996. Although the OECD Guidelines have no force of law they have provided guidance to MNEs as to which pricing methods tax administrations deem to be acceptable. Most transfer pricing regulations in Latin America and the world are based on the general principles stipulated in the OECD Guidelines.

In 1994, the United States issued formal transfer pricing regulations under Internal Revenue Code Section 482 (26 *U.S. Code*). Since then, countries around the world have followed this initiative and passed their own legislation. As of 2008, most countries around the world had or were in the process of effecting formal or informal transfer pricing requirements.

Most Appropriate Method

As stipulated under the OECD Guidelines, to determine what would be the price paid between independent parties, it is necessary to first select the most appropriate method. The most appropriate method will be the one that, given the facts and circumstances, provides the most reliable measure of the arm's length result.

The process of understanding the facts and circumstances involves a review of the characteristics of the transaction, including understanding the functions performed, assets employed, and risks borne by the parties to the transaction. In addition, the transfer price will also be affected by contractual provisions (such as payment terms), economic circumstances, and business strategies.

---

[6] The OECD, founded in 1961, is an international organization with 30 member countries, whose goal is to coordinate economic and social policies.

The OECD Guidelines establish that the most appropriate method for analyzing any transaction is the one that will provide the most reliable result and require the fewest adjustments. When the choice among methods is considered, the OECD Guidelines specify certain factors to be taken into account. First, there must be a close degree of similarity between comparable transactions and the transaction under analysis. Second, the method applied should allow a clear and accurate application. For this reason, complete and accurate data are important to ensure reliability of the results.[7]

Comparability and Range of Results

An operation does not have to be identical to the controlled operation to be considered comparable; however, an operation should be sufficiently similar to provide a reliable measure of an arm's length result.[8]

To be considered arm's length, the results of a controlled taxpayer should be within a range of results determined by two or more comparable uncontrolled transactions.[9] These concepts of comparability, reliability, and range of results are critical for the application of the arm's length principle.

The OECD Guidelines provide alternative methods to evaluate whether the prices between related parties are at arm's length. No one method shall be suitable for all situations and the most appropriate method will depend on the facts and circumstances of each intercompany transaction. The methods identified by the OECD Guidelines include traditional transaction methods as well as transactional profit-based methods.

Traditional Transactional Methods

Traditional transactional methods are considered by the OECD Guidelines to be the most direct way to evaluate intercompany transactions.

---

[7] See the OECD Guidelines, paragraphs 1.68 to 1.70.
[8] See the OECD Guidelines, paragraphs 1.15 to 1.30.
[9] See the OECD Guidelines, paragraphs 1.45 to 1.48.

Under the transactional methods, intercompany prices are compared directly to prices in the open market. However, there will not always be comparable transactions.

Comparable Uncontrolled Price Method

The comparable uncontrolled price (CUP) method compares the price charged for property or services in a controlled transaction to the price charged for property or services transferred in a comparable uncontrolled transaction in comparable circumstances.[10]

Comparability under the CUP method is closely linked to the degree of product similarity. To ensure reliability of the results, comparability adjustments should be limited and should have both a definite and a reasonable effect on price. Although there are no limitations on the use of comparable transactions in foreign markets, geographic differences can reduce the reliability of results. For example, the price paid for a manufactured good may be affected by the risk associated with shifts in currency value.

The CUP method can be used to benchmark intangible property such as brands, technology, know-how, and copyrights. When analyzing intangibles, comparability is based on the similarity of the intangible asset and its expected benefit or profit potential.

Resale Price Method

The resale price method (RPM)[11] is ordinarily appropriate in cases involving the purchase and resale of tangible goods in which the buyer/reseller does not add substantial value to the goods. Under the RPM, comparability is dependent primarily on the similarity of the functions performed and the risks assumed by the controlled and uncontrolled parties; it is less dependent on the similarity of the tangible goods bought and resold.

Application of the RPM involves the analysis of gross margins of the products being resold. The gross margin for applying this method is calculated as gross profit divided by net sales. Under the RPM the gross

---

[10] See the OECD Guidelines, paragraphs 2.6 to 2.13.
[11] See the OECD Guidelines, paragraphs 2.14 to 2.31.

margin is a measure of the functions performed by the reseller, including a return on its capital investment and the risks borne.

Cost-Plus Method

The cost-plus method (CPM)[12] tests the arm's length character of a transfer price in a controlled transaction by adding the gross profit markup to the product cost.[13] The CPM measures the value of functions performed and is ordinarily appropriate in cases involving the manufacture or assembly of tangible goods that are sold to a related party. The gross profit markup provides both compensation for the performance of manufacturing and/or assembly functions, and a return on capital invested and risks assumed by the manufacturer as well.

The reliability of the result can be affected by the degree of consistency in accounting practices between the controlled transaction and the uncontrolled comparables that materially affect the gross profit margin. Differences in inventory and other cost accounting practices would materially affect the gross profit markup. If possible, the appropriate gross profit markup should be derived by reference to the cost plus markup that the same supplier earns in comparable uncontrolled transactions.

Transactional Profit Methods

A transactional profit method examines the profits that may arise from particular controlled transactions. The transactional profit methods include the profit split method and the transactional net margin method.[14]

---

[12] See the OECD Guidelines, paragraphs 2.32 to 2.48.

[13] This method uses the cost of the sold product, excluding administrative costs.

[14] Although in the OECD Guidelines, traditional transactional methods are regarded as preferable over other methods and as methods of last resort, to be used in exceptional situations where there is limited availability of data, the trend seems to be changing. A recent OECD document states that in practice transactional profit methods are being used in more cases than would be expected given their last-resort status and suggests that transactional profit methods may indeed be more appropriate under certain circumstances. See "Discussion Draft for Public Comment," Centre for Tax Policy and Administration, Organisation for Economic Co-operation and Development, January 25, 2008.

Profit Split Method and Residual Profit Split Method

Where transactions are very interrelated, it may be difficult to evaluate them separately. The profit split method (PSM)[15] seeks to determine the division of expected profits that would have been agreed upon or negotiated by independent parties. The PSM first identifies the total profits and then splits those profits among the associated enterprises. The appropriate profit split may be determined by reference to the size of assets and risks assumed by each party directly transacting or indirectly participating in the transaction. The profit can also be split based on external market criteria—for example, profit split percentages observed among independent enterprises.

The residual profit split method (RPSM) is a variation on the PSM: from the total profit it deducts a minimum or routine profit using one of the previous methods. Keeping in mind the contribution of intangible assets from each party, the residual profit or loss is distributed among the related parties in the tested transaction.

One strength of the PSM is that it can be used in cases where no comparable uncontrolled transactions can be identified. It is very flexible and is easily adaptable to the most complicated set of facts. Under this method, it is also unlikely that either party to a controlled transaction will be left with extreme, improbable results.

Transactional Net Margin Method

The transactional net margin method (TNMM)[16] is one of the most commonly used methods, although the OECD Guidelines stipulate that it should be a method of last resort (see note 14). This method is based on comparing the profits earned by an entity in the transaction with the profits realized by comparable independent companies. The TNMM is frequently used because of its relaxed standards of comparability and easy application. This method is applicable both to transfers of tangible goods and intangible assets and to the provision of services.

---

[15] See the OECD Guidelines, paragraphs 3.5 to 3.25.
[16] See the OECD Guidelines, paragraphs 3.26 to 3.48.

The CPM established in the U.S. regulations is very similar to the TNMM. Both methods (TNMM and CPM) have won international recognition as essential ways of benchmarking related-party transactions. The TNMM has a distinct advantage over other traditional transactional methods. The OECD Guidelines indicate that in comparison with gross profit margins, the net margins can be more tolerant of functional differences between controlled and uncontrolled transactions. Differences in the functions performed among entities are often reflected in variations of specific operational costs, but not necessarily at the total cost level.[17]

Cost Sharing

Cost sharing agreements are contracts entered into by subsidiaries of an MNE to share costs and benefits of research and development in proportion to the reasonably expected benefits from the exploitation of the intellectual property. The United States issued detailed cost sharing regulations in 1995, with new proposed cost sharing regulations being issued in August of 2005. On September 27, 2007, The Internal Revenue Service issued a Coordinated Issue Paper (CIP) on buy-in royalties. The CIP presents many of the theories discussed in the proposed cost sharing regulations, and further indicates the intent of the IRS to apply such theories to examinations of current cost sharing arrangements under the existing regulations. The area of cost sharing agreements is one of the most controversial for tax authorities wanting to control intellectual property migrations to offshore locations.

Compliance

Formal documentation is the requirement that the taxpayer demonstrate it has made a reasonable effort to comply with the arm's length standard. In the United States, the requirement is that documentation

---

[17] See the OECD Guidelines, paragraph 3.27.

be contemporaneous (i.e., available) at the time of filing the tax returns. The OECD Guidelines make recommendations about the content and other requirements of the transfer pricing documentation, and these are defined in greater detail in each country's transfer pricing legislation.

Since their introduction in 1991, advance pricing agreements (APAs) have gained popularity with taxpayers in the United States and many OECD countries and emerging markets. Under this procedure, the taxpayer proposes a transfer pricing methodology and provides data to show that the proposed methodology should be accepted. The tax authority then evaluates the APA request. After discussion, if the taxpayer's proposal is acceptable, the taxpayer and the tax authority sign a written agreement that will hold for a number of years. The effect of an APA is that the tax authority will regard it as satisfying the arm's length standard as long as the taxpayer complies with the terms and conditions of the APA.

The Latin American Experience

General Observations

In general, transfer pricing regulations create a more stable invest-ment environment for MNEs. MNEs are accustomed to transfer pricing regulations, as they have been dealing with them in many countries for decades. Knowing what to expect reduces the uncertainty and fosters investment.

Once transfer pricing regulations and documentation requirements have been passed in a particular jurisdiction, the burden of proof shifts to the taxpayers, who must now demonstrate that they are transacting in accordance with the arm's length principle. Transfer pricing regula-tions also create new formal obligations such as contemporaneous docu-mentation requirements or transfer pricing information returns. These requirements need to be balanced in order not to create an excessive administrative burden for the taxpayers.

In general, most of the transfer pricing regulations in Latin America include internationally accepted rules. The adherence to the same or similar rules and methods around the world makes it easier for MNEs to meet their transfer pricing requirements around the world. Specifically, they can have one set of policies that will meet the requirements of all jurisdictions around the world. Any deviation from the basic set of principles and rules embodied in the OECD Guidelines can result in very painful and costly situations for taxpayers and may even result in double taxation.

Historical Background

Transfer pricing in Latin America began in Mexico (1997), followed by Brazil (1997), Chile (1997), Argentina (1999), Venezuela (2000), Peru (2001), Colombia (2004), Ecuador (2005), the Dominican Republic (2007), and Uruguay (2007). Several other Latin American countries, including Costa Rica and Honduras, have drafted transfer pricing laws that are undergoing discussion.[18]

Formal Obligations in Latin America

In Latin America the demand is generally for operations to adhere to the arm's length principle. Taxpayers may also be required to prepare contemporaneous documentation to be attached to tax returns or kept in files and presented to the tax authorities within a given period (often in 15 days). Transfer pricing documentation is sometimes also subject to independent third-party review, such as in Argentina. The more that formal obligations are required, the greater the shift of the burden of proof onto the taxpayers.

Countries differ as to whether the local tax authority imposes one or more of these requirements. Table 9.1 provides a comparative analysis of the transfer pricing documentation requirements across Latin American countries that have transfer pricing legislation. As the table shows, all the countries except Brazil adhere to the arm's length principle.

---

[18] At the time of writing (August 2007).

Table 9.1. Formal Transfer Pricing Obligations in Latin America

	Taxpayer requirement			
	Adherence to the arm's length principle	Contemporaneous documentation	Information return requirement	Independent third-party opinion
Argentina	✓	✓	Form 742 (semiannual) Form 743 (annual)	Certification of contemporaneous documentation
Brazil	No	Only invoices and safe harbor methods (June 30)	Yes, as part of tax return (June 30)	No
Chile	✓	No	No	No
Colombia	✓	✓ (June 30)	Forms 120/130	No
Dominican Republic	✓	No	No	No
Ecuador	✓	✓ (Six months after tax return)	✓	No
Mexico	✓	✓	Special Transfer Pricing Informative Return (Form 3560): due in mid-July	No
Peru	✓	✓	✓	No
Uruguay	✓	No	No	No
Venezuela	✓	✓ (Six months after tax return)	Form PT-99	No

Table 9.2 illustrates the methodologies and the type of economic analysis required by the transfer pricing legislation in place for each country listed. With the exception of Brazil, all the countries rely on the facts and circumstances and on internationally accepted methods. Adherence to the OECD Guidelines and their principles is voluntary because Mexico is the only country in Latin America that is a member

Table 9.2. Comparative Table on Transfer Pricing in Latin America

	Emphasis on facts and circumstances	Use of "safe harbors"	Use of internationally acceptable methods	Special documentation	Scope	Disclosure requirements	OECD member
Argentina	High	Low	✓	✓	Int'l	✓	No
Brazil	Low	High	Only CUP	No	Int'l	✓	Pending
Chile	High	Low	✓	No	Undefined	No	Pending
Colombia	High	Low	✓	✓	Int'l	✓	No
Dominican Republic	High	Low	✓	No	Undefined	No	No
Ecuador	High	Low	✓	✓	Domestic / Int'l	✓	No
Mexico	High	Low	✓	✓	Domestic /Int'l	✓	✓
Peru	High	Low	✓	✓	Domestic /Int'l	✓	No
Uruguay	High	Low	✓	No	Int'l	No	No
Venezuela	High	Low	✓	✓	Int'l	✓	No

of the OECD.[19] In most countries, transfer pricing legislation applies to international transactions only, but in some cases (Ecuador, Mexico, and Peru), transfer pricing also applies to domestic transactions among related parties.

Documentation Requirements in Latin America

Argentina

In general, the Argentinean legislation is in accordance with the OECD Guidelines and incorporates the methods established therein. Peculiarities of Argentina's legislation include requiring that the analyzed party under the TNMM always be the local entity. The motivation behind this requirement is probably to facilitate review by the local tax authority. However, this requirement in some circumstances results in analyses that are not in accordance with the OECD Guidelines. For example, consider an Argentinean manufacturing company that owns brands and processes and receives support services from a Uruguayan entity. Normally, we would test the results of the Uruguayan service provider, since it is the least complex of the parties—it does not own nonroutine intangible assets and bears minimal risks. However, given the requirement that we test the local entity, we may need to test the results achieved by the Argentinean manufacturing entity, even though its results may fluctuate significantly given the risks it bears.

Argentina introduced an additional method, not contemplated by the OECD Guidelines, for analyzing imports and exports. The motivation behind this method may be to neutralize the use of intermediary companies that sell goods at lower prices than those quoted on open commodity markets. Examples of such commodities include cereals, oilseeds, and by-products of the soil and hydrocarbons. In such cases, companies will consider the quoted value of a commodity in the commodity market on the day the good was invoiced. This method does not

---

[19] In May 2007, the OECD extended an invitation to five additional countries, including Chile, to open discussions for membership, and offered enhanced engagement, with a view to possible membership, to five other countries, including Brazil.

involve considering the price that would have been agreed upon with an international trade intermediary. In cases when the price agreed upon with the intermediary is higher than the quoted price on that date, the former should be used to assess the value of an operation.

In Argentina there is a clear definition of the interquartile range as the statistical measure normally used to analyze the results of a sample of comparable companies or transactions. Although this definition differs subtly from that established by the U.S. legislation, it is common to other Latin American countries.

Taxpayers in Argentina must submit their transfer pricing documentation to the tax authorities within certain time frames. Reports being submitted to the tax authorities must be notarized.

Argentina does not have a provision for APAs. Additionally, specific transfer pricing penalties apply if it is determined that a company was engaged in certain activities, including manipulating results, not providing the required information, or engaging in other irregularities.

Brazil

The transfer pricing rules in Brazil constitute the foremost exception in the region and are probably among the most peculiar in the world. From a practical perspective, Brazilian transfer pricing rules do not adhere to the arm's length principle. Brazil requires that safe harbors or fixed minimum and maximum profit margins be achieved for each transaction. For instance, when analyzing export prices, the average yearly price for a given transaction should be more than the cost of production plus a 15 percent markup, higher than 90 percent of the domestic market price, or higher than 85 percent of the resale price in the export market. Transactions can generally not be aggregated unless they relate to the same product. Brazilian law generally does not allow the use of profit-based methods.

The motivation behind the use of safe harbors may be to reduce the administrative burden for taxpayers. If a company can document that it achieved a given return, then it does not need to prepare transfer pricing documentation. The problem is that these fixed safe harbors are not flexible enough. For example, a taxpayer may need to artificially increase an export price in order to meet the safe harbor but at the expense of the importing jurisdiction. The foreign jurisdiction may impose an adjustment, which, because Brazil has limited treaties, may result in double taxation.

The definition of related parties under the Brazilian law is very broad. Companies that have a 10 percent share of ownership in the capital of another party are considered related parties. In some situations, this strict definition hinders compliance with transfer pricing rules. For instance, a company may own less than a 10 percent share of capital in a related party but practically operate as an independent party. In this case, although the Brazilian law considers the two entities related, they effectively negotiate their prices as independent parties. If companies are truly independent they may not share cost information. In such a case, the taxpayer will face greater difficulties as financial data necessary for the application of the safe harbors may not be available.

In 2005 Argentina and Brazil signed a bilateral agreement to share company information on transfer pricing and customs matters. This is part of a larger move by tax authorities around the world to share pricing information to reduce tax avoidance. Finally, transfer pricing penalties in Brazil are very significant and can amount to 100 percent of the amount of the tax an entity has failed to pay.

Chile

Currently Chile does not have formal transfer pricing documentation requirements. However, tax authorities can question the prices set between related parties if those prices do not comply with the arm's length principle—using the substance-over-form criterion in line with the characteristics of the operation. The Chilean tax authorities are expected to issue more stringent regulations in the near future.

Colombia

In Colombia both individual and consolidated returns are allowed. The method used will be the most appropriate one based on the information available and the nature of the operation. There are specific transfer pricing penalties, some of which were deferred to 2005. An APA authority was established in Colombia on January 1, 2006.

Dominican Republic

Transfer pricing legislation in the Dominican Republic became effective as of 2007 and the regulations that will provide additional details have not yet been released. In general, the transfer pricing legislation in the Dominican Republic adheres to the methods and principles of the OECD Guidelines. One peculiarity of the transfer pricing legislation in the Dominican Republic is that it contemplates the capacity for APAs in the tourism and other industries.

Ecuador

Similarly to Argentina, a peculiarity of the transfer pricing requirements in Ecuador is that the transfer pricing reports be provided to the tax authorities. To date, there are no specific transfer pricing penalties, and an APA mechanism has not yet been established.

Mexico

Transfer pricing regulations were first established in 1992 but it was not until 1996 that the Mexican Congress enacted a significant tax reform that included transfer pricing regulations. These changes represented a significant shift toward integrating Mexican tax rules with the other OECD member countries. In Mexico, there is an obligation to maintain contemporaneous documentation with the submission of the tax returns and provide an information return along with the tax return. The Mexican transfer pricing regulations also require the use of the interquartile range of arm's length results. Mexico has had an APA mechanism since 1997 and has concluded a large number of not only unilateral but also bilateral APAs. Between 2004 and 2007, Hacienda concluded 252 APAs of which 214 were unilateral and 38 were bilateral.

In addition to the transfer pricing legislation, there is a special regime for maquiladoras (toll manufacturers with a preferential customs regime). Besides promoting productive development through tax benefits, this system reduces a firm's administrative burden by establishing fixed profit margins. The maquiladora regime, for instance, establishes that companies that maintain a minimum taxable income of either 6.9 percent of assets or 6.5 percent of operating costs do not have to prepare transfer price documentation. To be included in this system, companies must seek authorization and meet a series of conditions (percentage of products exported, etc.). A presidential decree in October 2003 gave maquiladoras substantial tax benefits to further foster their competitiveness.[20] Although the required returns under the maquiladora regime are safe harbors, unlike in Brazil, where safe harbors are the only available alternative, in Mexico, companies may choose instead to use the TNMM method. This flexibility in the application of the safe harbors allows companies in adverse economic situations to face the risk of double taxation.

Peru

Since 2001, Peruvian income tax law has incorporated transfer pricing requirements. A taxpayer is required to maintain contemporaneous documentation in Peru. Peruvian legislation incorporates the OECD Guidelines and calls for the application of the most appropriate method. Other transfer pricing regulations include the use of the interquartile range, transfers by gratuitous title, and the dominant-influence criterion standard in assessing economic control. Modification to the transfer pricing rules came into effect for fiscal years beginning after January 1, 2006. Among other changes, Peruvian transfer pricing incorporated sophisticated APA mechanisms and specific transfer pricing penalties. Finally, Peru also requires a detailed transfer pricing information return for all transactions between related parties and with tax havens.

Uruguay

Transfer pricing legislation in Uruguay has come into effect recently, as of July 1, 2007. However, at this time, specific transfer pricing regulations

---

[20] On October 1, 2007, the Mexican Congress approved a tax bill for 2008 that replaces the previous asset tax with a new flat tax. The tax reform modified the income tax benefits for maquiladoras from 3 percent of the applicable safe harbor basis (i.e. assets or operating expenses) to 1.5 percent of foreign-owned assets.

which the law calls for, containing more detailed administrative applications, are not yet in existence. The Uruguay law does, however, incorporate the method developed in the Argentine tax law for commodities. Finally, another peculiarity of transfer pricing legislation in Uruguay is that the burden of proof is with the tax administration.

Venezuela

Venezuela requires contemporaneous documentation with the tax return. Although the regulations establish that the most appropriate method should be used, a taxpayer must consider the CUP method as the preferred method, in accordance with the OECD Guidelines. Venezuela has an APA mechanism and specific transfer pricing penalties.

Other Countries

Aruba enacted transfer pricing regulation in January 2008. Most other countries in Central America and the Caribbean still do not have transfer pricing rules.[21] El Salvador has general provisions but has not yet developed legislation. Costa Rica and Honduras have draft transfer pricing legislation that is being considered by their parliaments.

Like their counterparts in Chile, authorities in Costa Rica currently use their established principle of substance over form to conduct transfer pricing audits and enquiries. Substance over form is not a concept imposed by transfer pricing legislation but rather a principle similar to the commensurate-with-income standard in U.S. regulations. Under this principle, tax authorities may recast or recharacterize transactions entered into among related parties and provide alternative treatment for transfer pricing purposes.

Conclusions about Latin America

The region has a volatile economic environment and a changing legal framework. Hence Latin America needs a stable and predictable regula-

---

[21] This chapter was drafted in August 2006 and was last revised in February 2008. Transfer pricing rules in low tax jurisdictions are not as relevant given the lower incentive to shift income out of these countries.

tory framework that allows countries to attract foreign direct investment. MNEs are generally accustomed to preparing transfer pricing documentation in other countries where they operate, so documentation is not a significant burden, as long as the requirements are consistent with those in other jurisdictions.

In Latin America it is important to analyze and quantify factors such as economic cycles, competitive conditions, and country risk, because these have a significant impact on the profitability of local affiliates. Given the scarcity of local public company data, analysis often relies on comparable U.S. companies. However, Latin America is exposed to more abrupt business cycles than other markets. The "comparables" may need to be adjusted to better reflect the economic conditions in Latin American markets.

General Observations about Transfer Pricing

At the request of the Inter-American Development Bank and in preparation of this chapter, PwC conducted a survey[22] among members of the international transfer pricing network that sought opinions related to the best practices for introducing transfer pricing legislation in a given jurisdiction. The survey covered Argentina, Brazil, Colombia, Mexico, Peru, Portugal, Spain, the United States, Venezuela, and other countries.

In general, most practitioners agreed that adherence to the globally accepted OECD Guidelines helps facilitate trade among countries. The OECD Guidelines are incorporated into the legislation of most countries, allowing taxpayers to employ a consistent global transfer pricing policy around the world. This consistent legislation reduces the administrative burden and the risk of double taxation.

Members of the PwC network understand that it is important for tax authorities to strike a balance between their need for controls and information, on one hand, and the administrative burden on taxpayers,

---

[22] This survey was conducted during the first half of 2006.

on the other hand. If demands for information are excessive, they could entail undue cost for taxpayers. For example, tax authorities may want to require contemporaneous transfer pricing documentation only when transactions exceed a minimum amount. This de minimis rule focuses attention on significant transactions, such as those over $10 million. By establishing a minimum threshold on intercompany transactions, governments restrict the administrative burden to larger taxpayers. These taxpayers already have experience preparing transfer pricing documentation around the world, so the task is not especially onerous for them. However, for small exporters or entrepreneurs who might be ill-equipped to prepare the documentation, the de minimis rule obviates excessive costs.

Safe harbors or fixed profit margins are used in the Latin America region (in Mexico and Brazil) as a means of lowering the administrative burden on taxpayers. These safe harbors should not be vulnerable to accounting differences. An example of a safe harbor could be to request that companies meet a minimum profitability of 5 percent of their total costs. The best safe harbors are those that are optional and allow the use of traditional arm's length methods. In some cases, fixed profit margins are not flexible enough in the face of sudden economic changes. At the end of 2005, for example, Brazil had to modify its export safe harbors because of a substantial currency appreciation that reduced the profitability of exports in U.S. dollars.[23] Given the rise in production prices, most exporters were unable to meet the safe harbor requirements. Because Brazil amended the requirements toward the end of the year, only some taxpayers were able to take advantage of the relief. The beneficiaries were mostly taxpayers who had not made efforts throughout the year to meet the safe harbor requirements. Meanwhile, those who had taken the requirements most seriously exposed themselves to adjustments and double taxation in the other jurisdiction.

It is recommended that countries that are just starting to enact transfer pricing legislation should base their legislation on successful experi-

---

[23] In 2006 and 2007 Brazil issued similar amendments.

ences elsewhere. Probably the most efficient way of introducing transfer pricing legislation is to begin with basic principles and gradually increase the level of complexity and the number of demands. This allows the taxpayers as well as the tax authority to slowly increase their resources and capabilities in this area. For instance, although the legislation on transfer pricing in the United States dates back to 1968, documentation requirements were not in force until 1994.

It is also important to ensure the correct interaction of transfer price legislation within each country's regulatory framework, paying attention to legislation on indirect taxes, customs, and international agreements. In some countries, for instance, the mutual agreement clauses in tax accords allow for transfer pricing negotiation by tax authorities' competent authority teams to avoid the risk of double taxation in case of a transfer pricing adjustment, similar to the effect of a bilateral APA.

Tax Authorities and Transfer Price Audits

The Authorities Responsible for Overseeing Transfer Pricing

The officials assigned to transfer pricing typically come from local tax administration services. In Latin America there are specialized transfer pricing groups that usually consist of 10 to 60 people. The size of a team depends on how long each country's regulations have been in place and how many taxpayers are affected by transfer price legislation.

Officials of Latin American countries have become more specialized through national and international training courses. Officials who oversee transfer pricing are trained in accounting, economics, taxation, administration, and law. Inspectors generally work at a national or regional level. In countries like Argentina, tax authorities sometimes rely on external experts for particular issues.

There are formal and informal negotiations and mechanisms for resolving disputes within the region. In general, authorities in the region rely on private international and domestic databases for comparable financial information.

Transfer Pricing Audits in Latin America

Latin American tax authorities are giving increasing attention to transfer pricing and making enhanced efforts to audit transfer prices. Argentina and Mexico are considered the pioneers in this field. More recently, Brazil and Venezuela introduced exhaustive auditing processes and procedures and are being emulated by other Latin American countries.

Argentina

Argentina's tax authorities have focused on auditing transfer prices by sector. The pharmaceutical, automotive, and export commodity sectors are among the primary sectors of focus thus far. Companies are selected for inspection on the basis of income tax audits. Companies may also be chosen randomly or because of reports by government agencies such as the central bank, customs, the National Institute for Industrial Property, and special teams from tax authorities.

There have been more than 40 transfer pricing audits in Argentina. In several cases (especially in the pharmaceutical industry), a settlement was negotiated during the investigation stage, whereas other cases went to court. Tax authorities question numerous procedures and forms of economic adjustment that companies submit in response to various circumstances, such as the impact of an economic recession.

Brazil

Brazil has an aggressive plan for transfer pricing audits. Automated systems and specially created programs are used to select taxpayers for audit, and specialized inspectors conduct the investigations. As of August 2006, more than 160 audits had been completed in Brazil, with the fiscal year 2000 still being under audit.

Chile

Chile has no formal transfer pricing requirements. Tax authorities recently began to require submission of a sworn declaration containing information on transactions with related parties abroad. The Chilean tax authorities are expected to introduce more stringent transfer pricing regulations in the near future.

Colombia

Colombia's tax authorities recently introduced a series of transfer pricing documentation requirements covering fiscal year 2004 at the national level. Authorities try to identify those taxpayers who do not meet the formal transfer pricing requirements, which include the information return requirements and verifiable documentation. Authorities are expected to impose similar documentation requirements for later fiscal years.

Mexico

The Mexican authorities initially focused on APAs for the maquiladora industry. More recently, the tax administration was significantly restructured and reoriented. Resources were shifted from APAs to transfer pricing audits as part of a greater effort to increase the number of audits and review corresponding documentation. Taxpayers are selected for audit on the basis of an examination of income tax returns, tax reports, and other documents. Since 2006, Mexican tax authorities have focused on international restructurings and reorganizations and potential migrations of intellectual property. Several dozen transfer pricing audits are now under way, and an increase in audit activity in the coming months is expected. Tax authorities completed several audits leading to adjustments that brought additional income to the authorities.

Peru

Peruvian tax authorities recently started to require information on transactions with related parties, including specific data and corresponding documentation. These reviews focus on domestic operations and generally give companies 20 working days to provide the information.

Venezuela

Venezuelan tax authorities' transfer pricing reviews initially involved examining the information returns (Form PT-99). In 2005, authorities embarked on an aggressive inspection plan requiring documentation for several fiscal years (2001–2004). Taxpayers were given three days to produce the required documentation. In cases where companies lacked documentation, the operations were suspended. Given the importance of Venezuela's oil industry, tax authorities have focused closely on auditing this sector in general, including transfer pricing audits.

General Observations

Latin American tax authorities are beginning to focus on analyzing the substance and purpose of transactions among related parties. For instance, many Latin American countries receive corporate cost allocations. A company receiving a corporate allocation charge needs to demonstrate to tax authorities that a benefit is being perceived and a third party would be willing to pay for such service.

Matters that might be controversial in the future include:

- The appropriate level of aggregation among different types of transactions.
- The use of comparable companies with losses when applying profit-based methods.
- The use of multiyear averages, given the recent pronounced shifts in the Latin American economies, in order to smooth year-to-year results.
- Treatment of intellectual property rights.
- Inconsistencies in the forms and documentation, for example, in intercompany agreements, relative to the substance and how the taxpayers are actually operating.

Best Practices for Oversight Authorities

One of the main benefits of transfer pricing legislation is that it helps tax authorities administer transfer pricing matters. It also provides some basis for enabling tax authorities to prioritize among tax payers. For instance, when certain documentation requirements are imposed, the tax administration has a starting point for conducting an assessment.

Transfer pricing regulations often shift the burden of proof to the taxpayer, although it is not necessarily helpful to impose requirements on all taxpayers. A way of using the tax authority's resources more efficiently is to establish obligatory contemporaneous documentation requirements for companies that have significant or high-risk intercompany transactions. For instance, tax authorities typically introduce a minimum amount for intercompany transactions before a taxpayer is subject to a transfer pricing audit. In this case, tax authorities can also demand documentation from parties that transact with countries where fiscal control is weak or nonexistent (laws in Mexico and other countries make a provision for this).

Many countries also require a simple diagnostic form to be submitted with the tax return. This diagnostic form helps authorities undertake a quick transfer price control, with the option of requesting more information if needed. This form also allows tax authorities to determine if a transaction requires further investigation in case it is a high-risk or high-impact transaction. Additionally, the diagnostic form could be required from enterprises that have intercompany operations in excess of a certain threshold amount.

It is a common practice for tax authorities to focus their auditing resources on the most important local companies. For example, the Internal Revenue Service in the United States automatically audits the largest firms (the top 10 percent) each year. Tax authorities in countries such as the United States have specialized industry expertise in order to reduce taxpayers' frustration. Resolving disputes in due time and proper form is considered crucially important.

A practice that aids the transfer pricing administration is for each country to identify its industries or companies that are most sensitive to primary transfer pricing and to ensure that tax authorities have specialized inspectors for those industries.

Establishing a Working Group with the Country's Leading Companies

According to the PwC's experience, one way of successfully introducing transfer pricing is by initiating a dialogue between tax authorities and the main taxpayers. In this dialogue, both parties can ensure the feasibility of formal requirements and deadlines. Furthermore, they can require readily available information that the companies already possess, instead of creating burdensome requirements for new information. PwC also believes that it is imperative to inform companies beforehand about transfer pricing prerequisites and disclosure requirements. The goal should always be to attract investment and technology transfers of MNCs by minimizing the companies' inconvenience and burden. Good examples of aggressive and highly successful countries include Ireland and Singapore, which, in addition to maintaining a low effective tax rate, have eliminated red tape requirements and bureaucracy and have established offices in major cities around the world to attract and facilitate investment.

The Role of Multilateral Organizations

One way to avoid duplicating efforts is by relying on either a regional or an international multilateral organization. This organization could draw up drafts of transfer pricing legislation or unified model transfer pricing legislation and distribute the drafts among member countries. One advantage of starting with a single document is establishing closer consistency among the different laws. By ensuring greater consistency in the transfer pricing regulatory frameworks, multilateral organizations can foster trade and reduce the administrative burden of having to comply with different requirements in the jurisdictions where a particular multinational company may operate. A good example of these efforts is the European Union approach to standardized documentation for all its member countries.

Another way in which multilateral organizations could help is by offering technical and consultancy support. The principles of transfer pricing may be simple, but their application is often quite complex. In many cases, as discussed, there are no clear parameters on which to base prices. For this reason, economists may develop econometric models to address such complexities. Nonetheless, sophisticated resources are not affordable or necessary in every country. Hence, a multilateral advisory organization can be beneficial for smaller countries or countries with fewer resources. Working through such an organization to purchase databases and information sources can generate economies of scale. Data on comparables is usually public information found in costly source databases such as those of Standard & Poor's and Thomson Financial.

Finally, multilateral organizations can provide support to the competent authorities in settling disputes between the authorities in different countries. Competent authority can generally be invoked by a taxpayer who considers the actions of the tax authority in a given jurisdiction to result in taxation that is contrary to the provisions of a treaty. Thus, competent authority procedures will be available in countries with broad treaty networks, and they will be a resource available to taxpayers when they risk double taxation.

10

Exchanging Tax Information as a Tool to Curb Unfair Competition at the International Level

Claudino Pita

Politicians, social activists, ideologists and those who study society can be divided into three kinds: those who advocate the advantages of competition, those who support cooperation, and those who uphold a combination of the two.

The first group only sees permanent conflicts arising from group and individual interests. They are blind to solidarity. The second group only sees solidarity and its subsequent harmony. They are blind to conflict. And the third group pinpoints the dangers of unleashed competition and pure cooperation, and praises the benefits of regulated competition and partial cooperation between competitors.

The supporters of unleashed competition are individualists; those who support unpolluted solidarity are holists (pro-community); and those (we) who support the combination of both are systemists.

—Mario Bunge, *Cápsulas (translated from the Spanish)*

Introduction

Exchanging tax information to curb unfair competition at the international level means establishing a link between tax evasion, its effects on competition, and the exchange of information. This analysis is based on the premise that tax evasion, beyond its negative effects on tax collection and equity, may be compared to other unfair competition practices. Hence any tool used to combat evasion (in this case, the exchange of tax information at the international level) should be regarded as a means of strengthening markets and leveling the playing field.

This subject has not received the attention it deserves, especially in the face of growing globalization. It is still challenged by skepticism about its cost relative to its potential benefits for different tax administrations, as well as the practicality of enforcing exchange-of-information agreements when it is virtually impossible to impose penalties for noncompliance.

Background to the International Exchange of Tax Information

Basis for the Exchange of Information

In the current context of widespread globalization, tax administrations are restricted to their respective jurisdictions while businesses can plan and operate globally. This imbalance will not be resolved unless those agencies cooperate more closely. The international exchange of tax information can be crucial for developing control mechanisms that guarantee the effective enforcement of tax laws and leave little room for evasion. Tax evasion is difficult to curb when there is no access to data on the economic transactions taking place—partly or wholly—in other countries, on individuals resident in other countries, or on property located in foreign jurisdictions. Transfer pricing, tax havens, abuse of agreements, undercapitalization, and e-commerce are among the recurring issues of concern. If tax agencies do not give each other mutual assistance that provides them with reliable and timely international information, their mission becomes virtually impossible.

Information can be exchanged internationally without a formal agreement among countries.[1] However useful it may seem, this form of exchange is deficient because it is not backed by a legal instrument: it is

---

[1] Domestic legislation in some countries includes provisions to provide international fiscal assistance, even if no international conventions or agreements have been signed. In such cases, the countries operate under reciprocity and confidentiality conditions.

occasional and uncoordinated, subject to domestic legal limitations and based solely on the goodwill of the reporting country as to the extent and timeliness of the information and the manner in which it is supplied. For these reasons, it is now widely recognized that there is a need to encourage international agreements that guarantee the signatory states access to information that would not be available if they were to rely solely on their own methods and sources.

The international exchange of information may be assured by different means. For example, agreements may include provisions on the avoidance of double taxation, specific international accords may focus on information exchange, or international legal cooperation agreements may provide for the exchange of information in cases of tax crimes.

Provisions in Model Double Taxation Agreements

The most common way to agree on the exchange of information is by including clauses on the matter in broader international treaties on double taxation. From the outset, agreements and model accords on this issue have included provisions on the exchange of information. Initially, this was done with the sole purpose of supporting the implementation of the agreement itself, but gradually such provisions have been included in order to combat tax evasion, as shown by the evolution of the information exchange provision in Article 26 of the Model Tax Convention of the Organisation for Economic Co-operation and Development (OECD).

The OECD Model Tax Convention

As early as 1963, in its first draft, the OECD Model Tax Convention, which is the most commonly used framework for such agreements, included in Article 26 a provision on information exchange that read as follows:

> (i) The competent authorities of the Contracting States shall exchange such information as is necessary to carry out the provisions of this Convention or the domestic laws concerning the taxes comprised herein, insofar as the taxation thereunder is in accordance with the Convention. Any information thus

received shall be treated as secret and shall not be disclosed to any persons or authorities other than those concerned with the determination or collection of the taxes that are the subject matter of this Convention.

(ii) In no case shall the provisions of paragraph 1 be construed so as to impose on a Contracting State the obligation:

(a) to carry out administrative measures at variance with the laws and administrative practice of that or of the other Contracting State;

(b) to supply information which is not obtainable under the laws or in the normal course of the administration of that or of the other Contracting State;

(c) to supply information which would disclose any trade, business, industrial, commercial or professional secret or trade process, or information, the disclosure of which would be contrary to public policy (ordre public).

A revised version was published in 1977 and was intended, according to the commentaries, not to introduce substantial changes but to make the article more explicit in order to avoid misunderstandings about its scope. Thus the revision can be considered an expansion of the above-mentioned provisions. In particular, it clarifies the following:

- Information may be exchanged about individuals not resident in the contracting states.
- Information may be exchanged for the purpose of enforcing domestic laws provided it *is not contrary to* the Convention. (The previous wording was "is in accordance with.")
- The information received will be treated with the same degree of secrecy and "in the same manner as information obtained under the domestic laws" of the receiving state.
- The individuals and authorities who may have access to the information, and the purposes for which that information may be used, are spelled out.

▪ The information received may be disclosed "in public court proceedings or in judicial decisions." (This last item seems to be the only substantial amendment made.)

At the same time, it is worth pointing out that subsequent changes to Article 26 mitigated some of the limitations on the exchange of information included in previous versions—a clear sign of the growing importance attached to the exchange of information by the OECD, as well as by the international community.

Those limitations were softened after the report by the OECD Committee on Fiscal Affairs on the Model Tax Convention (2000 edition), which was approved on April 29, 2000. Among the modifications introduced, worth noting is the one making it possible to exchange information about all taxes imposed by all government levels.[2]

Moreover, the new version of Article 26 and its commentaries adopted by the aforementioned Committee on June 1, 2004, explicitly include some of the provisions already set forth in bilateral agreements that broaden the scope of the exchange of information prescribed in the article. The following modifications can be highlighted:

▪ With regard to the nature of the information to be exchanged, the expression "as is necessary" was changed to "foreseeable relevance." The aim was to provide for the widest possible exchange of information on tax matters, and, at the same time, to clarify that the signatory states are not at liberty to engage in "fishing expeditions"—that is, to request information that is unlikely to be relevant to the tax affairs of a given taxpayer.

▪ A paragraph was added whereby the signatories should obtain and exchange information whether or not they need it for their own tax purposes.

---

[2] Following the amendments, paragraph 1 of Article 26 currently reads: "The competent authorities of the Contracting States shall exchange such information ... concerning *taxes of every kind and description imposed on behalf of the Contracting States, or of their political subdivisions or local authorities*" (italics added).

- A new paragraph stipulated that banking confidentiality shall no longer be used as grounds to refuse to exchange information.
- The information exchanged is now made accessible to the signatories' higher-ranking officials responsible for supervising tax administration.

The United Nations Model

The exchange of information was also analyzed by the Group of Experts on Tax Treaties between Developed and Developing Countries, established pursuant to Resolution 1273 of the United Nations (UN) Economic and Social Council (ECOSOC). The mandate published by the Group in 1975 included a recommendation to broaden the scope of the provision on information exchange in the 1963 OECD model. The aim was to prevent fraud and tax evasion, as well to facilitate consultations among competent authorities with a view to developing the appropriate conditions, methods, and techniques for information exchange.

That mandate was included in the 1980 UN model, wherein the change (relative to Article 26 of the OECD model) is the express assertion that the exchange of information will take place "in particular for the prevention of fraud or evasion of such taxes" covered by the treaty. The following statement was also added: "The competent authorities shall, through consultation, develop appropriate conditions, methods and techniques related to the matters in respect of which such exchanges of information shall be made, including, where appropriate, exchanges of information regarding tax avoidance."

The Andean Pact Model

Provisions on information exchange are contained in Articles 20 and 19, respectively, of the Agreement among Member Countries of the Andean Pact and the Standard Agreement between Member Countries and other States outside the Subregion, approved by Decision 40 of the Cartagena Agreement in 1971. The two articles have the same wording:

> The competent authorities of the member countries shall hold consultations with each other and shall exchange the

information necessary to resolve by mutual agreement any problem or doubt that may result from the implementation of this agreement, and to establish the administrative controls needed to avoid fraud and tax evasion.

The information exchanged pursuant to the stipulation of the previous paragraph shall be considered confidential and may not be transmitted to any person other than the authorities responsible for the administration of the taxes that are the subject matter of this agreement.

For the purposes of this article, the competent authorities of the member countries may communicate with each other directly.

Given the provisions on the exchange of information in these two agreements, it can be said that, in a way, this is a step beyond the provisions of the OECD and UN Model Conventions. In other respects, the scope of the two Andean agreements is limited.

- The Andean provisions are broader in that they eliminate a series of express limitations set out in the OECD and UN models.
- The provisions are more limited in terms of the confidentiality of the information received and the individuals to whom the information can be disclosed (only the authorities responsible for the administration of the taxes that are the subject matter of the convention).

Provisions on Information Exchange Included in Double Taxation Conventions Currently in Force in Latin America and the Caribbean

At present, about 200 comprehensive international conventions to avoid double taxation are in force involving Latin American and Caribbean countries. Three of these are multilateral agreements: the Andean Pact, the Caribbean Community (CARICOM), and an agreement with the Netherlands.

As for bilateral accords with provisions on the exchange of information, five have no clause regarding double taxation: Argentina-Switzerland, Ecuador-Switzerland, Jamaica-Switzerland, Trinidad and Tobago-Switzerland, and Venezuela-Switzerland. The other agreements incorporate different versions of the OECD model provision,[3] with two exceptions: the Argentina-Bolivia and Argentina-Chile accords adopt the Andean Pact (Decision 40) model.

The provisions included in these conventions offer a wide range of alternatives on the scope of information exchange. The two bilateral agreements that follow the Decision 40 model (Argentina-Bolivia and Argentina-Chile) use the exact wording of the clause in that model. Various alternatives are evident in the conventions that follow the OECD model, but the dominant clause is the one in the 1977 version. The application of this clause might be only a partial solution to the need for the exchange of information, because of the following limitations:

- Consultations are to relate to the taxes covered by the convention, exempting the reporting state from providing information on any taxes outside the scope of the agreement.
- A state is entitled to deny the requested information if it is not sure that the receiving state will handle the data in line with the confidentiality rules imposed by its own legislation.
- No state is bound to adopt administrative measures that are contrary to its own domestic laws or administrative practices, nor to go beyond what is set forth in such laws or normal administrative practices. Furthermore, the parameters to determine the extent of the obligations of the state facing the request are confined not only to its own regulatory or material restrictions but also to limitations of the same kind in the requesting state. Hence the information that a state is obliged to provide to the other contracting state will be the minimum required (from the regulatory

---

[3] Given the similarities between the UN model and the OECD model, no distinction is made here as to which clauses of those agreements are based on the UN model.

or material viewpoint) by the states involved in the exchange of information.[4]

■ Disclosure of any trade, business, industrial, commercial, or professional secret or business processes, or of any information contrary to public policy, is excluded from all obligations. This gives primacy to specific domestic regulations and precludes the possibility of including in the agreements any provision that would restrict the scope of domestic regulations.

Moreover, an analysis of the exchange-of-information provisions adopted in the conventions on double taxation currently in force in Latin America and the Caribbean shows that the most relevant limitations in the OECD model (1977 edition) are either maintained or tightened. In this regard, the following can be highlighted:

■ Almost all of the provisions clearly state that the exchange of information and the use of the information received shall cover only the taxes specified in the convention.

■ In several cases, the exchange of information is restricted to whatever is necessary for the implementation of the agreement's provisions.

■ In most cases, there is a reciprocity obligation, both de jure and de facto.

These limitations indicate that it might be useful, even for countries that already have comprehensive treaties on double taxation, to sign specific agreements on the exchange of tax information. Such agreements could have a broader scope than the mere exchange of information and could establish other mutual administrative assistance mechanisms, such

---

[4]This circumstance was recognized in paragraph 18 of the commentary on that article, which states that if two contracting states have information systems that are very different in structure, the conditions under subparagraphs (a) and (b) of the second paragraph of Article 26 will result in those states exchanging very little information, or perhaps none at all.

as assistance on tax collection, as set out in subsequent versions of the OECD Model Tax Convention.

The exchange proposed in a provision of a double taxation convention, whose purpose is to combat tax evasion and avoidance, does not seem to be the most suitable means of meeting the tax agencies' information needs, especially if the above-mentioned limitations are taken into account. Obviously, this does not mean that double taxation agreements should exclude provisions on information exchange. Their inclusion will always be necessary to ensure that agreements are properly implemented, and in the absence of a better solution (such as a specific agreement), these provisions foster at least some exchange of information.

It should be kept in mind, however, that double taxation agreements have a primary and immediate objective—to avoid double taxation. Information exchange is a secondary goal, and one that is solely geared to the application of the agreement's provisions, as prescribed in most of the accords in force. Hence, when they also refer to another purpose (that the exchange of information is to help combat tax evasion and avoidance), they are conditioned by a series of limitations that restrict their effectiveness. For that reason, therefore, the battle against tax evasion and tax avoidance, as a main objective, should be pursued through specific agreements on exchange of information.

Specific International Agreements on Tax Information Exchange

Specific agreements on the exchange of tax information are recommended when the aim is to develop instruments intended to fight tax evasion and avoidance. This is more effective than including a provision on the exchange of tax information in double taxation agreements, for several reasons:

- Globalization makes it essential that tax administrators have guaranteed access to cross-border information to effectively control tax liabilities.
- Taxes covered by double taxation agreements are those levied on income or on both income and net worth—that is, the areas in

which most international double taxation problems arise. With a few exceptions, which might increase with the new wording of Article 26 of the model, effective since 2000, the exchange of information under such agreements is limited to these taxes. This is the case despite the fact that substantial tax frauds have been committed with indirect taxes, particularly the value-added tax and other indirect taxes subject to "border tax adjustments," by means of false export or credit operations resulting in the improper reimbursement of alleged export credit balances.

▪ Preventing double taxation and combating tax evasion and avoidance are two distinct objectives. A country may very well be interested in entering into an agreement to attain one of these objectives but not both. For instance, Germany—the OECD member with the largest number of conventions with Latin American and Caribbean countries—seems interested only in avoiding double taxation. All the conventions it has signed provide for information exchange only through the "limited information exchange" clause—that is, exclusively for the application of the provisions of the agreement. In contrast, the United States seems to emphasize information exchange agreements, at least in Latin America and the Caribbean, where it has concluded nine tax information exchange agreements and five double taxation agreements.

▪ The use of a single instrument to serve two distinct purposes always introduces a certain degree of inflexibility that is detrimental to one purpose or the other. In the case of the agreements designed to prevent international double taxation, the adverse impact is evidently on information exchange.

▪ In the pursuit of a framework of mutual assistance to combat tax evasion and avoidance, it is difficult for a simple clause to overcome the differences that contracting states have in their legislation, administrative practices, and material capabilities to exchange information. It is even harder when the states involved have different levels of development. The legal and, particularly, material reciprocity criteria traditionally embodied in double taxation agreements seem to be an inappropriate and therefore inadvisable solution for the exchange of information, especially when the countries involved are at different development stages and the difference is reflected in their tax administrations.

■ The officials who are best qualified to weigh the needs, possibilities, and formalities required for the exchange of information with other countries are those responsible for managing taxes—that is, the tax administrators. In many countries, however, the negotiation and drafting of agreements designed to avoid international double taxation are entrusted to officials who are foreign to the tax administration. In many other countries, the participation of tax officials is only tangential or limited to the mere application of such agreements. Since the exchange of tax information is meant to help fight tax evasion and avoidance, it seems appropriate that tax administrators play an active role in developing agreements—determining their scope and, in particular, identifying and recommending the mechanisms and instruments necessary to ensure their operational effectiveness.

The OECD and most of its member countries seem to share a concern that the information exchange clauses based on Article 26 of the OECD model are inadequate to fully respond to the growing need for such exchange. This explains why countries that already have a broad double taxation agreement network have also ratified other agreements dealing with the exchange of tax information. The following instruments can be mentioned in this respect:

■ The 1977 EEC Directive, which—following successive expansions—has come to rule the exchange of information on both direct and indirect taxes, making specific reference to different aspects of such exchange, some of which might be understood to be implicit in the wording of Article 26.

■ The Multilateral Convention on Mutual Administrative Assistance in Tax Matters between the Council of Europe and the OECD, concluded in 1988. This 32-article convention covers many different ways of cooperating administratively to assess and collect taxes. These range from the exchange of tax information to the recovery and enforcement of tax claims abroad, with a view to fighting tax evasion and avoidance.

■ The Nordic Convention on Mutual Administrative Assistance in Tax Matters, derived from the 1972 treaty that served as the basis for the Council of Europe–OECD multilateral convention. The new version of the Nordic Convention, which accompanies the terms of the aforementioned multilateral convention, has been in force since 1991.

Reference should also be made to European Union Council Directive 2003/48/EC of June 3, 2003, on taxation of savings income in the form of interest payments. Individuals who are residents of member states are often able to avoid paying their state of residence any taxes on interest they receive in another member state, because of the absence of coordination of national tax systems for the taxation of savings income in the form of interest payments. This circumstance creates distortions in capital movements. Hence Directive 2003/48/EC provides for the automatic exchange of information on interest payments between member states.[5]

Most Latin American and Caribbean countries do not have a long history of information exchange agreements. Twelve such agreements are currently in force, including nine that the United States has concluded with the following countries: Barbados, Bermuda, Costa Rica, the Dominican Republic, Honduras, Jamaica, Mexico, Peru, and Trinidad and Tobago. The other three agreements now in force are the Canada-Mexico, Spain-Argentina, and Argentina-Peru agreements, the last being the only information agreement between two Latin American countries. The latter

---

[5] Since Austria, Belgium, and Luxembourg cannot apply the automatic exchange of information at the same time as the other member states, during a transitional period these three countries should apply a withholding tax to the savings income covered by this directive, so as to ensure a minimum level of effective taxation on that savings income. In addition, the directive provides that agreements with third countries are to be made, to ensure the application of measures equivalent to those imposed on member states.

two accords were negotiated and signed in 2004, on the basis of the Inter-American Center of Tax Administrations (CIAT) Model Agreement for the Exchange of Tax Information.

Since CIAT's main mission is to encourage all forms of international cooperation among tax administrations, the exchange of information is commonly dealt with in all its activities. For more than two decades, information exchange has been included on the agenda of CIAT's general assemblies and technical conferences, a circumstance that has helped raise awareness of this crucial topic.

In addition, drawing particularly on the Council of Europe's Convention and the United States Model Treaty on Tax Information Exchange, in 1990 CIAT drafted its first Model Convention on Tax Information Exchange. This agreement was intended to serve as a comprehensive framework for all its member countries.

CIAT subsequently established a Working Group on International Taxation, made up of tax officials from Argentina, Brazil, Canada, Italy, Mexico, Spain, and the United States. One of the group's duties was the promotion of tax information exchange through specific activities such as:

■ Reviewing the previous CIAT Model Agreement on the Exchange of Information to clarify, specify, and complement its provisions. The outcome of this review was the CIAT Model Agreement for the Exchange of Tax Information, adopted by its Thirty-Third General Assembly in El Salvador in 1999.

■ Drafting the explanatory notes to the reviewed model, which were completed and approved by the Thirty-Fifth General Assembly in Chile in 2001.

■ Establishing strategies and implementation manuals.

■ Assessing the organization's needs for carrying out information exchange activities.

■ Identifying and scheduling technical assistance and training mechanisms to promote the development of tax information exchange.

The aim of such work, as pointed out in one of the CIAT documents, is to facilitate the conclusion and implementation of information exchange arrangements. Yet however crucial these are for combating tax evasion, they have not been used to the desired extent by the CIAT members, especially those from Latin America.

In this respect, the actions undertaken by the Working Group aim to establish parameters that go beyond the mere existence of a model agreement, seeking to provide support and solutions for its effective implementation and application by tax administrations.

Basic Features of Tax Information Exchange Agreements and Requirements to Ensure Their Effectiveness

Agreement Components

Tax information exchange agreements typically fit into the category that international law calls "executive agreements." Unlike conventions and treaties, these generally do not require legislative approval because they are intended to regulate or specify the administration's powers or terms of reference as already prescribed by legislation or by a convention or treaty that is in force.

To serve their purpose fully, these agreements must properly delineate the powers or terms of reference provided for in the corresponding legislation or convention, including the operational matters required for the exchange of information. The procedures and scope of these agreements may vary by country, depending on the legal system. But they should contain, and specify in some detail, a number of elements that may enhance the effectiveness of information exchange.

Persons about Whom Information May Be Exchanged

The exchange should not be limited to information related to residents of the signatory countries. A tax administration may be interested in information about someone residing in a third country who has incurred tax obligations as a nonresident in the country requesting the information.

Objective of the Exchange and Taxes Covered by the Agreement

The purpose of the agreement is the exchange of information necessary to administer and enforce tax obligations, and thus it is an effective means of combating tax evasion. Given the objective, the scope of the taxes covered should be as broad as possible. The current trend is to include both direct and indirect taxes. But in the case of information exchange clauses in double taxation treaties, some countries' legal systems restrict the taxes covered to those specifically mentioned in each treaty.

Types and Methods of Information Exchange

Agreements should expressly establish the forms or methods of exchange that are to be applied. These should be defined as broadly as is practicable. They may include exchange of information on request (or specific exchange), automatic exchange, spontaneous exchange, exchange of general information on business sectors, simultaneous tax audits, and tax audits abroad. The latter two—simultaneous audits and audits abroad—should be understood as forms of cooperation to acquire information and facilitate exchange, rather than as methods of exchange.

Exchange of Information on Request (Specific Exchange). One country may ask another for specific information, but only when it has exhausted all of its own information sources. This means of consultation is deemed to be complementary to those domestically available to the tax administration, all of which must be previously exhausted. The request should clearly indicate the name of the person about whom information is sought, the type of information requested, and the purposes thereof. These steps are intended to preclude "fishing expeditions," thereby ensuring that no information that is unlikely to be relevant to the tax affairs of a given taxpayer is requested.

As for the country being asked for information, it should, among other things, examine the accounting books, documents, records, and any other sources that may be relevant to the investigation. If necessary, it should also interview anyone possessing knowledge of or information about the matters under investigation.

Automatic Exchange of Information. The automatic exchange of information involves the regular provision of information on, for instance, specific categories of income (interests, royalties, and so on) obtained in one country by residents of another country, as previously agreed upon by both countries. This type of exchange will increasingly be made via digital means.

In addition, certain types of activities or transactions warrant the routine transmission of information, such as the opening of business branches or the establishment of permanent facilities, the creation or dissolution of a company or trust, and the opening or closing of corporate bank accounts.

One of the greatest advantages of the automatic exchange of information is that it makes it possible to gather information on taxpayers or income sources unknown so far, without the need to submit any special request.

Spontaneous Exchange of Information. The signatory countries transmit information to each other on a spontaneous basis if one of them gains access to information that may be relevant to the other. During an audit, for example, an official may uncover information suggesting the need for another country to impose taxes. Based on that information, the official may assume that inappropriate tax advantages are being obtained in the other country. In such an event, that information should be sent to the other country without awaiting a request from it.

The information may consist of details of a resident's particular circumstances, or operations connected to the resident's tax liabilities in the other country, or any type of activity or transaction that is directly or indirectly related to individuals or firms resident in the other country.

The authorities themselves must determine whether this type of exchange should conform to the conventional directives regulating such exchange or, by contrast, whether the country transmitting information should define when and how to do so.

With this method, it is important to provide for feedback on the outcome of the information forwarded to the other country, since that outcome may be of interest to the country that forwarded the original information. An example is the verification in the country of residence of the nonexistence of income from the payment of fees, recorded as expenses in the country that spontaneously forwarded the information.

Exchange of General Information on Business or Industry Sectors. In this case, the exchange of information concerns not specific taxpayers but a business or industrial sector as a whole, such as the petrochemical, automobile, or pharmaceutical sector. One aim is to allow the signatory countries to learn about and compare tax avoidance trends and schemes, pricing policies, and financial systems related to that sector.

Simultaneous Tax Audits. This form of cooperation is very important for mutual assistance and information exchange. It is an arrangement between two or more countries to examine simultaneously, each in its own territory, the tax affairs of a person or persons in whom they have a common or related interest, with a view to exchanging any relevant information they uncover.

This form of cooperation is particularly useful for analyzing transfer pricing and for examining cases where tax-avoidance schemes with countries classified as tax havens either exist or are presumed to exist, provided that the effort helps both competent authorities coordinate and control the audits. In certain circumstances, moreover, this procedure may also prove useful for taxpayers, because simultaneous audits may help reduce administrative costs by avoiding the duplication of tasks that would otherwise be undertaken by each of the competent tax authorities involved at different stages of the procedure.

Tax Audits Abroad. This method involves the tax officials of a signatory country being present during an audit conducted in another country. These audits may spring from an invitation to take part in assessing the scope of a request for information, or to join in an interview with a local taxpayer in connection with the requested information. In that case, the presence of a foreign official may, depending on the applicant country's interest, lend accuracy to the information to be forwarded. Furthermore, the visit may be made at the request of the taxpayer, if he or she prefers that inspectors from another country examine his or her records in situ rather than take them abroad, which in some circumstances may be difficult.

Definitions

To facilitate the interpretation and application of agreements, it is customary to include definitions of certain terms, among which "competent authority" is worth mentioning. This refers to the person or institution appointed by each country to manage the exchange of information, as well as the terms under which that authority may be delegated. Given the nature and scope of information exchange agreements, it is recommended that the authority be delegated to the highest-ranking official of the tax administration—usually the individual who signs the agreement.

A referral clause is usually included, in order to construe terms not defined in the agreement. Under the referral clause, undefined terms are to be interpreted according to the signatory countries' domestic legislation, with precedence given to tax laws.

Obligation to Exchange Information: Procedures and Forms

It should be noted that the exchange of information is mandatory, with the exceptions explicitly listed in the agreement. Hence the obligation to provide information is not limited to the data held in the files of the tax administration to which the request is made. When the information sought is not available in those records, the country receiving the request must take all relevant information-gathering measures to provide the applicant country with the requested information. This may be done, for example, through audits of or investigations into the taxpayer and other related parties. In addition, information must be exchanged without regard to whether the country to which the application is made needs or is interested in the information for its own tax purposes.

One of the most crucial matters that should be addressed, either in the body of the agreement or in an annex, is what formalities must be met when forwarding the information requested. These should be examined and determined individually for each of the signatory countries, to ensure that all procedures are followed and that the information received meets evidentiary or other legal requirements. This provision is included even though the exchange of information is made upon request; the formalities may be specified in the request for information so that the competent authority takes account of them—to the extent allowable by its own laws—when sending or acquiring the information.

Use of Single Taxpayer Identification Numbers

There is no doubt that a common, single taxpayer identification number for all signatory countries would greatly facilitate the exchange of information. The process might be complicated to implement, but significant headway could be made by adopting some system of correlating the taxpayer identification numbers used by the participating countries, at least in connection with firms operating regularly in both jurisdictions. This system would, in particular, expedite the implementation of automated data cross-reference software and the automatic exchange of information.

It would be necessary to establish a minimum requirement as to the taxpayer particulars to be indicated in the information requests and deliveries. The aim here would be to increase the accuracy of the identification of taxpayers and avoid any confusion that might arise in the event of individuals having the same name.

Time Considerations

Information exchange agreements typically apply to information that existed before the agreements entered into force.

Information Exchange Limitations

Agreements may provide for limitations on the exchange of information. If a request is covered by the stipulated limitations, the countries shall not be obliged to exchange the information. For example:

- Tax secrecy may limit disclosures. Furthermore, the country receiving information is obliged to treat it with a similar degree of confidentiality as the country providing the information.

- The existence of de jure or de facto reciprocity may limit the exchange of information, although there is currently a tendency to rule out de facto reciprocity, particularly when the agreement is between countries with disparate resources.
- No information disclosure should be contrary to public policy (the *ordre public*). That is, information provided should not run counter to a country's vital interests.
- Information exchange should not result in the disclosure of any business, industrial, professional, or other secrets, which are not to be interpreted broadly. If the laws of one of the parties were too broad and strict as to the secrets protected, the agreement might fail to meet its purposes. In this respect, therefore, the scope of the rules on such secrecy should be expressly defined, so as to obviate the danger of conflicting interpretations. For example, professional secrecy should not apply to ownership information with tax implications.
- No administrative procedures at variance with a country's domestic laws or administrative practices should be carried out.

Confidentiality of the Information Received

To ensure the confidentiality of the information received, it is advisable to clearly identify the persons and authorities to whom it may be disclosed. It should also be expressly indicated whether the information may be disclosed to other jurisdictions and, if so, the procedure for doing so (for example, with the express written consent of the competent authority of the party to whom the request is made).

Rights and Safeguards

Many countries' legislation establishes that persons about whom information is being exchanged shall enjoy certain rights and safeguards, such as a right to notification, to challenge the exchange following notification, and so forth. It is important that the countries involved be mutually aware of these rights and safeguards and, if possible, set out the necessary provisions to limit them. In cases of tax fraud, for instance, the obligation to notify should not be applicable, or notification should be postponed until the information has been exchanged.

Use of the Information for Other Purposes

The information obtained through tax information exchange agreements is generally subject to the express condition that it may be used only for the purposes laid down in the agreement. This is another important matter to be considered when countries negotiate and enter into such agreements. They may stipulate that if it is necessary to use the information for other purposes, the competent authority of the country that provided it should be consulted and, if circumstances allow, should authorize its use.

Cost Incurred in Exchanging Information

Agreements generally establish how the costs incurred in exchanging information are to be allocated, distinguishing between ordinary and extraordinary costs. In general, ordinary costs are borne by the country to which the request is made, while the extraordinary costs are borne by the applicant country.

Terms for Gathering and Forwarding the Information

Agreements should specify the maximum periods permitted for gathering and forwarding the information requested. Time limits are necessary because if the information exchange is to be effective, not only should the formalities be met, but the information should be made available to the applicant country in a timely fashion. Hence agreements should establish a short initial period for countries to respond to information requests, informing the applicant country whether they can meet the request and, if so, how quickly. If the response time will be too long for the applicant country, it may take alternative steps.

Exchange Transparency and Requirements to Ensure Effectiveness

While information exchange agreements should provide for the details mentioned above, the signatory countries, too, should have certain characteristics. If they do not, the agreements will be unable to meet their goal of ensuring effective information exchange. These characteristics are transparency and the willingness and capability to carry out an effective exchange of information.

Lack of transparency and unwillingness to exchange information in a jurisdiction may be regarded as an indication of harmful tax competition by that jurisdiction, especially if extremely low nominal income taxes are applied.

Transparency

In this context, transparency implies that a jurisdiction's tax system and administrative practices enable taxpayers to have a clear idea of the tax treatment they receive and the criteria applied when assessing the taxes imposed on a taxable transaction or estate. The factors that affect any tax jurisdiction's transparency are related to a wide range of matters concerning the jurisdiction's laws and tax administration.

To some extent, tax transparency is related to legal certainty. For taxpayers, transparency is ensured when they can clearly anticipate the tax consequences of their businesses' development—not only the treatment prescribed by law but also the criteria applied by the tax administration. If the applicable standards are inaccurate or unpredictable, and/or if the administration exercises its functions with a high degree of discretion, there will be a direct impact on taxpayers' legal certainty and thus on the system's transparency. Obviously, if there is no transparency for taxpayers, there will be no transparency for the other countries' tax administrations.

Tax transparency may also be adversely affected by the insufficiency of the legal powers vested in the tax administration, particularly the power to identify and/or control taxpayers and gain access to their tax records and tax-relevant information. For example, legal obstacles may be expressly established in special regulations (bank secrecy laws, stock anonymity, and so on). It is also evident that if a tax administration cannot rely on the transparency required in its own jurisdiction to impose its taxes, no transparency will be ensured for other countries' tax administrations either.

The circumstances affecting transparency addressed so far relate to the legal sphere—that is, they stem from legal shortcomings (legal uncertainty, the administration's high degree of discretionary power to levy taxes, or the insufficiency of the administration's legal powers). But a tax system's transparency may also be affected by other factors, such as significant administrative deficiencies resulting in arbitrary practices or a pervasive lack of control of tax compliance. There is no doubt that when a lack of transparency affects a country's administration, regardless of its causes, no information can be exchanged effectively.

Effectiveness of the Information Exchange

A precondition of information exchange is that the data of interest to the requesting administration be available to the authorities in the jurisdiction where the data exist. The information may relate, for instance, to ownership interests; to the nature, amounts, and assets involved in a commercial transaction that is subject to verification; to bank account movements; or to an individual's status or place of residence. As already mentioned, an absence of transparency is the first and most obvious obstacle to the effective exchange of information. Nobody can provide information of which he or she is unaware.

Other hurdles are the provisions included in various tax secrecy laws, whereby the use and disclosure of information is permitted only under certain conditions, which do not include the international exchange of information.

Finally, it is worth mentioning that in many cases, in order to exchange information with foreign tax administrations, there must be a formal commitment to do so. This is a necessary but perhaps not a sufficient condition. The mere existence of a convention or agreement does not itself guarantee that its provisions will consistently and clearly include the key elements required to support effective information exchange.

Conclusion: Possible Strategies to Strengthen the Exchange of Tax Information in Latin America

Tax evasion in all its forms entails the loss of legitimate tax revenue, affects the equitable distribution of the tax burden, and distorts market competition. The loss of revenue often prompts the application of simplistic solutions, such as the exemption of certain taxable bases—which are real manifestations of taxpaying capacity but are difficult to control—and the use of other, more readily collectable taxes (mainly on salaries and consumption). Or, even worse, revenue loss might lead to the imposition of taxes that are both inequitable and highly resource-distorting but that are also easier to control (taxes on bank checks, for instance).

It should be underscored again that because tax evasion is a form of unfair competition on the part of the companies that engage in it, in addition to infringing the law, it distorts the market's level playing field by giving tax evaders an undeserved and illegitimate advantage.

Tax evasion may be related to or even equated with other unfair competition practices. Hence any instrument designed to combat it—in this case, the exchange of information that is relevant to tax affairs—should be viewed as a market-strengthening tool. As mentioned earlier, although much has been written on the subject of this chapter, authors have not given the matter the importance it deserves, especially in light of intensifying international economic relations stemming from globalization and thus the greater number of opportunities for tax evasion.

Tax evasion is particularly harmful to economic integration processes. In addition to the distortions attendant on asymmetries in the participating countries' tax systems (in terms of both competition conditions and the location of investments), tax evasion involves an inherent, undesirable risk: the possibility of gaining a larger market share on the basis of unfair competition rather than efficiency.

Full awareness of the above-mentioned negative effects of tax evasion, and a thorough understanding of the ways in which it operates, are the starting point for identifying viable solutions.

Since tax evasion is an international phenomenon, the exchange of information between tax administrations is unquestionably one of the key instruments available to combat it and to eradicate, or at least mitigate, its negative effects on tax revenue and equity. Information exchange is also important in restoring the foundations of healthier market competition.

This is a particularly challenging aspiration for Latin American countries, which so far have been unable to make proper use of the information exchange mechanism as a means of combating tax evasion. A strategy is needed that would enable the countries of the region to take better advantage of the benefits of exchanging information. This strategy could be based on three main courses of action:

▪ Adjust their domestic legislation, and their administrative structures and procedures, to ensure an effective exchange of information.

Implementation of a strategy geared to strengthening information exchange should begin by adjusting domestic laws in order to remove any obstacles they pose for effective information exchange. This might entail amending them—for instance, to make tax secrecy exceptional; to entitle tax agents to give information to tax administrations in foreign jurisdictions with which exchange agreements have been concluded; to vest the highest-ranking tax administration official with the power to conclude information exchange agreements with foreign tax administrations; to remove or restrict other information confidentiality rules, especially those concerning tax secrecy; to accept information received from foreign tax administrations as evidence when certain formalities are met; and so forth.

In addition to regulatory matters, each domestic tax administration should be prepared to engage effectively in the exchange of information. This requires action on several fronts. For one thing, structural changes should be made. In addition to identifying the official or body that is to act as the "competent authority," a unit to coordinate and supervise tasks related to the exchange of information should be created. Moreover, appropriate procedures should be established for the proper handling of the requests for information sent and received; it might even be advisable to prepare information exchange manuals. Finally, with respect to human resources, it is important to raise awareness of the existence and significance of information exchange, particularly among officials in oversight areas; to develop training programs on the importance of information exchange as an instrument of control; and to foster its use.

▪ Survey, complement, and strengthen information exchange provisions in the international conventions and agreements in force.

There are cases in which the different prevailing agreements providing for the exchange of information among countries have not yet been surveyed, analyzed, and systematized. A first step in that direction would be to identify the clauses in the various agreements in force, and then analyze their current scope and the extent to which they can support the exchange of information with other countries.

This exercise would also be useful in determining the adjustment needs mentioned above, and in establishing whether it is necessary to supplement, for instance, the current conventions with other protocols so as to add greater strength and effectiveness to the exchange of information already agreed upon.

▪ Promote further international agreements on the exchange of information.

Because of the limited value accorded to information exchange clauses in double taxation agreements, it seems advisable in the proposed strategy to implement a policy that favors the conclusion of specific administrative agreements on information exchange. Such efforts should first target countries whose economic interrelations—both commercial and financial—are currently or potentially significant.

Among these countries, special consideration should be given to those participating in the same regional economic integration process, even if they are not the closest partners. This is because participation in an integration scheme presupposes cultural affinity and a greater propensity for cooperation, and because it is necessary to ensure that the market expansion resulting from the integration process contributes to the progress of the region rather than to the expansion of the opportunities for tax evasion.

Additional Reading

CIAT (Inter-American Center of Tax Administrations). 1999. *Modelo de acuerdo de intercambio de informaciones tributarias del CIAT.* Panama City: CIAT.

———. 2006. *Manual CIAT para la implantación y práctica del intercambio de informaciones tributarias del CIAT.* Panama City: CIAT.

Jackson, John. 1999. *The World Trading System—Law and Policy of International Economic Relations.* Cambridge, MA: MIT Press.

McLure, Charles, and Giampaolo Corabi. 1999. *L'imposizione fiscale sul commercio elettronico.* Milan: IPSOA Editore SRL.

OECD (Organisation for Economic Co-operation and Development). 2003. *Model Convention on Income and on Capital.* Paris: OECD.

———. 2004. *Outcome, Conclusion of the Meeting of the OECD Global Forum on Taxation.* Berlin: OECD.

———. 2006. *Tax Co-operation: Towards a Level Playing Field.* Paris: OECD.

Pita, Claudino. 1989. "El intercambio de información bajo tratados tributarios." Paper presented at the 22nd CIAT General Assembly, Brasilia, 1988. In *Administración, política y enfoques cooperativos entre las administraciones tributarias para desestimar la elusión y evasion.* Madrid: Instituto de Estudios Fiscales.

———. 1997. "Intercambio de información y administración tributaria." *Revista Iberoamericana de Derecho Tributario* (Editoriales de Derecho Reunidas, Madrid) 6:577–605.

———. 2001. "Transparency and Effective Exchange of Information." Discussion text for the Global Forum on Taxation Meeting on Harmful Tax Practices. Paris: OECD.

———. 2003. "El intercambio de información." *Comercio Internacional e Imposición* (Editorial Ábaco, Buenos Aires), 1077–1104.

———. 2004. "El intercambio de informaciones tributarias." Paper presented at the CIAT Technical Conference, Lisbon, September 29–October 2, 2003. In *Aspectos claves en las acciones de control de las administraciones tributarias.* Madrid: Instituto de Estudios Fiscales.

———. 2005. "Tributación y precios de transferencia, el punto de vista de las administraciones tributarias." *Revista Impuestos—Asociación Interamericana de Contabilidad* (Andean Development Corporation, Lima), 66–78.

Tanzi, Vito. 2002. "Globalization, Tax Competition by the Future of Tax Systems." In *Corso di Diritto Tributario Internazionale,* 2nd ed. Padua, Italy: Casa Editrice Dott. Antonio Milani (CEDAM).

Uckmar, Antonio. 2003. "Tributos aduaneros y subsidios en la OMC." *Comercio Internacional e Imposición* (Editorial Ábaco, Buenos Aires), 325–49.

UN (United Nations). 2002. *United Nations Model Double Taxation Convention between Developed and Developing Countries.* New York: UN Department of Economic and Social Affairs.

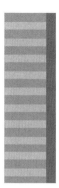

11

Economic Integration and Pensions: The European Union, Latin America, and the Caribbean

Francisco José Delmas González

Introduction

A large number of countries with different economic systems and levels of development coexist in the world, conducting economic relations among themselves and exchanging goods and services. There are different forms of economic relations among countries. Simplifying, economic relations can be structured as follows: free exchange, bilateralism, aid, and economic integration. These, perhaps, correspond to the different stages of global economic development.

Of these related forms, perhaps the one of most interest here is integration, a process whereby two or more national markets, previously separated, join to become a single market in order to become more efficient. The process requires an adjustment period while countries undertake a series of activities to close the gap in their economic structures. This usually entails the creation of an infrastructure, which is superimposed on the countries wishing to integrate, and from which decisions arise.

Integration can progress through certain stages: customs preference systems, free trade areas, customs unions, and economic unions that might become the embryo of a political union. Depending on the kind of integration pursued, there will be greater or lesser transfers of sovereignty. In an economic union, therefore, the degree of interrelation between the economies and markets will be very important and will entail closing the gap between tax, commercial, and labor legislation, such that citizens in each member state will be able to demand similar economic benefits upon retirement. Hence it is clear that the realm of labor is affected by economic integration processes, since the latter affect labor legislation, employment rates, social protection and welfare, productivity, competitiveness, and so forth.

Circumstances in the European Union

Examining Labor Mobility: Adopted Solutions

The European Union (EU) has passed through various stages in its integration process: free trade area, customs union, common market, and economic union. With the completion of the common market, the hurdles for the movement of productive factors were eliminated. The free movement of workers consists of allowing equal conditions for workers regardless of their country of origin. But how is this free movement organized?

The Treaty of Rome, the founding treaty of what is now the EU, established the basic principles of the European Community and stated that Community action entails the abolition, among the member states, of obstacles to the free movement of people, services, and capital. Thus the free movement of people is one of the fundamental pillars on which the EU is based.

The free movement of workers is an aspect of the free movement of people, since it concerns immigrant workers who perform salaried work in another member state. The relevant regulations have three goals: [1]

■ To ensure the right to enter and live in a member state in order to perform a job there, and to abolish any possible discrimination concerning employment and labor conditions.

---

[1] There are two relevant regulations of the Council of the European Union. One is Council Regulation (EEC) No. 1408/71, dated June 14, 1971, on the Application of Social Security Schemes to Self-Employed Workers and Their Families Moving within the Community. The other is Council Regulation (EEC) No. 574/72, dated March 21, 1972, fixing the procedure for implementing Regulation (EEC) no. 1408/71 on the Coordination of the Social Security Schemes for People Moving within the Community.

▪ To foster the exchange of young workers.
▪ To establish a system through which immigrant workers can maintain their social security benefits and not suffer a reduction in them.

The aim is to build a common labor market that coordinates and compensates the supply of and demand for labor in the integration area. The EU's social policy has two objectives: to improve workers' living and working conditions and to foster collaboration among countries in matters such as employment, the right to work, working conditions, professional training and upgrading, social security, protection against accidents and sickness, hygiene in the workplace, and so forth. But it must be stressed that these matters are derived subsidiary regulations that have been arrived at through necessity, as a consequence of compliance with the basic mandate to attain the free movement of workers.

One of the ways through which the EU tackles the free movement of workers is the establishment of a system whereby migrant workers can maintain their right to social security benefits and not suffer a reduction in those rights. The system is implemented through coordination of the member states' various social security systems, so as to ensure that displaced workers do not suffer social security disadvantages because they have moved to work in another member state. The goal of the coordination is to ensure that:

▪ Each migrant worker receives treatment equal to that accorded to the nationals of the member state where he or she works.
▪ Contributions made by the workers in other member states are added together in order to preserve the workers' right to pension benefits and the basis for benefit calculation.
▪ Pensions may be transferred to beneficiaries of the social security system residing in any member state.

From a coordination standpoint, as regards the regulations on joining and contributing to the system, the law is applied where the job is performed (*lex loci laboris*). However, in the case of workers who are displaced for a limited period in order to perform professional activities in a member state other than the one where they were working previously, EU regulations allow the social security law of the original work location to continue to be applied—that is, the legislation of the member state in which the workers were making contributions before moving. It must be underscored that maintaining that association with the legislation in the country of origin is exceptional and applies for a maximum of five years.

But the question arises as to why harmonization, which is simply regulatory coordination, has been used instead of regulatory standardization. The answer lies in the degree of social protection that each state has developed over its history. On the basis of the numerous variables that affect each society's historical evolution, the different countries have been granting greater or lesser importance to the protection of their citizens, a circumstance that has led to a greater or lesser development of public protection systems. Indirectly, however, it has also affected the degree of development of complementary systems. In short, each country has created a guarantee system on the basis of certain agreements established with economic and social actors, and it is enormously complex and costly to undo the system. The latter was built over many years in order to establish arrangements that, on occasion, would be completely unrelated to the state's idiosyncrasy and structure.

In short, harmonization offers a system of guarantees for workers on the move. In principle, workers in different member states all enjoy the same disability, retirement, and death benefits (pensions). Additionally (within specific limits and under strict conditions), a worker who is wholly unemployed and meets the benefit entitlement requirements of a member state, and who moves to another member state to seek work, remains entitled to those benefits. Finally, EU regulations provide for the possibility of portable health care. European citizens who reside in a member state other than the one where they are registered may be treated for illness or receive maternity care in their state of residence under some conditions.

The Viability of Public Pensions: Solutions Adopted

Pension systems perform an essential function in modern societies, since they provide economic benefits. Their main task is to compensate wholly or partly for the income-generating capacity that workers or their dependents lose because of age or some contingency.

Pension systems can be public or private and fall into three categories or pillars of welfare: basic public schemes, professional schemes, and individual plans. Each of these has advantages and disadvantages. Most income for elderly people in all the member states comes from public pension schemes.

The constant increase in life expectancy poses the question of how to defray pension expenditures linked to extended life expectancy. Demographic trends will greatly affect the above-mentioned three pillars of welfare, although the greatest impact will occur in the first pillar (public pensions). That might entail certain risks: for instance, there might be a great imbalance between contributions and benefits, a circumstance that might destabilize the process of tax consolidation in the EU member states and disrupt public finances. The final objective is to guarantee decent pensions, but assuring their viability poses a triple challenge:

- Safeguarding the capacity of pension systems to meet social goals and provide adequate income and insurance to those who have retired.
- Maintaining the financial viability of pension systems so that the future impact of aging on public finances will not endanger budgetary stability.
- Increasing the capacity of pension systems in order to respond to developments in the needs of society and of individuals, and helping to foster labor market flexibility, enhance equal opportunities for women, and strengthen social protection.

The need is to guarantee adequate income for the elderly while maintaining a reasonable and acceptable level of contributions and taxes. There is also a belief that privately financed pension schemes will curb increases in public pension spending.

For pension schemes to become viable, it is important to tackle the basic problem of the growing imbalance between the numbers of working and retired people—in other words, between the number of contributors and the number of beneficiaries. This is the dependency rate, which measures the proportions of active and passive individuals in the system. There is a need for reform strategies that will allow this problem to be tackled. Moreover, pension systems must be modernized and adapted to the needs of individuals in society.

The challenge posed by aging requires coordinated efforts in broad policy spheres: welfare, employment, and public finances. Welfare policies must guarantee that all citizens will enjoy adequate pensions without imposing an excessive burden on the working population. In this regard, it is important to heighten the incentives for people to extend their working lives. The strategy regarding employment must improve job opportunities, especially for women and older workers.

Open Method of Coordination

The open method of coordination is a mechanism to guarantee the feasibility of pension systems. Logically, this method must be combined with the current political procedures under way in each member state. Moreover, it should not alter the level of political responsibility at either the European or the national level. The goal is an integrated framework of information exchange on national strategies, so as to guarantee pensions that are adequate and viable over the long term.

This method entails defining common objectives, transferring those objectives to national political strategies, and undertaking periodic oversight, all in the framework of a mutual learning process, on the basis of indicators that have been jointly agreed upon and defined. The method offers a series of advantages:

▪ The common objectives will help the member states focus on the necessary reforms and will provide greater transparency to pension policy, allowing citizens to adapt to planned changes.

- These objectives will help build consensus on the necessary reforms, which will strengthen people's confidence in the future of pension systems.
- The exchange of experiences, based on good practices and innovative approaches, will foster mutual learning and broaden the political operations considered in each member state.
- Finally, the jointly agreed indicators will help clarify the progress made in other member states and progress on the common objectives.

For example, a country might not dare, on its own, to raise the retirement age or extend the period used to determine the level of benefit. However, if other countries have introduced such measures, the public might find them more acceptable, and weaker-willed governments might find the justification for acting.

Political Process of Reforming the Basic Universal System

Pensions are a fundamental element of the welfare system in modern societies. They are used to pursue some clear goals: obviating the danger of poverty among the elderly, helping maintain certain standards of living after retirement, and promoting intergenerational solidarity and social cohesion. Current problems and new circumstances make it necessary to reform all the welfare systems in the EU, for several reasons:

- New social and economic circumstances arising from changes in the labor market (job instability, the growing informal economy, part-time jobs, and increasing female labor participation).
- Demographic changes and their consequences—and not only because people live longer, with all that entails. It must be kept in mind that longer life spans entail significant expenditure: dependency. Also, the aging of the population has come in tandem with a low birth rate.
- The relentless growth of the informal economy.

These and other matters make it hard to transfer resources from the working to the nonworking population. All of the member states must undertake reforms in order to provide adequate public provision, and must foster complementary systems, so that both variables—public and private pension benefits—are close to the amount paid during the individual's working life. Hence many measures focus on:

- A gradual reduction of public benefits.
- Transferring resource management to the private sector in an effort to cut costs.
- Rationalizing expenditures on pensions and health care benefits in order to tighten eligibility requirements.
- Establishing more stringent conditions to qualify for unemployment benefits.

Economic policymakers have concluded that efforts must be refocused, because otherwise the growth of spending items may stifle budgetary items. The main question, however, is whether enough is being done, since political leaders rarely carry out drastic reforms that might jeopardize their electability.

Promoting Complementary Systems

To a greater or lesser degree, all of the member states that are aware of the above difficulties with welfare systems pursue the coexistence of complementary systems, so that citizens can receive income that supplements their public pension. This goal is pursued using a basic tool: tax incentives. In an economic integration area, however, use of that tool poses problems. The presence of strong incentives can lead to different treatment in different countries and can distort the international movement of people and services. An analysis of the cross-border taxation of pensions must address certain phenomena: (1) distortions stemming from the existence of different tax schemes in different countries (or from the varying levels of incentives in different countries); and (2) the possibility of discriminatory treatment among countries that do not apply the same incentives to contributions or benefits. The European Commission highlighted both matters in a 2001 document (Commission of the European Communities, 2001).

Three kinds of transnational movements affect cross-border pensions:

- Workers who move to other member states. Their employers continue to pay the contributions. An initial problem could be the possibility of not making those contributions. From a fiscal standpoint, what is also interesting is the danger that those contributions are not deductible for the workers' income taxation.
- Workers who have been working in a country other than their own for some years. They have accumulated some resources in a pension fund. They return to their own country during their working life and try to move the resources accumulated in the pension fund from the other country.
- Workers who decide to change their place of residence upon retirement, and who begin to collect their pensions in a country other than the one in which the pension fund was set up.

Perhaps all of these issues could be resolved within the EU's own regulatory framework, but the adoption of fiscal harmonization measures currently poses significant difficulties. Nonetheless, some notable regulatory progress has been made on the creation of a competitive financial environment for employment and professional systems.

First, there is a regulation removing obstacles to the free movement of employed and self-employed workers—one that preserves their rights to a complementary pension when they move from one member state to another (Council of the European Union, 1998). This regulation is not applied to schemes dependent on public social security; it applies to members of complementary pension schemes and to other possible beneficiaries of these schemes who have acquired or are acquiring rights in one or more member states.

Second, with the adoption of a directive on the activities and supervision of "occupational pension funds" (European Parliament and the Council of the European Union, 2003), the EU has taken a great step toward an internal market for occupational pensions. By subjecting these financial institutions to specific conditions for their activities, the directive guarantees a high degree of protection to the funds' participants and beneficiaries. The creation of a specific framework for occupational pension funds allows these institutions to act with the greatest security and efficiency. Henceforth, moreover, they can accept businesses in other member states as participants and can manage pension plans for them. They will also be able to apply an investment strategy adapted to the characteristics of their pension plans. The directive allows the host member state (where the company paying for the contributions is located) to request the member state of origin (where the pension fund is located) to reciprocally apply certain regulations in cross-border pension plans. However, the directive scrupulously respects the member states' prerogatives on welfare and pension plans.

This regulation establishes the measures related to access to the activities and the operations of pension fund institutions. It seeks to guarantee a high level of protection for future retirees (participants and beneficiaries of the pension funds) and to ensure the effectiveness of the investment.

Some issues must be addressed further, especially as regards third-level complementary instruments. Studies are being conducted on a proposal to facilitate the transferability of economic rights from one member state to another when a worker or citizen moves. This proposal is not without difficulties, but its approval would resolve many of the tax-related problems stemming from the existence of different tax schemes in the member states.

Assessment of Latin America and the Caribbean

Introduction

An economic integration process seeks to foster and harmonize the economic development of all its member countries and thus insert itself into the global economy under the best possible conditions. Integration must be based on agreements among the members to establish closer links among their economies, thereby ensuring stronger and more balanced economic growth.

However, although economic growth is the starting point, integration must become something more than that. Attention should be paid, even if somewhat tangentially in the initial stages, to possible processes for improving workers' social conditions, so as to minimize existing differences and coordinate matters that could disturb the proper functioning of economic policy. This, therefore, should also be a process that provides broad social cohesion that makes possible the modern society. Hence economic integration is a means to development, one that takes into account policies in the labor field and in all the areas that allow a transition to a form of economic integration that is more complete from the viewpoint of economic theory.

In a developed integration process, workers should be able to decide where they want to work, and they should have a greater number of jobs to choose from, since they face a much wider labor market with greater opportunities. Workers would therefore adjust to a labor supply and demand that transcends a single country. In sum, labor is affected by different processes of economic integration and trade liberalization. In the EU, as mentioned, these processes have led to the standardization of economic policies, entailing the establishment of common guidelines on social and labor policy among the member states. We turn now to an assessment of integration in Latin America and the Caribbean (LAC).

The Scale of Labor Mobility

What has happened in Latin America's various economic integration processes?[2] Among them, the following are notable:

---

[2] Pere Puig, a professor of economics at ESADE, published a recent article highlighting the regional integration deficit arising from mounting tensions in the current political climate. He states that "the integration of the region is . . . not at its finest moment and the future of the economies and the welfare of the societies in the area greatly depend on it" (Puig, 2006: 23). He adds, "Latin America itself has also demonstrated quite a high level of economic imbalance and internal problems, partially related to the modest progress of economic and social reforms and the clear lack of progress of some ambitious integration projects, largely publicized a long time ago" (44).

- Southern Common Market (MERCOSUR): Argentina, Brazil, Paraguay, Uruguay, and Venezuela. (Bolivia and Chile are associate members.)
- Andean Community (CAN): Colombia, Ecuador, and Peru.
- Central American Integration System (SICA): Costa Rica, El Salvador, Guatemala, Honduras, and Panama.
- Caribbean Community (CARICOM): Antigua and Barbuda, Bahamas, Barbados, Belize, Dominica, Grenada, Guyana, Jamaica, St. Kitts and Nevis, St. Lucia, St. Vincent and the Grenadines, Suriname, and Trinidad and Tobago.

It is important to consider how the social dimension, an essential aspect of such forms of economic integration, is addressed—not to mention the potential impact of the Free Trade Area of the Americas (FTAA), a process that has not flourished for various reasons.

The existence of different development levels among member states poses a significant challenge to the creation of integration groups. This problem is substantial in regions with extensive experience of economic integration, such as the EU—which features long transition periods and structural funds that help finance nominal and real convergence among the members. In less developed areas, the problems to be overcome are even more significant.

The adoption of a free trade structure does not pose great difficulties, since it is based on removing tariffs on a series of specific products during a first stage, and then adding other products at later stages. As mentioned earlier, economic integration agreements undeniably affect specific aspects of the labor field, including the adaptation of labor and tax regulations; labor costs and attendant matters; training; and the free movement of workers. Additionally, and as important, attention must be paid to the effect of any sort of integration on welfare.

MERCOSUR is the integration process with the most developed social and labor dimension.[3] The preamble to its founding treaty states

---

[3] MERCOSUR Subgroup 11 (now Subgroup 10), which was created under Annex V of the Treaty of Asunción, examined the situation in the region in order to harmonize the labor force, social security, salaries, and employment.

that "the expansion of [the member states'] domestic markets, through integration, is a vital prerequisite for accelerating their economic development with social justice." This statement is an embryonic form of the latent concern for economic development that is sustainable and compatible with an improvement in the labor environment.

The Andean Community has what is known as the Andean Social Security Instrument. Its goal is to foster the establishment of a common policy on the rights of individuals who are covered by social security and receive benefits in another Community country in case of maternity, work-related accidents, and illnesses, in addition to benefits for old age, disability, and death (Martínez, 2004). Another CAN document, the Labor Migration Instrument, establishes a common policy on the rights and duties of workers who emigrate to another Community country for work-related reasons; it also outlines the procedures for these workers to follow.

SICA has paid very little attention to labor issues (Martínez, 2004). As for CARICOM, the preamble to its founding treaty asserts the Caribbean Community's interest in the labor and social dimension of integration, stating that the governments of the member states must concern themselves not only with economic development but also with ensuring that such development translates into improved living for citizens. Hence the agreement underscores the members' willingness to "fulfill the hopes and aspirations of their peoples for full employment and improved standards of working and living" (Martínez, 2004).

But what is the impact of economic integration—which, as has been seen on a theoretical level, is good for the social and labor environment and, as regards social protection, improves essential aspects of citizens' lives?

In the various integration systems, very significant structural problems undermine the theoretical model of the advantages conferred by any economic integration: greater efficiency of business and labor structures, with higher employment and contributions, and thus greater institutional stability for social protection. In fact, the regional integration processes seem to be experiencing some difficulties, as is the FTAA, which has not yet led to an agreement (Sangmeister and Taalouch, 2003).

Labor markets are suffering substantial difficulties. In Latin America the percentage of salaried workers contributing to social security has diminished because of the significant growth of the informal economy. Another troubling effect is the increase in poverty rates, a circumstance that poses a serious problem for welfare instruments and their viability and increases the need to allocate resources properly.

Another matter is the migration of more people to countries with a higher level of development in search of new and better job opportunities.[4] The receiving countries are Canada, the United States, and the countries in the EU and the Southern Cone, where apparently there is some social resistance to these migration flows. Clearly, this migration has nothing to do with the opportunities that stem from or should be produced by economic integration procedures. It arises from something different and is related to people's need to seek opportunities outside their countries of origin. It seems that free movement of the kind that prevails in the EU, or to a greater degree in the United States, does not happen in Latin America or does so only rarely.

Hence the need to give more thought to the free movement of workers, which would begin with the more dynamic economic sectors and could extend to other groups of workers. Moreover, unlike in the EU, language should not be a barrier to such movements.

There will be a need to coordinate social security systems among countries. That coordination is enormously complex in its early stages, but it should make the systems easier to administer, allow for the accumulation of services provided in the different countries, and give workers access to benefits generated in one country while they or their families live in another one.

Aside from this coordination in the area of social security, it is crucial to consider the transformation of the welfare systems that has taken place in LAC, and how it has affected integration processes.

---

[4] High percentages of the populations of Bolivia, Ecuador, El Salvador, Guatemala, Honduras, Nicaragua, and Peru live abroad.

The Viability of Public Pensions

There are three essential aspects of social and labor problems and how they affect public pensions: demographic aging; structural poverty; and problems with labor markets and free movement. These problems are interrelated, and they all affect the structure of social protection in Latin America.

Demographic Aging

The aging of the population is a clear trend in the EU, and it causes concern about its budgetary impact and the way in which the likely increases in budgetary expenditures will be financed: through taxes, social security contributions, and the issuance of debt. All of these options pose problems in a context of integration because undoubtedly they would affect the productive competitiveness of a country that tackled them unilaterally.

In recent decades, the LAC region has undergone substantial demographic changes that alter the population profile and the way in which resources are transferred between generations. The most profound demographic change is the aging of the population. This has an important effect on the welfare systems, as does poverty in certain social strata. According to Jorge Bravo (2000), people over the age of 60 are the fastest-growing population group in the region, although the proportion of the population over that age is still small in comparison to developed countries. Bravo adds that LAC countries diverge widely with respect to the age makeup of the population.[5]

The matter to be explained is whether institutional pension systems have the necessary structure and coverage to support the elderly. The struc-

---

[5] Bravo (2000) states that Bolivia, Honduras, and Nicaragua have a younger population structure. Many other countries are in the intermediate stages of demographic transition, and they are expected to have a greater rate of aging over the next few decades. Brazil and Mexico, the two most populated countries, are in this group. Another group of countries with relatively older populations includes Argentina, Uruguay, and some Caribbean countries.

ture has undergone significant changes throughout the region. Indeed, the welfare model developed worldwide after World War II was based on a quasi-perfect labor market that defined the contributions of the employer, the worker, and the government. In Latin America, however, this model has not worked well because of the extent of the informal economy, recurring economic crises that have hampered the operation of the labor market, and extreme poverty among some sectors of the population.

To a greater or lesser degree, all these variables have intensified the need to reform the institutional systems because of the enormous problems involved in maintaining universal benefits on the basis of solidarity or distribution criteria. Hence welfare reforms have boosted the private sector's role in the management and provision of services, and social programs have been introduced to support the most disadvantaged sectors and to rationalize spending. As mentioned earlier, there were several reasons for these reforms: difficulties in ensuring comprehensive coverage, inefficiencies in collecting contributions, the lack of reserve funds, the need to adjust benefits in order to guarantee the system's stability, structural economic crises, and so forth. In Latin America, as in the rest of the world, most public systems are or were distributive and had modest reserve funds.

Public spending on pensions has grown throughout the world. For 2003, expenditure in the 25-member EU was 12.6 percent of gross domestic product (GDP) (see Appendix Table 11A.1). In Latin America, by contrast, spending was about 2–3 percent of GDP (Bravo, 2000).[6] The gap remains very wide.

The future prospects for spending on pensions are not very encouraging. Forward-looking assessments in the EU are always risky because their parameters and initial hypotheses are not always wholly valid, but they suggest a worrying trend in future spending. The impact of spending is not known with any certainty because of various difficulties in con-

---

[6] The figures vary by country and are perhaps a little outdated now. To get a more accurate picture of the current situation, the impact of social spending in the region, in GDP terms, should be considered.

ducting assessments, but without doubt it will be very substantial. This concern has spurred some reforms in the EU; in all of the economic policy documents, the European Commission repeatedly expresses its concern in regard to this area.

According to the United Nations, by 2050, 45 percent of Europe's population will be over the age of 65. In North America the share will be 35 percent, and in Latin America and the Caribbean it will be 28 percent. The population is aging in a delicate economic context where the economic integration model has yet to be determined (the scope of the FTAA is still being discussed) and where there are deficiencies in the labor market—which are reflected in a very high unemployment rate and increased work in the informal economy.

Without doubt, demographic and economic circumstances could pose significant institutional difficulties, but they should not necessarily cause the closing of the pension system or its bankruptcy. The solutions include restructuring the system in order to guarantee its viability, strengthening the complementary systems (as in the EU), and creating more efficient management systems. Thought could also be given to the establishment of an individual capitalization system. Some countries have taken this approach, but for those that have not done so, this is a very complicated matter and the debate is often marred by ideological factors.

Without venturing too far into the issue, since it is beyond the scope of this chapter, it is inadvisable to establish a pure capitalization system for several reasons: (1) the significant transition costs (Mesa-Lago, 2000), (2) the need to organize a contribution system for people lacking income or bordering on poverty, and (3) the substantial loss of focus on intergenerational solidarity. Perhaps a more reasonable solution would be a partial capitalization system that encourages the most dynamic sectors. What is clear is that any adjustment to welfare instruments must made after broad debate among the political parties in each country's parliament, and hence the agreement must be a social pact.

In any case, the decisions made must take account of annual pension spending in GDP terms and of social expenditure in general terms. Furthermore, the decisions must be underpinned by forward-looking cost-benefit analyses that are conducted with the greatest degree of transparency, so that all the political and social actors have all necessary information in the debate. In this regard it is important to note the difficulties involved in obtaining appropriate statistical data to support decision making.

Poverty

Extreme poverty is widespread in Latin America and should concern the region's policymakers for two reasons: first, social justice; and second, how that justice is expressed. Resources (noncontributory in most cases) are needed to address these issues, but they are either absent or modest. Provision has to be made for the pertinent budgetary items. In Latin America, 37 percent of the rural population and 13 percent of the urban population live in poverty. Since 2000, however, the number of urban poor has surpassed the number of poor in the countryside.[7]

Labor Market

There is broad agreement that the best way to guarantee social justice is to provide a job to every job seeker. But the region's labor markets have been unable to do this. Between 1990 and 2003, moreover, contribution coverage declined (see ECLAC, 2006, chap. 2). Additionally, social protection covers only a fraction of workers (see Table 11A.3). The prospects of extending welfare coverage through contributory schemes have been constrained by the growth of unemployment and by the structure of the labor market, which is affected by economic growth rates and their erratic behavior. Furthermore, the labor environment has been characterized by unstable employment and the spread of the informal economy.

Pension Systems in Latin America and the Caribbean

Pension systems have been unable to provide adequate protection to substantial sectors of the population. Many different solutions have been adopted, as illustrated in Table 11.1.

---

[7] According to ECLAC (2006) estimates through 2004, 52 million of 96 million people in extreme poverty live in urban areas.

Table 11.1. Latin America and the Caribbean: Models and Characteristics of Pension Reform

Model, country, and start date of reform	Financial regime	Calculation of benefits	Management
Structural reforms			
Substitute model of individual capitalization Chile: May 1981 Bolivia: May 1997 Mexico: September 1997 El Salvador: May 1998 Dominican Republic: 2003–2005	Individual capitalization	Defined contribution	Private
Parallel model of individual capitalization (workers can opt for the system of their preference) Peru: June 1993 Colombia: April 1994	Pay-as-you-go Individual capitalization	Defined benefit Defined contribution	Public Private
Mixed model of individual capitalization (workers contribute simultaneously to both systems)	Pay-as-you-go Individual capitalization	Defined benefit Defined contribution	Public Private
Parametric reforms or no reform			
Brazil (general welfare scheme, private sector workers): 1999	Pay-as-you-go	Defined contribution	Public
Brazil (public sector): 2003 Costa Rica (distribution component): 2005 Cuba Guatemala Haiti Honduras Nicaragua Panama Paraguay Venezuela	Pay-as-you-go	Defined benefit	Public

Sources: Mesa-Lago (2000); Paddison (2005).

The systems that have tried to reform the factors affecting the assessment of benefits (parametric reforms) face important fiscal constraints in financing retirement pensions. In the countries that have undergone structural reforms, there are problems with the solidarity scheme that is characteristic of traditional systems. Additionally, they have been unable to increase coverage of the population because of the difficulties of the labor market. Hence several factors pose substantial problems for the institutional systems: the process of demographic aging; the coverage deficit, which stems from the deficiencies of the region's labor market; and the systems' insolvency problems.

The distribution systems have always been criticized for their modest financial viability, deficits, poor management, and lack of transparency in transfers. These circumstances have spurred a transformation: the development of individual capitalization systems, wherein the economic and financial risks can be transferred to workers and the elements of solidarity of the distribution models are eliminated. Additionally, the contributions are invested in financial instruments of indeterminate profitability, and thus the worker assumes a substantial risk stemming from market instability.

It is essential that such transformations be accompanied by complementary instruments implemented by the state, either through fiscal incentives along with guaranteed (noncontributory) pension schemes, or through schemes in which workers participate even though the basic system in some countries is individual capitalization.

Conclusions

The goal of economic integration is to improve the living conditions of the citizens of the countries involved. Hence economic integration areas must consider the whole range of labor and tax issues. As well as improving the capacity of national economies to create an efficient labor market, progress must be made on measures that guarantee the viable and stable financing of welfare systems, in order to safeguard social peace and economic equilibrium. The two factors, therefore, are closely related: the proper functioning of the labor market in the region, and the efficient operation of welfare systems so that workers who move will continue to receive benefits.

As regards welfare, the population of Latin America is beginning to age. This phenomenon is not as marked as in developed countries, such as those in the EU, but the aging segment of the population does not enjoy the same level of protection as in developed countries. It is essential that the region's countries seriously take account of this issue and adopt institutional measures and reforms in line with their respective economic structures and real possibilities.

In the not-too-distant future, public spending could reach levels similar to those in developed countries, with all that implies for the budgets of countries in the region. This calls for decisions on highly complex matters. First is the need to become aware of the growing problem and to acknowledge that institutional systems are perhaps not ready to sustain over many years the level of spending that can offer citizens decent living standards—especially those who have not been properly covered by the system during their working lives.

First and foremost, therefore, economic policymakers must be aware of the problem. This is the case in the EU, where reforms are being adopted so that countries can face future increases in pension spending—and can do so in such a way that budgetary consolidation processes and procedures (where maneuvering room is very narrow because of the requirements of the single currency) are unaffected or affected as little as possible.

The matter cannot be tackled in some universal way. That is, there is no magic formula for all, because each country has created its own level of welfare with its own structure, establishing a specific level for its citizens, one that in many cases stems from public debates among social and political actors. Thus solutions must consider each country's particular structure.

A labor contribution capitalization system has been implemented in several Latin American countries, and its possible adoption is discussed whenever a reform process begins in all of the countries. The capitalization system is justified by its enormous potential to reduce pressure on budgetary spending and to increase labor market effectiveness. It can do that by reducing the level of labor contributions, which sometimes act as a tax on the labor market. The capitalization system also offers huge advantages by strengthening the development of financial markets, fostering capital accumulation, and providing protection against the aging of the population, considering that an adequate labor market is not always present. However, if the labor market does not work properly, if there are significant costs involved in moving from a pay-as-you-go system to a capitalization system, if a very generous guarantee system is established, or if the system does not offer the profitability promised, inefficiencies ensue. These can entail a significant loss in the adoption of a system based on capitalization, with the possible ulterior demand that the state cover the loss of economic rights.

If the labor market is not well developed, the consequences of applying a capitalization system will be that substantial sectors of the population do not have adequate protection or any coverage at all. In fact, reforms should consider a number of matters:

- A minimum threshold of welfare for all citizens. Each country must determine for itself how to cover and gradually raise this minimum, given its own circumstances.
- The greatest possible institutionalization of the pension or welfare system. Concentrated decision making should be discarded so as to obviate fluctuations in the systems' operation as a result of policymakers' ideological outlooks.
- The establishment of a minimum level of solidarity that is separate from immediate circumstances—that is, creating a permanent solidarity system that is not confined to a particular period, so that citizens can participate and can appreciate that everyone shares responsibility for improving living conditions and enhancing the dignity of people. This will strengthen and legitimize the institutions.

The LAC countries face the challenge of expanding social security coverage to their entire population and guaranteeing the system's short- and long-term financial sustainability. Keeping in mind the lack of savings capacity among large sectors of the population, the extent of the informal economy, and the shortcomings of the labor market, future approaches must focus on the development and consolidation of noncontributory schemes that provide people with a basic pension, regardless of their contribution record. This effort must therefore focus on people living in poverty. There are clear constraints because of the scarcity of public resources in most cases. Hence good information and good decisions about where to target spending are crucial.

As regards pension system reform, and in addition to strengthening the noncontributory schemes, all the countries should enhance solidarity in the contributory system in such a way that the two systems are truly complementary. The basic guidelines must focus on the following:

- The combination of a pay-as-you-go component with parametric reforms.
- A capitalization scheme, perhaps partial, with limited administrative costs.
- A guaranteed, noncontributory component for people living in poverty.
- Consolidated pay-as-you-go components for countries that have mixed parallel models. Countries that have only pay-as-you-go systems must consider, along with parametric reforms, the advisability of introducing a capitalization component, and they should take account of and incorporate the transition cost.

In Latin American and the Caribbean there is enormous concern, even more so than in the EU, about uncertainties in the labor sphere, health care, social security coverage, and the availability of revenue for specific groups of the population. In a context of economic integration, these institutional mechanisms must be perfected in order to provide the region with protection equal to that in the EU. The aim is to provide viable pensions that continue to meet social needs while also attaining other important objectives: financial, public, social, and intergenerational justice.

Viability should be pursued from an overall perspective. Economic growth and more jobs are essential and will contribute greatly to pension viability, but substantive reforms in the pension schemes themselves are crucial. Several countries have undertaken reforms, but since the systems differ from one country to another, it is neither advisable nor realistic to provide a general answer. Nonetheless, there are a series of common and crucial problems, particularly population aging, that could cause an exponential increase in public expenditure in GDP terms. Hence joint reflection and an exchange of experiences and ideas, covering the range of practices, can help broaden the political options for every country, both in the EU and in the Americas.

The most important challenge is population aging. In this regard, it is important to note that economic growth and job creation can give rise to opportunities to solve the problem. Additionally, pension schemes must be more efficient, both in meeting their social objectives and in supporting employment and growth objectives. In short, the pension system cannot become dead weight for employment and growth.

Demographic trends, and everything they entail, pose a problem, particularly in the increase in life expectancy, the decline in fertility rates, and population aging. These are worrying developments, but to assess the future viability of the pension schemes, the actual number of employed people relative to those who do not work (the economic dependence coefficient) must be kept in mind.

Reforms should be based on the maximum possible consensus and on an economic growth strategy, which is possible within an economic integration context. Maintaining a viable system in a context of swift aging entails striking a balance between contributions and benefits, and between the active and nonworking population. A consensus between the generations is needed.

Pay-as-you-go public pension schemes give rise to widespread concern, since the sensitivity of population aging is much greater in these systems, while in capitalization schemes the impact is more difficult to predict. Therefore, a possible course of action is to promote complementary systems through fiscal policies, as happens in the EU.

A solid macroeconomic policy and structural reforms that foster growth, thereby creating a favorable economic and entrepreneurial environment, are essential for the viability of pension schemes.

With regard to addressing the mobility of production factors, specifically labor, coordinating the wide-ranging systems in the Americas would be hard but not impossible. Progress would have to be made little by little, through an initial agreement among the more dynamic countries. The accord should be one of minimum requirements that at all times favors workers, who would not lose their benefits as a result of moving from one country to another. It should facilitate access to social security systems under the same terms as in workers' country of origin, and workers should not, of course, lose their rights to a private or public pension.

Clear rules on coordination are needed, so that in the event of unemployment, illness, maternity, or simple health care needs, workers who have moved will not face problems obtaining benefits. In most cases, the worker's country of residence is responsible for providing the benefits, although in some cases it might be the worker's country of origin or the one in which the original contributions were made. The aim of coordination is to make the different options clear and certain, establishing the benefit rules that the countries require but without affecting workers or their benefits.

Appendix

Table 11A.1. Pension Expenditure in European Countries
(percentage of GDP)

Group or country	1992	1993	1994	1995	1996	1997	1998	1999	2000	2001	2002	2003
EU25[1]	—	—	—	—	—	—	—	—	12.5	12.5	12.4	12.6
EU15[2]	12.5	12.9	12.9	12.8	12.9	12.9	12.6	12.7	12.6	12.5	12.5	12.7
Eurozone[3]	12.6	13.1	13.1	13.0	13.1	13.1	12.9	13.0	12.8	12.8	12.9	13.0
Austria	13.7	14.1	14.1	14.3	14.4	14.5	14.4	14.4	14.2	14.4	14.6	14.7
Belgium	12.3	13.0	12.8	12.1	12.1	11.8	11.7	11.5	11.1	11.3	11.4	11.5
Cyprus	—	—	—	—	—	—	—	—	—	6.4	7.0	—
Czech Republic	—	—	—	7.3	7.6	8.5	8.5	8.7	8.7	8.7	8.9	8.8
Denmark	9.6	10.0	11.4	11.3	11.4	11.1	11.0	10.8	10.5	10.6	10.8	11.1
Estonia	—	—	—	—	—	—	—	—	6.9	6.2	6.1	6.3
Finland	13.3	13.8	13.4	12.7	12.7	11.9	11.1	11.2	10.7	10.8	11.2	11.4
France	12.7	13.2	13.2	13.4	13.5	13.5	13.4	13.4	13.0	12.8	12.9	13.0
Germany	11.9	12.3	12.4	12.5	12.7	12.8	12.8	12.8	13.0	13.1	13.3	13.4
Greece	10.8	11.3	11.1	11.2	11.7	11.7	12.4	12.6	12.5	13.2	12.9	12.9
Hungary	—	—	—	—	—	—	—	9.1	8.7	8.9	9.0	9.3
Iceland	5.3	5.6	5.6	5.8	5.8	5.8	5.8	6.0	6.4	6.3	6.9	7.6
Ireland	5.8	5.6	5.4	5.0	4.7	4.3	4.0	3.8	3.6	3.7	3.8	3.9
Italy	14.5	14.9	15.0	14.5	14.8	15.3	14.8	15.1	14.7	14.7	15.0	15.1
Latvia	—	—	—	—	—	—	—	—	9.6	8.6	8.3	7.5
Lithuania	—	—	—	—	—	—	—	—	7.8	7.3	7.0	6.8
Luxembourg	12.5	12.5	12.3	12.7	12.5	12.0	11.1	10.7	9.7	10.1	10.5	10.9
Malta	—	—	—	8.1	8.9	8.8	—	8.5	8.2	9.1	9.1	9.4
Netherlands	15.0	15.0	14.4	14.1	14.0	13.7	13.1	13.2	13.0	12.4	12.7	12.6
Norway	8.9	8.8	8.7	8.5	8.2	8.0	8.7	8.7	7.6	7.8	8.5	8.8
Poland	—	—	—	—	—	—	—	—	13.0	13.9	14.2	14.3
Portugal	8.7	9.6	9.9	9.8	10.0	10.0	10.2	10.2	10.5	10.9	11.4	11.9
Slovakia	—	—	—	7.4	7.3	7.3	7.4	7.5	7.5	7.5	7.5	7.5
Slovenia	—	—	—	—	11.2	11.2	11.2	11.2	11.4	11.5	11.7	11.2
Spain	9.8	10.3	10.4	10.3	10.5	10.3	10.1	9.9	9.6	9.4	9.3	9.2
Sweden	—	13.8	13.5	12.8	12.8	12.5	12.3	12.1	11.7	11.7	12.0	12.7
Switzerland	9.8	10.5	10.7	11.1	11.5	11.8	12.1	12.3	12.2	12.7	12.8	13.2
United Kingdom	11.9	12.2	12.0	11.9	11.9	12.0	11.4	11.5	12.2	11.8	11.1	11.0

Source: Eurostat.

Note: — = Data not available.

[1] Includes the 25 countries that were members of the EU as of May 2004 (those listed in note 2, plus Cyprus, the Czech Republic, Estonia, Hungary, Latvia, Lithuania, Malta, Poland, the Slovak Republic, and Slovenia).

[2] Includes the 15 countries that were members of the EU as of 1995 (those listed in note 3, plus Austria, Finland, and Sweden).

[3] Includes the 12 countries that were members of the EU as of May 2004 (Belgium, Denmark, France, Germany, Greece, Ireland, Italy, Luxembourg, the Netherlands, Portugal, Spain, and the United Kingdom).

Table 11A.2. Total Expenditure on Social Welfare in European Countries
(percentage of GDP)

Group or country	1992	1993	1994	1995	1996	1997	1998	1999	2000	2001	2002	2003
EU25[1]	—	—	—	—	—	—	—	—	26.9	27.1	27.4	28.0
EU15[2]	27.6	28.7	28.4	28.2	28.4	27.9	27.5	27.4	27.2	27.5	27.7	28.3
Eurozone[3]	27.2	28.2	28.0	27.9	28.1	27.8	27.4	27.4	27.1	27.3	27.8	28.1
Austria	26.9	28.2	28.9	28.9	28.8	28.7	28.4	28.8	28.3	28.6	29.2	29.5
Belgium	27.7	29.3	28.7	28.1	28.6	27.9	27.6	27.3	26.8	27.7	28.8	29.7
Cyprus	—	—	—	—	—	—	—	—	—	15.2	16.4	—
Czech Republic	—	—	—	17.2	17.6	18.6	18.6	19.3	19.6	19.5	20.2	20.1
Denmark	29.7	31.5	32.5	31.9	31.2	30.1	30.0	29.8	28.9	29.2	29.9	30.9
Estonia	—	—	—	—	—	—	—	—	14.4	13.6	13.2	13.4
Finland	33.6	34.5	33.8	31.4	31.4	29.0	26.9	26.6	25.3	25.5	26.2	26.9
France	28.7	30.4	30.2	30.3	30.6	30.4	30.0	29.9	29.3	29.5	30.2	30.9
Germany	27.2	27.8	27.7	28.2	29.4	28.9	28.9	29.2	29.3	29.3	29.9	30.2
Greece	21.2	22.0	22.1	22.3	22.9	23.3	24.2	25.5	26.3	27.0	26.4	26.3
Hungary	—	—	—	—	—	—	—	20.7	19.8	19.8	20.7	21.4
Iceland	18.6	19.1	18.7	19.3	19.1	18.9	18.7	19.4	19.6	20.0	22.2	23.8
Ireland	20.3	20.2	19.7	18.8	17.6	16.4	15.2	14.6	14.1	15.0	15.9	16.5
Italy	26.2	26.4	26.0	24.8	24.8	25.5	25.0	25.2	25.2	25.6	26.1	26.4
Latvia	—	—	—	—	—	—	—	—	15.3	14.3	13.8	13.4
Lithuania	—	—	—	—	—	—	—	—	15.8	14.7	14.1	13.6
Luxembourg	22.5	23.3	22.9	23.7	24.1	22.8	21.7	21.7	20.3	21.3	22.6	23.8
Malta	—	—	—	17.5	18.8	19.0	—	17.4	16.9	17.7	18.0	18.5
Netherlands	31.9	32.3	31.7	30.9	30.1	29.4	28.4	28.0	27.4	26.5	27.6	28.1
Norway	28.2	28.2	27.6	26.7	26.0	25.3	27.1	27.1	24.6	25.6	26.2	27.7
Poland	—	—	—	—	—	—	—	—	20.1	21.5	21.9	21.6
Portugal	18.4	21.0	21.3	21.3	20.4	20.6	21.2	21.6	21.7	22.8	23.7	24.3
Slovakia	—	—	—	18.7	19.8	20.0	20.2	20.2	19.5	19.1	19.2	18.4
Slovenia	—	—	—	—	24.0	24.5	24.8	24.7	24.9	25.3	25.2	24.6
Spain	22.4	24.0	22.8	22.1	21.9	21.2	20.6	20.3	19.6	19.4	19.6	19.7
Sweden	37.1	38.2	36.8	34.6	33.8	32.9	32.2	31.9	31.0	31.5	32.5	33.5
Switzerland	23.2	24.8	25.0	25.7	26.6	27.5	27.7	27.6	27.4	28.1	28.7	29.8
United Kingdom	27.9	29.0	28.6	28.2	28.0	27.5	26.9	26.4	27.0	27.5	26.4	26.7

Source: Eurostat.
Note: — = Data not available.
[1] Includes the 25 countries that were members of the EU as of May 2004 (those listed in note 2, plus Cyprus, the Czech Republic, Estonia, Hungary, Latvia, Lithuania, Malta, Poland, the Slovak Republic, and Slovenia).
[2] Includes the 15 countries that were members of the EU as of 1995 (those listed in note 3, plus Austria, Finland, and Sweden).
[3] Includes the 12 countries that were members of the EU as of May 2004 (Belgium, Denmark, France, Germany, Greece, Ireland, Italy, Luxembourg, the Netherlands, Portugal, Spain, and the United Kingdom).

Table 11A.3. Latin America and the Caribbean—Social Security Coverage

(percentage of workers who contribute to social security)

Country	Total, national	Total, urban areas	Total, rural areas	Urban formal sector[1]	Wage-earning urban informal sector[2]	Non-wage-earning urban informal sector[3]	Total, men	Total, women
Argentina[4] (2002, urban areas)	—	56.0	—	68.5	22.7	—	59.0	52.5
Bolivia (2002)	14.5	21.2	4.6	42.8	6.8	10.4	13.8	15.4
Brazil (2001)	47.8	54.3	17.4	78.3	34.4	17.1	48.4	47.0
Chile (2003)	64.9	67.0	48.8	81.6	50.8	20.7	66.6	62.1
Costa Rica (2002)	65.3	68.2	60.5	87.7	43.3	35.0	68.5	59.3
Ecuador (2002, urban areas)	—	32.3	—	57.4	12.8	10.9	32.4	32.0
El Salvador (2001)	32.9	43.4	14.5	78.5	10.9	11.0	30.9	35.9
Guatemala (2002)	17.8	31.1	8.5	63.6	10.0	0.3	18.4	16.7
Mexico (2002)	55.1	64.8	30.8	81.9	25.5	—	52.9	59.1
Nicaragua (2001)	18.3	25.1	7.6	53.8	7.4	1.3	16.3	21.9
Panama (2002)	53.8	66.6	29.3	88.4	36.5	26.4	48.6	63.4
Paraguay (2000)	13.5	20.2	5.0	48.9	4.1	0.8	13.1	14.2
Peru (2001)	13.0	18.7	2.6	43.8	3.8	3.2	15.0	10.4
Dominican Republic (2002)	44.7	48.0	32.7	52.6	14.8	—	43.4	46.6
Uruguay (2002, urban areas)	—	63.8	—	88.2	43.9	24.7	63.6	64.0
Venezuela (Bolivarian Rep.) (2002)	61.5	—	—	75.5	19.9	—	58.0	67.1
Simple average	38.7	45.4	21.9	68.2	21.7	13.5	40.06	41.7

Source: Economic Commission for Latin America and the Caribbean (ECLAC), based on home surveys in the respective countries.

Note: — = Data not available. The variables used to define contributions to social security vary based on the surveys conducted in each country: contribution to or affiliation with a pension system (Argentina, Bolivia, Brazil, Chile, Colombia, Mexico, Paraguay, Peru, Uruguay); contribution to a national social security system (Costa Rica, Ecuador, El Salvador, Guatemala, Nicaragua, Panama); entitlement to social benefits (Bolivarian Republic of Venezuela); and work with a signed contract (Dominican Republic).

[1] Includes wage-earning workers from the public sector and from businesses with more than five employees, self-employed professionals and technicians, and the owners of businesses with five or more employees.

[2] Includes wage earners from businesses with fewer than five employees, as well as domestic service workers.

[3] Includes technical or nonprofessional self-employed workers, non-wage-earning relatives, and the owners of businesses with fewer than five employees.

[4] The rate corresponds to the social security contributions of wage-earning workers, except for self-employed workers, non-wage-earning relatives, and business owners.

References

Bravo, Jorge. 2000. "Envejecimiento de la población y sistemas de pensiones en América Latina." *Revista de la CEPAL* 72 (diciembre):121–46.

Commission of the European Communities. 2001. *Communication from the Commission to the Council, the European Parliament and the Economic and Social Committee: The Elimination of Tax Obstacles to the Cross-Border Provision of Occupational Pensions.* COM (2001) 214. Brussels: Commission of the European Communities. Available at http://eur-lex.europa.eu/LexUriServ/site/en/com/2001/com2001_0214en01.pdf.

Council of the European Union. 1998. "Council Directive 98/49/EC of 29 June 1998 on Safeguarding the Supplementary Pension Rights of Employed and Self-Employed Persons Moving within the Community." *Official Journal of the European Union* L-209 (July 25):46–49.

ECLAC (Economic Commission for Latin America and the Caribbean). 2006. "La protección social de cara al futuro: Acceso, financiamiento y solidaridad." Thirty-First Period of Sessions of ECLAC, Montevideo, Uruguay, March 20–24.

European Parliament and the Council of the European Union. 2003. "Directive 2003/41/EC of the European Parliament and of the Council of 3 June 2003 on the Activities and Supervision of Institutions for Occupational Retirement Provision." *Official Journal of the European Union* L-235 (September 23):10–21.

Martínez, Daniel. 2004. *El mundo del trabajo en la integración económica y la liberalización comercial: una mirada desde los países americanos.* Lima: International Labour Organisation.

Mesa-Lago, Carmelo. 2000. "Estudio comparativo de los costes fiscales en la transición de ocho reformas de pensiones en América Latina." Serie Financiamiento del Desarrollo 93. Santiago: United Nations Economic Commission for Latin America and the Caribbean.

Paddison, Oliver. 2005. *Social Security in the English-Speaking Caribbean.* LC/CAR/L.64. Port of Spain, Trinidad and Tobago: Subregional Headquarters of ECLAC for the Caribbean.

Puig, Pere. 2006. "La falta de integración regional en América Latina." *Diario Expansión de Madrid* (May 17).

Sangmeister, Hartmut, and Karim Taalouch. 2003. "¿Quiénes pueden beneficiarse del ALCA? Potenciales de comercio exterior no aprovechadas en ambos Américas." Estudios sobre el ALCA 18. Berlin: Friedrich Ebert Stiftung.

12

Capital Income Tax Coordination in the European Union: A Blueprint for Latin America?

Harry Huizinga

Introduction

The history of the European Union (EU) is one of gradually closer coordination of national tax policies. The EU's predecessor, the European Economic Community (EEC), completed a customs union with a common external tariff in 1968. In the 1960s the EEC also introduced a common framework for value-added tax (VAT), to replace the national sales taxes that had been applied previously. Plans for far-reaching European coordination of corporate income tax date from the 1970s. A proposal for a European directive to introduce a 45 to 55 percent band for the top corporate income tax rate, and to standardize the corporate income tax base, was introduced in 1975 but was not adopted. Several EU directives were adopted in 1990, dealing with the double taxation of dividend payments inside multinationals, and with international mergers and acquisitions. These were followed by the adoption of a code of conduct to fight harmful corporate income tax competition in 1997, and by a directive on the international taxation of savings income in 2003. In 2001, the European Commission announced a strategy to provide European multinationals with a common consolidated tax base, but no proposal for a directive to this effect has been tabled yet. Instead, in recent years the Commission has made further proposals that aim to smooth the operation of Europe's current corporate tax systems based on separate accounting.

Increased economic integration in Europe, stimulated by the introduction of the euro in 1999, has heightened interest in the international
implications of capital income tax in the EU. The recent decline in top
statutory corporate income tax rates in Europe is commonly attributed
to greater corporate income tax competition. Average capital income
taxes in the EU, however, have not declined in recent years. Paradoxi-
cally, greater economic integration—leading to the increased foreign
ownership of firms—may have contributed to the maintenance of relatively high average corporate income tax rates, since foreign ownership
allows countries to export part of their corporate income tax burden
to the foreign owners of domestic corporate assets. In the absence of
a more obvious "degradation" of the corporate income tax because of
international competition, it remains to be seen whether the EU will
be able to make much progress toward rationalizing its current system
of corporate income tax in the coming years. The need for consensus
among member states on EU tax policy directives—a requirement laid
down in the Nice Treaty, as well as in the draft EU constitution—is a formidable barrier to further progress on EU tax policy. At the same time,
in recent years the European Court of Justice (ECJ) has been quite active on international tax issues, and is forcing changes in national tax
policies that are seen as obstacles to the international capital mobility
guaranteed by the Maastricht Treaty. Recently, for instance, the ECJ
forced countries to revise "thin capitalization rules" that limit the interest deductibility for corporate income tax purposes to the subsidiaries
of foreign multinationals.

Latin America, of course, differs from Europe in many respects.
Average per capita income levels are lower in Latin America than in
Europe, which may partly explain why countries in Latin America rely
relatively heavily on indirect rather than direct taxation. Latin America
and Europe, however, are similar in that both regions consist mostly of
small, open economies that are highly integrated. In Latin America, as in
Europe, capital income tax has immediate international repercussions,
and perhaps those repercussions are a reason for the rather low taxes
on capital income in most Latin American countries. In both regions,
the existence of multiple and separate capital income tax systems entails

large efficiency costs—for instance, in the form of high compliance costs for internationally active companies. There thus appears to be a case for greater capital income tax coordination in Latin America, as there is in Europe. The EU experience, as reflected in economic studies and in the policy debate, might therefore be useful for Latin America.

Of course, if capital income tax coordination is introduced in Latin America, it will differ from the EU experience in several ways. Latin America, for example, lacks the equivalents of European institutions such as the European Commission and the ECJ that have been supranational catalysts in the international tax debate. In Latin America, capital income tax coordination would instead have to be proposed, approved, and eventually enforced by a group of nation-states. That circumstance makes such coordination relatively difficult in Latin America. On the other hand, economic integration is now advancing faster worldwide than in previous decades, which suggests that any Latin American cooperation in this area may evolve much faster than it did in Europe.

The purpose of this chapter is to review developments in personal and corporate income tax policy in the EU, with a view to informing the debate about possible capital income tax policy coordination in Latin America.[1] The chapter first reviews recent trends in capital income tax in the EU. National capital income tax policies have direct international repercussions if there is considerable cross-ownership of corporate and other assets. To shed light on this, the chapter presents some data on the foreign ownership of direct investment, portfolio investment, and bank liabilities. The chapter then lists some of the problems that arise with uncoordinated national capital income tax policies, which potentially can be addressed through international cooperation. Next comes a description of some of the supranational political infrastructure that guides the international tax debate in the EU, in the form of EU treaties and the European institutions. The chapter goes on to describe the EU capital income tax policies that have been adopted in the past or are

---

[1] See also Cnossen (2001) and Gorter and de Mooij (2001) for recent surveys of capital income taxation in the EU.

being debated at present. The penultimate section aims to assess the applicability to Latin America of the EU approach to capital income tax coordination. Finally, the chapter offers a brief conclusion.

Capital Income Tax Burdens in the EU

Capital income tax rates, and their dispersion among a set of countries, can be measured in several ways. First, "forward-looking" tax rates are measures of taxation that are based on statutory tax information, such as tax rate schedules and depreciation allowances for certain asset classes. Second, "backward-looking" tax rates are calculated ex post as ratios of realized tax liabilities and the corresponding income or expenditure measures.

Taking the forward-looking approach, the European Commission (2001a) published a comprehensive study of corporate income tax in the EU using 1999 data. Using statutory information, tax rates were calculated for domestic investments and for cross-border investments as financed by debt, equity, or retained earnings (or a combination thereof). To summarize the study, the highest corporate tax burdens were found to be in France and Germany, while the lowest were in Finland, Ireland, and Sweden. Despite the potential for double taxation of cross-border activities, the effective taxation of such activities was frequently lower than that of domestic activities, if the most tax-favored form of financing was chosen. Overall, the Commission study found that the most important determinant of cross-country differences in effective tax rates is the top statutory tax rate (rather than, say, depreciation rules). Harmonization of top statutory tax rates in the EU, therefore, would do much to reduce the dispersion of effective corporate income tax rates. The introduction of common depreciation rules, in contrast, would serve to increase the dispersion of those rates.

Table 12.1 provides some recent forward-looking information on top corporate and personal income tax rates for 2004. In that year, the average top corporate income tax rate in the 25-member EU (EU25) was 27.4 percent. This reflected an average top corporate income tax rate of 31.4 percent in the 15-member EU (EU15), and a lower average

Table 12.1. Top Statutory Tax Rates in 2004
(percent)

Country or group	Corporate income	Personal income	Interest income[1]
EU15[2]	31.4	46.2	34.1
Austria	34.0	50.0	25.0
Belgium	34.0	50.0	60.6
Denmark	30.0	47.6	59.7
Finland	29.0	53.0	29.0
France	35.4	49.6	24.0
Germany	38.3	45.0	36.9
Greece	35.0	40.0	10.0
Ireland	12.5	42.0	24.0
Italy	37.3	45.0	27.0
Luxembourg	30.4	38.0	43.0
Netherlands	34.5	52.0	None
Portugal	27.5	40.0	20.0
Spain	35.0	45.0	48.0
Sweden	28.0	56.0	30.0
United Kingdom	30.0	40.0	40.0
NMS10[3]	21.5	32.8	
Cyprus	15.0	30.0	
Czech Republic	28.0	32.0	
Estonia	26.0	26.0	
Hungary	17.7	38.0	
Latvia	15.0	25.0	
Lithuania	15.0	33.0	
Malta	35.0	35.0	
Poland	19.0	40.0	
Slovak Republic	19.0	19.0	
Slovenia	25.0	50.0	
EU25[4]	27.4	40.9	

Sources: Corporate and general personal income tax rates are from European Commission (2004b: 46); personal income tax rates on interest income are from Cnossen (2001, Table 9).
[1] Data are for 2001.
[2] Includes the 15 countries that were members of the EU before 2004.
[3] Includes the 10 new member states accepted into the EU in 2004.
[4] Includes the EU15 and the NMS10 (the 25 EU members as of May 2004).

of 21.5 percent in the 10 new member states (NMS10). Even among the EU15, top corporate tax rates varied considerably, from a high of 38.3 percent in Germany to a low of 12.5 percent in Ireland. Among the NMS10, Latvia, Lithuania, and Cyprus shared a low rate of 15 percent. The EU25 had an average top personal income tax rate of 40.9 percent in 2004. The average top personal rate was 46.2 percent in the EU15 and, again, somewhat lower in the NMS10 (32.8 percent). These rates apply to labor income and, depending on the country, to certain types of capital income. Several EU countries tax capital income such as interest at a reduced rate. As the table shows, the average personal income tax rate on interest income was a relatively low 34.1 percent in 2001.

The prospect of tax competition with the NMS10 is one of the factors that has caused the EU15 countries to cut their top corporate tax rates aggressively over the last decade, as reflected in Figure 12.1. The EU15 countries cut their average top corporate rate from 38.1 percent in 1995 to the above-mentioned 31.4 percent in 2004. Over the same period, the NMS10 cut their average top corporate rate from 30.4 percent to 21.5 percent.

With regard to backward-looking measures of tax burdens in Europe, Table 12.2 provides information on corporate and other tax burdens relative to gross domestic product (GDP) in the EU. For the EU25, the average total tax burden was 40.4 percent of GDP in 2002. This reflects an average total tax burden of 40.5 percent of GDP for the EU15, which is somewhat higher than the average tax burden of 37.3

Figure 12.1. Effective Top Statutory Tax Rates on Corporate Income in the EU, 1995–2004

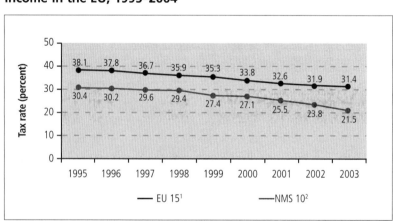

Source: European Commission (2004b, Graph I-2.2.1.4).
[1] Includes the 15 countries that were members of the EU before 2004.
[2] Includes the 10 new member states accepted into the EU in 2004.

Table 12.2. Tax Burden Relative to GDP
(percent)

Country or group	Total, 2002	Difference, 1995–2002	Consumption, 2002	Difference, 1995–2002	Labor, 2002	Difference, 1995–2002	Capital income, 2000	Difference, 1995–2002	Environmental,[1] 2002	Difference, 1995–2002
EU15[2]	40.5	-0.1	11.6	0.1	20.6	-0.8	8.3	0.6	2.6	-0.1
Austria	44.4	2.1	12.6	1.0	23.4	-0.6	8.5	1.6	2.6	0.6
Belgium	46.6	1.5	11.4	0.3	25.4	0.4	9.8	0.8	2.3	0.0
Denmark	48.9	-0.4	15.9	0.4	26.7	-1.2	6.2	0.5	4.8	0.4
Finland	45.9	-0.1	13.7	-0.2	24.2	-1.9	8.0	2.0	3.1	0.2
France	44.2	0.2	12.1	-0.6	22.8	-0.1	9.3	1.0	2.0	-0.4
Germany	40.2	-0.7	10.1	0.0	24.4	-0.4	5.6	-0.2	2.6	0.2
Greece	36.2	3.6	13.1	-0.3	13.6	1.8	9.6	2.1	2.6	-0.9
Ireland	28.6	-4.8	11.1	-2.0	10.2	-3.5	7.4	0.8	2.3	-0.8
Italy	41.7	0.6	10.3	-0.2	20.2	1.7	11.2	-0.9	2.9	-0.7
Luxembourg	41.9	-0.4	11.7	0.2	16.2	-1.5	14.1	0.9	2.9	-0.4
Netherlands	39.5	-1.1	11.7	0.9	19.2	-2.9	8.5	0.9	3.6	0.1
Portugal	36.3	2.8	12.5	-0.1	15.1	1.1	8.7	1.7	3.2	-0.5
Spain	36.2	2.7	10.0	1.1	16.8	0.1	9.3	1.6	2.2	-0.1
Sweden	50.6	1.1	13.0	-0.5	31.6	0.6	6.0	0.9	3.0	0.1
United Kingdom	35.8	0.5	13.4	-0.1	14.0	0.0	8.5	0.5	2.8	-0.2

(continued on next page)

Table 12.2. Tax Burden Relative to GDP *(continued)*
(percent)

Country or group	Total, 2002	Difference, 1995–2002	Consumption, 2002	Difference, 1995–2002	Labor, 2002	Difference, 1995–2002	Capital income, 2000	Difference, 1995–2002	Environmental,[1] 2002	Difference, 1995–2002
NMS10[3]	**37.3**	**0.8**	—	—	—	—	—	—	—	—
Cyprus	32.5	—	—	—	—	—	—	—	—	—
Czech Republic	35.4	-4.5	—	—	—	—	—	—	—	—
Estonia	35.2	—	—	—	—	—	—	—	—	—
Hungary	38.8	—	—	—	—	—	—	—	—	—
Latvia	31.3	-5.9	—	—	—	—	—	—	—	—
Lithuania	28.8	0.2	—	—	—	—	—	—	—	—
Malta	31.3	3.6	—	—	—	—	—	—	—	—
Poland	39.1	4.8	—	—	—	—	—	—	—	—
Slovak Republic	33.0	-8.5	—	—	—	—	—	—	—	—
Slovenia	39.8	-1.5	—	—	—	—	—	—	—	—
EU25[4]	**40.4**	**-0.2**	—	—	—	—	—	—	—	—

Source: European Commission (2004b: 239, 276, 277, 282, 288).
Note: — = Data not available.
[1] Environmental taxes include energy taxes, transport taxes, and pollution taxes. This is a subcategory of indirect or consumption taxes.
[2] Includes the 15 countries that were members of the EU before 2004.
[3] Includes the 10 new member states accepted into the EU in 2004.
[4] Includes the EU15 and the NMS10 (the 25 EU members as of May 2004).

percent of GDP for the NMS10. In the EU15, the overall tax burden relative to GDP ranged from 50.6 percent in Sweden to 28.6 percent in Ireland in 2002. The table also shows that the average tax burden relative to GDP fell by only 0.1 percent in the EU15 during the 1995–2002 period, while it increased by about 0.8 percent in the NMS10. Note that changes in the average tax burden relative to GDP may arise from tax reforms, but equally from the business cycle or economic growth. Economic growth, specifically, can push some taxpayers into higher tax brackets, which would serve to increase the average tax burden relative to GDP.

Table 12.2 also provides a breakdown of taxes on consumption, labor, capital, and the environment, all relative to GDP. European Commission information of this kind is available only for the EU15. The data show a surprising variation in the importance of these main tax categories across EU member states. Consumption taxes, for instance, are relatively important in Denmark, reflecting the fact that Denmark has the highest VAT rate in the EU (25 percent). Luxembourg has the lowest VAT rate among the EU15 (15 percent), but it still takes in a considerable 10.3 percent of GDP in the form of consumption taxes. This could reflect significant cross-border shopping by citizens of neighboring countries. Turning to labor taxation, Denmark and Sweden have the highest labor taxes in the EU: 26.7 and 31.6 percent of GDP, respectively. As regards capital income tax, Luxembourg receives somewhat high taxes relative to GDP (14.1 percent), while Denmark, Sweden, and Germany are at the bottom with 6.2, 6.0, and 5.6 percent, respectively. In the case of Germany, this low capital income tax intake is certainly not due to a low corporate income tax rate, since the country's top corporate income tax rate was the highest in the EU in 2004 (see Table 12.1). To some extent, low capital income tax revenues in Germany may reflect tax evasion by corporations domiciled in Germany—for example, through manipulation of international transfer prices. Finally, note that environmental taxes (that is, taxes on energy, transport, or pollution, which are a subcategory of consumption taxes) amounted to 2.6 percent of GDP in the EU15 in 2002, 0.1 percent lower than in 1995.

Table 12.3 provides an alternative backward-looking measure of tax burdens on consumption, labor, and capital income in the form of implicit tax rates. These rates, also calculated by the European Commission (2004b), are obtained by dividing the tax revenues in a certain category by the pertinent tax base using information from national accounts. The implicit consumption tax rate is thus the ratio of the revenues from the indirect taxation of consumption (mostly through VAT), divided by the value of consumption. The implicit labor tax rate, analogously, is the sum of taxes on labor (as paid by individuals and firms) divided by labor income, while the implicit capital income tax rate is the sum of capital income taxes (paid by individuals and companies) divided by capital income. The table indicates that the average implicit tax rate on consumption was 20.3 percent in the EU15 in 2002, unchanged from 1995. The implicit tax rate on labor was 36.3 percent in the EU15 in 2002, about 1 percent less than in 1995. Finally, the implicit tax rate on capital income was 28.4 percent in 2002, which was 4 percent higher than in 1995. Hence fears that tax competition in the EU would lead to a degradation of capital income taxation—with a "race to the bottom" in capital income tax rates—have not been realized.

The tax system data presented so far do not distinguish between the taxation of domestic and international activities, even though multinationals' cross-border activities are very important in Europe. As indicated by the European Commission (2001a), the effective taxation of cross-border activities may be higher or lower than that of domestic activities for different modes of financing. In the case of equity financing, there is the potential for double taxation by both parent and subsidiary countries. To prevent double taxation, parent countries typically exempt foreign-source income from domestic taxation, or they provide a domestic tax credit against taxes paid abroad, or they allow parent companies to deduct foreign-source income from domestic taxable income.

EU member countries typically have a general rule for alleviating potential double taxation of cross-border activities (the exemption, credit, or deduction rule), which may or may not be amended bilaterally through a tax treaty. The resulting pattern of double tax relief in the EU, as represented in Table 12.4, is rather haphazard. Some countries, such

Table 12.3. Implicit Tax Rates, 2002
(percent)

Country	Consumption, 2002	Difference, 1995–2002	Labor, 2002	Difference, 1995–2002	Capital income, 2002	Difference, 1995–2002
Austria	22.0	1.4	39.2	0.5	28.5	5.0
Belgium	21.9	0.7	43.5	-0.7	30.1	6.3
Denmark	33.7	2.4	39.9	-0.8	28.8	2.4
Finland	28.0	-0.2	43.9	0.0	30.3	2.4
France	21.9	-1.0	41.8	-0.3	36.6	5.6
Germany	18.3	-0.5	39.9	0.4	20.9	-0.2
Greece	18.1	0.6	37.8	3.7	18.1	6.1
Ireland	25.8	0.5	25.9	-3.9	32.0	10.3
Italy	17.1	-0.5	41.1	3.3	28.1	1.7
Luxembourg	23.7	2.0	28.0	-1.5	32.0	7.1
Netherlands	24.2	1.6	31.9	-3.1	29.6	6.6
Portugal	20.1	0.6	33.7	2.7	—	11.1[1]
Spain	16.3	2.0	30.0	1.1	29.6	8.9
Sweden	30.6	2.2	46.6	-1.7	31.5	13.4
United Kingdom	21.3	-0.5	24.6	-1.1	30.8	3.0
EU15	20.3	0.0	36.3	-0.9	28.4	4.0

Source: European Commission (2004b: 293–94).

Note: — = Data not available.

[1] Calculated for 1995–2001.

Table 12.4. Bilateral International Double Taxation Relief Conventions

Location of subsidiary firm

Location of parent firm	Austria	Belgium	Cyprus	Czech Republic	Denmark	Estonia	Finland	France	Germany	Greece	Hungary	Ireland	Italy	Latvia	Lithuania	Luxembourg	Netherlands	Poland
Austria		E	E	E	E	E	C	E	E	E	E	E	C	C	C	C	E	E
Belgium	E		E	C	C	C	C	E	E	C	E	C	C	C	C	E	E	E
Cyprus	E	E		E	C	C	C	C	E	C	C	C	E	C	C	C	E	E
Czech Republic	E	BD	C		C	C	C	E	E	E	E	E	E	C	C	E	E	E
Denmark	E	E	C	E		E	C	E	E	E	E	E	C	E	E	E	E	C
Estonia	E	BD	C	C	C		E	C	C	C	E	C	C	C	C	E	E	E
Finland	E	E	C	C	C	C		E	E	C	E	C	C	C	C	E	E	C
France	E	E	E	C	E	E	E		E	E	E	E	E	E	E	E	E	E
Germany	E	E	C	E	C	C	C	E		C	E	C	E	E	E	E	E	E
Greece	E	E	C	E	C	C	C	E	E		E	D	C	C	C	E	E	E
Hungary	E	E	E	E	E	E	E	E	E	E		C	C	E	E	E	E	E
Ireland	C	C	C	C	C	C	C	E	E	E	E		C	C	C	E	E	E
Italy	C	E	E	E	E	E	E	E	E	E	C	E		C	C	E	E	E
Latvia	E	BD	C	C	E	C	C	E	C	C	C	C	C		E	E	E	E
Lithuania	E	BD	C	C	E	C	E	C	C	C	C	C	C	E		C	E	E
Luxembourg	E	E	E	E	E	E	E	E	E	E	E	C	C	C	C		E	E
Netherlands	E	E	C	E	C	C	C	E	E	E	E	C	C	C	C	E		C
Poland	E	E	C	E	E	C	C	E	E	C	C	C	C	C	C	E	E	

(continued on next page)

Table 12.4. Bilateral International Double Taxation Relief Conventions *(continued)*

Location of subsidiary firm	Portugal	Slovak Republic	Slovenia	Spain	Sweden	Switzerland	United Kingdom
Austria	E	E	C	C	C	E	C
Belgium	C	C	C	C	C	E	C
Cyprus	C	E	E	C	E	E	C
Czech Republic	C	C	C	E	C	E	C
Denmark	C	E	E	E	C	E	C
Estonia	C	C	C	C	C	E	C
Finland	C	C	C	E	C	E	C
France	C	E	E	E	C	E	C
Germany	C	E	E	C	C	C	C
Greece	C	E	C	C	E	E	C
Hungary	C	C	E	C	C	E	C
Ireland	C	C	C	C	C	E	C
Italy	C	E	E	C	C	E	C
Latvia	C	C	C	C	C	E	C
Lithuania	C	C	C	C	C	E	C
Luxembourg	C	E	C	C	C	E	C
Netherlands	C	E	E	E	C	E	C
Poland	C	C	C	E	C	E	C
Portugal		E	C	C	C	E	C
Slovak Republic	C		E	E	C	E	C
Slovenia	C	E		C	E	E	C
Spain	C	E	E		C	E	C
Sweden	C	E	E	C		E	C
Switzerland	C	C	E	C	C		C
United Kingdom	E	C	C	E	C		

Source: Huizinga and Laeven (2005, Table 2).

Note: E = exemption; C = credit; D = deduction; BD = Belgian deduction. The rule applies to income received by a parent firm in a country listed at the left from a subsidiary in a country listed at the top. For example, income received by a parent firm in France is exempted from tax in France regardless of its foreign origin.

as France and the Netherlands, exempt all foreign-source income; other countries, such as Italy and the United Kingdom, provide a foreign tax credit in all cases. Austria provides an exemption for income from some countries and a credit for taxes paid in other countries. Note that Belgium and Ireland apply the deduction method to some foreign-source income. The pattern of double tax relief displayed in the table is clearly unsystematic and an unnecessary barrier to the smooth taxation of cross-border corporate income in the EU.

Economic Integration in the EU

National capital income tax policies have international repercussions if capital markets are integrated internationally. In that case, a higher corporate income tax in one country, for instance, can cause a relocation of investment to another country. Similarly, a higher tax on savings in one country can reduce the pool of funds available for investment worldwide. With international capital mobility, therefore, national tax policies potentially have positive or negative external effects on other countries, creating a rationale for international tax policy coordination.

Capital mobility and financial market integration in the EU can be measured in a variety of ways. European Commission data (2001b), for example, show that correlations among national savings and investment rates in the EU have declined over time—evidence of increased international capital mobility. Such mobility is likely to lead to substantial cross-border investments, entailing considerable cross-ownership of national assets. Thus ratios of international investments to GDP and foreign ownership rates of national assets can serve as useful quantitative measures of international capital mobility.

Table 12.5 summarizes some of these measures for the EU15. First, the table shows that foreign direct investment (FDI) liabilities averaged 14 percent of GDP in 1998. FDI liabilities were quite high in Belgium, at 77 percent of GDP, but relatively low in Germany and Italy, at 4 and 9 percent, respectively. The table also provides the foreign ownership share of nontraded equities (these are either equities of independent firms without an exchange listing or equities of other firms' subsidiar-

Table 12.5. Investment Liabilities and Foreign Ownership Shares

Country	Foreign direct investment (% of GDP)	Foreign ownership of nontraded equities, 1997 (%)	Portfolio investment liabilities, 1998 (% of GDP)	Foreign ownership of traded equities, 1997 (%)	External bank liabilities, 1999 (% of GDP)
Austria	13	21	7	21	5
Belgium	77[1]	37	8	14	37
Denmark	17	24	12[1]	19	5
Finland	15	—	63	37	4
France	16	13	20	27	4
Germany	4[2]	12	9[2]	20	13
Greece	—	29	—	13	—
Ireland	—	—	—	64	28
Italy	9	34	6	26	1
Luxembourg	—	—	—	—	768
Netherlands	36[2]	27	62[2]	40	14
Portugal	20	16	18	30	10
Spain	22	31	13	27	13
Sweden	24	—	42	27	4
United Kingdom	24	9	49	18	28
EU15	14	22[3]	16	27[3]	13

Sources: Direct and portfolio investment data are from Huizinga and Nielsen (2005, Figure 1). Data on external bank liabilities are from Huizinga (2004, Table 2). Shares of foreign ownership of nontraded equities are computed using data from the Amadeus database. Shares of the foreign ownership of traded equities are computed using data from the Coordinated Portfolio Investment Survey as published by the International Monetary Fund, along with data from the International Federation of Stock Exchanges.
Note: — = Data not available.
[1] Includes data for Luxembourg.
[2] Data are for 1997.
[3] Data are arithmetic averages.

ies). The average foreign ownership share for these firms was 22 percent. The table indicates that portfolio investment liabilities as a share of GDP were 16 percent on average in the EU. Finland and the Netherlands had rather high portfolio investment liabilities, at 63 and 62 percent of GDP, respectively. Again, Germany and Italy had fairly low portfolio investment liabilities, at 9 and 6 percent of GDP, respectively. The foreign ownership share of traded equities averaged 27 percent in the EU. Finally, the table indicates that, on average, external bank liabilities were 13 percent of GDP. Among individual countries there was a wide variation in this measure of financial openness: external bank liabilities were 768 percent of GDP in Luxembourg, but only 1 percent in Italy. Overall, capital and bank markets in the EU appear to be quite international, such that national capital income tax policies potentially affect other European economies.

Inefficiencies of International Capital Income Taxation

National tax policymakers typically do not take account of how their policies affect other countries. As a result, national income tax policies can spur outcomes that are collectively undesirable. Some of the potential inefficiencies of international income taxation are reviewed in this section. The solution to these inefficiencies, if they arise, has to be found in international tax policy coordination. In the EU, this has taken the form of common tax policies (discussed in a later section, "EU Initiatives in the Area of Capital Income Taxation").

Insufficient Total Tax Revenues

The literature on international tax competition typically indicates that tax revenues, and hence government spending, are too low in the absence of international cooperation. (For recent surveys, see Gordon and Hines, 2002, and Wilson and Wildasin, 2004). To understand why this is the case, note that a lower corporate income tax in a country may serve to attract additional investment from abroad. Reduced investment abroad also leads to lower corporate income tax revenues abroad. This involves a negative externality for the foreign country, since that country can no longer offer the same level of government services. National tax authorities typically ignore the negative externality of a lower corporate income tax on a foreign country, and therefore, in the noncooperative equilibrium, tax rates and tax revenues are too low.

In Verona in 1996, at an informal meeting of the member states' economics and finance ministers (commonly known as the Ecofin Council), EU policymakers stated that protecting total tax revenues is a goal of EU tax policy, not least to maintain the European socioeconomic model characterized by significant income redistribution (see European Commission, 1996). Total tax revenues as a percentage of GDP declined by only 0.2 percent in the EU25 between 1997 and 2002. Hence total tax

Figure 12.2. The Corporate Tax Burden and Foreign Ownership of Equities, 1996–2000

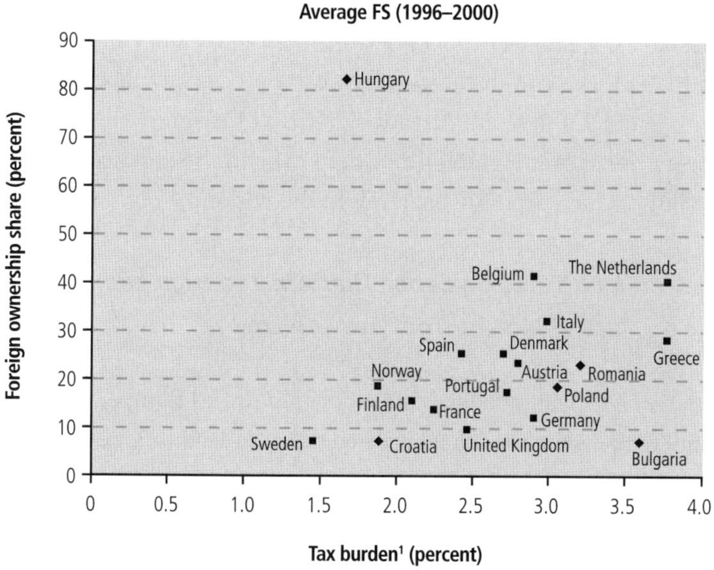

Average FS (1996–2000)

Source: Huizinga and Nicodème (2006, Figure 1).
Note: Data are averages of yearly averages. For a given country in a given year, the foreign ownership share was computed only if there were at least 35 observations. In that case, the corresponding tax burden was computed as well.
[1] Calculated as corporate taxes divided by assets.

revenues do not appear to be under pressure in the EU. One reason for this may be that a high foreign ownership of equities provides countries with an incentive to raise rather than lower their corporate income tax rates, since the resulting higher corporate income tax will be paid in part by the foreign owners of domestic assets.[2] Huizinga and Nicodème (2006) offer some evidence that higher foreign ownership rates are indeed associated with higher corporate tax rates in Europe. As an illustration of this, Figure 12.2 plots the foreign ownership share for European countries over the 1996–2000 period against their average corporate tax burden, defined as taxes paid as a share of assets.

---

[2] See Huizinga and Nielsen (1997, 2002) for theoretical papers on how foreign ownership affects corporate tax policy in a small, open economy, and what the scope is for tax coordination in a multicountry world.

The scatter displays an apparently positive relationship between foreign ownership rates and average corporate tax burdens. Econometric results suggest an economically significant relationship between these two variables: a 1 percent increase in the foreign ownership share appears to lead to a rise in the average corporate income tax rate of between 0.5 and 1.0 percent. Already significant foreign ownership levels in Europe (as shown in Table 12.5) help explain the absence of a "race to the bottom" in corporate tax levels in the region.

A Skewed Mix: Taxes on Labor That Are Too High and Taxes on Capital Income That Are Too Low

International capital mobility is already significant in Europe, while labor mobility remains limited. As mentioned, this can lead to lower capital income taxes. Subsequently, labor income taxes could be raised to offset the capital income tax shortfall. If so, the overall tax mix will be tilted toward labor taxes, with possibly negative implications for employment and investment in human capital. At the Verona Ecofin meeting in 1996, EU member states expressed their desire to counter this perceived trend by reshuffling the tax mix towards higher capital income taxes (and higher environmental taxes) and lower labor taxes (see European Commission, 1996). As Table 12.3 shows, the EU has been able to increase its average implicit tax rate on capital income and lower its average implicit tax rate on labor income since 1995. Hence a tax mix that is progressively tilted toward labor taxes has not materialized. As discussed in more detail later, since 1997 the EU has developed several tax policy initiatives to increase capital income taxes. These may have contributed to the revealed higher capital income taxes. One contributing factor, already discussed, may also have been higher capital income taxes in response to high foreign ownership of domestic assets.

Economic Distortions Resulting from Double Taxation or No Taxation of International Capital Flows

The international tax system potentially entails the double taxation of capital income flows for several reasons. First, the income of multinationals' subsidiaries can be subject to taxation in both the country of the subsidiary and that of the parent company if the latter country provides incomplete double taxation relief for taxes already paid in the country of the subsidiary. Withholding taxes on dividend and interest payments that apply only to nonresidents can similarly lead to relatively high taxation of international capital income streams. Finally, countries that have imputations systems (to impute corporate income taxes to shareholders) typically do not provide foreign shareholders with personal income tax credits for domestic corporate income taxes. Hence international dividend streams are taxed relatively heavily. Instead of overtaxation, the international tax system may equally well give rise to the undertaxation of international capital flows. For instance, the system can undertax international capital income if the recipients are able to evade domestic taxes on such income.

There is evidence that the international tax system imposes either double taxation or none at all on international capital income streams. Hines (1996), for example, offers evidence that investors from countries with worldwide taxation systems (and foreign tax credits to offset foreign-source corporate income taxes) invest relatively heavily in U.S. states with high tax rates. The reason is that the double taxation suffered by these foreign investors—relative to domestic U.S. investors—is relatively small in high-tax states. Hence, the (potential) double taxation of international corporate income in this case distorts FDI flows.

Similarly, Huizinga and Nicodème (2004) provide evidence that international bank depositing patterns are affected by international taxation, and especially by the desire to evade domestic income taxes on foreign-source interest income. The evidence suggests that a higher interest income tax led to higher nonbank deposits abroad during 1983–91, but not during 1992–99. This may indicate that incentives to place deposits abroad, so as to evade domestic interest taxation, were particularly high in the 1980s because both tax rates and interest rates were then high. On the other hand, there is no robust evidence that either wealth taxes or nonresident withholding taxes affected international deposit flows. In addition, external deposits are estimated to have increased by 28 percent following the introduction of the reporting of domestic interest payments to domestic tax authorities. There is no evidence, however, that the international exchange of information on interest payments to nonresidents has affected international deposit flows (using 1999 data).

Distortions as a Result of Different National Tax Rates

Even in the absence of discriminatory international taxation, the international tax system can distort investment and company location decisions in the international economy. A relatively low average corporate income tax in a country can serve to attract new investment, possibly at the expense of locales with higher taxes. A relatively large literature confirms that FDI flows are affected by taxation (see Gresik, 2001, and de Mooij and Ederveen, 2003). For example, Devereux and Griffith (1998) investigate the decisions made by U.S. multinationals that invest in Europe. The authors find that tax rates do not affect the choice as to whether to invest abroad, but they do influence the choice among potential FDI destinations. A harmonization of (effective) international corporate income tax rates would serve to eliminate inefficient location and investment outcomes arising from the present dispersion in national tax rates. On the basis of a simulation model, Sørensen (2004) concludes that a harmonization of corporate tax rates in the EU can yield a welfare gain equivalent to 0.35 percent of GDP.

Tax-Motivated International Profit Shifting

Differences in international corporate income tax rates can lead to tax-motivated international profit shifting. Profits can be shifted internationally through a variety of techniques. These include the manipulation of international transfer prices, international debt shifting, and the assignment of the multinational's common expenses (such as research and development costs) to high-tax locales. A significant body of literature has investigated potential profit shifting, mostly with U.S. data (for surveys, see Hines, 1999, and Newlon, 2000). Huizinga and Laeven (2005) investigate the scale of international profit shifting within European multinationals. Using regressions based on micro data, these authors find that the semi-elasticity of reported profits with respect to the top statutory tax rate is 1.43 on average in Europe. As a result, international profit shifting leads to a substantial redistribution of the corporate income tax base and of corporate income tax revenues in the EU.

Specifically, Huizinga and Laeven estimate that multinationals active in Germany shift 27 percent of their tax base out of Germany. The reason is that Germany has the highest corporate tax rate (at 54 percent in 1999) in the sample of 32 European countries considered in the study. At Germany's expense, most other European countries are estimated to gain tax revenues as a result of international profit shifting. Table 12.1 shows that by 2004, Germany had reduced its corporate tax rate to 38.3 percent, no doubt in an effort to stop the hemorrhaging of tax revenues because of outward international profit shifting.

High Compliance and Enforcement Costs

The present system of separate national tax bases creates high compliance costs for internationally active firms, and it involves high enforcement costs because of the myriad options for international tax avoidance and evasion. The European Commission (2004a) recently conducted a survey of 700 European companies to gain information on their compliance costs related to corporate income tax and VAT. Econometric analysis, based on the survey results, shows that compliance costs are higher for companies with at least one subsidiary in another EU member state than for companies without such subsidiaries. At the same time, compliance costs increase with the number of subsidiaries abroad. The study also yielded some qualitative results that indicate that transfer pricing requirements are a major difficulty in the company tax area. Specifically, 82.8 percent of large companies with international operations report that transfer pricing is an important issue, while documentation requirements in this area are difficult for 81.9 percent of large companies. This no doubt reflects the fact that firms have to incur substantial costs in order to comply with existing profit-shifting regulations, but perhaps it also indicates that firms need to incur costs so as to shift profits internationally through noncompliance. Huizinga and Laeven (2005) estimate that the (noncompliance) costs of profit-shifting activities incurred by European multinationals amount to 1.5 percent of their tax base.

Decision Making on Tax Policy in the EU

The treaties establishing the EU set out the ground rules in the EU tax policy debate. The EC Treaty of Rome defines the scope of EU tax policy. Article 93 calls for the harmonization of indirect taxes, since these may create an immediate obstacle to the functioning of the internal market. Article 94 provides only for the approximation of direct taxes insofar as income taxes directly affect the establishment or functioning of the common market. In principle, EU treaties allow countries to discriminate in their income taxes on the basis of the national source of the income or the national residence of the income recipient. Counterbalancing this, the Maastricht Treaty elevates the freedom of capital movements within the EU to treaty level. It remains to be seen to what extent the guaranteed freedom of capital movements will be deemed to be consistent with any remaining international discrimination in the area of capital income taxation.

EU treaties also define the roles that European institutions and member states are to play in the EU tax policy debate. The European Commission has the right to propose directives and regulations in the area of taxation. The Council of Ministers can subsequently adopt such legislation after consultation with the European Parliament. In tax matters, the Nice Treaty and the draft EU constitution maintain the requirement of unanimity in the Council of Ministers. Needless to say, this requirement amounts to a formidable hurdle for EU tax policy in a union currently consisting of 27 member states. Consequently, progress on EU tax legislation is bound to be slow.

The relative legislative inaction increases the weight of the ECJ in tax matters. European citizens or companies can appeal directly to the ECJ if they feel that national tax policies breach the treaty or some other piece of European legislation. Traditionally, European international corporate tax law has had important discriminatory aspects, and these are increasingly challenged at the ECJ. As an example of discrimination, countries have traditionally limited the deductibility of interest from taxable income available to the subsidiaries of multinational firms. One way to do this is to use thin capitalization rules, whereby thinly capitalized foreign subsidiaries are denied interest deductibility. In a recent case (Lankhorst-Hohort, C-324/00), the ECJ struck down Germany's formulation of its thin capitalization rule as being discriminatory. This has prompted countries throughout the EU to review their rules. The potential consolidation of losses for tax purposes within multinational firms is another area in which ECJ action may come to play an important role in shaping national tax policies in the EU.

EU Initiatives in the Area of Capital Income Taxation

As indicated earlier, cooperation among national policymakers within an EU framework may be necessary to address inefficiencies in capital income taxation. Cooperation can take several forms. Harmonization would lead to equal tax policies in different countries. More limited coordination could impose minimum standards on tax policies in EU members, such as a prescribed band for a certain tax rate. Proposals for EU tax directives, whether or not they have been adopted, generally define a range within which national policies are to be applied. For example, in 1975 the European Commission proposed a directive on corporate income tax that called for a tax band of between 45 and 55 percent. This proposal, like several similar suggestions in the area of corporate income tax, was not adopted (see Devereux, 2004: 71).

This section provides an overview of the EU directives on capital income tax that have been adopted to date, and it reviews some of the Commission's current initiatives in this area. In the last several decades, there have been three waves of activity in EU capital income tax policy. First, in 1990, an initial set of agreements arose in the form of two directives (the Parent-Subsidiary Directive and the Merger Directive) and an arbitration convention related to international transfer pricing. Second, in 1997, the EU launched its "tax package," including an initiative against harmful tax competition and a call for the common taxation of international savings income in the EU. Finally, starting in 2001, the EU renewed its efforts to improve the functioning of the EU corporate income tax system. An important feature of this latest initiative is the desire to introduce a consolidated tax base for internationally active companies in Europe.

Table 12.6 summarizes the three waves of EU policymaking on capital income taxes. It lists the main directives already adopted, along with current initiatives, and indicates the primary objectives of each.

The 1990 Initiatives

In 1990 the EU adopted the Parent-Subsidiary Directive. As Table 12.6 shows, the main purpose of this directive was to reduce tax barriers to the completion of the common market—in this case, by addressing double taxation of the profits of multinational corporations. First, the directive provides that each member state must adopt some method of alleviating

Table 12.6. Capital Income Tax Policies and Initiatives in the EU

Objective	Parent-Subsidiary Directive, 1990	Merger Directive, 1990	Arbitration Convention, 1990	Code of Conduct, 1997	Interest and Royalties Directive, 2003	Savings Directive, 2003	Revision of Parent-Subsidiary Directive, 2003	Revision of Merger Directive, 2005	Cross-Border Loss-Offset Directive	EU Tax Treaty	Common Tax Base Directive
Safeguard tax revenues				X		X					
Alter tax mix				X		X					
Eliminate tax barriers to common market (double taxation/no taxation)	X	X	X		X	X	X	X	X	X	X
Reduce tax rate differences				X							X
Reduce compliance costs/enforcement costs											X

the potential double taxation of foreign-source profits. Specifically, it offers member states two options in this regard: countries can exempt foreign-source income from taxation, or they can provide a foreign tax credit for foreign-source taxes against domestic taxes on foreign-source income. As Table 12.4 shows, both methods are now widely applied in the EU. Second, the Parent-Subsidiary Directive eliminates nonresident withholding taxes for dividend payments among related parties in different member states. This applies if the parent firm owns at least 25 percent of the stock of a foreign subsidiary.

The Merger Directive was also adopted in 1990. It aims to eliminate tax barriers in the form of capital gains taxes on cross-border mergers and acquisitions. More specifically, any capital gains taxes are to be deferred until a later disposal of the assets. This directive applies to capital gains taxes on a company that sells assets, and to shareholders who tender their shares to enable an acquisition.

As a final measure in 1990, the EU adopted an arbitration convention. This sets out the procedures that tax authorities are to follow to reach an agreement on international transfer prices to be used by a multinational firm. The aim is to eliminate the possibility that different transfer prices may be applied in the calculation of taxable income by the tax authorities in the exporting and importing countries. Differences in the transfer prices applied by member states can lead to international income being taxed twice or not at all. A main objective of the arbitration convention, therefore, is to reduce the double taxation of international corporate income.

The EU has continued to build upon the 1990 initiatives. In 2003, it adopted a directive on the taxation of interest and royalty payments among related parties. This can be seen as an extension of the Parent-Subsidiary Directive applying to dividend payments among related parties. In 2005 the EU revised the Merger Directive.

The Tax Package of 1997

As mentioned earlier, at an informal Ecofin meeting in Verona in 1996, the European Commission addressed several challenges confronting

EU tax policy. These include safeguarding total revenues, preventing the tax mix from becoming skewed toward labor taxation, and establishing a single market without tax barriers. To meet these challenges, the Commission drafted a tax package in 1997 (see European Commission, 1997). The package consisted of three policy initiatives:

- A code of conduct against harmful tax practices in the area of corporate income taxation.
- A stated intention to develop a common approach to the taxation of cross-border interest payments accruing to individuals.
- A stated intention to eliminate nonresident withholding taxes on interest and royalty payments among related corporate parties.

The code of conduct on corporate income taxation of 1997 and the savings tax directive of 2003, which provides for information exchange on cross-border interest payments, are discussed separately below.

The Code of Conduct

The code of conduct is a political, nonlegislative agreement to limit harmful tax competition. The code aims to protect the corporate tax base and to bring about a fair division of that base among member states. It outlines several criteria to identify harmful tax competition. Harmful measures, for instance, may involve relatively low taxes that are limited in their application in the sense that they are available only to nonresidents or they apply only to activities undertaken by nonresidents. Other harmful measures are those that potentially shift the tax base without affecting the location of real activity. Such shifting can occur by granting low levels of taxation to firms (or to parts thereof, such as the headquarters), while being lenient about the rules for allocating the profits of multinationals internationally. Tax policy can also be harmful if it is not transparent and might thus discriminate in favor of foreign firms.

To identify harmful tax practices in the EU, in 1998 Ecofin established the Code of Conduct Group, chaired by the British Paymaster-General, Dawn Primarolo. In 1999 this group published its report, which enumerated 66 harmful tax measures. Among these was the low corporate tax rate of 10 percent for manufacturing in Ireland. This low rate encouraged firms to manufacture or assemble goods in Ireland for sale elsewhere in the EU, thus shifting the EU-wide profits to Ireland by charging relatively high export prices to the sales organizations elsewhere in the EU. Also listed as harmful were special tax regimes for coordination centers in Belgium and holding companies in the Netherlands. Member states have pledged to scrap these tax practices through a "rollback," and to refrain from introducing additional harmful practices by way of a "standstill."

Ireland, for instance, agreed to replace its dual corporate income tax system with a single tax rate of 12.5 percent for all industries. Plainly, this hardly eliminated the incentive for multinational manufacturing firms to shift profits to Ireland; it even created incentives for firms in industries other than manufacturing to do the same. Hence the proscription of a special tax regime may be welfare-reducing if it leads a country to reduce its overall tax rate (Keen, 2002).[3] Nonetheless, the elimination of the special 10 percent tax rate for manufacturing in Ireland should eliminate distortions related to, for example, the allocation of capital in Ireland between manufacturing and other industries.

It is hard to gauge whether the harmful tax initiative has met its main goal of preventing a degeneration of the corporate tax base. Table 12.3 indicates that the implicit tax rate of capital income in the EU rose by 4 percent between 1995 and 2002. It may well be that this stems partly from the EU's fight against harmful tax competition. Indirectly, the harmful tax competition initiative may have contributed to the view that erosion of the corporate tax base is to be prevented. If so, it may have contributed to a better enforcement of corporate income taxation generally, which would lead to a higher intake of measured corporate tax revenue.

---

[3] Janeba and Peters (1999), however, show that eliminating preferential tax regimes can be welfare-improving if it sufficiently reduces competition for an internationally mobile tax base.

Table 12.7. International Automatic Exchange of Information on Bank Interest in the EU15, 1999

Providing country	Receiving country														
	Austria	Belgium	Denmark	Finland	France	Germany	Greece	Ireland	Italy	Luxembourg	Netherlands	Portugal	Spain	Sweden	United Kingdom
Austria		0	0	0	0	0	0	0	0	0	0	0	0	0	0
Belgium	0		0	0	0	0	0	0	0	0	0	0	0	0	0
Denmark	0	0		1	1	0	0	0	0	0	0	0	1	1	1
Finland	1	1	1		1	1	1	1	1	1	1	1	1	1	1
France	1	1	1	1		1	0	0	1	0	1	1	1	1	1
Germany	0	0	0	0	0		0	0	0	0	0	0	0	0	0
Greece	0	0	0	0	0	0		0	0	0	0	0	0	0	0
Ireland	0	0	0	0	0	0	0		0	0	0	0	0	0	0
Italy	0	0	0	0	0	0	0	0		0	0	0	0	0	0
Luxembourg	0	0	0	0	0	0	0	0	0		0	0	0	0	0
Netherlands	0	0	0	0	0	0	0	0	0	0		0	0	0	0
Portugal	0	0	0	0	0	0	0	0	0	0	0		0	0	0
Spain	0	0	0	0	0	0	0	0	0	0	0	0		0	0
Sweden	0	0	1	1	1	0	0	0	1	0	0	0	1		1
United Kingdom	—	—	—	—	—	—	—	—	—	—	—	—	—	—	—

Source: Huizinga and Nicodème (2004, Table 6).
Note: 0 = Country does not provide information; 1= country provides information; — = data not available.

The Savings Tax Directive

By 1997 there was concern in the EU that cross-border interest payments to individuals largely escaped taxation. Nonresident interest withholding taxes had been reduced or eliminated in previous decades, and enforcement of interest income taxation in the country of residence was difficult in practice. For 1999, Table 12.7 additionally shows that there was only a patchy network of (automatic) information exchange on nonresident interest payments among EU member states. Only Finland provided such information automatically to all other EU15 countries. (Finland provides information to all its tax treaty partners.) Three other EU15 countries—Denmark, Sweden, and France—provided information automatically to 5, 6, and 11 EU15 partners, respectively. The other 11 countries did not provide interest information to any other EU15 country in 1999. Luxembourg, for example, which harbors a large volume of external deposits (see Table 12.5), refrained from doing this entirely.

There are two means of ensuring an adequate level of taxation of cross-border interest: higher nonresident withholding taxes (on interest), or expanded, generalized information exchange. In the last two decades, there have been several proposals for interest taxation in the EU that have put different stresses on withholding taxes and information exchange as possible solutions. The thinking among policymakers has shifted from favoring withholding taxes to championing generalized information exchange as the best way forward.[4] An early proposal for an EU directive in 1989 (predating the 1997 tax package) called for a common minimum interest withholding tax of 15 percent.[5] In 1998, as part of the Tax Package, the European Commission proposed a system involving both withholding taxes and information exchange: countries would be free to choose a withholding tax with a minimum rate of 20 percent or to institute information exchange. In 2001 this coexistence model was abandoned in favor of generalized information exchange. After years of indecision, Ecofin finally reached agreement in 2003 on the implementation of a modified version of the 2001 proposal, taking effect on July 1, 2005.[6] All EU member states except Austria, Belgium,

---

[4] Information exchange may look better over time because of technological progress. Note, moreover, that information exchange enables countries to impose interest income taxation according to the residence principle. This benefits capital-exporting countries. Hence information exchange will favor the EU15 in an enlarged EU if the EU15 are net exporters of capital, through banks, to the new member states.

[5] The imposition of a minimum nonresident withholding tax can be mutually beneficial if it also prompts countries with withholding taxes above the minimum to raise their rates. See Huizinga and Nielsen (2000).

[6] Another agreement providing for countries to exchange information on direct and indirect tax matters is the Convention on Mutual Administrative Assistance in Tax Matters. The Convention, produced jointly by the Organisation for Economic Cooperation and Development and the Council of Europe, has been ratified by eight countries (Denmark, Finland, Iceland, the Netherlands, Norway, Poland, Sweden, and the United States). Additionally, the Nordic Convention on Mutual Administrative Assistance in Tax Matters allows the Nordic countries to exchange bank and other information for all kinds of taxes except import duties. The Nordic Convention calls for the automatic exchange of bank information.

and Luxembourg are to move to information exchange. These three countries are allowed to levy withholding taxes at a rate of 15 percent for the first three years (2005–2007), 20 percent for the next three years (2008–2010), and 35 percent from 2011 onward.[7] Interestingly, the three countries are to transfer 75 percent of the withholding tax revenues to the depositor-state treasury. This suggests that their adherence to withholding taxes stems less from the prospect of higher tax revenues than from their banks' guaranteed ability to withhold information on the identity of their international customers.

The preference for information exchange presents economists with the puzzle of trying to explain why it may be in a county's interest to willingly give valuable tax information to other countries. The literature presents several potential answers. Bacchetta and Espinosa (1995) argue that it may be in a country's interest to provide information about bank interest payments to nonresidents, since this enables the interest-receiving country to increase its own income tax rate. That, in turn, reduces the incentive for residents of the information-providing country to place their savings abroad. In a repeated game framework, Bacchetta and Espinosa (2000) further study the joint determination of taxes on international investment income and information exchange clauses in double taxation treaties. They find that information exchange may be part of a (sustainable) taxation treaty if there is a reciprocity requirement, if there is a high cost of negotiation, or if capital flows are one-way.

Also in a repeated game setting, Huizinga and Nielsen (2003) examine countries' exclusive choice between nonresident withholding taxes and information exchange (as provided for by the European Commission's draft directive of 1998). Two countries choosing the same regime (either withholding taxes or information exchange) and a mixed regime (one country choosing withholding taxes and the other choosing information exchange) are all possible equilibriums of the regime selection game.

---

[7] These three member states, however, will also implement information exchange once several third countries, including Switzerland and the United States, have agreed to exchange information with the EU. Switzerland so far has agreed only to withhold tax at the same rates as Austria, Belgium, and Luxembourg and to transfer 75 percent of the revenue to the affected EU member state.

Information exchange performs relatively well, and is more likely to be chosen in equilibrium, if governments apply a relatively low discount rate to future outcomes. In principle, countries can simultaneously levy withholding taxes and exchange information, as examined by Keen and Ligthart (2006). These authors find that the availability of both instruments can increase countries' capacity to raise revenues.

The Push for a Consolidated Corporate Tax Base Starting in 2001

In 2001, the European Commission (2001c) published a communication that set out its strategy for corporate income taxation following a major Commission study of the topic (European Commission, 2001a). Policy efforts were to be directed at reducing the tax-related obstacles and inefficiencies related to cross-border economic activity in the EU, rather than at increasing overall corporate tax revenues or changing the overall tax mix. To meet these objectives, the Commission presented a two-track strategy—a recent update of which is presented in European Commission (2003).

The first track consists of proposals to reduce the frictions of international corporate income taxation, given that member states currently maintain separate tax bases for corporate tax purposes. This track included proposals for revisions of both the Parent-Subsidiary and Merger Directives (adopted in 2003 and 2005, respectively). The Commission also stated its intention to improve the rules affecting cross-border loss offset within multinational firms. At the same time, the Commission contemplated ways of reducing the difficulties faced by businesses in the area of international transfer prices, and it studied means of streamlining the existing pattern of bilateral tax treaties in the EU.

The second track of the Commission's strategy paves the way for introducing a consolidated corporate tax base for the EU-wide activities of European companies. A consolidated tax base would be a radical solution for several hard-to-solve problems inherent in taxation based on separate accounting. These include an inadequate offset of losses associated with foreign activities and international profit-shifting.

While the two tracks address some of the same problems, their outcomes of course differ. A first major difference is that the introduction of a consolidated tax base requires that the corporate tax base be allocated to member states according to some allocation rule. A second major difference is that a common tax base presumably would yield substantial savings in compliance and enforcement costs, which are high under the current system of separate accounting. The main features of the Commission's two-track approach are described in detail below, followed by an assessment of the Commission's current drive to introduce a common consolidated tax base.

The First Track

The first track consists of several disparate proposals and initiatives that all aim to improve the functioning of the current system for the corporate taxation of international activities in the EU. Extending existing legislation, the Commission adopted proposals to enlarge the scope of the Parent-Subsidiary Directive and the Merger Directive. Specifically, the Parent-Subsidiary Directive, as revised in 2003, is to apply to a wider range of company types (including, for instance, the newly created "European Company"). It is also to gradually reduce the required minimum shareholding rate of the parent company from 25 to 10 percent. The revised Merger Directive (adopted in 2005) similarly widens the application of this directive.

As indicated by European Commission (2001a: 317–30), EU member states now offer only limited loss-offset to parent companies for losses suffered abroad. Countries that exempt foreign-source income from taxation, naturally, do not allow their multinationals to deduct foreign losses from their taxable income. Countries with worldwide taxation systems generally allow their multinationals to take account of losses suffered by foreign branches but, unfortunately, not losses suffered by foreign subsidiaries. Exceptions are Denmark and France, which generally also allow loss-offset for losses suffered by foreign subsidiaries. In contrast, immediate loss-offset is generally available to holding companies for losses suffered by domestic subsidiaries. Hence an incomplete loss-offset for foreign losses means that cross-border activities are tax-disadvantaged, thus forming a barrier to the single market. The discriminatory nature of current loss-offset treatment in the EU is being challenged in the ECJ, and EU case law in this area is developing. Early on, the Commission attempted to take a legislative approach to solving the problem of inadequate cross-border loss-offset. An early proposal for an EU directive to this effect, however, had to be withdrawn in 1991. Now, the Commission is counseling member states on their obligations in this area in the light of developments in EU case law.[8]

A third main plank of the first-track approach is the creation of an EU Joint Forum on Transfer Pricing, which is a working group consisting of high-level tax experts and representatives of the business community. The Forum seeks to provide pragmatic, nonlegislative recommendations on transfer pricing issues in the EU. For instance, it has addressed problems in the application of the arbitration convention relating to disputes on transfer prices between tax authorities. In addition, it has discussed documentation requirements regarding transfer prices for businesses, as well as possible ways of avoiding double taxation in the area of transfer pricing—for instance, through advance pricing agreements between firms and tax authorities.

A final first-track goal is to eliminate the inefficiencies arising from the existing set of bilateral and multilateral tax treaties in the EU. In addition to helping member states to interpret the implications of ECJ case law in this area, the Commission is studying the options of developing an EU model tax treaty or, alternatively, concluding a multilateral tax treaty among all EU member states. This would do away with the erratic pattern of double taxation relief currently evident in the EU (see Table 12.4). Specifically, an EU tax treaty would presumably mainstream either the exemption method or the foreign tax credit method as the way to alleviate the double taxation of foreign-source income in the EU. According to the European Commission (2001a), however, such harmonization would do little to reduce the dispersion of effective tax rates in the EU.

---

[8] Also in other areas, new case law on taxation provided by the European Court of Justice tends to have ramifications for all EU member states, not only for those that were party to the case.

The Second Track

The second track of the Commission's strategy aims for the introduction of a consolidated corporate income tax base for multinational firms in the EU. As is presently the case in the United States and Canada, a common tax base has to be allocated to individual member states according to some apportionment formula. In this regard, the European Commission (2001c) does not go beyond listing a range of options. At present, it does not envision a harmonization of tax rates to accompany the consolidated tax base.

A common tax base, clearly, presents a radical, once-and-for-all solution to some of the problems addressed by first-track measures. Specifically, the potential for EU firms to engage in international profit shifting would be eliminated, since there would no longer be separate national tax bases. For the calculation of the consolidated tax base, similarly, it would no longer be an issue whether losses within the overall group were incurred domestically or abroad. Further, the potential for double taxation of cross-border activities at the company level would be obviated, since the common tax base would apply equally to income from separate national sources. Not least, a common tax base presumably would establish significant gains in terms of lower compliance and enforcement costs on the part of firms and tax authorities alike.

In practice, there are several ways to bring about taxation by way of a consolidated tax base for firms with cross-border activities. A first issue is whether firms with parent companies in different countries would have to apply the same consolidated tax base. A second and related question is whether the consolidated tax base for multinational firms would coexist with different national tax base definitions for purely domestic firms. If so, a third question is whether internationally active firms could choose between two possibly coexisting tax base definitions. A fourth matter is whether taxation by way of the consolidated tax base would be administered by national tax authorities or at a central EU level. The European Commission (2001c) distinguishes among four ways of implementing a consolidated tax base for internationally active firms that differ in some way along these four dimensions (see also Hellerstein and McClure, 2004; Sørensen, 2004; Mintz, 2004). The four options are:

- Home-state taxation. EU multinationals can apply the tax base definition of their home state to their EU-wide activities. The application of this consolidated tax base definition is optional. Taxation is administered by national tax authorities.
- Common consolidated tax base. A new, single, common corporate tax base is made available for all EU multinationals. Application of this tax base is optional. Administration is by national tax authorities.
- Compulsory harmonized corporate tax base. A single corporate tax base for all EU firms. Administration is by national tax authorities.
- European Union company tax. This is a single corporate tax base for large EU multinationals. Other firms continue to use their national tax bases. The EU company tax could be administered at the EU level, with some of the revenue going to the EU budget.

Home-state taxation and a common consolidated tax base would allow international firms to choose between two or more tax base definitions, which presumably would involve high transaction costs and require rules for limiting frequent changes among tax base definitions. Notably, only the compulsory harmonized corporate tax base involves the application of a single tax base definition to all EU firms. Home-state taxation has the advantage that it does not require new tax base definitions and international agreement on them. It is based on the principles of mutual recognition and home-state control that are commonly applied in other areas of cross-border activity in the EU, such as the regulation and supervision of international banking activities. It is not clear, however, that this parallelism will make it easier for EU member states to reach a political agreement on home-state taxation than on any of the other proposals.

To implement a consolidated tax base, several technical issues must be resolved. These include answers to the following questions (see also Mintz, 2004: 228):

■ What types of income should be included in the common tax base? Should this include income solely from business activities or also passive income from financial investments?

■ How should a business group be defined for the purposes of the consolidated tax base? Firms could be included in a business group on the basis of ownership and control or, alternatively, on the basis of the perceived integration of actual business activities.

■ What apportionment formula should be used to assign the common base to individual member states? There are several options. Using firm-level data, a formula can be based on sales, payroll, or capital in the various countries where the multinational operates (as is the case among U.S. states). Alternatively, firm-level data on value added could be used (on either an origin or a destination basis—that is, on the basis of where goods and services are produced or purchased). A formula based on macro-level value added is also an option (see, for instance, Hellerstein and McLure, 2004).

■ How should income generated outside the EU be dealt with? Worldwide apportionment according to some EU formula is likely to face opposition from third countries. Hence the separate bookkeeping approach will probably prevail, to divide income to the EU as a group from that to third countries individually. The EU as a whole would have either to exempt non-EU income from EU taxation or, alternatively, to tax this income while providing a foreign tax credit for non-EU taxes.

Since the publication of the Commission's report on the need for a consolidated tax base (European Commission, 2001c), no corresponding directive has been proposed. To gain further insights, the Commission has suggested to member states that a pilot study be conducted on home-state taxation for small and medium-sized enterprises (SMEs). The European Commission (2003) provides several arguments for limiting such a pilot study to SMEs. Small enterprises would stand to gain much from a common international tax base, since they face relatively high compliance costs in dealing with multiple tax base definitions. At the same time, relatively few SMEs have international operations. This suggests that with a case study of this kind, tax authorities would have limited risks (in terms of lost tax revenues).

In preparation of an eventual directive, the Commission is considering what might be an appropriate common tax base definition for the EU. Important in this regard is the introduction of international financial reporting standards (IFRS) for exchange-traded firms as of January 1, 2005. These firms now have to provide consolidated accounting statements according to IFRS rules. Hence a natural question is whether and how consolidated accounting statements according to IFRS could serve as a starting point for defining a common tax base. IFRS rely heavily on market valuation, which is traditionally not the case—and is not intended to be the case—with tax accounting, and this difference poses some problems. In addition, IFRS accounting statements need only reflect (changes in) data that are considered of material importance. As a result, IFRS accounting statements may provide less information than is necessary for taxation purposes.

A Consolidated Tax Base versus Harmonization of Tax Rates

At present, the Commission aims only for a common tax base definition for internationally active EU firms, not for tax rate harmonization. It has even described tax rate competition as potentially beneficial (European Commission, 2001c). The drive for a common tax base without tax rate harmonization, however, may do little to reduce the present dispersion of effective tax rates in the EU. The European Commission (2001a) finds that the harmonization of capital depreciation allowances in the EU—an important aspect of the tax base—would have little effect on this dispersion. The introduction of home-state taxation would even increase the dispersion of effective tax rates. On the other hand, harmonization of the statutory tax rate results in a significant reduction in effective tax rate variation in the EU. Therefore, it may seem surprising that the Commission currently favors the introduction of a consolidated tax base without tax rate harmonization. However, this choice is no doubt influenced by political reality: a proposed directive aiming for tax rate harmonization in the EU would in all likelihood fail to be adopted.

Harmonization of tax base definitions or tax rates, of course, makes sense only if it brings significant welfare gains. On this issue, Sørensen (2004) provides some evidence based on a simulation model. In the simulations, he considers the harmonization of the tax rate and depreciation rules to the EU average. Clearly enough, such an equalization brings higher corporate tax revenues in some countries and lower revenues in others. Sørensen considers, alternatively, that either public transfers or labor taxes are adjusted to maintain government budget balance. In these scenarios, the average change in GDP in the EU is found to be 0.22 percent or 0.32 percent, respectively. The changes in consumer welfare are even smaller—0.12 percent and 0.18 percent, respectively. These welfare changes are so small that it is questionable that by themselves they can sway the argument in favor of tax rate harmonization. In this regard, it should be noted that calculations of this kind do not take account of the potential gains from lower compliance and enforcement costs. Mintz (2004) argues that these gains are the main benefit of introducing a common tax base definition in the EU. Harmonization of the tax rate would arguably entail a significant simplification of the EU corporate tax system as well, which could also yield non-negligible reductions in compliance and enforcement costs.

The introduction of a common tax base could well affect corporate tax rates in the EU, even without explicit efforts to harmonize them. In fact, the introduction of a common tax base could lead to downward pressure on tax rates. Note, first, that the introduction of a common tax base will not eliminate the potential for tax rate competition in the EU. According to Gordon and Wilson (1986), the introduction of a common tax base could intensify tax rate competition, resulting in lower tax rates. To understand why, note that under separate accounting, a lower tax on profits increases investment and thus reduces the pre-tax rate of return to capital. The concomitant decrease in taxable profits forms a disincentive to lower the tax rate. Under a common tax base, a lower national tax rate similarly may increase national investment, which again leads to lower pre-tax profits. These lower profits, however, are now shared among several countries. As a result, the taxable profits assigned to the country that raises its tax rate are affected relatively little. With a common tax base, therefore, there is a relative incentive to lower the tax rate. Hence tax competition with a common tax base may well result in relatively low tax rates—and low levels of public goods.

As a related matter, the introduction of a common tax base increases international transparency about effective levels of taxation in different countries. Thus small tax rate differences—with a common tax base— could lead to relatively large reallocations of international activity. If so, the introduction of a common tax base could similarly lead to more intense tax rate competition, again resulting in lower tax rates and lower levels of public goods. In this scenario, it is possible that the introduction of a common tax base might lead to a "race to the bottom" in corporate tax rates. That, in turn, could prompt calls for a minimum corporate income tax or tax rate harmonization at a reasonable level. An outcome of this kind, while possible, is of course highly uncertain. In any case, it is unlikely to be a main motivation for the Commission's current drive for a common tax base in the EU.

Applicability to Latin America of the EU Approach to Capital Income Taxation

On average, countries in Latin America reveal a lower "tax effort" (share of tax revenues in GDP) than the EU. Another important difference is that Latin American tax authorities rely relatively heavily on indirect taxes, as evidenced by a simple comparison of some key tax burden figures in Table 12.8.

Panel A of the table shows that total tax revenues as a share of GDP were 17 percent in Latin America in 1999/2000, and 38 percent in the EU. At the same time, direct taxes in Latin America amounted to 22 percent of total tax revenues, compared with 38 percent in the EU. Indirect taxes instead were 61 percent of tax revenues in Latin America, while they were 31 percent of tax revenues in the EU. Social security contributions, finally, were 18 percent of the total in Latin America and 32 percent in the EU.

Table 12.8. Tax Burdens in Latin America and the EU

A. Tax revenues, 1999 or 2000

	Latin America		EU15	
	Percentage of GDP	Percentage of total tax revenues	Percentage of GDP	Percentage of total tax revenues
Direct taxes	4	22	15	38
Indirect taxes	10	61	12	31
Social security contributions	3	18	12	32
Total	17	100	38	100

B. Effective tax rates (percent), 1999 or 2000

	Latin America	EU
Capital income	6	24
Labor	11	42
Consumption	12	21

Source: Martner and Tromben (2003, Figures 1 and 8).

In Panel B, a similar picture emerges from a comparison of implicit tax rates in Latin America and the EU. The effective rate of taxation of capital income was relatively low in Latin America, at 6 percent, as against 24 percent in the EU. Countries in Latin America taxed labor income somewhat higher, at 11 percent, while the rate in the EU was 42 percent. The average tax on consumption, finally, was 12 percent in Latin America, compared with 21 percent in the EU.

There are several reasons for the historically low reliance on direct taxation, and especially capital income taxation, in Latin America relative to the EU:[9]

▪ Historically, substantial barriers to international trade in Latin America have provided authorities with significant tariff revenues, thereby lessening the need to levy income taxes.

---

[9] On this subject, see also Tanzi (2000: 24–28) and Lledo, Schneider, and Moore (2004: 32).

- Latin America is less developed than the EU. A large share of agriculture in total output, a sizeable informal sector, and the relatively limited technical capacity of tax administrations have reduced the reliance on direct taxation, and in particular on capital income taxes.

- Latin America has a history of macroeconomic instability (with high inflation) and financial sector instability (with banking crises). These circumstances have encouraged capital flight and hence reduced the tax base for capital income taxation.

- Some countries in Latin America have significantly unequal distributions of income and wealth. Unlike European countries, however, countries in Latin America have made limited use of capital income taxes to redistribute income and wealth.

- Latin American countries originated as colonies that were meant to provide resources to their colonial rulers. More recently, several Latin American countries were under authoritarian governments. These features of Latin America's political history have reduced the perceived legitimacy of government, thereby harming the tax authorities' ability to raise revenues through direct taxation.

Some of these explanations of historically low capital income taxation in Latin America are now losing their relevance. First, increasing trade integration in the region has greatly reduced tariff revenues (IDB, 2004). Higher VAT revenues, but also higher direct tax revenues, now have to make up for the lower tariff revenues. Second, because of economic growth and the development of tax administrations in Latin America, the relative costs of raising tax revenues by way of direct taxation have fallen. Third, capital flight will decline because of improved macroeconomic and financial stability in recent years, leading to a larger capital income tax base in the region. Fourth, the spread of democracy in Latin America gives governments the political legitimacy to levy higher direct taxes. All of these developments suggest that desired capital income taxes in Latin America are likely to increase in the future.

The will to levy higher capital income taxes may be present but, as in the EU, the ability to do so is eroded by ongoing financial market integration and the internationalization of business. This suggests that in Latin America, as in the EU, there is a rationale for international cooperation on capital income taxation. In the European Community, trade integration was completed in the 1960s, while the first European directives on capital income taxation were adopted only in 1990 (as noted earlier). Since the 1960s, however, financial and capital market links between countries have become much stronger everywhere. Latin America, therefore, may proceed more quickly from trade integration to some form of international coordination on capital income tax policy than did the EU.

One of the main differences between Latin America and the EU, of course, is that the EU has its treaties and supranational institutions, particularly the European Commission and the ECJ. The Commission can prepare and propose common policies, and, once these are adopted, the Commission can enforce them by undertaking infringement procedures against member states that do not implement them. Meanwhile, the ECJ is evolving into an important force to root out those parts of corporate income taxation that are deemed discriminatory. Latin America lacks supranational institutions of this kind, which makes agreement on and enforcement of capital income tax coordination more challenging.

As in the EU, the gains from prospective tax policy cooperation in Latin America have to be balanced against the costs. The gains would be the savings reaped by addressing the shortcomings outlined earlier under "Inefficiencies of International Capital Income Taxation." To inspire proposals for tax coordination in Latin America, of course, it would be useful to have estimates of the costs, based ideally on pertinent economic studies. An important cost of tax policy coordination (but one that is hard to quantify) is reduced national discretion in setting tax policy objectives. As in the EU, tax policy coordination among all or some Latin American countries will have to be based on consensus. In the EU, this requirement has made it difficult, but not entirely impossible, to make progress on tax coordination. It remains to be seen whether, in due course, Latin America will follow the EU example.

Conclusion

Increasing financial market integration and the internationalization of business activities magnify the costs of a lack of cooperation on capital income taxation. In particular, a single market for capital without tax barriers may fail to materialize without international cooperation. In addition, tax competition may limit governments' ability to raise sufficient tax revenues by way of capital income and other taxation. There are similarities as well as differences between Europe and Latin America. Both regions consist of many economies that are mostly small, open, and highly integrated with each other and with the rest of the world. A key difference is that Latin America has a lower level of economic development, and tax authorities rely relatively little on raising revenues through direct taxation, especially capital income taxation. Over time, however, continuing economic development may increase the desire to raise additional tax revenues through capital income taxation in Latin America, while closer economic integration will make this increasingly difficult. This suggests that in Latin America, as in the EU, there is a rationale for the coordination of capital income tax policies. If so, the EU offers an interesting example of how such coordination could proceed.

References

Bacchetta, Philippe, and Maria Paz Espinosa. 1995. "Information Sharing and Tax Competition among Governments." *Journal of International Economics* 39(1–2):103–21.

———. 2000. "Exchange-of-Information Clauses in International Tax Treaties." *International Tax and Public Finance* 7(3):275–93.

Cnossen, Sijbren. 2001. "Tax Policy in the European Union: A Review of Issues and Options." *FinanzArchiv* 58(4):466–558.

de Mooij, Ruud A., and Sjef Ederveen. 2003. "Taxation and Foreign Direct Investment: A Synthesis of Empirical Research." *International Tax and Public Finance* 10(6):673–93.

Devereux, Michael P. 2004. "Debating Proposed Reforms of the Taxation of Corporate Income in the European Union." *International Tax and Public Finance* 11(1):71–89.

Devereux, Michael P., and Rachel Griffith. 1998. "Taxes and the Location of Production: Evidence from a Panel of U.S. Multinationals." *Journal of Public Economics* 68(3–4):335–67.

European Commission. 1996. "Taxation in the European Union." Discussion paper for informal meeting of Ecofin ministers, SEC(96) 487. Brussels: European Commission.

———. 1997. "Towards Tax Co-ordination in the European Union: A Package to Tackle Harmful Tax Competition." COM(97) 495. Brussels: European Commission.

———. 2001a. "Company Taxation in the Internal Market." Commission Staff Working Paper, SEC(2001) 1681. Brussels: European Commission.

———. 2001b. "Financial Market Integration in the EU." In *The EU Economy: 2001 Review.* Brussels: European Commission.

———. 2001c. "Towards an Internal Market without Tax Obstacles: A Strategy for Providing Companies with a Consolidated Corporate Tax Base for Their EU-Wide Activities." COM(2001) 582. Brussels: European Commission.

———. 2003. "An Internal Market without Company Tax Obstacles: Achievements, Ongoing Initiatives and Remaining Challenges," COM(2003) 726. Brussels: European Commission.

———. 2004a. "European Tax Survey." Taxation Paper 3. Brussels: European Commission, Directorate-General Taxation and Customs Union.

———. 2004b. "Structures of the Taxation Systems in the European Union." Brussels: European Commission, Directorate-General Taxation and Customs Union.

Gordon, Roger H., and James R. Hines, Jr. 2002. "International Taxation." NBER Working Paper 8854. Cambridge, MA: National Bureau of Economic Research.

Gordon, Roger, and John D. Wilson. 1986. "An Examination of Multi-jurisdictional Corporate Income Taxation under Formula Apportionment." *Econometrica* 54(6):1357–73.

Gorter, Joeri, and Ruud de Mooij. 2001. *Capital Income Taxation in Europe: Trends and Trade-Offs.* The Hague: Netherlands Bureau for Economic Policy Analysis.

Gresik, Thomas A. 2001. "The Taxing Task of Taxing Multinationals." *Journal of Economic Literature* 39(3):800–38.

Hellerstein, Walter, and Charles E. McLure, Jr. 2004. "The European Commission's Report on Company Income Taxation: What Can the EU Learn from the Experience of the U.S. States?" *International Tax and Public Finance* 11(2):199–220.

Hines, James, Jr., 1996. "Altered States: Taxes and the Location of Foreign Direct Investment in America." *American Economic Review* 86(5):1076–94.

———. 1999. "Lessons from Behavior Responses to International Taxation." *National Tax Journal* 52(2):305–22.

Huizinga, Harry. 2004. "The Taxation of Banking in an Integrating Europe." *International Tax and Public Finance* 11(3):551–86.

Huizinga, Harry, and Luc Laeven. 2005. "International Profit Shifting within European Multinationals." Unpublished. Tilburg University, Tilburg, Netherlands.

Huizinga, Harry, and Gaëtan Nicodème. 2004. "Are International Deposits Tax-Driven?" *Journal of Public Economics* 88(6):1093–1118.

———. 2006. "Foreign Ownership and Corporate Income Taxation: An Empirical Evaluation." *European Economic Review* 50(5):1223–44.

Huizinga, Harry, and Søren Bo Nielsen. 1997. "Capital Income and Profit Taxation with Foreign Ownership of Firms." *Journal of International Economics* 42(1–2):149–65.

———. 2000. "The Taxation of Interest in Europe: A Minimum Withholding Tax?" In *Taxing Capital Income in the European Union: Issues and Options for Reform*, ed. Sijbren Cnossen. Oxford: Oxford University Press.

———. 2002. "The Coordination of Capital Income and Profit Taxation with Cross-Ownership of Firms." *Regional Science and Urban Economics* 32(1):1–26.

———. 2003. "Withholding Taxes or Information Exchange: The Taxation of International Interest Flows." *Journal of Public Economics* 87(1):39–72.

———. 2005. "Must Losing Taxes on Saving Be Harmful?" Unpublished. Tilburg University, Tilburg, Netherlands.

IDB (Inter-American Development Bank). 2004. "Integration and Trade in the Americas: The Fiscal Impact of Trade Liberalization in the Americas." Periodic Note, Integration and Regional Programs Department and Institute for the Integration of Latin America and the Caribbean. Washington, DC: Inter-American Development Bank.

Janeba, Eckhard, and Wolfgang Peters. 1999. "Tax Evasion, Tax Competition and the Gains from Non-Discrimination: The Case of Interest Taxation in Europe." *Economic Journal* 109(452): 93–101.

Keen, Michael. 2002. "Preferential Regimes Can Make Tax Competition Less Harmful." *National Tax Journal* 54(4):757–62.

Keen, Michael, and Jenny E. Ligthart. 2006. "Incentives and Information Exchange in International Taxation." *International Tax and Public Finance* 13(2–3):163–80.

Lledo, Victor, Aaron Schneider, and Mick Moore. 2004. "Governance, Taxes and Tax Reform in Latin America." Unpublished. University of Sussex, Brighton, U.K.

Martner, Ricardo, and Variana Tromben. 2003. "Tax Reforms and Fiscal Stabilization in Latin America." Unpublished. United Nations, New York.

Mintz, Jack. 2004. "Corporate Tax Harmonization in Europe: It's All about Compliance." *International Tax and Public Finance* 11(2):221–34.

Newlon, Scott T. 2000. "Transfer Pricing and Income Shifting in Integrating Economies." In *Taxing Capital Income in the European Union: Issues and Options for Reform,* ed. Sijbren Cnossen. Oxford: Oxford University Press.

Sørensen, Peter B. 2004. "Company Tax Reform in the European Union." *International Tax and Public Finance* 11(1):91–115.

Tanzi, Vito, ed. 2000. "Taxation in Latin America in the Last Decade." Unpublished. International Development Bank, Washington, DC.

Wilson, John Douglas, and David E. Wildasin. 2004. "Capital Tax Competition: Bane or Boon?" *Journal of Public Economics* 88(6):1065–91.

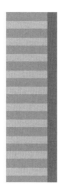

13

Globalization, Tax Systems, and the Architecture of the Global Economic System

Vito Tanzi

Introduction

Modern tax systems developed largely between 1930 and 1960, a period when major restrictions on trade were erected (at the time of the Great Depression and during the Second World War and its aftermath). In addition, capital movements were limited; there was little cross-country investment and, consequently, a limited role for multinational enterprises; there was little international mobility of people, except as emigrants; and individuals did almost no cross-country shopping. During these decades, most countries' tax burdens were relatively low because governments had not yet assumed many social and economic responsibilities that they would assume in later years, especially after 1960. The tax burdens were generally lower than 30 percent of the industrial countries' gross domestic product (GDP), and half that level in developing countries. In Brazil, for example, where the tax burden exceeded 36 percent of GDP in 2004, it was less than 16 percent of GDP before 1961.

Between 1930 and 1960, two important "technological" innovations that were introduced in the tax area came to have a great impact on the tax systems of most countries. These were (1) the introduction and affirmation of the concept of the "global and progressive" income tax; and (2) the introduction of the value-added tax (VAT). The first of these developments was especially significant in industrial countries. The second was significant in all countries. In later years, these two developments contributed a great deal to the rise in tax levels, which exceeded 40 percent of GDP in many countries of the Organisation for Economic Co-operation and Development (OECD). Of course, some incomes had been taxed for a long time in various countries. For example, wages, presumptive profits, or rents from properties (imputed or not) had been taxed separately with low and proportional rates. This was the "schedular approach" to income taxation that had been popular in some of the continental countries of Europe. A century ago, the Italian economist Antonio de Viti de Marco argued that for various reasons (facility of eva- sion for some forms of income, differential efforts required to earn the income, durability of income flows, different costs of earning incomes), the rates applied proportionally to the various income categories (the schedules) should be differentiated among them.

In a very influential book published about 70 years ago, Henry Si- mons (1938), a University of Chicago professor, made a strong case for taxing all sources of income of individuals *as a whole* (the global income) and for taxing this total with *progressive* rates. This approach, it was ar- gued, would better satisfy equity considerations. Coming during the Depression and soon after the New Deal (and just before the Second World War), this "global income tax" became very popular in the United States, where it helped finance the war. The concept was exported to other countries, and in the 1950s and 1960s, U.S. tax consultants were trying hard to promote this tax in developing countries.

The VAT originated in France and hence is a European invention. It replaced the turnover (cascade) taxes on transactions that had existed in many European countries, including the six members of the European Coal and Steel Community (ECSC). It was welcomed by the members of the ECSC because it allowed the zero-rating of exports and the imposition of imports without discord. The countries were thus free to impose the tax rate they liked or needed without interfering with trade flows. This feature made the VAT welcome in countries that formed part of a customs union. The VAT has proven itself to be a major revenue source for all countries.

In industrial countries, the two developments mentioned above had profound effects. In conjunction with taxes that were levied on labor income to finance pensions (social security contributions), they made it possible for many countries' tax systems to finance the large demands for public revenue that the growing functions of government, especially in the so-called welfare states, were creating.

The Growing Role of Globalization

In recent decades and especially since the 1980s, important developments have been changing the economic landscape that characterized earlier decades. These developments have potentially great implications for tax systems. The most important of them are as follows:

1. Economies have opened and international trade has skyrocketed. World trade has been growing at double the rate of world GDP, such that the world economy is now much more integrated than it was in the past.

2. The growth in trade has been accompanied by a phenomenal increase in cross-border capital movements. This increase has been promoted by the removal of obstacles to capital mobility imposed by policy, and by technological innovations (such as powerful computers and the Internet) that have made communications cheap and rapid. Hence there has been extraordinary growth in the amount of capital that now crosses borders each day to finance direct investment, feed portfolio investments, cover current account imbalances, and provide needed currency to travelers.

3. The importance of multinationals has grown enormously, both in the financing of direct investment and in promoting trade among parts of the same enterprise located in different countries. The time has long passed when most enterprises produced and sold their output in the country or region where they were located. Trade among related parts of the same enterprise located in different countries has become a large part of total world trade. This trade creates special problems for tax authorities.

4. These international activities, accompanied by higher per capita incomes, falling transport costs, and policy changes, have greatly

heightened the mobility of individuals as economic agents and as consumers. A large and growing number of individuals now earn all or part of their incomes outside the countries where they have their official residence. And a large and growing number spend part of their income outside the countries where they live.

The implications of these developments for countries' tax systems are not yet fully understood by policymakers or economists. Mounting evidence and much theory, however, suggest that the developments described above are creating significant difficulties for tax administrators in some countries and opportunities for those in others. Because of these developments, a country's potential tax base is no longer limited by that country's territory, but in some sense has extended to include parts of the rest of the world. A country can now attract and tax (1) foreign financial capital; (2) foreign real capital in the form of foreign direct investment (FDI); (3) foreign consumers; (4) foreign workers; and (5) foreign individuals with high incomes, including pensioners.

These circumstances are fueling "tax competition" among countries. Tax competition implies that, to some extent, a country's tax burden can be exported. A country, and especially a small country, may now be able to "raid" the tax bases of other countries in a way that was not possible in earlier times. Like the ocean and the atmosphere, the "world tax base" is becoming a kind of "commons," a shared resource that all countries can try to exploit to their advantage. At present there is no global institution that, like a government, can establish rules to regulate this competition. The process so far is very messy and clearly incomplete.

Tax competition is related in part to the importance of taxation for location. By lowering the burden of taxation on some sensitive activities, tax competition aims to make a particular location (say, Ireland or Lichtenstein) more attractive than other locations for those activities. The attractiveness of a location depends on several elements, such as (1) nominal or statutory tax rates; (2) tax burdens—that is, the ratio of taxes to GDP or to other specific tax bases (profits, sales, payroll, and so on); (3) tax practice (administrative and compliance costs); (4) the predictability of the tax system ("tax certainty") over time, to limit time consistency problems; (5) legal transparency—that is, clarity of the tax laws; (6) the use of tax revenue—that is, the services that the residents or the enterprises get from the government in exchange for the taxes paid; (7) fiscal deficits and public debt, because these may forecast tax increases in the future; and more generally, (8) the country's economic or investment climate.

All other things being equal, a low level of taxation can attract business activities and financial capital, or even consumers and pensioners, to a particular location by making it more attractive to them from a tax viewpoint. Rarely, however, are all other things equal. An unpredictable tax system or high compliance costs, for example, can neutralize a low tax level. A particular location's "tax climate" can influence the amount of investment in that location, the choice of investment, the financing for it, and the legal form that the enterprises will choose.

When people face high tax rates or an unfriendly tax climate in today's environment, they may (1) "vote with their feet" and move to a friendlier tax environment; (2) "vote with their portfolio" by sending their financial assets abroad to safer and lower-tax jurisdictions; (3) remain in the country but exploit tax avoidance opportunities; or (4) engage in, or increase, explicit tax evasion. Tax competition is making it easier to engage in all these options.

Tax competition is creating frictions and diplomatic problems between countries and groups of countries. It has been a hot topic in the European Union (EU); between some EU countries and Switzerland; between the EU and the United States; between China, Europe, and the United States; between the Caribbean countries and OECD countries; and so on. Clearly, it is slowly poisoning the diplomatic environment.

A question often raised is whether tax competition is ultimately a positive or negative global development. Should policymakers welcome it or not? Views diverge sharply on this question. Some economists (especially theoretical economists) and those with a public-choice bent tend to see tax competition as beneficial for several reasons. By contrast, ministers of finance, directors of taxation, and policy-oriented economists often tend to see it as a problem. Finance ministers in France, Germany, and Italy have sometimes been sharply critical of this phenomenon. The arguments in favor of tax competition are the following:

1. It forces countries to lower their high tax rates, especially on mobile tax bases such as financial capital, highly skilled workers, and so on. The very high rates levied on these incomes in previous decades would be impossible today. Theory has taught that lower tax rates imply lower welfare costs and thus contribute to more efficient economies.

2. By reducing total tax revenue, tax competition would force governments to reduce inefficient public spending. Several studies have shown that public spending is very inefficient in some countries. This "starve-the-beast" theory was favored by, and made popular during, the Reagan administration.

3. It allocates world savings toward areas where, it is claimed, the savings are used more productively. This claim was commonly made by representatives of the U.S. government in the first half of the 1980s and in recent years.

4. Because of lower tax revenue, tax competition may force policymakers to rethink the economic role of the state so as to make it more focused and efficient.

5. It leads to a tax structure that is more dependent on immobile tax bases. Economic theory considers the taxation of these bases less distortionary for the economy.

Naturally, these arguments in favor of tax competition are counterbalanced by arguments against it. The main arguments in this regard are as follows:

1. Because public spending may be politically or legally inflexible downwards, especially in the short run, tax competition can lead to increased fiscal deficits and high public debts.

2. When governments are forced to cut public spending because of revenue reduction due to tax competition, there is no assurance that they will cut the inefficient part of public spending. Inef-

ficient spending may be protected by strong political constituencies.

3. Tax competition may lead to tax "degradation" because the government may try to maintain public revenue by introducing bad taxes to replace lost revenues, or it may replace public spending with inefficient public regulations, recognizing that regulations can sometimes be substituted for spending.

4. The shift of the tax burden from mobile factors (such as financial assets and highly skilled individuals) to immobile factors (largely labor income) will make the tax system less fair and may increase pressures for redistributive public spending.

5. The increased taxes on labor income obtained from employment in the official economy are likely to stimulate the growth of the underground economy and, consequently, the growth of tax evasion and different kinds of distortions.

6. Tax competition (and reactions to it) could make tax administration and tax compliance more difficult. It could also reduce the predictability of specific countries' tax systems, thus negatively affecting the investment climate.

In a quantitative sense, it is still difficult to identify fully the impact of globalization on tax revenue because that impact is, so far, neither strong nor obvious in total tax revenue terms. Closer observation, however, reveals effects that point to potential future difficulties:

1. In OECD countries, where the ratio of tax revenue to GDP grew at a significant pace in earlier decades, that ratio has stopped growing recently, even though large fiscal deficits called for higher revenue. Furthermore, in an increasing number of OECD countries, the average tax ratio has started to fall.

2. The rates of both personal income taxes and corporate income taxes have been reduced substantially in most countries, in part because of tax competition.

3. The rates of excise taxes on luxury products have been sharply reduced in most countries, leading to substantial falls in revenue

from these taxes. These reductions are partly the consequence of increased foreign travel by taxpayers and the possibilities that such travel offers for shopping in places where excise taxes on expensive items are lowest.

4. The global income tax, which had been very popular among tax experts and considered the fairest of all taxes for many years in the 1950s and 1960s, has been losing popularity. A progressive return to a schedular tax system is evident, one that distinguishes between taxes on labor (a nonmobile factor) and taxes on capital (a mobile factor). The dual income taxes introduced by the Scandinavian countries and some others are an example of the waning attractiveness of global income taxes.

5. There is a growing interest in flat-rate taxes. Several countries (Estonia, Latvia, Russia, Ukraine, and others) have introduced such a tax, while others (Belarus, El Salvador, Georgia, Guatemala, the Kyrgyz Republic, Paraguay, and Poland) have been considering introducing it. In the United States, there is also increasing talk of replacing income taxes with consumption taxes.

The Rise of Fiscal Termites

"Fiscal termites" arise from the interplay of globalization, tax competition, and new technologies. Like biological termites that damage physical structures, fiscal termites are weakening the foundations of current tax systems. They are making it ever more difficult for countries to maintain high levels of taxation. Evidence of them is apparent almost daily. There follows a brief outline of some of them. For more detail on this issue, see Tanzi (2001).

The first of these termites is *electronic commerce*, which has been growing fast both within and among countries. It has been growing for consumer goods and services, as well as for trade in inputs of intermediate and capital goods. Its growth has been accompanied and facilitated by the growing shift, in the countries' GDP, from physical to digital products. This kind of commerce leaves fewer traces than the previous invoice-based commerce and is much more difficult to tax. The growth of electronic commerce is creating enormous difficulties for tax administrators and legislators, who seem to be at a loss as to how to deal with it.

A second termite is *electronic money* (credit cards, ATM cards, and others). Progressively, real money is being replaced by electronic money exchanged through electronic cards. A "purse" software may be purchased especially through deposits in foreign banks or even from secret bank accounts. This makes it difficult to trace and tax various transactions.

A third important termite originates in transactions that take place between different parts of the same multinational enterprises: *intracompany transactions*. Since these transactions are internal to a company, they require the use of transfer prices—that is, the prices at which one part of the enterprise located in a given country "buys" products or services from another part of the same company located in another country. Obviously, the tax systems and tax rates can differ in the various countries where a multinational company operates. Furthermore, the products or services bought may not be traded in the open market, so they may not have a market or "arm's length" price that can be used as a reference. These are almost like transactions between members of the same family. Some items may have just family value and family prices. Problems arise especially with (1) inputs that are made specifically for a final product (say, a particular jet aircraft), since there may not be an arm's length price established by the market for these products; (2) use of copyrights, trademarks, and patents for which a value must be assessed; (3) the allocation of headquarters research and development costs; and (4) interest on loans made from one part of a multinational corporation to another part, for which determining a market rate is difficult. The determination of these costs or the prices of the goods and services traded within the enterprises is often difficult and arbitrary. It lends itself to manipulation by enterprises seeking to show higher profits in those countries where taxes on enterprise profits are low (such as Ireland), and less profit in countries where the taxes on enterprises are high (such as Germany and Italy). The strategic use of transfer prices by multinational enterprises can significantly reduce the total taxes they pay.

Another termite is the existence and rapid growth of *offshore financial centers and tax havens*. Various studies have estimated the total deposits in these tax havens at levels that may approach the annual GDP of the United States. The distinguishing characteristics of the tax havens are (1) low tax rates to attract foreign financial capital; (2) rules that make it difficult or impossible to identify the owners of the deposits in these countries (no-name accounts, banking secrecy, and so forth); and (3) lack of regulatory powers and information on those deposits on the part of the countries where the real owners of the deposits reside. These tax havens allow individuals and enterprises from the countries where the capital originates to receive income in ways that make it difficult for national authorities to tax them.

Another termite consists of new, *exotic and complex financial instruments* that continually enter the financial market. It has been a long time since ordinary citizens could understand and easily choose from among the financial instruments in which they could invest savings. New financial instruments, such as various categories of derivatives, are far more complex. Many of these are specifically designed to avoid (if not evade) paying taxes. Consequently, it is ever more difficult for the employees of tax administrations, who have basic training and modest salaries, to keep up with these developments. Imagine how difficult it must have been for the tax authorities to determine the income of Parmalat and Enron.

Increasing foreign activity by individuals, both as workers and as consumers, is also creating difficulties for national tax administrations. Incomes earned abroad are often not reported to the national or home-country tax authorities. Foreign travel allows individuals to buy expensive items (jewelry, cameras, and so on) in countries where excise taxes are lower. Competition for mobile consumers has encouraged some countries, and especially small countries, to lower these excise taxes in order to attract foreign consumers. Airports have become huge shopping centers. The consequence of these trends, once again, is the greater difficulty faced by many countries in raising the high tax revenue they collected in the past.

In addition to these termites, other developments merit inclusion on the above list. Furthermore, it is possible that some of the termites may combine or mutate to create even greater difficulties. Over the years, these developments will have ever greater impact on tax revenue, tax structures, and the use of particular tax bases. The net result will be a world with lower tax revenue and different tax systems. It would be wise for the governments of many countries to anticipate these developments and take the necessary actions to offset their effects.

The Need for a New Global Architecture for Tax Systems

The previous discussion calls attention to the widening gap between the tax systems that some countries' policymakers might wish to have and those that global forces are forcing them to adopt. For a growing number of countries, the latter are now, or soon will be, less capable of generating the same level of tax revenue as in the past. These countries will be forced to scale down the economic role of the state, at least inasmuch as that role is manifest through public spending. Many observers feel that this reduction in public spending is desirable, but not all policymakers would agree. This is happening at a time when global social needs are becoming more urgent and visible in the areas of poverty, pandemics, multicountry catastrophes, major disasters in poor countries, genocide and civil wars, the need to eliminate atomic material that could be acquired by terrorists, environmental disasters, and so forth. The costs of dealing with these global needs are now covered through the generosity of individual governments. But these governments inevitably pursue their own political interests, which may not match those of the world. And the resources made available seem to fall far short of the needs. The net result is that some of these global social needs are not met or are met only partially.

A striking aspect of these situations, and one that goes directly to the core of the architecture of global economic and social arrangements, is that at present there is no international institution charged with monitoring world fiscal developments to prevent tax "degradation" and contain the more damaging aspects of tax competition. No global organization has the power to levy taxes, even if limited to activities that generate global negative externalities, so as to help finance global public goods and lessen the creation of negative externalities.

About two decades ago, and then again a decade ago, this author suggested that there was a need for the creation of an International Revenue Service, or perhaps a Global Tax Organization (GTO), that could help close this important gap in the existing global economic architecture (see Tanzi, 1988, 1999). If there were a world government, there would be no need for such an institution because that government would deal with the problem. But a world government may never materialize, while global social needs are becoming more evident every day. In the absence of a world government, the international community has created various institutions that are entrusted with playing some of the roles that a global government would fulfill if it existed.

The role that could be assigned to a GTO could be modest or ambitious. The more ambitious that role, the more difficult it would be to secure the agreement of, in particular, the largest countries. A modest but still important role would be to provide a forum for debating national tax actions that have significant cross-country implications. Hence a modest role for a GTO would be to follow fiscal developments around the world, identify trends, collect statistics, and provide a global forum for discussion of these developments. In this scenario, the GTO would have no power to levy taxes or impose sanctions on countries. Its role would be strictly one of surveillance over national tax systems so as to assess their international implications and perhaps to exercise some moral suasion to discourage countries from using taxes that could damage other countries. Strange as it may seem, at present no international organization performs this function. A more ambitious role for the GTO, of course, would involve tax collection. The revenue would be earmarked for the provision of global public goods or the reduction of global "public bads." The possibilities are many, but the most justifiable would be the imposition of taxes on activities that have clear and negative cross-country externalities.

Many years ago, James Tobin (1978) proposed a tax on exchanges between the currencies of different countries. Over the years, this so-called Tobin tax has attracted a lot of attention, support, and criticism. A very small tax levied on the growing and enormous tax base created by foreign exchange transactions would generate a high level of revenue. One problem with this tax (and there are several problems) is that many economists do not see it as a tax on a negative externality. They do not accept the view that cross-currency transactions are necessarily speculative and thus involve negative externalities.

An alternative that has been attracting some political backing is a tax on airplane tickets. The tax, promoted by the so-called Quintet against Hunger (Brazil, Chile, France, Germany, and Spain) would tax these tickets and use the proceeds to fight global hunger. There is no question that airplanes generate negative externalities (air pollution), but the link between the tax cost of the ticket paid by passengers and the amount of pollution that their travel creates is very indirect at best. Thus it is easy to criticize this tax. Another alternative could be a tax on energy use, on the grounds that most energy use generates some negative externalities. There are other options as well, all with some justification and all with some shortcomings. It is clear that any of the possible alternatives will meet opposition from some countries. If the opposing countries are powerful, they will be able to prevent the introduction of the tax. The United States is likely to continue to have a de facto veto power on these issues.

Concluding Remarks

This chapter has discussed the relationship between various global trends and national tax systems. It has argued that the existing tax systems were created in a period when the world was very different. Thus modern tax systems have started to reflect the effects of these global trends.

At the same time, many public goods and "public bads" have crossed national borders and become global. Hence, while governments will face growing difficulties in financing their current national public needs, there seems to be no mechanism for guaranteeing that global public needs will receive the financing and attention they deserve. It is clear that the current architecture of the international economic system is deficient on two grounds: it provides no monitoring or coordinated reform of tax systems that may negatively affect other countries; and it provides no mechanism to finance international public goods.

An option would be to create a new international organization with specific responsibility for tax developments. This responsibility might be limited to the surveillance of tax reforms with international implications; or it could extend to the collection of particular taxes, with the revenue being earmarked for the financing of particular public goods.

References

Simons, Henry C. 1938. *Personal Income Taxation: The Definition of Income as a Problem of Fiscal Policy.* Chicago: University of Chicago Press.

Tanzi, Vito. 1988. "Forces That Shape Tax Policy." In *Tax Policy in the Twenty-First Century,* ed. Herbert Stein. New York: Wiley.

———. 1999. "Does the World Need a World Tax Organization?" In *The Economics of Globalization: Policy Perspectives from Public Economics,* ed. Assaf Razin and Efraim Sadka. Cambridge: Cambridge University Press.

———. 2001. "La globalización y la acción de las termitas fiscales." *Finanzas y Desarrollo* 38(marzo):34–37.

Tobin, James. 1978. "A Proposal for International Monetary Reform." *Eastern Economic Journal* 4(3–4):153–59.

Index

A

administrative cooperation, 83, 88

advance pricing agreements (APAs), 110, 273, 278, 280–282, 285

Africa, 71

aging of population, 178, 337–340, 342–343, 346

air ticket taxes, 413

alcoholic beverages, 91

Alliance for Progress, 63

Andean Community (CAN): common external tariffs, 92–93; crises in, 124; double taxation, 95–98, 105*n27*, 106*n30*; exchange of tax information, 10; integration and tax harmonization, 5; intra-Andean FDI, 97–98; Labor Migration Instrument, 335; membership of, 334; Social Security Instrument, 11, 335; tax competition, 213; tax structure, 26; tax treaties, 238–241, 251, 298–300; trade liberalization's effect on tax revenue, 149; VAT harmonization, 40, 97, 100–103;

VAT statistics, 102*tab*

Andean Community Court of Justice, 96

Argentina: abandonment of regional policies by, 119; aging of population in, 337*n5*; business assets tax, 233; double taxation agreements, 110*n35*, 116; economic crisis (late 1990s), 135–136; fiscal decentralization experiences, 135–136, 146, 150; free zones, 237; gross exports tax, 233; information exchange treaties, 111, 300, 305; minimum not-profit-related business taxes, 203; social security income, 27; state and local business taxes, 233; state tax as percentage of GDP in, 27; state tax exemptions, 18; tax incentives, 186, 196–197; tax shares by level of government, 136*tab*; tax treaties, 231–232, 239–241, 261; transfer pricing, 274, 277–279, 283, 286; U.S. treaties with, 182

arm's length principle in transfer pricing, 266–267, 272–273, 278

Aruba, 282

Asian miracle, 197

assets-based taxes, 203, 233

assurance games, 187

ATM cards, 409

Audit Manual (CIAT), 112

audits, 259, 285–289, 310–311

Australia, 241*n11*

Austria: bank secrecy regulations, 91; double taxation, 366; exchange of information, 381,

U

unemployment benefits, 326
United Kingdom: arm's length
principle in transfer pricing,
266; double taxation, 366; tax
treaties, 240*n10*, 241*n11*
United Nations (UN): double
taxation model, 104–105,
298–299; exchange of tax
information, 10; Joint Tax
Program, 63; tax competition,
188; tax treaty model of,
246–247, 298–299; worldwide
cost of basic social services, 179
United Nations Conference
on Trade and Development
(UNCTAD), 19
United Nations Economic and
Social Council (ECOSOC), 298
United States: abolishment of
withholding tax, 174, 187; arm's
length principle in transfer
pricing, 266–267, 272–273;
auditing of large companies,
289; Convention on Mutual
Administrative Assistance in
Tax Matters, 381*n6*; cost-plus
method in transfer pricing,
272; exchange of information,
382*n7*; immigration to,
336; information exchange
agreements, 303, 306; Internal
Revenue Code, 250*n24*, 267;
interstate tax competition in,
210–212; as main source of
FDI in LAC, 15–16; Mexican
treaties with, 8, 182, 231–232,
305; Model Treaty on Tax
Information Exchange,

306; political integration
of, 1; sovereignty, 188; tax
competition, 405; tax sparing,
91, 182–183; tax treaties,
8, 182, 231–232, 240*n10*;
transfer pricing, 283; Uniform
Commercial Code, 250*n24*; veto
power on taxation proposals,
413
Uruguay: aging of population in,
337*n5*; loss of tariff revenue
from U.S. trade agreements,
33–35; public spending, 132;
"small country" tax strategy of,
119, 122; social security income,
27; state monopoly income as
important in, 27; tax secrecy
laws in, 90; transfer pricing,
274, 281–282
Uruguay Round, 22, 188
user fees, 51

V

value-added taxes (VAT): CAN
harmonization of, 40, 97,
100–103; CAN statistics on,
102*tab*; Central American
proposal, 107*n33*; effectiveness
of broad base in, 73; EU
harmonization of, 2, 220, 353;
export-promotion model and,
21; in non-OECD countries,
177; origins and introduction
of, 401–402; in states of Brazil,
90; as substitute for tariffs, 3–4,
42, 46, 51–52, 72, 219; tariff
reduction's effect on, 29; trade
liberalization's effect on, 61
Velayos, Fernando, 5, 79